THE
JFK
FILES

Peter Kross

Adventures Unlimited Press

To the memory of my aunt, Jewel Josephs,
teacher and mentor to so many.

Books by Peter Kross:

The Vatican Conspiracy
American Conspiracy Files
Tales From Langley
The Secret History of the United States
JFK: The French Connection
Spies, Traitors and Moles
The Encyclopedia of World War II Spies
Oswald, the CIA and the Warren Commission

THE
JFK
FILES

Adventures Unlimited Press

The JFK Files

ISBN: 978-1-948803-04-5

Published by:
Adventures Unlimited Press
One Adventure Place
Kempton, Illinois 60946 USA
auphq@frontiernet.net

Printed in the United States of America

Cover illustration by Terry Lamb

AdventuresUnlimitedPress.com

THE
JFK
FILES

President Kennedy and Jackie arrive in Dallas on November 21, 1963.

TABLE OF CONTENTS

THE
JFK
FILES

President Kennedy in Dallas, November 22, 1963.

History will be kind to me,
for I intend to write it.

—Winston Churchill

INTRODUCTION

It has been fifty-five years since John F. Kennedy was gunned down in Dealey Plaza in Dallas, Texas. No one who lived through that time had any idea just how much that one event would change the history of our country. The world changed dramatically after the assassination of JFK, with the war in Vietnam rocking the nation to its core, with the assassinations of two of America's most valued leaders, Robert Kennedy and Rev. Martin Luther King, race riots across the nation, the Watergate scandal during the Nixon administration, the Pentagon Papers affair, and scandals like Iran-Contra, and the impeachment of President Bill Clinton, after a sexual affair he had with a White House intern.

The information gleaned from the release of documents via the JFK Records Act of the early 1990s opened the floodgates for researchers to delve into the assassination of the president. We learned about the plans of the United States to work with certain Mafia figures to assassinate Fidel Castro, as well as other foreign leaders. The newly released files gave us new insights into the cold war mentality that prevailed inside the Kennedy administration *vis á vis* Cuba and other international hotspots. But those files were just the tip of the iceberg as to what the government was holding back regarding the assassination. There were more documents still to be released, but just how long it would take to release them was the open question.

In October of 2017, the National Archives released almost 3,000 documents (some which had been previously released years before). There was no "smoking gun" revelation in that batch of documents, but there were just enough tidbits of information to make the researcher yearn for more.

In this book, *The JFK Files,* I will try to pinpoint the most relevant files and what they mean in the documentary history of the Kennedy assassination. Along with describing the newly released documents, I will give the reader the historical background of the documents, and how they relate to what was put on the record. Some of the new files that will be described are the following: the Soviet reaction to the president's death, the deportation of Carlos Marcello from the United States under orders from Robert Kennedy, new information regarding the activities of Valerie Kostikov and his association with Lee Oswald in Mexico City, the goings on in Louisiana of anti-Castro organizations and the CIA's operation called JMMOVE, Operation Tumbleweed regarding Oswald's contacts with the Russians in Mexico City, the elusive figure called "El Mexicano" who was supposed to be in Mexico City, and what his activities might have been, a phone call that was intercepted by Britain's MI-5 regarding the fact that Kennedy would be killed, new information on Yuri Nosenko, and the relationship between James Angleton and Oswald, a possible link with Marilyn Monroe and Robert Kennedy, Robert Mahue's underworld connections, the possibility that Kennedy was killed in retaliation for the assassination of President Diem of South Vietnam, the role played by Frank Sturgis in his anti-Castro crusade, the Polish threat against JFK, Kennedy's two-track approach to Castro, the CIA's Miami Station, and many more.

This is just a start in the process of revealing the secret Kennedy files that have been hidden away for over fifty years. Allan Dulles, who participated in the Warren Commission, said that "people didn't read," describing the public's reaction to the publication of the Warren Report in 1964. He was wrong. The American people do read, thus the continuing interest in the Kennedy assassination. Maybe, with the final release of the remaining files by the government, we will finally have a better idea of just what happened, 55-years ago that forever changed our nation's history.

Peter Kross
North Brunswick, New Jersey

Oswald and Marina with their daughter in 1962.

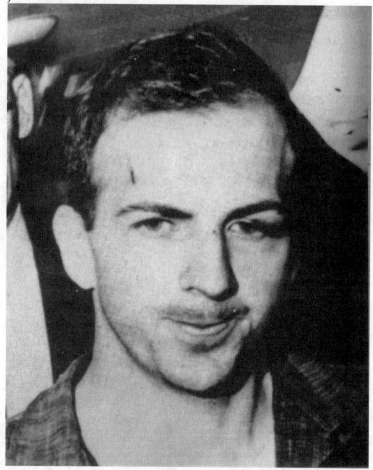

Lee Harvey Oswald after his arrest on November 22, 1963.

Oswald and Marina in St. Petersburg in 1961.

Chapter 1
The Polish Threat against Kennedy

There were many threats to the life of President Kennedy in the years before his assassination, some real, some not. One of the newly released documents tells of a threat to the President that was made on November 14, 1963, from an anonymous telephone call to the United States embassy in Canberra, Australia, relative to the planned assassination of the president.

The memorandum was sent to US government officials by J. Lee Rankin, one of the counselors to the Warren Commission which was investigating the assassination. The message from Mr. Rankin was sent to the CIA which began its own investigation to determine if the report was accurate or not.

"On 24 November 1963," the memo reports, "CIA received from the Department of the Navy a copy of a cable from the Naval Attaché in Canberra, Australia, reporting a telephone conversation the previous day with an anonymous individual who had described himself as a Polish chauffeur for the Soviet Embassy in that city. This individual, while discussing several matters of intelligence interest, touched on the possibility that the Soviet Government had financed the assassination of President Kennedy. Reference was made in this cable to the receipt of a similar anonymous telephone call on 15 October 1962."

Upon getting the gist of the cable from Australia, the CIA took the following actions to determine its validity. The CIA cabled someone in the government, probably a person in the intelligence community, to give the full details of the phone call of November 23 and also, the call that was made on October 15, 1962, one year previously. According to the cable, the CIA did not know about the October 1962 call. When the CIA looked into the 1962 call, they came up with the following information. "It appears that source on that occasion (November 27) stated that "Iron Curtain Countries" planned to pay a hundred thousand dollars for the assassination of President Kennedy. On 27 November, the (blank) also furnished complete detail on the anonymous telephone call of 23 November

1963. On 29 November, CIA disseminated this information, as supplied by its (blanked out) to the White House, Department of State, and Federal Bureau of Investigation, with a copy to the Secret Service."

After going over all the information at their disposal, the CIA came up with the following determination. "In the opinion of the (blank), the caller was a crank. In any event, they were not able to identify any Polish employee of the Soviet embassy, the automobile described by the caller as the one he drove, or the license plate number given to him. No further information on this call has been received. Available evidence would tend to show that the caller was some type of crank. This conclusion, however, cannot be confirmed." The person who signed the above-mentioned memo was none other than Richard Helms, the Deputy Director for Plans at the CIA. Helms' name would become prominent in the story of the Kennedy assassination, and his name will crop up again in the documents that will be described in later chapters.[1]

One has to wonder, if the above-mentioned report was true, why a Polish national who worked as a driver for the Soviet Embassy in Canberra would have access to such information. If he was telling the truth, maybe this person, while driving his superiors around the city, heard such a conversation. If he did hear such a discussion, why didn't he report it to the Americans? Who knows what may have been in this person's mind, if and when he heard what was being discussed? The early 1960s were the height of the Cold War between the United States and the Soviet Union and any small incident could have triggered an all out war.

But why would the Soviet Union want to eliminate President Kennedy? If it were proven to be true, the potential outcome would be an all out nuclear war between the United States and the Soviet Union in which there would be no winners. One possible scenario was that Premier Nikita Khrushchev was so humiliated after the Cuban Missile Crisis of 1962 that he ordered the president's assassination. Another factor that has to be included in any "Russia did it" scenario, is the fact that the president's alleged assassin, Lee Harvey Oswald, had lived in the Soviet Union for a number of years under mysterious circumstances, married a Russian woman, and

1 RIF Number 104-10440-10035: Anonymous Telephone Call to US Embassy in Canberra, Australia, Relative to Planned Assassination of President Kennedy.

then abruptly, and without much effort, returned to the United States whereupon he took up various pro-Castro causes in places such as Dallas and New Orleans. The Oswald saga upon his return home is still a story that has not been fully unraveled.

The "Russia did it" angle has focused much heated debate in assassination circles, but like the Castro thesis, holds little water. Yes, Oswald was a believer in Marxist philosophy starting as a young man, was an admirer of Castro and Cuba, and read Marxist literature while in the Marine Corps (a strange thing, to say the least). Some people say that Oswald's defection to Russia was his chance to become a part of Russian society, disclaiming his American nationality. There is also a crazy belief that the "Oswald" who was shot by Jack Ruby in Dallas was a Russian-born KGB agent who was a doppelganger of the real Oswald. But at the time of Oswald's defection to the Soviet Union, the United States had a false defector program going on. Was Oswald part of this program?

Another link to Russia came in September 1963, when Lee Oswald made a short trip to Mexico City where "Oswald" tried to get a visa to return to the Soviet Union. It was common procedure for the CIA to bug the Cuban Consulate and the Soviet Embassy where 'Oswald" went to get the necessary travel documents.

Oswald made contact with Valery Kostikov in the Soviet Embassy. Kostikov was a high-ranking KGB agent who had been serving in the Soviet's Mexican compound since 1960. As described by recent CIA documents, it is believed that Kostikov was a member of the top secret Soviet Department 13 that was responsible for assassination activity in the Western Hemisphere. Using this highly tenuous link (it is unclear whether it was even the real Oswald in Mexico City) certain members of the CIA tried to paint Oswald as a member of the Communist Party (which he was not) and more important, as a Soviet agent in touch with Kostikov. Thus, they tried to falsely tie the Soviet Union to the president's assassination. As far as Valery Kostikov is concerned, the latest batch of documents released, in October 2017, paints a broader picture of him and his activities in Mexico City at the time that Oswald was there. I will tell that part of the story as this book continues.

After the assassination, Soviet intelligence did its own digging into the events in Dallas and came up with its own version of what happened that day. In November 1963, a reliable Polish intelligence source, an American who owned some businesses, said that he learned that the assassination was carried out by three wealthy Texas businessmen, all of whom hated JFK. The men were H.L. Hunt, Sid Richardson, and Clint Murchinson. All these men hated Kennedy, who was instrumental in having a law passed in October 1962 which put new tax provisions on their lucrative oil business.

Further evidence compiled by the KGB implicated H.L. Hunt in the president's death. Their informant was a reporter for the *Baltimore Sun,* Paul Ward. Ward told the KGB that H.L. Hunt was the point man for the group that planned the assassination. Ward said that Hunt had instructed Jack Ruby to offer Lee Oswald money to kill Kennedy. Oswald was instructed not to inform his wife or mother about what he was about to do.

According to the story, "Oswald was a most appropriate figure staging the terrorist attack against Kennedy because of his past—he implicated the USSR, Cuba, and the Communist Party of the US. Ward said that after Oswald was arrested, their sources informed them that he was going to spill his guts at trial and he had to be killed before that could happen. Ruby was then dispatched to kill Oswald."[2]

The Russians were not the only ones who believed that a right-wing conspiracy killed JFK. The French had the same view. The KGB said that their informers in the French government had come to the conclusion that Kennedy had been killed as a result of a right-wing plot because of Kennedy's domestic and foreign policy pronouncements, along with his detente with the Soviet Union. The French ambassador to the UN said Soviet intelligence "believed that the assassination was a carefully organized act by a determined group on the far right of American politics."

As we shall see, the Polish warning was not the only one to come to light in the months and years before the president's death on November 22, 1963.

2 Fursenko, Alexander, & Naftali, Timothy, *One Hell of a Gamble: The Secret History of the Cuban Missile Crisis, Khrushchev, Castro & Kennedy,* 1958-1964, W.W. Norton & Co., New York, 1997, Page 348.

Chapter 2
The MI-5 Warning

Among the newly released files is an intriguing document about a call to a London-based newspaper called the *Cambridge News* 25-minutes before the president was killed in Dallas, Texas at 12:30 p.m. local time. The call was received at the newspapers office at 18:05 GMT on November 22, 1963, less than a half hour before the assassination.

No one knows who the caller was and even today, no one in the newspaper has any idea whether or not it was genuine in nature. The memo reads in part, "The caller said only that the *Cambridge News* reporter should call the American Embassy in London for some big news and hung up. After the word of the President's death was received the reporter informed the Cambridge police of the anonymous call and the police informed MI-5. The Cambridge reporter had never received a call of this kind before, and MI-5 stated that he is known to them as a sound and loyal person with no security record."

The memo in question also stated in a rather cryptic fashion that "similar anonymous phone calls of a strangely coincidental nature have been received by persons in the UK over the past year," particularly in the case of a Dr. Ward. The reference to a Dr. Ward might have been referring to the Profumo scandal that rocked England in the early 1960s that involved a doctor named Stephen Ward.

The pertinent parts of the memo, which was dated November 26, 1963, days after the assassination, read thusly:

1) The following cable from the CIA Station in London was reported orally to Mr. Samuel Papich at 0930 on 23 November.

2) The British Security Service (MI-5) has reported that at 1805 GMT on 22 November an anonymous telephone call was made in Cambridge, England, to the senior reporter for the *Cambridge News*. The caller said only that the *Cambridge News* reporter should call the American

Embassy in London for some big news and then hung up.

3) After the word of the President's death was received the reporter informed the Cambridge police of the anonymous call and the police informed MI-5. The important point is that the call was made, according to MI-5 calculations, about 25-minutes before the President was shot. The Cambridge reporter had never received a call of this kind before and MI-5 stated that he is known to them as a sound and loyal person with no security record.

The memo was sent to J. Edgar Hoover, the director of the FBI at the time of the Kennedy assassination, by none other than James Angleton the deputy director (Plans) at the CIA.[3]

In the years following, the name of James Angleton would come up prominently in the events surrounding the president's assassination, with Angleton and his counter-intelligence staff at CIA headquarters taking an active interest in the president's alleged shooter, Lee Harvey Oswald. Angleton took part in some of the most important CIA activities from the days of the Cold War and was also an OSS agent in Rome during World War II in which he had covert ties to the Vatican in its secret war against the Hitler regime in Berlin. During the Cold War era, he was an ally of an important British intelligence officer named Kim Philby who was stationed in Washington and was the liaison between the British intelligence services and the CIA. What Angleton and the rest of the US intelligence community did not know was that Philby was in fact a double agent who had been working for the Soviet Union since World War II. Angleton and Philby had become very close. When the CIA found out that Philby had defected to the Soviet Union, Angleton was crushed. Philby's defection would color Angleton's view of the secret war between the Soviet Union and the United States, and he started a mole hunt inside the agency to try to locate a suspected mole who had penetrated the CIA, but was never found.

When the above-mentioned document was released last year, the current staff of the *Cambridge News* began an investigation to see who the reporter who took the call might have been. Anna Savva, a current reporter for the paper, said her reaction when she heard

3 RIF No. 104-10404-10307: Assassination of President Kennedy—Reported Anonymous Telephone Message Date 11/26/1963.

the news of the MI-5 memo and her paper was "completely jaw-dropping." She stated, "It would have been common knowledge in the office who took the call, but we have nothing in our archive—we have nobody here who knows the name of the person who took the call."

Another person who works for the paper today, the chief reporter Chris Elliot, said, "no one has ever been able to establish whether that call was actually made" but the fact that it might have been made came to light in the 1980s.

Sam Papich, the man who the document says was contacted by the American Embassy in London, was the FBI's liaison to the CIA during the time of the CIA-Mafia plots to kill Fidel Castro. It was from his very close-up seat that Papich was able to see for himself the intricate machinations between the Bureau and the CIA.

By 1961, FBI Director J. Edgar Hoover had discovered, to his surprise, the secret dealings between the CIA—in the person of Sheffield Edwards—and Johnny Rosselli and Sam Giancana of the Mafia. Hoover discovered the genesis of the anti-Castro plots in an indirect way—the bugging of singer Dan Rowan's hotel room in Las Vegas by Robert Mahue and Arthur Belliti. Hoover had been going after the mob in Las Vegas for some time and when the CIA and his own investigation learned of the botched job against Rowan, the secret of the CIA vs. Castro came spilling out.

Hoover was angry that his investigation of the mob was being compromised by the CIA and he immediately sought an answer from Sheffield Edwards. A meeting between Hoover and Edwards took place on May 3, 1961 at which time the CIA head of security told Hoover of the agency's relationship with both Rosselli and Giancana and "Phase One" of the Castro plots. On May 21, 1961, Hoover sent a memo to Robert Kennedy telling him of his meeting with Edwards and the information gleaned from that sitting.

It was at this time that Sam Papich was informed by Hoover of his meeting with Edwards. Papich, who was dealing with both intelligence agencies at the same time, told Bill Harvey of the news. Harvey asked Papich to tell him if Hoover was going to tell John McCone, the new head of the CIA, about the Castro plots. It was now almost certain that McCone did not know of his own agency's involvement with the Mob.

9

William Harvey was one of the most pivotal spies in the Cold War era and his name comes up numerous times in the events relating to the assassination of President Kennedy, both in the Cuban angle to the crime, and in the CIA's assassination program called ZR/RIFLE-Executive Action.

In 1947, Harvey worked for the FBI, got into an altercation with the powerful boss, J. Edgar Hoover, and was transferred to the minor post of Indianapolis where he decided to leave the Bureau and join the CIA. He found he newly created CIA much more to his liking and wound up in Staff C, the Agency's counterintelligence unit. One of his early duties was to unmask the top Soviet mole, Kim Philby, who worked for the British intelligence service in Washington, D.C. In 1952, Harvey was given the sensitive post of CIA Station Chief in Berlin at the heart of the Cold War between the Soviet Union and the United States. It was Harvey who supervised the CIA's "Project Gold," the Berlin tunnel operation which allowed the West to monitor all intelligence calls from the Soviet Union to its allies in Eastern Europe.

By 1961, Harvey was recalled to Washington where he took over the newly created Executive Action assassination program. It was in this work for this most secret operation that Harvey would get highly involved in the Agency's attempts to kill Castro, which would make him a marked man within the Kennedy administration.

Bill Harvey was head of the super-secret group called "Staff D" which was responsible for communication intercepts. All of the CIA's covert activities were given coded IDs with letters for designation. Staff A was foreign intelligence; B, operations; C, counterintelligence. But Staff D was different, its doors physically guarded around the clock by armed Marines. To insure maximum security, Harvey brought in his own safe to supplement the other three that were already in the office.

It was after the Bay of Pigs invasion in April 1961, that Harvey took over the CIA's efforts to eliminate Castro:

> After Harvey took over the Castro operation he ran it as one aspect of ZR/RIFLE, however, he personally handled the Castro operation and did not use any of the assets being developed by ZR/RIFLE. He says that he first came to

think-of the Castro operation and the ZR/RIFLE as being synonymous. The overall Executive Action program came to be treated in his mind as being synonymous with QJ/WIN, the agent working on the overall program. He says that when he wrote of ZR/RIFLE, QJ/WIN the reference was to Executive Action capability, when he used the cryptonym ZR/RIFLE alone, referring to Castro.

As the covert war against Castro continued during the Kennedy administration, called Operation Mongoose, William Harvey became a thorn in the side of the Kennedy brothers. He repeatedly had harsh words with Robert Kennedy who oversaw the entire operation. The men repeatedly got into shouting matches that tended to turn ugly.

During the height of the Cuban Missile Crisis in 1962, Harvey and a group of his men made their way into Cuba to try to foment hit-and-run attacks against Cuban military installations, just at the time when the president was trying to defuse the situation that might have led to nuclear war.

According to author Gus Russo, in his book *Live By the Sword,* Papich told the HSCA (House Select Committee on Assassinations) that the FBI kept Robert Kennedy informed of its information on the plots to kill Castro. According to Papich, Robert Kennedy did not disapprove of the plots but was concerned that the news did not get out.

Another point of interest in the MI-5 memo is a puzzling reference to a "Dr. Ward." The Dr. Ward in question might have been Dr. Stephen Ward who was involved in the Profumo scandal that rocked Great Britain at the time and led to the resignation of Prime Minister Harold Macmillan.

Dr. Stephen Ward was a prominent artist-osteopath who treated some of the most important people in British society, both politicians and businessmen. For a period of time, Dr. Ward was having relationships with two young and attractive women, Christine Keeler and Mandy Rice-Davies. Keeler, it seems, was having an affair with two important people: John Profumo who was the Secretary of State for War, as well as a Russian intelligence officer named Captain Yevgeny Ivanov who was the assistant Soviet naval attaché.

Captain Ivanov came to London in March 1960 and soon met

Dr. Ward. It is not known who introduced him to Dr. Ward or if Ward was treating him as one of his patients. Both Keeler and Rice-Davies were working as dancers in a club and were soon to move in with Dr. Ward. Ivanov met Keeler in the spring of 1961 and an affair took off.

Dr. Ward did not know that his new Russian friend was an intelligence officer and he quickly introduced him to many of his uppercrust friends in the British government, including Lord Astor, Winston Churchill, Prince Philip, and John Profumo, among others. Profumo would soon be at the center of the upcoming scandal that rocked Britain to its core.

John Profumo was an army veteran of World War II, and won a seat in Parliament at age 24. He was a successful businessman and he entered the government of Harold Macmillan. Macmillan appointed Profumo as Secretary of State for War in 1960. Profumo first met Christine Keeler on July 9, 1961 and an affair soon blossomed.

Soon, things began to get interesting as far as secret affairs of state were concerned. It seems that Ward told a man who worked at MI-5 that Ivanov had asked him questions regarding the placement of US missiles in West Germany (just how Dr. Ward was supposed to know about the placement of these missiles in hard to understand). This undisclosed MI-5 officer told his superiors, but then something untoward happened. The information was relayed to Sir Roger Hollis who was the Director General of MI-5. It seems that for whatever reason, Hollis did not relay this information to his colleagues in the Foreign Office, and thus, no action was taken against Ivanov. After the Profumo affair died down, there were persistent rumors in England as to why Hollis did not tell the Foreign Office about Ivanov. There was talk among many people in British intelligence that Hollis might have been a Soviet mole who had infiltrated the British government and was thus trying to protect Ivanov from capture. In time, Hollis was to take a more active interest in Ivanov when, in April 1960, a Russian mole named Oleg Penkovsky, a GRU agent in place in Russia who was then working secretly for the West, told his handlers about a naval attaché who was working secretly in Great Britain. That man turned out to be Ivanov, and MI-5 agents began tracking him. Ivanov led them to the home of Dr. Ward.

Hollis ordered his men to follow Dr. Ward and on June 8, 1961, they warned Dr. Ward that Ivanov might be using him for his own devious ends. One of the MI-5 officers said of Dr. Ward, "Ward was not a person we can make use of because of his political ideas were exploitable by the Russians."

The Profumo affair came about via information from a man called George Wigg who was member of the Labor Party and was a member of Parliament. While lunching with a friend, Wigg got a call from a stranger who told him, "Forget about the Vassall case! You want to look at Profumo." Wigg believed that the mysterious caller was Vitali Lui, a KGB agent who was posing as a freelance Russian journalist called Victor Louis. Wigg somehow found out that Dr. Ward was having an affair with Christine Keeler. Wigg did not like nor did he trust John Profumo, and he now had the ammunition to discredit him in public.

As time went on, Keeler began telling anyone who'd listen that she believed that Dr. Ward was acting as an intelligence officer for Ivanov, and she even stated that she had seen him deliver packages to the Russian Embassy in London.

It seems that John Profumo had secret access to classified information on the types of nuclear missiles that the United States was giving Great Britain, including the Skybolt and Polaris, via his attendance in cabinet meetings to discuss the delivery of these weapons systems beginning in 1962 and 1963. One person who had documents on Christine Keeler's relationship with Profumo was a reporter named Michael Eddowes, a writer and lawyer who knew Keeler, Ward, and Ivanov. A statement that Eddowes took from Keeler on December 14, 1962, said that Ivanov had asked her to discover the date when Great Britain would obtain nuclear weapons from the US. "Ivanov had asked her directly to obtain from Profumo the date of delivery of nuclear warheads to West Germany."

In January 1963, the Profumo scandal came to a head. It seems that Christine Keeler was about to publish her account of her affair with Profumo, Ivanov, and Ward. Profumo then spoke to Roger Hollis in the hope of having the story quashed. It wasn't. Profumo then spilled his guts to Hollis and told him the whole, sordid story (Profumo had broken off his affair with Keeler in late 1961). Things were getting so hot for Ivanov that he left England for Russia to escape the ever-growing scandal.

With the Keeler-Ward-Profumo scandal ready to erupt in full view, Roger Hollis did something rather unusual: he gave orders to MI-5 agents not to further investigate the matter. He probably did so after considering the fact that his name would probably come to light as being an acquaintance of Dr. Ward. His subordinates were incredulous of Hollis's decision and they took the order reluctantly.

Things got out of hand when on February 7 the commander of Scotland Yard's Special Branch went to MI-5 and told them that he had learned that Keeler had told the police that she had an affair with Profumo as well as Ivanov who had now returned to Russia. The report also said that Ward had asked Keeler to find out the release date of the nuclear warheads to Britain. By now, Prime Minister Harold McMillian had heard rumors of the affair but took no action.

On March 21, 1963, George Wigg made a speech in parliament hinting about a scandal at the highest levels of the British government but did not name names. Profumo then made a comment in public denying any links to what Wigg had said (Wigg did not mention Profumo by name).

On May 7, 1963, Hollis met with Prime Minister Mcmillian and told him the awful truth that the rumors of Profumo's affair with Keeler were true. He also told him that he (Hollis) had sat on the information for five months. He also told McMillian about the Ivanov connection with Keeler and Ward. Things got even tenser when Hollis told him about the story of Ward and the delivery date of the nuclear missiles to England. The Prime Minister was shocked and now had to figure a way out of the brewing scandal.

The final stages of the scandal began when Profumo said in public that he lied about not having an affair with Keeler. In June, the newspaper *The News of the World* began printing Keeler's story and the scandal was now out in the open.

The Prime Minister then went to Parliament to explain the story. He said that MI-5 had not told him the entire story about the Keeler-Ward-Profumo affair and said that Hollis told him that the affair was "not of great importance."

The Prime Minister asked his security services to mount an investigation to see if the Russians were behind the affair and they came up with no solid information to back that claim.

In the United States, President Kennedy was informed of what was going on by the US Ambassador to England, David Bruce. The president, after reading the report, told his aides that he believed that Prime Minister Mcmillian was so badly wounded that he probably would have to resign.

In the end, John Profumo resigned his position in the cabinet, admitting that he had lied all along. In October 1963, Prime Minister Macmillan also resigned. "A government report published at the time, concluded that connections between Profumo, Ward, Keeler and Ivanov had not damaged British security—although Ivanov was to proclaim differently."

As the trial of Stephen Ward came to a close in late summer, he took an overdose of sleeping pills and was unconscious during the final proceedings. He was found guilty of prostitution charges. Stephen Ward died on August 3, 1963. Keeler also went to trial and was found guilty and sent to prison. She died at age 75 in London in December 2017. Mandy Rice-Davis became a cabaret singer and opened a series of restaurants.

If the reference to Dr. Ward in the newly-released document is to Dr. Stephen Ward, then it is one of the most interesting items to be revealed to the public in the release of the Kennedy files.

Earle Cabell, mayor of Dallas.

Allen Dulles, Gen. Ed Lansdale, Gen. Charles P. Cabell, Mr. Nathan Twining.

Chapter 3
Dallas 63 Mayor was CIA Asset

One of the first of the new documents to be released by the National Archives is an interesting piece regarding the Mayor of Dallas, Texas in November 1963, Earle Cabell. What was not known all these years was Mayor Cabell had been a CIA asset beginning in 1956.

Over the years, there had been persistent rumors in the assassination research field that Mayor Cabell, along with other members of the government of Dallas, may have changed the route that President Kennedy took when his open motorcade passed through the crowded streets of Dallas, winding up in Dealey Plaza where the shots that killed the president were fired. The route that the presidential motorcade took was through the maze of narrow streets that wound up in Dealey Plaza, a perfect place for a potential assassin to wait in ambush. The buildings surrounding Dealey Plaza were not guarded, and the windows were open, which was against Secret Service rules at the time. If the proper procedures were adhered to, it is possible that the assassination may have been prevented.

The document revealing that Mayor Cabell was acting as a CIA asset does not tell us what he did or for how long. We don't know whom he worked with in Dallas, whom he saw during his work for the Agency, or whom his contacts might have been. What was revealed however was a copy of the CIA's secrecy agreement, his CIA 201 file, which is a personality file. The existence of such a file means that the CIA had an interest in a particular person for some sort of work. What was also revealed was a CIA personality file request indicating that the House Select Committee on Assassinations (HSCA) reviewed his file. The reason for the file not being released sooner was because it was "Not Believed Relevant" to the history of the assassination. While the file lacks substance as to what Mayor Cabell did for the CIA during that time, it opens up a window to who the CIA used as an asset during that time. One of the questions to ask is whether, as an asset of the CIA in Dallas in 1963, Mayor Cabell knew about Lee Harvey Oswald when the alleged assassin was living in Dallas and Fort Worth? If it ever came to light that Cabell knew about Oswald, that would shake up the case even further. But the file makes no mention of that or anything else in that regard.

What is interesting in the story of Earle Cabell is that his brother Charles P. Cabell was the Deputy Director of the CIA, and, along with Allen Dulles, was one of the most important members of the CIA during the administrations of both Presidents Eisenhower and Kennedy. After the disastrous Bay of Pigs invasion of Cuba in April 1961, both Dulles and Cabell were fired by JFK.

Earle Cabell became a US congressman when he defeated Bruce Alger in the 1964 election. He was able to get funding for the federal center in Dallas, which is today called the Earl Cabell Federal Building and Courthouse.

The city of Dallas at the time of the Kennedy assassination was a hot-bed of ultra-right wing sentiment. The city was basically conservative in its political leaning and the Kennedy's were not well liked to say the least. Even Vice President Lyndon Johnson was beginning to get out of favor with these same people and his once robust star was beginning to fade.

The atmosphere was so toxic in Dallas that when UN Ambassador Adlai Stevenson came to Dallas to make a speech, he was booed and heckled by a noisy crowed. After his return to Washington, Stevenson told the president of his encounter with the demonstrators, and warned him not to make the Dallas trip.

After the assassination, the Mayor's office began receiving hate mail from across the country. One of the telegrams said, "Dallas, the city that spawns the lunatic fringe of the far right. Dallas, the City of Hate."

Another hate filled message read as follows: "As with your ridiculous and nauseating auto slogan stickers we see—Made in Texas by Texans—I suppose a similar one can be adopted pertaining to the assassination."[4]

After the murder of Lee Oswald by Jack Ruby two days after the assassination, Mayor Cabell said of the events that had just taken place in his city, "It could have happened in Podunk as well as Dallas."

4 Minutaglio, Bill and Davis, Steven, *Dallas 63,* 12 Publishing Co., New York, 2013, Page 316.

Earle Cabell's family were well connected in Dallas politics for years. His father and grandfather were also mayors of Dallas. His grandfather was a Confederate general and Earle was a member of the ultra-right John Birch Society. Another person in Dallas who was a member of the John Birch Society was retired army general Edwin Walker who was fired by JFK for insubordination. The men were close friends and shared their anti-Kennedy political views. It was General Walker who would take part in a still disputed incident involving Lee Harvey Oswald in the months before the assassination. Historians writing about the assassination believe that Oswald took a shot at General Walker while he was at his home (he missed). Others believe that Oswald was not the shooter and that there were other people who may have been behind the event.

At one point in time, Walker and Mayor Cabell were at the same event where both men spoke. For his part, General Walker was all bombast and fire, attacking the Kennedys and the anti-communists in the United States at the same time. He told the crowd that the reason he left the military was because "he could no longer be a collaborator." He attacked the media and said that the growing communist conspiracy would soon be taking over the nation's schools and churches. He said that the generals would have taken care of the communist threat (Russia) "if they hadn't been throttled by the meddlesome politicians in Washington."

As most of the south in the 1950s and 60s, the policy of integration of the schools and public accommodations went slowly at best. Most southern politicians were reluctant to force integration and that was the case in Dallas. But things were taking a different turn in Dallas. The city fathers, including Mayor Cabell, working with African-American leaders in the city, decided to integrate the city's schools, one grade at a time. The first school be integrated was the Travis Elementary School starting with its first grade class. In subsequent years, the other grades in the Dallas public school system were integrated, making Dallas less backward than other southern cities when it came to desegregation.

In the wake of the trip to Dallas by Adlai Stevenson where he was horribly treated, Mayor Cabell in late 1963 had a change of heart when it came to the radicals who were fomenting trouble in his city. Why he did this is not known but in a speech he said, "These are radicals. Dallas cannot ignore the existence of this element any more than we can allow it to continue as our spokesman. The cancer of the body politic must be removed."

The city of Dallas would now have a second chance to make up for the attack on Adlai Stevenson. The White House announced that the president was going to make a trip to Dallas in November to boost the fates of the Democratic Party leaders in Texas. President Kennedy's civil rights program was not loved by many people in the city who saw Kennedy's fight for civil rights as a blow to their endorsement of him in 1960. Many of these same people disagreed sharply with Kennedy's policy of detente with the Soviet Union, especially the president's call for a nuclear test ban treaty with the Russians, which he announced at the American University commencement some time before.

Prior to the president's trip to Dallas, the *Dallas Morning News* wrote the following, "The president's security team will compile a full report on who might be demonstrating where and why. By the time the President arrives in Dallas, the men assigned to that segment of his Texas trip will be very knowledgeable about his zealous critics. The federal agents are sharp-eyed, alert and cat-like in their quickness. They know what they are watching out for and, usually whom." It seems that someone in Dallas did not get that message.

According to author Anthony Summers in his book *Conspiracy,* three people in the president's motorcade smelled gunpowder in Dealey Plaza during the assassination. These people were Mayor Cabell's wife, Senator Ralph Yarborough, and Congressman Ray Roberts. This is important because they smelled the smoke near the grassy knoll; a number of people heard what sounded like gunshots coming from that direction. It is highly improbable that they could have smelled the gunpowder from a rifle being fired from the sixth floor of the Texas School Book Depository Building.

The mayor's wife, along with two photographers saw the barrel of a rifle sticking out of the widow from which the shots that killed the president were supposed to have been fired.

Earle Cabell's brother, Charles, was a world away from the goings on in Dallas that his brother had to deal with. At the time that Earle was secretly working for the CIA in Dallas, Charles

Cabell was one of the highest ranking members of the CIA. This was during the early years of the Kennedy administration, and as a military officer (he was a General), he served as the deputy director of the CIA at the time of the Bay of Pigs invasion of Cuba. As CIA Director Allen Dulles' right hand man, General Cabell was privy to a host of top-secret Agency operations including the Bay of Pigs invasion, and to a lesser extent, the CIA's plots to kill Fidel Castro.

Because of his military experience, General Cabell had the dubious distinction of running the CIA while its director, Allen Dulles, left the country to go to Puerto Rico where he was to address a convention of the Young President's Organization to discuss doing business with Iron Curtain countries. Skeptics would argue that by being out of the United States at a time when the Cuban brigade was in its death throes, Dulles left his deputy to take the blame for the invasion's failure while he was conveniently away from the storm. Dulles was aware that certain members of the Kennedy team did not like General Cabell and yet they decided to put him in the driver's seat during a highly contentious and dangerous military operation.

When it was obvious that the exiles were going to be defeated, a request came from the exile leaders to the administration for another air strike against the remainder of Castro's air force. The president's National Security Advisor, McGeorge Bundy, cancelled the strike on the orders of the president and relayed that information to General Cabell and his boss, Richard Bissell. Furious at the president's cancellation of another air attack, General Cabell and Richard Bissell debated whether to appeal directly to the president to change his mind. JFK refused. In the aftermath of the Bay of Pigs invasion, JFK fired Richard Bissell and General Cabell.

The aftermath of the Bay of Pigs invasion did not go so well for Allen Dulles either. President Kennedy asked that a detailed report be written on just how the invasion was planned and executed. Kennedy was ambushed by the old men at the CIA who had assured the new president that the invasion would be a success and that once the rebels invaded Cuba, the local population would rise up in revolt against Castro. That, of course, did not happen.

The man who Kennedy asked to write the post-Bay of Pigs report was Lyman Kirkpatrick who was one of the "Old Boys" of the postwar CIA, having served in the wartime OSS as a Major. He was a Princeton graduate, a scholar and a man whose rising star in the Agency was tragically cut down by his acquisition of polio, which he contracted in 1952 while on assignment in Thailand.

He joined the CIA in 1947 and served as a division chief until 1950. He was then appointed to the position of assistant director for special operations from 1950 to 1953. He was then given the important job of Inspector General of the CIA from 1953 to 1961 and was in the position after the failed Bay of Pigs invasion. A number of years ago, the CIA finally declassified its own secret report on the Bay of Pigs invasion written by Lyman Kirkpatrick which was a devastating critique of itself concerning the operation. The report took a direct swipe at both Dulles and Cabell, putting them on notice for the failure of the operation. When Kirkpatrick handed the men a copy of the secret report, Dulles called it a "hatchet job." Dulles and Cabell were both exceedingly shocked and upset, irritated and annoyed, and mad and everything else "Kirkpatrick recalled." Speaking years later about his father's report, Lyman Jr., a retired Army intelligence colonel, said, "When you speak honestly about what people did wrong, you're going to step on toes."

The president was so enraged at the intelligence establishment in the wake of the Bay of Pigs fiasco that he fired a number of high-ranking CIA and Pentagon staffers. Besides firing both Cabell and Dulles, the president also sacked Admiral Arleigh Burke and General Lyman Lemnitzer, who was replaced as head of the Joint Chiefs by Maxwell Taylor, who was a close confidant of Robert Kennedy (both Lemnitzer and Burke were well known critics of the Kennedy brothers).

According to author David Talbot in his book *The Devil's Chessboard,* after his firing by Kennedy, Dulles was still working the phones, dredging up anti-Kennedy propaganda and meeting at his home in Washington with his old pals, including Charles Cabell and ex-CIA officer Frank Wisner. Other members of the intelligence community who came calling were James Angleton, Cord Meyer, and Desmond Fitzgerald. Also among the callers to Dulles's home was CIA officer E. Howard Hunt, along with Thomas Karamessines and CIA Director John McCone, who replaced Dulles.

While the document regarding Earle Cabell is historically noteworthy, it gives the reader little else of substance. However, there are many unresolved questions as to just what Earle Cabell did as an agent in Dallas, while he was Mayor of the city where JFK was killed. What kind of intelligence relationship did he have with the CIA and his brother Charles, while Charles was deputy director? Did Charles give Earle any secret information from Langley headquarters that he could use while as an asset? Did Mayor Earle have any knowledge of Lee Harvey Oswald prior to the assassination, and if he did, what did he do with it? All these questions will have to wait until further information is released on his activities.

Chapter 4
Soviet Reaction to the Assassination

In the aftermath of the president's assassination, the Soviet Union began a comprehensive internal investigation of the circumstances surrounding the events of November 22, 1963. This involved almost all the relevant elements of the Soviet government including its intelligence services, the press, and its diplomatic corps. Some of its conclusions mirrored those of some of the critics of the Warren Report in the United States, and much to the surprise of many historians who did not know about the Soviet reaction, it took on the findings of the Warren Commission when it made its internal report. Their report also made reference to the time that Lee Harvey Oswald lived in the Soviet Union and their reaction to him while he was there. They also were very interested in finding out as much as they could on the new president, Lyndon Johnson, about whom they had very little information. All this must be taken in context with the high-stakes tensions then going on between the two countries at the height of the Cold War that had been going on since the mid-1950s.

In a memo dated December 2, 1965 from J. Edgar Hoover to Marvin Watson, who was the Special Assistant to President Johnson, the FBI leader sent information from sources that the FBI had inside Russia and other places in the Soviet government. The memo is comprehensive in nature and covers many secret topics that were of interest to the US after the assassination.

Minutes after the news of the president's assassination was made public, it was flashed to the citizens of the Soviet Union. "It was greeted by great shock and consternation and church bells were tolled in the memory of President Kennedy."

The report starts out by saying:

> According to our source, officials of the Communist Party of the Soviet Union believed there was some well-organized conspiracy on the part of the "ultra-right" in the United States to effect a "coup." They seemed convinced

that the assassination was not the deed of one man, but that it arose out of a carefully planned campaign in which several people played a part. They felt that those elements interested in utilizing the assassination and playing on anticommunist sentiments in the United States would then utilize this act to stop negotiations with the Soviet Union, attack Cuba, and thereafter spread the war. As a result of these feelings, the Soviet Union immediately went into a state of national alert.

Our source further stated that Soviet officials were fearful that without leadership, some irresponsible general in the United States might launch a missile at the Soviet Union. It was the further opinion of the Soviet officials that only maniacs would think of the "left" forces in the United States, as represented by the Communist Party, USA, would assassinate President Kennedy, especially in the view of the abuse the Communist Party, USA, has taken from the "ultra-left" as a result of its support of the peaceful coexistence and disarmament policies of the Kennedy administration.[5]

The report then goes into the possible relationship between Lee Oswald and the Soviets while he was living in Russia. "According to our source, Soviet officials claimed that Lee Harvey Oswald had no connection whatsoever with the Soviet Union. They described him as a neurotic maniac who was disloyal to his own country and everything else. They noted that Oswald never belonged to any organization in the Soviet Union and was never given Soviet citizenship."

On November 23, 1963, Nikolai Fedorenko, the Permanent Representative to the Soviet Mission to the United Nations, held a brief meeting with all diplomatic personnel employed at the Soviet Mission. He told the assembled staff that the president's death was a terrible thing and was "regretted by the Soviet Union." Fedorenko stated that the Soviet Union would have preferred to have had President Kennedy at the helm of the American government. He added that President Kennedy had, to some degree, a mutual understanding with the Soviet Union, and had tried seriously to improve relations between the United States and Russia.

5 RIF No. 178-10003-10131: Reaction of Soviet and Communist Party Officials to the Assassination of President John. F. Kennedy, December 1, 1966.

It was now time for the KGB to get into the act investigating the background of the assassination and they wasted little time in doing so:

According to our sources, Boris Ivanov, Chief of the Soviet Committee for State Security (KGB) Residency in New York City, held a meeting of KGB personnel on the morning of November 25, 1963 (the day of the president's funeral). Ivanov informed those present that President Kennedy's death had posed a problem for the KGB and stated that it was necessary for all KGB employees to lend their efforts to solving the problem.

According to our source, Ivanov stated that it was his personal feeling that the assassination of President Kennedy had been planned by an organized group rather than being an act of one individual assassin. Ivanov stated that it was therefore necessary that the KGB ascertain with the greatest possible speed the true story surrounding President Kennedy's assassination. Ivanov stated that the KGB was interested in knowing all the factors and all of the possible groups which might have worked behind the scenes to organize and plan this assassination.

Ivanov told his men to find out as much information as they

Yuri Nosenko.

could on the new American president, Lyndon Johnson. They were to trace his political background, as well as his personal life in order to try to figure out where he came from and what his political views were. They were also asked to look into his views on the Soviet Union, because they had little to go on. The report now makes a startling revelation concerning what the Russians believed were the connections between LBJ and the president's murder.

> Our source added that in the instructions from Moscow, it was indicated that "now" the KGB was in possession of data purporting to indicate that President Johnson was responsible for the assassination of the late president John Kennedy. KGB headquarters indicated that in view of this information, it was necessary for the Soviet Government to know the existing personal relationship between President Johnson and the Kennedy family, particularly that between President Johnson and Robert and Ted Kennedy.[6]

The narrative goes on to mention information provided by a Russian defector to the United States named Yuri Nosenko who, while a KGB officer, handled the Oswald case when Oswald defected to the Soviet Union. Much has been written and discussed about the case of Yuri Nosenko regarding the Kennedy assassination, Lee Harvey Oswald, and the Cold War intelligence war between the Russians and the United States during that time. The author will write about Nosenko later in this book.

Suffice it to say that Nosenko was in charge of all investigations of tourists coming to the Soviet Union and Oswald was no exception. Nosenko said that Oswald came to the attention of the KGB when he arrived in Russia and wanted to defect. The KGB decided that Oswald was "mentally unstable" and told their Kremlin bosses that in their opinion, Oswald should be returned to the United States. Oswald then slashed his wrists in his hotel room, was taken for medical treatment and wound up living in Russia for over two years. Nosenko also revealed that Oswald came to their attention after his return to the States when he went to Mexico City in September 1963 and went to the Soviet Embassy in order to get a visa back to Russia via Cuba (he was turned down).

6 Ibid.

According to Nosenko, Oswald's case was a routine one in which the KGB had no interest until he assassinated President Kennedy. He was not approached or recruited for espionage by the KGB nor was his wife, Marina. Nosenko said Marina was regarded as a woman who possessed little intelligence and he added that she had once been a member of the Communist Party but had been dropped for failure over a long period of time to pay her dues.

According to the report, Nosenko said that JFK was held in high esteem by the Soviet government despite the political differences that separated the countries.

After the assassination, Anatoli Dobrynin, the Soviet Ambassador to the United States, turned over to the Secretary of State a file alleged to be the complete consular file on Lee Oswald and Marina Oswald that the Russians had in their possession. This included his medical records as well as the information on his attempted suicide in his hotel room.

Officials of the Soviet Union, under the leadership of Premier Nikita Khrushchev, took a long look at the Warren Report on the Kennedy assassination and were very critical of its findings (like many people in this country). In an article in the newspaper *The Worker*, which was a communist newspaper in the United States, called "Warren Report Brushes Off Ultra Rightist Conspiracy," the authors says that the Warren Report gives comparatively very little space to the material that came before it indicating that a right-wing conspiracy was in the making and that Oswald was a "Left-painted" undercover instrument of such forces or of a Government agency.

Other pro-communist newspapers in the US also wrote articles attacking the findings of the Warren Commission. The *Progressive Labor,* the official publication of the Progressive Labor Party, published a special supplement dated November 27, 1963, which contained an article taking exception to the WC's findings that Oswald killed the president without any outside help. The article said that Oswald had been "framed."

Once the Warren Commission issued its findings on September

24, 1964, Russian reaction was swift in its condemnation. The official Soviet newspaper, *Pravda,* published an article in its September 28, 1964 edition summarizing the WC's report. The article stated that that the WC report did not dispel all doubts and suspicions about the "crime of the century." The article also noted that "not everything mysterious has become public and pointed out that at the beginning of the work of the WC, Mr. Warren declared that some facts connected with the assassination of President Kennedy may not be revealed in the lifetime of this generation."

In the Russian publication *Izvestia* for September 21, 1965, reporter V. Zorin attacked the WC's conclusions and wrote about the growing number of American writers who had published books on the WC's report and concluded that "the assassination in Dallas has many riddles to offer and that the mystery remains a mystery."

Another Soviet publication called *New Times* took issue with the findings of the WC in its September 1966 issue. The writer wrote about Richard Popkin who had published book reviews regarding a number of books by American authors who were critical of the WC's report, including books called *Whitewash* by Harold Weisberg and *Inquest* by Edward Jay Epstein. The *New Times* emphasized that "the Kennedy assassination was the outcome of a carefully laid plot in which influential quarters were implicated."

The Soviet reaction to the assassination of JFK was just one part in the mysterious saga linking Oswald to the Russians. Years after the assassination, rumors spread among certain circles in the United States that Oswald might have been an intelligence asset for the United States government. None of that speculation proved out, one way or another, but it just added fodder to the mystery of Oswald.

Oswald was considered a rather odd character by his fellow Marines, many of whom began calling him "Comrade Oswald." In his spare time, he learned Russian and tended to keep to himself. Oswald's military record says nothing about his officially learning Russian but the Warren Commission had other ideas. In 1974, chief counsel J. Lee Rankin said of Oswald's possible training in the Russian language, "We are trying to find out what he studied at the Monterey School of the Army in the way of languages." Most members of the armed forces who are taught a foreign language go into some sort of intelligence work. Was Oswald slated for some kind of operation that we are not aware of?

Over the years there have been constant rumors about whether or not Oswald attended the Defense Language Institute in Monterey. It is interesting to note that when Marina Oswald met Lee in Minsk she thought he was a Russian because of his fluency in the language. While the verdict is still out as to Oswald's attendance at the Monterey language school, it is certain he did more in Monterey than take the 17-Mile Drive.

After leaving the Marine Corps under highly unusual circumstances, Oswald made his way to the Soviet Union where he promptly showed up at the American Embassy. There he met with the Counsel Richard Snyder and Vice Counsel John McVicker and told them that he was renouncing his US citizenship and pledged allegiance to the Soviet Union. He told them of his work as a radar operator in Japan and offered to give them whatever information he had on the U-2 spy plane. While he was in the Soviet Union, U-2 pilot Francis Gary Powers was shot down over Russia. After his capture, Powers said that the information Oswald gave the Soviets might have been responsible for his shoot down. Prior to his departure for Russia, Oswald did not have enough money to afford the trip but he somehow made it to Russia, even though there were no commercial means of transportation that could have gotten him there in the time he arrived. This leaves open the possibility that he took some sort of military transport to Europe and then made his way to Russia.

In 1957, Lee Oswald was stationed at the highly secret Marine Corps base located in Atsugi, Japan as part of the Marine Air Control Squadron One, knows as "MACS-1," which controlled air traffic for the units of the 1st Marine Aircraft Wing. Soon, the men at MACS-1 saw the arrival of a sleek, modern plane that they had never seen before. The men began speculating just what kind of plane it was. However, their curiosity did not last long. The plane was the CIA's super-secret U-2 reconnaissance aircraft which was to be flown out of Atsugi to take photos of the Soviet Union and China. Oswald was one of the radar operators who got a good look at America's newest spy plane and reveled in its scope. The U-2, dubbed "Race Car," could fly at 90,000 feet, well above any enemy missiles that lay in wait. Oswald and his fellow radar operators were now privy to one of America's most important secrets and had a bird's-eye view of just what the U-2 could do in its spying against our enemies. We do not know what, if anything, Oswald gave to the Russians while he was living in that country. If he told what he knew, then the Russians would have had a wellspring of information on the U-2 that they never would have had before. We also don't know if any information that Oswald handed over to the Russians regarding the U-2 may have played a part in the downing of Gary Powers' plane.

The Soviet reaction to the Kennedy assassination was one of shock and sorrow, despite the growing tensions between the United States and Russia during the Kennedy administration. JFK took power at the height of the Cold War between the US and the Soviet Union, when one mistake by either side could have caused a nuclear war. Tensions were high between the two nations, with Kennedy warning Khrushchev not to interfere in Berlin and other hotspots around the globe where both sides had opposite interests. In the short one thousand days of Kennedy's presidency, Russia was at the forefront of US foreign policy, one that would dominate his time in office. Events in such places as West Berlin and Cuba would pit the US against the Soviet Union in a game of high-stakes chicken where the one who blinked first, might lose everything.

At John Kennedy's inaugural on January 20, 1961, he stood before the nation in freezing temperatures and called for a "New Frontier" in American foreign policy and said the US "would pay any price, bear any burden for the defense of liberty." It was a rallying cry for millions of people around the world who saw in Kennedy a new type of leader, after eight years of the administration of Dwight Eisenhower. The new president brought in to his cabinet a host of new leaders, such as Robert McNamara at Defense and Dean Rusk at State. But Kennedy wanted to be his own Secretary of State, pulling the strings controlling US foreign affairs.

The two major themes of Kennedy's foreign policy were Cuba and Russia. Cuba, located 90 miles off the coast of Key West, had been taken over in 1959 by Fidel Castro when he overthrew the corrupt government of Batista. At first, Castro promised free elections but as time went on, dropped his pretense and allied himself with the Soviet Union who provided most of Cuba's money. As the new president, Kennedy would have to take on Castro in a battle of wits and see who blinked first. Kennedy did not know, as he started his administration, just how much he'd have to deal with Cuba and Castro, with the Soviet Union acting as their main ally against the US. The first major standoff between Cuba—with Soviet backing—was the ill-fated Bay of Pigs invasion of Cuba in April 1961, only three months into his presidency. This was not to be, as the exile-backed invasion had to be put back until after the November elections.

The April 1961 Bay of Pigs invasion of Cuba had its roots in the last days of the Eisenhower administration. With Castro now in the Soviet orbit, Eisenhower ordered the CIA to come up with a plan to oust Castro, preferably before the 1960 presidential election in the US.

The point man for the Cuban invasion was Vice President Richard Nixon, who was then running for president against Senator John Kennedy. The men at the CIA who were in charge of the Bay of Pigs invasion were: Richard Bissell, the director of the CIA's Clandestine Service, J.C. King, head of the Western Hemisphere Section, Tracy Barnes, Bissell's assistant, and Jacob Esterline, the Task Force Director. The Cuban exiles began their invasion training at a secret base in Guatemala called Camp Trax. An airstrip at Retalhuleh was built for the invasion's air force and a secret radio station called Radio Swan was established to broadcast propaganda into Cuba.

"Operation Zapata," was originally scheduled for late March at Trinidad, along Cuba's southern coast. But the site was cancelled and a new landing point called the Bay of Pigs was chosen instead. It was hoped that when the exiles landed in Cuba a spontaneous exile revolt among the mass of the Cuban population would take place, thus causing the downfall of the Castro regime. That failed to happen.

The invasion force left its base at Puerto Cabezas in Nicaragua on April 17, 1961. Shortly before the landing took place, a number of exile bombers based in Nicaragua attacked the small Cuban air force. But the raid failed to take out all of Castro's bombers and the remaining aircraft wreaked havoc at the landing site, killing hundreds of exiles and sinking their ships offshore.

The CIA asked JFK to call an air strike from American ships

offshore but he refused, thus sealing the fate of the exiles as they were now stranded on the beaches at the Bay of Pigs. Over 1,000 men were captured by Castro's forces and were imprisoned for almost a year before being ransomed. Speaking before the now freed members of the Bay of Pigs invasion at Miami's Orange Bowl, President Kennedy promised that their flag would someday fly in a free Havana.

The Bay of Pigs defeat was the first major drubbing of the young Kennedy administration and it set the stage for the administration's later efforts to oust Castro, including the use of the mob and the CIA's covert/overt plan called Operation Mongoose.

Kennedy had been humiliated in the eyes of the world after the failure of the Bay of Pigs adventure, especially when viewed from the perspective of Soviet Premier Nikita Khrushchev. Looking from his balcony atop Red Square he saw, in his opinion, a weak, vacillating young president who could not control his own administration (in this case, the CIA).

The next major crisis between the US and the Soviet Union came in October 1962 in what was called the Cuban Missile Crisis. The world came ever so close to nuclear war during those terrifying 13-days in October (the Soviets had battlefield nuclear weapons on hand in Cuba and were going to use them if the US invaded the island).

The Cuban Missile Crisis had its roots in the period right after the June, 1961 summit meeting in Vienna, Austria between JFK and Soviet Premier Nikita Khrushchev. In what turned out to be an utterly fruitless meeting to discuss the world's crises, the wily Russian leader believed he had the young American president over a barrel. Khrushchev told Kennedy that the Soviet Union was planning to sign a separate peace treaty with East Germany within six months even at the risk of war. If Kennedy refused to cooperate, the western allies were threatened with losing their occupation rights in Berlin. Khrushchev then built the Berlin Wall to keep the eastern population from escaping to the west.

Kennedy said privately to his advisors in summation of the latest Russian move, "It's not a very nice solution, but a wall is a hell of a lot better than a war." But all of Kennedy's soft sounding words suddenly changed on October 15, 1962. On that date, an American reconnaissance plane flying over Cuba photographed the beginnings of a rapid Soviet deployment on Cuban soil of intermediate missiles capable of carrying nuclear weapons. This was the start of the 13-day Cuban Missile Crisis that almost led to nuclear war between the two superpowers.

It is believed that Khrushchev allowed the installation of nuclear weapons in Cuba as a way of countering the American superiority in nuclear weapons. Before introducing the missiles into Cuba, the Soviet Union had never allowed its missiles in any of her satellite nations in Eastern Europe. But the Soviet arms buildup in Cuba did not happen overnight. For months the Navy and the CIA had been monitoring the ever-increasing shiploads of military equipment arriving in Cuban ports, carrying MIG aircraft and thousands of "technicians" to man these new weapons. After consulting his top military and political leaders, the president ordered a naval blockade that would prevent any further military shipments from entering Cuba.

President Kennedy, in a nationally televised speech, told the American people and the world that any Soviet missile launched against the United States would trigger an immediate American response against the Soviet Union.

Thousands of American soldiers began pouring into the southeast for a possible invasion of Cuba. On October 27, 1962, the crisis grew deeper as an American U-2 spy plane was shot down over Cuba. The pilot was Major Rudolf Anderson, and his death created a firestorm among Kennedy's military leaders. They wanted an immediate attack on the missile site that was responsible for the death of Major Anderson, but the president decided not to take any action, which infuriated the generals even more. They saw Kennedy as a weak leader, ready to cave to Russian blackmail. Using so-called "back channel" negotiations, as well as responding to Khrushchev's less belligerent messages during the crisis, the Russians agreed to remove their missiles from Cuba. In return, the United States pledged not to invade Cuba, and also to remove our aging nuclear weapons from Turkey. Per US demands, this part of the deal was not mentioned in public and the Turkish weapons were secretly taken down. In the early 1990s, it was learned that the Soviet Union had about twenty nuclear missiles in Cuba but they were not mounted on the rockets at the time of the crisis. It is evident that if the Americans did invade Cuba, then these nuclear missiles would have been launched (both New York and Washington were on the target list). The big loser in the entire affair was Fidel Castro who was not told of the Soviet-American agreement until it was over. Thus, the only nuclear confrontation the world had ever seen was peacefully ended.

Johnson and Kennedy had a difficult relationship.

Chapter 5
The Richard Helms Testimony

On April 23, 1975, Richard Helms, who had been a key figure in the plots to assassinate Fidel Castro of Cuba and had become the Director of Central Intelligence from 1966 to 1973, gave a deposition to the Senate Committee that was investigating the assassination of President Kennedy, as well as other illegal activities of the intelligence community in the 1960s. The interview took place at the offices of the CIA at Langley, Virginia, at 9:37 a.m. The interview was recorded by a stenographer named S. Susan Hanback and was transcribed under her direction.

Helms had testified before in front of the HSCA on other occasions and his testimony is available on the web for further review. In his testimony which was released in October 2017, Mr. Helms was questioned on a number of important matters including the assassination of South Vietnamese Premier Diem, as well as the Castro plots. But what caught most of the attention of historians of the era is what he did not say at the very end of the document as it related to the possible ties between Lee Oswald and any connections he may have had with the various US intelligence agencies. The document ends before Mr. Helms can answer that question.

One of the questions that Mr. Helms addressed was the assassination of South Vietnamese President Ngo Dinh Diem in late 1963. Diem and his brother Ngo Dinh Nhu, and his flamboyant wife, Madam Nhu, ran South Vietnam with an iron fist. In the last summer of his life, JFK was focusing more and more on the ever-changing situation in South Vietnam. At that time, there were 16,000 US "advisors" training the South Vietnamese Army and already there were causalities among US troops. US advisors were even going on search-and-destroy missions with their counterparts, a fact that was being kept secret from the American public.

As president, Kennedy would face an ever-unraveling political and military situation in Vietnam which he had little control over, and where the stakes were extremely high.

Over time, the ruling generals in South Vietnam were growing more restless with the corruption of the Diem family and they took concrete steps to overthrow him. The catalyst for the eventual coup occurred on May 8, 1963, when an unforeseen event took place in South Vietnam that changed the entire military/political landscape. During a demonstration in the city of Hue, South Vietnamese soldiers under the direction of President Diem fired into a crowd of Buddhist monks who were celebrating the birthday of Buddha. In the ensuing gunfire, nine were killed and fourteen wounded. This incident triggered a nationwide Buddhist protest and a decline in support among the people for the Diem regime. Things got so bad that a number of Buddhist monks openly killed themselves by setting themselves on fire in pubic. These horrific scenes were sent across the world and the Kennedy administration had no choice but to back a coup against Diem that was planned by dissident generals. US officials in Saigon pleaded with Diem to change his ways but he refused. That set off the final plans for his ouster.

On the morning of November 1, 1963, units of the South Vietnamese army attacked the presidential palace. The US Embassy was given only four-minute's notice of the coup. CIA officer Lucien Coenin brought three million piasters ($42,000) to his office that would be used to pay for food for the troops and pay death benefits to those killed in the coup.

The generals met with Diem and guaranteed him and his family safe passage out of the country if they left immediately. Diem called US Ambassador Henry Cabot Lodge and asked what the US position was. Lodge said that as far as he was concerned, the US had no view and said he was concerned for Diem's safety. After Diem refused to resign, the air force began bombing the palace and troops quickly moved in.

No one is sure what happened next, but by 10:30 that night, the bodies of President Diem and his brother Nhu were found. Coenin opined that the brothers escaped to a Catholic Church in Chalon. He said that they might have been recognized and shot. It is also possible that they took their own lives, but as they were good Catholics, that is doubtful. An Inspector General's Report on foreign assassinations said that on November 8, "a field-grade officer of unknown reliability gave the CIA two photographs of the bodies of Diem and Nhu, in which it appeared their hands were tied behind their backs. The source reported that Diem and Nhu had been shot and stabbed while being conveyed to the Joint General Staff headquarters."[7]

Three weeks later, President Kennedy himself was assassinated in Dallas, Texas while riding in an open motorcade. Over the years, there have been persistent rumors that the two assassinations were somehow linked, although no solid proof has ever been revealed to back up that theory.

In his deposition that day, Helms was asked by one of the committee members about the Diem assassination. "And I think you have already testified about that." Answer—"I just did, because President Johnson had raised the cases with me and I thought that since he had done it he might have raised them with President Nixon, and early in his administration I wanted to get him straightened out on this. You know, to this day I am not persuaded that President Nixon doesn't still believe that the Agency didn't have something to do with the demise of President Diem of Vietnam and there is

Richard Helms.

7 Kross, Peter, *Tales From Langley: The CIA from Truman to Obama,* Adventures Unlimited Press, Kempton, Ill., 2014, Page 173.

absolutely no evidence of this in Agency records and the whole thing has been, I mean, rather—what is the word I want—heated by the fact that President Johnson used to go around saying that the reason President Kennedy was killed was that he had assassinated President Diem and this was just justice. He certainly used to say that in the early days of his presidency and where he got this idea from I don't know. I don't know how many of you had the privilege of trying to argue with presidents about things like that but you tend to be a loser."[8]

The questioning then diverted to the events surrounding the election in Chile of the leftist leaning President, Salvador Allende.

Salvador Allende was elected President of Chile in 1970 in a democratic process which was as free as could be in a non-democratic nation. Allende won a plurality, not a majority, in the election over two other candidates. Under the constitution of Chile, the congress would declare the winner between the two top vote getters. Allende was chosen and he took the nation on a new course, wanting to make Chile into a Marxist state, one that Washington was not too thrilled about. Allende called for the nationalization of American companies such as Anaconda Copper and ITT. At the White House, the Nixon administration took notice and they began planning for the ouster of Allende under the right circumstances. Henry Kissinger, whose fingerprints were all over the Allende operation, said, "I don't see why we need to stand by and watch a country go Communist due to the irresponsibility of its own people."

The planned Chilean adventure was not the first attempt by the United States to oust a dictator in South America. In 1954, Operation PBSUCCESS was run by the CIA to remove the democratically elected president Jacobo Arbenz in Guatemala. The operation was run by DCI Allen Dulles with the blessing of President Eisenhower.

In 1961, the CIA teamed up with the Mafia to try to kill Fidel Castro of Cuba. Richard Helms was front and center at the Bay of Pigs planning and Dulles's deputy for plans, Richard Bissell, was the man most responsible for the invasion of Cuba at the Bay of Pigs. The CIA's fingerprints were all over these two covert operations; so why would the plans to topple Allende be any different?

Richard Helms was right in the middle of the Nixon administration's plans to oust Allende. On September 15, 1970,

8 RIF No. 178-10003-10272: Deposition of Richard Helms, April 23, 1975.

Nixon asked Helms to come to the White House for a strategy session on the Allende coup. The CIA's budget for the operation was $10 million but more could be available if needed. Helms later told the Church Committee who investigated the affair that, "The president came down very hard. If I ever carried a marshal's baton in my knapsack out of the Oval Office, it was that day."

However, the coup plan was not the first US attempt to meddle in Chilean elections. In 1964, the CIA persuaded the opposition to Allende to unite behind the Christian Democratic candidate, Eduardo Frei, and gave some $3 million to the effort. In 1970, John McCone, who was the CIA Director at the time of the Kennedy assassination and was then a director of ITT (International Telephone and Telegraph) asked Helms to make a joint ITT-CIA plan in which ITT would provide a million dollars to prevent an Allende victory. Helms refused the offer.

There were some in the CIA who did not want to attempt the coup, but the higher-ups prevailed and the CIA gave the dissident generals ammunition and equipment for the coup. On September 11, 1973, the army staged a coup by attacking the presidential palace called La Moneda in Santiago, with British-made Hawker jets which pounded the palace. The CIA plan was called Operation Fubelt and it was a total success. Allende was overthrown and was replaced by the dictatorship of Augusto Pinochet who ruled that nation with an iron fist.

Another part of Helms' deposition was on his views of how open the intelligence community would have to be with the oversight committees of congress. In parts of his testimony he said, "If I was going to talk to Congress I talked to those congressmen. I testified before other committees, I tried to avoid lying or being guilty of any illegality, but I also tried in some cases to duck these questions so that I wouldn't be in the position of having to come forward in a different context with a different committee on matters which I thought were the proper business of the oversight committee."

The most interesting part of the deposition, and one which opens more questions than answers, came in the comments of David Belin who was the Warren Commission's Chief Counsel. In 1978, Mr. Belin made the following statement, "The CIA withheld from the Commission information which might have been relevant in light of the allegations of conspiratorial contact between Oswald and agents of the Cuban government."

Belin, despite his many later critics, wanted to find out as much as he could, in light of the allegations of involvement by the Cubans in the president's death. At one point he said, "At no time did the CIA disclose to the Warren Commission any facts which pertained to alleged assassination plots to kill Fidel Castro which might have been relevant in light of the allegations of conspiratorial contact between Oswald and agents of the Cuban government."

He also said, "I don't know of any member of the Commission, other than Dulles, that knew that the CIA had been involved in the plots to kill Castro, and I have specifically discussed this with some of the living members."

Belin later wrote a book on the Kennedy assassination and the Warren Commission called *Final Disclosure,* in which he opined on what Robert Kennedy knew regarding the assassination. He wrote, "Robert Kennedy did not respond until August 4, nearly two months later, when he wrote that all information relating in any way to the assassination of President John F. Kennedy in the Department of Justice has been referred to the Warren Commission."

He wrote that, "I would like to state definitely that I know of no credible evidence to support the allegations that the assassination of President Kennedy was caused by a foreign or domestic conspiracy. I have no suggestion to make at this time regarding any additional investigation which should be undertaken by the Commission prior to the publication of its report."

Belin was hard on Robert Kennedy following the assassination. He said that, perhaps Robert Kennedy could not decide whether to tell the Warren Commission about the assassination plots against Castro. He eventually decided to withhold the information."

In *Final Disclosure,* Belin has a lot to say regarding Richard Helms and the Castro plots. After the CIA-mob attempts to kill Castro which were called Phase I, Phase II of the operation took shape. Phase II was run by CIA officer William Harvey, whose name has been mentioned in this book. Helms knew about Phase II and this is what he had to say when Belin asked him about the sending of poison pills to the agent who was to kill Castro, "I don't have any question that we tried to line them up in Cuba, to bring

41

down the government or kill anybody they could lay their hands on." But he did recall that a specific project was approved which was designed for a man to go to point B and actually shoot or poison or do something to Castro.

Helms testified before Congress that he "was not aware of the CIA ever having assassinated any foreign leader. I certainly never authorized the execution of any such operation while I was Director or Deputy Director and when I was Deputy Director for Plans, I don't remember it coming forward. I certainly never recommended such an action to the Director."

While Belin believed that Lee Oswald was the man responsible for the president's assassination, he also believed that the CIA did not have "clean hands" in the information it gave to the Warren Commission. He writes in his book, "So far as the investigation of the assassination of President Kennedy is concerned, the CIA did not have clean hands. The CIA had been guilty of withholding information from the Warren Commission—information that the CIA had been involved in assassination plots directed against Castro, which was a legitimate area of concern for the Warren Commission.

"The CIA also withheld knowledge of the fact that Castro was probably aware of these plans. Existence of the plans was also withheld from the Department of Justice and the FBI. Such information would have been relevant to the investigation of the Warren Commission in light of the allegations of conspiratorial contact between Oswald and agents of the Cuban government. Therefore, I thought it might be interesting if the CIA were to face the problem of losing the protection of secrecy where it operated without clean hands."[9]

At the end of his book, Belin says that he believed that "when Oswald shot Kennedy, he felt he was acting on the man he idolized, the man whose first name was adapted by Oswald to form his alias—A.J. Hidell—Fidel Castro. I also believe there is a substantial possibility that Oswald was influenced by the extreme anti-Castro rhetoric of the Kennedys and perhaps by Castro's call for retaliation."

It is with this background of David Belin in mind, that we return to the Helms deposition and it startling and abrupt ending. The questioning went like this:

9 Belin, David, *Final Disclosure: The Full Truth About the Assassination of President Kennedy,* Charles Scribner's Sons, New York, 1988, Page 174-75.

Mr. Belin: "Well, now, the final area of my integration relates to charges that the CIA was in some way conspiratorially involved with the assassination of President Kennedy. During the time of the Warren Commission you were Deputy Director of Plans is that correct?"

Mr. Helms: "I believe so."

Mr. Belin: "Is there any information involved with the assassination of President Kennedy which in any way show that Lee Harvey Oswald was in some way a CIA agent or an agent..."[10]

This is where the document abruptly ends. There is no more text, as if whoever was taking the notes decided not to reveal the rest of Mr. Helms' testimony. It is also possible that there was no more testimony Helms had to give and we should take no further notice of it. But maybe there's more to the story.

For years, there has been speculation that Oswald was some sort of intelligence asset for some department in the US government. When asked this question, the WC emphatically denied any connection between Oswald and either the CIA or the FBI. But the more researchers delved into the possibility of an Oswald-government connection, the murkier the story got.

Over the past 50 years, there has been much speculation that Oswald might have been a "false defector" sent by US intelligence to the Soviet Union to find out as much as possible on Russian intelligence systems. A former Chief Security Officer at the State Department, Otto Otepka, said that in 1963 that his office was working on a program to study American defectors that included Oswald. Otepka said that in the months before the Kennedy assassination, the State Department did not know if Oswald "had been one of ours or one of theirs."

When Oswald returned from the Soviet Union with Marina, his new wife, he was not charged with desertion by the Navy. Why? By defecting to the Soviet Union, Oswald should have been considered a traitor but there was no disciplinary action taken against him. The Office of Naval Intelligence told the FBI that they had no intention of taking any further action against one of their own. Once back

10 RIF No. 178-10003-10272.

in Texas, the FBI opened a "security case" on him because of his defection; the Bureau sent agents to interview him and found him to be "cold, arrogant, and difficult to interview." Since the FBI did not have any evidence that Oswald had given any secrets to the Soviets, they left him alone.

After the Kennedy assassination, the FBI would learn that Oswald had brought a note into its Dallas office. There is no way to know for certain just what was in the note Oswald delivered because it was destroyed after Oswald was killed by Jack Ruby. Conspiracy theorists say that Oswald was delivering a note to warn the Bureau of the impeding assassination because he was working for them as an agent. Both the CIA and the FBI denied any link to Oswald.

Before Oswald arrived in Russia, he was in Helsinki, Finland for a brief time. It was there that Oswald got a visa to travel to Russia in days instead of the usual one week time period. We know about this via a CIA memo from a vice consul/CIA officer named William Costille. During this time period, Costille met with his Soviet counterpart, Gregory Golub, and they began to trust each other, swapping stories, among other things. According to CIA records, the REDCAP project was "originally designed in 1952 to deal with the results of uprisings in the Soviet satellites, with a special focus on defectors and refugees." One CIA employee said of the REDCAP mission, "First priority went to recruit Soviets as sources or, as the Redcap sloganeers put it, to encourage them to defect in place. Failing that, those who insisted in defecting outright would be brought to the west where their intelligence knowledge could be tapped."[11]

The information we have on the REDCAP/REDSKIN program might have something to do with Oswald's "defection" to the Soviet Union. This information is given in a memo written by the CIA's Deputy Director of Plans, Richard Bissell, on September 2, 1959, days before Oswald left the US for Russia. In the memo, Bissel wrote that the CIA needed to expand efforts by the clandestine service against Russia and that, "One way was to monitor activities of Soviet personnel and installations (REDCAP) and to negate their activities outside of the USSR, and the other was all the operations aimed inside the USSR itself, including REDSKIN."

11 Simpich, Bill, *Lee Harvey Oswald's First Intelligence Assignment*. World-wide-web, September 25, 2010.

It is very possible that Oswald was to be part of the REDSKIN program. The State Department listed Oswald as a "tourist" when he made his application to go to Russia. In the late 1950s, there were at least twenty REDCAP agents sent to the Soviet Union. It is not out of the realm of possibility that Oswald was part of the REDCAP program, sent to the country in order to find out as much information on the Soviet Union as he could.

It is now known that the CIA had a longstanding interest in Lee Oswald, but this was not shared with the Warren Commission. Almost immediately after the president's death, the CIA began its own, internal investigation of the events in Dallas. The man who was put in charge of the operation was John Whitten, a.k.a. "John Scelso." John Whitten worked for the CIA for twenty-three years as an officer in the clandestine operations service. At the time of the president's death, Whitten was a branch chief responsible for operations in Mexico City and Central America, including Panama. His branch was called WH-3 or Western Hemisphere 3. Through the release of thousands of pages of Kennedy assassination information via the JFK Records Act, the 188-page "Scelso Report" was declassified, and tells the story of the CIA's probe into the Kennedy assassination.

For a lone nut that the Warren Commission made Oswald out to be, the CIA had a keen interest in him. New information shows that four important CIA officials kept track of Oswald prior to the assassination. These four people read a lot of information on Oswald, and by October 1963, all of them said he was "maturing." The names of these four people were Jane Roman, William Hood, Tom Karamessines, and John Whitten. These individuals were responding to a cable that they received from the CIA's Mexico City station about Oswald. They told their colleagues in Mexico City that they were aware of Oswald's defection to Russia and his return to the US in 1962. They said that Oswald's stay in the Soviet Union had a "maturing effect on him." If they knew that his stay abroad had a "maturing" effect on him, what did they know about him before his trip to Russia?

If Lee Oswald was not some sort of intelligence operative for the US government (wittingly or unwittingly), why then were there so many important people in the CIA interested in his whereabouts and actions? He associated with various people in Dallas (George de Mohrenschildt) and New Orleans in the summer of 1963 (David Ferrie, Guy Banister and Clay Shaw) before his return to Dallas. Then there is his mysterious trip to Mexico City in late September-early October 1963 when he tried to get a visa to return to Russia via Cuba. The CIA knew that someone was impersonating Oswald while he was in Mexico City and in an interesting development, the pictures of people entering the Cuban and Russian embassies when Oswald was supposed to have been there have, quite by accident, disappeared.

There were rumors that Oswald may have been an informant with the FBI and the Warren Commission took a look at that possibility. The subject came up on January 1, 1964, during the Commission's Executive Session. The Commission's legal counsel, J. Lee Rankin, started the conversation by telling his fellow commissioners the following story. He said that he had a telephone conversation with Waggoner Carr, the Attorney General of Texas, in which he was told that Oswald was an FBI informant and was given the designation 179. Oswald was supposed to have been paid two hundred dollars a month from September 1962 to the time of the assassination. When asked by Rankin how Carr had gotten the information, he said that the news had been given to the defense team for Jack Ruby. Rankin said that he immediately told Chief Justice Warren and that Warren broached the possibility of bringing Carr up to Washington for further testimony.

During their session, the commissioners talked among themselves as to the possible ramifications of such a thing being true. Rankin said that, "Now it is something that would be very difficult to prove out. There are events in connection with this that are curious, in that they might make it possible to check some of it out on time. I assume the FBI records would never show it, and if it is true, and of course we don't know, but we thought you should have the information."

Commission member John Sherman Cooper asked Rankin if it would be possible to absolutely prove that Oswald was not an FBI informer. Rankin responded by saying:

It is going to be very difficult for us to establish the fact in it. I am confident that FBI would never admit it, and I presume their records will never show it, or if their records do show anything, I think their records would show some kind of number that could be assigned to different people according to how they wanted to describe them. So that it seemed to me if it truly happened, he (Oswald) did use postal boxes practically every place he went, and that would be an ideal way to get money for anything that you wanted as an undercover agent, or anybody else that you wanted to do business with without having any particular transaction.[12]

Commissioner Hale Boggs had many lingering questions about Oswald being the killer of the president. He famously said, "Of course it is conceivable that he may have been brought back from Russia you know."

Allen Dulles, another commission member and head of the CIA who was fired by Kennedy, replied, "They (the FBI) have no facilities, they haven't any people in Russia. They may have some people in Russia but they haven't got any organization of their own in Russia. They might have their agents there. They have some people, sometimes American Communists who go to Russia under their guidance and so forth and so on under their control."

It is evident from this conversation that the members of the panel were concerned about Oswald's stay in Russia and the possibility he might have been sent under the auspices of the FBI in some undercover capacity. If Dulles knew of any relationship Oswald might have had with the CIA in Russia (or anywhere else), he never would have mentioned it in open session.

There is a large amount of circumstantial evidence that points to the fact that Lee Oswald was in fact a member, one way or another, in some branch of US intelligence. The CIA and the FBI took an active interest in him while he was in Russia and upon his return home. He actively associated with both pro- and anti-Castro organizations and people in New Orleans in 1963 and the CIA knew of his travels to Mexico City where someone impersonated him. Four important people in the CIA hierarchy kept track of him and knew his every move. For someone unimportant, he had a lot of eyes on him.

And so, it seems appropriate that David Belin would ask whether

12 Warren Commission Executive Session, 1/22/64, 5:30-7 PM.

or not Oswald was associated with any branch of US intelligence to Richard Helms. Helms was one of the most controversial directors of the CIA in agency history, and was deeply involved in the Castro assassination plots,— "the man who kept the secrets," as one author described him.

He was a veteran of the wartime OSS, serving in England and France, and was under the employ of Allen Dulles. After the war, Helms worked for the Central Intelligence Group and later for the CIA. At the height of the Cold War, Helms worked in Germany with the former head of the Nazi intelligence service, Reinhard Gehlen, keeping track of Soviet intelligence operations in Europe.

In the 1960s, he got directly involved in the Castro assassination plots after the Bay of Pigs invasion of 1961 when he was appointed as Director of Plans for the CIA, taking over from Richard Bissell.

Throughout the Kennedy administration's efforts to topple Castro, Helms, like the good soldier he was, followed his orders to the letter, even though he deeply disagreed with many of the policies he was asked to carry out. In later years, Helms refused to testify before various Congressional committees into abuses of the CIA and the Castro assassination attempts, even after leaving government service. For that, he was cited for perjury for his involvement in the coup that toppled the government of President Salvador Allende in Chile.

As "the man who kept the secrets," he stuck to his guns when Mr. Belin asked him about Oswald and US intelligence. Maybe he had one more secret to keep.

Chapter 6
The Cubana Airline Incident

In the minutia of the Kennedy assassination, there are incidents that have been left out of the tale or not researched enough to give a proper presentation. One of these stories is the so-called Cubana Airline Incident that took place on the evening of November 22, 1963 in Mexico City. that has been disputed by many researchers over the years with no concrete answer. What is not in dispute is that the Cubana Airline Incident came to the attention of the Warren Commission, the House Select Committee on Assassinations, and the CIA that wanted to find out just what happened. An ancillary fact that surrounds this incident was a large-scale CIA wiretapping operation that took place in Mexico City that was targeting the Soviet Union and may have picked up some information regarding the alleged presidential assassin, Lee Oswald. Also involved in the wiretapping operation were a number of high-ranking CIA officers whose names are well known to assassination researchers, but whose whole story is still not told.

On the evening of November 22, 1963, only hours after the president was shot, as wild rumors were circulating around the world, an official Cubana Airlines plane (the national airline of Cuba) en route from Mexico City to Havana was delayed for five hours until 9:30 p.m., until a small, private twin engine plane could land. It is alleged that upon arriving, an unidentified man exited from the small plane, got into the larger Cubana airline without going through Mexican customs, and entered the pilot's cabin for the flight to Cuba.

Records declassified concerning the Cubana incident revealed a large-scale covert CIA surveillance operation at the Mexico City airport that was called "LITEMP." According to the written record, the agency operated a concealed camera and photographed incoming passengers from most Cubana Airline flights into Mexico City. There were no photographs of outgoing flights, however. The purpose of the surveillance was to identify all Soviets arriving in Mexico City.

Another interesting incident that took place on that night was the arrival in Havana, Cuba of a plane with Mexican markings that landed at an isolated area in a field. A source allied with the United States said that he saw two men, whom he recognized as Cuban "gangsters," alight, enter the rear entrance of the administration building and disappear without going through the normal customs procedures. His curiosity aroused, he was able to learn that the aircraft had just arrived from Dallas, Texas, the site of the assassination, via Tijuana and Mexico City. The plane had been forced to land in Tijuana due to engine trouble. By comparing the date, the origin of the flight, and the known reputation of the two men, the source theorized that the two men must have been involved somehow in the assassination of JFK. He speculated that Lee Harvey Oswald had acted in the pay of Castro, and that the two Cubans had been in Dallas to organize or oversee the operation. Unfortunately, the source died following his report to the CIA and thus, his allegations could not be substantiated.

During the Cold War era, Mexico City was one of the major hotspots of international espionage. Located between the United States and South America, it was a vital listening post for spies of both NATO and the Warsaw Pact. A book by author Pete Early called *Confessions of a Spy: The Real Story of Aldrich Ames,* gives a vivid description of how the spy game was played in Mexico City. During the 1960s, says Early, the US Defense Intelligence Agency (DIA) began flooding the Soviet embassy with double agents, i.e., volunteer spies, to glean any information they could get. At that time, the US had over one hundred double agent programs on a world-wide basis with a majority of them taking place in Mexico City. This is important to know in light of the obvious impersonation of Oswald in that city.

When the HSCA (House Select Committee on Assassinations) began its investigation into the Kennedy assassination and its ancillary aspects, one of the areas they looked into was the Cubana Airline affair. In a document dated March 27, 1979 titled "November 22, 1963, Cubana Flight," the committee wrote a five-page memo on the topic. After describing the basic details of what happened, they wrote, "The Senate Intelligence Committee wrote that the CIA had no information indicating that a follow up investigation was conducted to determine the identity of the passenger, and had no further information on the passenger, and no explanation for why a follow up investigation was not conducted."[13]

The memo continues by asking four major questions:

a) Did the CIA write the Senate Intelligence Committee that no investigation of the November 22, 1963 Cubana flight was conducted?
b) Did the CIA further investigate the allegation?
c) What were the results of the CIA's investigation?
d) Were the results of the CIA's investigation forwarded to the Senate Intelligence Committee?

The staff of the HSCA took the following measures to answer these questions. They conducted an extensive review of the CIA's files that pertained to the Cubana Airlines flight: they reviewed portions of the Staff Report which included a section on the November 22, 1963 Cubana flights; and they reviewed the February 4, 1976 CIA letter to the Senate Intelligence Committee.

Referring to the February 4, 1976 CIA letter to the Senate Intelligence Committee, "the House Select Committee on Assassinations has determined that the Senate Intelligence's interpretation of the letter is misleading. The CIA wrote the Senate Intelligence Committee that the Mexican authorities were asked about the reported flight delay, although there was no recorded response."

The next question to be asked in this investigation was whether the CIA further investigated the flight allegations. The report tells an interesting story about what was going on in Mexico City at that time:

The CIA conducted regular surveillance of Cubana flights, filing cable reports to headquarters. There was one unilateral CIA surveillance team that observed arrivals and departures of Cubana flights, reporting any unusual incidents and providing copies of flight manifests. The Mexican authorities also had a surveillance team of its own at the airport which provided the CIA with photographs

13 RIF No. 180-10142-10485: November 22, 1963, Cubana Flight.

of passports and copies of passenger lists. A telephone tap operation (LIENVOY) against the Cuban Embassy provided transcripts of conversations with the Cubana office and the Mexican Airport Control office.

Records from that time reveal several CIA operations against the Mexican government in regard to Cubana Airlines at the airport. One of these operations was called LIFIRE:

These sources observed arrivals and departures of Cubana flights. They reported any unusual incidents and provided copies of the flight manifests. This travel was routinely reported to Washington by cable. A copy of the manifests was sent by dispatch to Washington with the same reporting crypt.

LITEMO and LIENVOY were handled (on the policy level) by the COS [the rest of the line is blanked out]. I made the daily pick-up meetings with Career Agent Jeremy K. Benadum for LITEMPO and Staff Agent Arnold Arehart for LIENEVOY. LITEMPO was a surveillance team. They operated a concealed passport camera and photographed incoming passengers. Incoming passengers were photographed because the facilities for departures were located at the other end of the airport and not feasible for the number of available agents at our disposal. Further, the purpose of the passport camera operation was to identify the Soviets arriving in Havana. They also provided us with a list of the incoming passengers on the Cubana flights. LIENVOY was a telephone tap operation against the Cuban Embassy and provided transcripts of conversations with the Cubana Office and the Mexican Airport Control Office.

The CIA was able to ascertain that in late 1963, the Commercial Office of the Cuban Embassy was shipping large quantities of automobile parts, food, and medicine from Mexico City to Havana by Cubana Airlines.[14]

The November 22, 1963 memo that we are referring to talks about when the Cubana flight arrived and departed:

14 RIF No. 104-10404-10423: Cubana Flights.

The LIENVOY transcripts record a series of discussions about the status of the November 22, 1963 Cubana flight— when it arrived and when it departed. The transcripts show that the flight arrived at the airport at 1620 hours (Mexican time). Prior to the arrival of the aircraft, one person stated that the aircraft was due at 1630 hours and "it will go" at 1730, suggesting a quick turnaround that would have reduced unloading and loading time, as well as servicing to a relatively short period. However, the key report on the departure of the aircraft was a statement at 2040 hours that the aircraft had departed for Cuba five minutes earlier, i.e., 2035 hours.

The memo then gives different findings of both the Senate Intelligence Committee and the HSCA. The House's findings were as follows:

> The Cubana flight was on the ground in Mexico City for a total of four hours and about ten minutes. It was not delayed five hours as reported in Book V. The Cubana flight departed at 2035 hours Mexico City time, 55 minutes ahead of the alleged arrival at 2130 of a private flight with a secret passenger. The 2035 departure also contrasts further with the Senate Intelligence Committee Report that the Cubana flight departed at 2200.
>
> No record of a November 22, 1963 twin-engine aircraft carrying a lone passenger exists. In addition, no record exists of a passenger traveling to Havana in the pilot's cabin. In view of the surveillance coverage of the Cubana flight, it is doubtful that the alleged activity involving the private twin-engine aircraft and passenger would have gone unnoticed or unreported had it occurred.
>
> The CIA gave the Senate Intelligence Committee only the informant allegations. The Senate Intelligence Committee did not review the LIFIRE or LIEVOY records. Relying solely on the informant's allegations, the Senate Intelligence Committee could not have reported the story

any differently. (RIF No. 180-10142-10485).

The question is, if there was a mystery man who was on the Cubana flight, who was he? Author Henry Hurt wrote in his book called *Reasonable Doubt: An Investigation into the Assassination of John F. Kennedy* that the identity of the man in question is Miguel Casas Saez. Documents on Saez reveal that he was born in Cuba and was either 21 or 27 at the time of the assassination and that he was fluent in Russian. He was an admirer of Raul Castro, the brother of Fidel (Raul would, years later, become president of Cuba after the retirement of Fidel). The CIA was well aware of Casas and they said that he entered the United States under the alias of Dominiguez Martinez Casas in early November 1963. The CIA documents say that he was on a "sabotage and espionage mission" inside the US. There were rumors that he, along with two other men were in Dallas at the time of the assassination, and that shortly thereafter he returned to Cuba.

A US government source, who was not named, told the agency that he had received information from Casas's aunt and gave the following story. "The aunt said that Casas went by the nickname of Miguelito who had just arrived from the US; he was in Dallas, Texas on the day of the assassination of Kennedy but he managed to leave through the frontier of Laredo. Already in Mexico, a plane brought him to Cuba. You know that he is one of Raoul's men. Miguelito was very brave."

The documents on Casas say were revealed in November 1983 said that a Cuban sources "learned that Casas had firing practice in militias and is capable of doing anything." The CIA assigned two men to investigate Casas and they released a report that "confirms that Casas was indigent and poorly dressed prior to disappearing for several weeks. He now dresses well, has much money, owns large amounts of T-shirts, jackets and shoes, all American." If anything regarding Casas is true then we have to ask the following questions. How and where did he get the money and who gave it to him? How did he leave the US and return to Cuba?

Information gleaned from CIA files on Saez came from an undercover program called AMOT. "AMOT'S were Cubans in Miami, controlled by JMWAVE (the CIA base in Miami) Station who gathered information on Cubans, primarily from debriefing of Cuban refugees."

The AMOT program ran for several years and had about two dozen people working for it at its height. It is believed that the person who ran AMOT was David Morales, a name that is familiar to JFK researchers. Morales was anti-Kennedy in his politics and in later years declared that he knew a lot about the Kennedy assassination. Further information on Saez came from AMOT-28. "Saez belonged to the Communist shock troops, and the G-2 and DIT Cuban intelligence agencies. AMOT-28 even noted that Saez took a course on the Russian Language in the University of Santa Clara." Another source from the CIA said, "Saez speaks Russian quite well."

The information released on Saez says that he left Cuba by small boat and wound up in Puerto Rico. He then arrived in Miami and "tried to buy a boat for unknown purposes." He got the attention of the Immigration and Naturalization Service days before the president was supposed to make a trip to Chicago. New information revealed years later showed that an assassination attempt on Kennedy's life was planned for Chicago. The Secret Service got wind of the plot and it was foiled before it could get off the ground. The documents say that Saez left Miami for Chicago and was possibly in the city when Kennedy's trip was being planned. The information on Saez makes one wonder if he was being set up to put the blame on Castro for the president's assassination. The fact that he was associated with Cuban intelligence and was supposed to have been in Dallas on the day of the assassination makes the "Castro did it" scenario plausible.[15]

One of the most important CIA officers in Mexico City at the time of the Cubana Airline Incident was its Station Chief, Winston Scott. Scott was one of the most promising and influential members of the CIA in the decades of the 1950s and 1960s. He was a poet, a writer, a veteran of the OSS, and served as CIA Station Chief in Mexico City from 1956 to 1969. He also wrote a personal memoir of his life in the CIA that mysteriously disappeared within days of his sudden and premature death.

Winston Scott was born in Alabama in 1909. Well-built and very athletic, he played football at the University of Alabama. He

15 Waldron, Lamar and Hartmann, Thom, *Ultimate Sacrifice,* Carroll & Graf, New York, 2005, Page 606-7.

later graduated from the University of Michigan where he got his PhD in mathematics. He was such a talented baseball player that the New York Giants offered him a professional contract as a catcher. He declined the offer, and instead, joined the FBI at the beginning of America's entry into World War II. During his stint in the Bureau, Scott found time for his passion, writing. He published poetry and wrote a few math textbooks under the pen name "Ian Maxwell."

His first overseas posting for the FBI was in Havana, Cuba. As the war progressed, Scott transferred to the US Navy and he was commissioned as a lieutenant commander. Finding his interest lay in the mundane tools of the intelligence craft, he was sent to the OSS office in London where he was given detailed instructions by the British secret service.

After the war ended, Scott returned to London to become the CIA's first Station Chief (from 1947 to 1950). This was at the height of the Cold War in Europe and Scott was on the firing line of some of the most important operations of the day. He returned to the US and was appointed to the job of CIA Inspector General. In 1956, Scott was given one of the top assignments the CIA could hand out. He left for Mexico City as the new Station Chief.

It was during Scott's tenure as Station Chief in Mexico City that he became embroiled in the secret machinations of Lee Harvey Oswald, the alleged assassin of President Kennedy. In late September and early October 1963, Oswald came to Mexico City seeking a visa to return to the Soviet Union. The CIA later learned that Oswald, or someone pretending to be him, went to the Cuban and Soviet embassies loudly demanding that he be given travel permits for him and his wife to leave the United States, via Cuba.

It has been speculated over the years that the CIA had a recording of Oswald's voice at the Soviet Embassy, although it has never turned up. How, then, does Win Scott fit in all these speculations?

Information concerning Winston Scott's role in the Oswald trip to Mexico City in September 1963 comes in a book by Michael Kurtz called *The JFK Assassinations Debates: Lone Gunman verses Conspiracy* (University Press of Kansas, 2006). According to author Kurtz, Scott told a CIA contact officer named William George Gaudet to meet with Oswald when the latter arrived on September 25, 1963 and checked into the Hotel Comercio in the city.

Oswald's trip to the Mexican capital was arranged by Guy Banister and Hunter Leake in New Orleans. Leake said that Oswald was to be used as a courier to bring information to anti-Castro people in Mexico City. Scott then ordered Gaudet to tell Oswald to return to Dallas on September 27, 1963 and visit the home of Sylvia Odio, whose family was a leader in the anti-Castro cause.

It is interesting to note that William George Gaudet was issued a Mexican tourist card to enter Mexico on the same day as Oswald (September 17, 1963), and at the same location. The number of Gaudet's tourist card was one number before that of Oswald. Over the years, Gaudet was associated with the CIA but denied that he met with Oswald in Mexico City.

On November 23, 1963, President Johnson met with CIA Director John McCone who told the new president that according to Win Scott, Oswald had met in Mexico City with KGB officer Valery Kostikov. McCone told Johnson that Kostikov was a member of the KGB's Department 13 which dealt in assassinations. This meeting began a high-tension mindset inside the new administration that tried to link Oswald to the Soviet Union.

The previous day, on the afternoon of the assassination, a high-level meeting took place at the United States Embassy in Mexico City. In attendance were Winston Scott, US Ambassador to Mexico Thomas Mann, and Clark Anderson, who was the FBI's legal attaché. Their discussion concerned new information that Oswald visited the Cuban and Russian embassies. Clark Anderson fumed at Scott because Scott had not told him of the Oswald visit. Anderson was given the photos and tapes of Oswald's visits to the two embassies. These material were then flown immediately to Dallas where FBI agents were in the process of interrogating Oswald. The agents were surprised to learn that the photos of the man who visited the embassies was not Oswald. "The photographs depicted a man about forty years old, around six feet tall, with a stocky, muscular build, and sporting a receding hairline and a square jaw." This was the picture of the so-called "Unidentified Man" who was impersonating Oswald (the identity of the man has never been revealed).

Scott and Ambassador Mann tried to tie Oswald with pro-Castro forces. They championed a version of events that centered on Gilberto Alvarado, a Nicaraguan intelligence agent who said he had seen Oswald meeting in Mexico City with a "tall Negro with reddish hair" and a "blonde haired girl with a Canadian passport named Maria Luisa." Alvarado said that the Negro gave Oswald $6,500 as payment to kill JFK.

When LBJ was preparing to organize a commission to look into the president's assassination, he ignored pleas from Scott and others to at least consider the fact that Oswald might have been involved with Cuba.

In his testimony to the HSCA, former Ambassador Mann voiced his reservations about what took place in Mexico City on the weekend of the assassination. Mann said that "instructions were received from Washington to stop investigative efforts to confirm or refute rumors of Cuban involvement in the assassination. Mann said that his instructions came from Dean Rusk who was Secretary of State, and he believed that Scott, CIA Station Chief, and Anderson, FBI Legat, had received similar instructions from their respective directors."

When Scott retired from the CIA in 1969, he remained in Mexico City and went into private business, creating a firm called Diversified Corporate Services. He also kept most of his private files that he had accumulated over the years. He told many of his colleagues that he was writing his memoirs but most of them did not really know what was going to be included in the book. Some people who knew about Scott's book said it contained information about his life in the OSS and the FBI. The book was referred to as an autobiographical "novel" about Scott's life. The working title of the book was *Foul Foe*. The manuscript, which was never released to the public, has numerous, candid references to the CIA's relationship with Oswald during the September-October 1963 time period. Furthermore, after Scott's death, his manuscript was seized, along with all his personal papers.

The circumstances surrounding Scott's death are interesting and tragic. He fell from a ladder at his home, fell off the roof, and received a number of cuts and bruises. He didn't seem too fazed by the injury and resumed his normal activities. On April 26, 1971, one day after his fall, his wife found him dead in their home.

In the wake of Scott's death, the CIA, which had been notified of the event shortly after it happened, moved quickly. In circumstances that are still unknown today, James Angleton, the agency's legendary counterintelligence chief, made a hurried trip to Mexico City to retrieve all of Scott's personal papers, including the cryptic manuscript he had written. What could have made Angleton go to Mexico in such a hurry? Could it have been Scott's very extensive information that he had about Oswald's visit to Mexico, and any potential CIA involvement?

Thomas Mann, who served as JFK's ambassador to Mexico at the time of Scott's residence as CIA Station Chief, had some rather interesting remarks concerning Scott's death. In an interview Mann gave later to a reporter, he said, "But that was one of the things that makes me a little bit suspicious about Win Scott dropping dead like that. Well, I always suspected that he might have been murdered. He started running some kind of his own personal intelligence organization. They wanted to use his expertise and knowledge of Mexico, especially the intelligence side of it. When you get involved in that sort of thing, one is not surprised, if you know that world, when people drop real quick. I wouldn't want to write a life insurance policy on some of the people I've known connected to that organization."

In 1985, Michal Scott, Winston's son, tried to get the CIA to allow him access to his father's papers, as well as the secret report. The younger Scott paid a visit to CIA headquarters in Langley, Virginia. There, he was treated with respect by the people he talked to. However, they refused to release any of his dad's material to him. According to Michael Scott, one of the CIA men whom he met told him that, "There may be information you know from outside sources that might seem to be public knowledge, but we can't officially release it to you."

To this day, Winston Scott's unpublished narrative and any explosive material it may contain relating to the Oswald trip to Mexico City (and other topics) is still under wraps.

Chapter 7:
The Secret Soviet Murder Program

One of the little known documents that came out in October 2017, which was mostly unread by many of the Kennedy assassination researchers, was a newspaper article written by Robert Allen and Paul Scott in the "Inside Washington" column (he name of the newspaper in not mentioned in the article) called "CIA Withheld Vital Intelligence from Warren Report." The gist of the article is that there was a top-secret Soviet plan that began in the 1940s whose goal was the elimination of American political leaders who did not share Soviet views. The method of eliminating these Western leaders was the use of various exotic weapons whose development was kept a secret in Moscow. This intelligence story was not given to the Warren Commission members when they were investigating the president's assassination. In light of any possible Soviet involvement in the assassination, the Warren Commission was not able to verify or investigate this explosive story.

Whether or not the story had any relevance to the Kennedy assassination investigation, the CIA kept this information to itself, never revealing any of it to Chairman Earl Warren or any of his fellow commissioners.

The origin of the story was a national intelligence estimate provided by the CIA "that it is Kremlin policy to remove from public office by assassination Western officials who actively oppose Soviet policies."

The title of the national estimate was "Soviet Strategic Executive Action." The suppressed CIA document went into the shocking details of how agents of the KGB, the Soviet secret police, are trained to do away with Western leaders, including officials in the US, and to make their deaths appear to be due to natural causes." The article says that one of the American leaders who was targeted for elimination was John McCormack who was the Speaker of the House of Representatives under the administration of President Lyndon Johnson and was in the line of succession to the presidency.

The United States itself had a secret assassination program

called Executive Action-ZR/RIFLE which was run by the CIA.

Project ZR/RIFLE first came to light during the Church Committee hearings in 1975 that dealt with both illegal CIA domestic activities and the committee's parallel investigation of the Kennedy assassination. This program, originally established in the early days of the new Kennedy administration, was originally set up to get rid of Fidel Castro, turned into a nightmare, but finally involved plots to kill Patrice Lumumba of the Congo, as well as other foreign heads of state whose policies ran counter to US interests. Project ZR/RIFLE had its domestic ramifications as well, involving militant anti-Castro Cubans whose goal was to reestablish their old business interests in Cuba.

Besides the Cubans, this top-secret project may have had tenuous links to the assassination of JFK on November 22, 1963. The Executive Action purview included "the development of a general, stand-by assassination capability." This program included research into the long-term possibilities and capabilities of killing foreign leaders. Despite all the intensive planning for Executive Action, in reality, the program was never actually carried out.

The man who was put in charge of the Executive Action-ZR/RIFLE program was a James Bond-type CIA officer named William Harvey. Harvey was well equipped to deal in this new type of operation, having been one of the key players in the CIA's secret war against Castro, later called Operation Mongoose. At one point Harvey called ZR/RIFLE "the magic button," and "the last resort beyond and a confession of weakness." In the notes he left behind, Harvey never used the word "assassination." Instead, when dealing with ZR/RIFLE, his favorite expressions "maximum security" and "nonattributability."

The files on the program show that the Kennedy administration was well aware of ZR/RIFLE as early as February, 1961. In the CIA's Inspector General's Report on the plots to kill Fidel Castro, "Project ZR/RIFLE was covered as an operation (ostensibly to develop a capability for entering safes and for kidnapping couriers). Harvey has a note dated November 15, 1961, in which he discussed with Richard Bissell the application of the ZR/RIFLE program to Cuba.

Despite all the preparations at the CIA in regards to the operational nature of Executive Action, this program was never directly used against Castro or Cuba. Bill Harvey was head of the super-secret group called "Staff D" which was responsible for communication intercepts. All of the CIA's covert activities were given cover names with letters for designations. Staff A was foreign intelligence, B-operations, C-Counterintelligence. But Staff D was different, its doors physically sealed and guarded by armed Marines. The CIA cryptonym for the ZR/RIFLE project was KUBARK, which was used for internal use. Nothing was written down, it was only "word of mouth" and "strictly person to person, singleton ops, no projects on paper."

The ZR/RIFLE also had parallel ties to the CIA-Mafia efforts to kill Castro and was in operation at that time. The agency hired two mercenaries to become part of a team and were forever known by their code names, WI/ROGUE and QJ/WIN.

It now seems clear that President Kennedy and probably his brother Robert were aware of the ZR/RIFLE-Executive Action program (that issue is still hotly debated among researchers). Whether JFK ordered that Fidel Castro be "terminated," or knew of the CIA-Mafia plots (the Mahue-Rosselli-Trafficante-Giancana connection) is still in dispute. It is very possible that the forces unleashed via Executive Action, as they affected the Cubans, QJ/WIN, WI/ROUGE, and the various plots to paint Lee Harvey Oswald as a follower of the Castro regime, thus making him a Castro dupe in the assassination of the president, may have led to the tragedy in Dallas.

The article mentioned above goes on to describe what kind of weapons these Soviet assassins used in their deadly tasks. One was a "pneumatically operated poison ice atomizer which leaves no wound or other evidence of the cause of the person's death."

The authors say that at the time that the article was written, they had no evidence that any high Western leader was executed by Soviet agents, but that hundreds of KGB agents covertly operated outside of Russia and had been supplied with a pocket-size gun, "awaiting only orders from Moscow to use it."

Part of these agents' job was "arranging for the dismissal of such persons from public office, at other times even having them eliminated physically."

Such activities are known to be undertaken against other types of persons in the West, notably defectors from the USSR and from other countries of the Soviet bloc.

One way in which these KGB assassins did their dirty work was to lure their victim to a telephone booth that was connected to a high-voltage wire during a thunderstorm. Another method used by these people was a pistol which projected a poison gas in liquid form. Once a person was killed in this way, an autopsy would not be able to find any trace of the poison in the person's system.

The article by Allen and Scott makes reference to misleading information coming from the US State Department regarding one of its employees and Lee Oswald. They write that the State Department suppressed information "linking Oswald with one of its employees, who according to security files, presented strong pro-Soviet views on every question that came up in the Department's USSR country committee while he was a member."

"This State Department official's name also appears in the address book of a suspected Soviet agent who arrived in the US in 1943, according to government files."

As mentioned earlier in this chapter, one of the targets of Soviet assassins was Speaker of the House John McCormack. The FBI told Speaker McCormick that he was on the target list, but the CIA took a different tack in that regard. "No CIA authority has shown the No. 2 man in government [McCormack] the CIA report listing these secret Soviet assassination methods." Why Speaker McCormack was not told this information is hard to imagine. McCormack was finally told about the Soviet operation by congressional staffers who were looking into this secret operation.

The article ends with information on Oswald's trip to Mexico City in September-October 1963. Here is what they wrote:

> The investigators also are trying to determine why the CIA in its pre-assassination report to the State Department on Oswald's trip to Mexico City gave details only of the defector's visit to the Russian embassy and not the Cuban embassy. The CIA did not report the latter visit until after Kennedy's assassination in Dallas.

63

The US State Department was well aware when young Lee Harvey Oswald left the United States for Russia. His mother, Marguerite, wrote a letter telling of her worry that her son had not been heard from since he arrived in Russia and that she was worried about his safety. On the advice of an FBI agent named Fain, Mrs. Oswald wrote to her congressman Jim Wright, telling him of her son's predicament. The congressman then contacted the State Department which sent a copy of Mrs. Oswald's letter to the American embassy in Moscow, asking that a copy of her letter be sent to Lee.

While we don't know anything more about the unidentified State Department person the article references, it is just another clue in this very mysterious case.

The concept that a special section of KGB assassins had a hit list on prominent American and Western leaders, and were ready to take them out if necessary, adds fuel to the theory of a possible Russian connection to the president's assassination. The "Russia did it theory" has been bandied about for years, but it is not very plausible. If it had been verified beyond a doubt that the Russians did it, then a nuclear war between the US and Russia would have been inevitable, with consequences far beyond our thinking.

The fact that the KGB had such an operation on the books for so many years was probably just a legacy of the Cold War between the two superpowers that was not put into effect.

Chapter 8
The Robert Rawls Allegation

In the months before the assassination of President Kennedy, there were numerous reports of assassination attempts being planned. Most of this information was gleaned from records and personal accounts after the assassination by groups like the HSCA (House Select Committee on Assassinations) whose mandate was to look into the deaths of both JFK and Martin Luther King, Jr., as well as to evaluate statements from people who were alleged to have made threats against the president. One such statement came from a New Orleans resident by the name of Robert Collum Rawls, who was interviewed on November 27, 1963 by a member of the US Secret Service.

Shortly after the president's assassination, the District Intelligence Office, Charleston, South Carolina was informed that Robert Rawls had information regarding the events in Dealey Plaza just a few, short days ago. It seems that Robert Rawls was a patient at the US Naval Hospital in Charleston, SC. and was there for back problems. He was interviewed by a representative of the Office of Naval Intelligence for less than an hour. Here is what the report had to say.

Robert Rawls said he was in a bar in New Orleans about ten days to two weeks before the assassination. He said he had just gotten off work as an attendant at Mayfield's Gulf Service Station on Canal and Broad Streets in New Orleans. He said that while he was in the bar, he heard another patron attempt to place a bet on the life of the president and said that JFK would be dead within two weeks. The amount of money he was betting was $100.00. Mr. Rawls said that he had never seen the person before and that it was unlikely he could even remember what he looked like. When he was asked by his interviewer about his sobriety at that time, he said that he was "somewhat intoxicated" and said the man who made the remark was in a similar state. Rawls said that he paid no attention to the man's remarks at the time because, "It was just drunk talk and a drunk will bet on anything." He said that after the assassination, he remembered the incident and notified federal authorities. He said the man in question was dressed like a "working man," but could not describe him any further.

It is now that Mr. Rawls' story gets complicated, and possibly not really credible. He said that he did not remember the name of the bar he was in but did recall that it was located just off Canal Street. He also said that he sometimes frequented other bars in the area, called Freddie's Bar and the Straight Day Bar.

On the night in question, Mr. Rawls said he was in the company of two other people, an ex-Navy friend named Bob Tanner and his girlfriend whose name he did not mention. He said that he does not know if either of them heard the remark that the stranger allegedly made because none of them ever discussed the matter. "He thinks Tanner and his girl-friend may have been away from the table or at the booth at the time the remark was made. The man offering the bet was not at a table, but was at the bar. He did not hear anyone call this man by name. He does not know Tanner's New Orleans address and does not know the name of Tanner's girl-friend. He said, however, that she works as a waitress at the Meal-a-Minute on Canal Street."

Rawls, a white male, said his address at the time of the incident was 2037 Cleveland Street, New Orleans, LA. He told authorities that he was a former Navy quartermaster third class, and that his Navy serial number was 636-84-38.

When the Secret Service looked into Rawl's allegations, they reported that he had been treated at the US Naval Hospital in Charleston, S.C. where he was getting an evaluation physical. "They stated when results of this physical are compiled, a disability evaluation board will study said results to determine the extents of Rawl's handicap. The authorities advise Rawl's medical problem was mainly orthopedic, however, they said he does have a psychiatric past of passive-aggressive reaction with hostile tendencies. They stated persons with this psychiatric problem are generally reliable and are considered to be sane."[16]

The story purportedly told by Robert Rawls, while really not credible on its face, is just a part of a larger operation that took place in New Orleans in the months before the president's death. This was

16 Letter to Mr. Lewis Huff, US Secret Service, Columbia SC from E.L. McIntosh, Jr. 27 November 1963.

investigated by Jim Garrison, the DA of Orleans Parish, Louisiana, andinvolved a number of nefarious and curious persons who lived in New Orleans at that time, among them, David Ferrie, Guy Banister, and the president's alleged assassin, Lee Oswald. While the entire story of the New Orleans connection to the JFK assassination is too long to be told in this chapter, a few words about the participants are in order.

Guy Banister's name comes up time and again in the New Orleans chapter of the Kennedy assassination saga, as he was directly linked in one way or another with many of the other suspects in the Kennedy drama: David Ferrie, Lee Harvey Oswald, and the anti-Castro Cubans who made New Orleans their home in the summer of 1963. During his professional life in law enforcement, Banister had ties with the FBI, the CIA and the Office of Naval Intelligence. He was an ex-FBI agent, the head of the Bureau's Chicago office. He was one of the FBI agents who arrested the notorious criminal John Dillinger. In World War II, Banister worked for Naval Intelligence and kept his contacts in the decades after the war. After the hostilities ended, he came to New Orleans and was appointed Deputy Police Chief. He was forced to resign in the late 1950s after an

Guy Bannister.

Oswald in New Orleans handing out pro-Cuba leaflets.

incident in which he pulled a pistol on a civilian.

Banister was a rabid anti-Communist, an anti-Castro proponent and was also a member of the ultra right-wing John Birch Society. He was also a member of the Louisiana Committee on Un-American Activities, kept large files on left-wingers in New Orleans, and was tight with the numerous anti-Castro groups working in the city in the early 1960s.

According to Jim Garrison, Banister was celebrating after the assassination, had too much to drink, and pistol whipped his co-worker, Jack Martin. Martin, according to Banister, was a spy in his office who was talking too much and not keeping Banister's private dealings private. Martin later said that Banister's associate in the anti-Kennedy, anti-Castro crowd, an ex-pilot and homosexual named David Ferrie, was linked to the assassination and was supposed to be the getaway pilot after the president's death.

Banister ran his private detective agency out of an address at 544 Camp Street in New Orleans. This address was the home of his anti-Castro operation in the city where guns and ammunition were stored and subsequently passed to members of the anti-Castro cause then training in the swamps outside the city for an invasion of Cuba.

In the summer of 1963, Lee Harvey Oswald was passing out his Fair Play for Cuba Committee leaflets in the city and got into a confrontation with an anti-Castro passerby. Written on the leaflets was the address 544 Camp Street. It has also been reported by Banister's secretary that Oswald was working for Banister and that he was frequently in his office in the summer of 1963.

Banister's links with the various anti-Castro elements in New Orleans were rock solid, as well as his relationship with the law enforcement and federal intelligence agencies working out of downtown New Orleans in the summer before JFK's death.

Another one of Banister's associates in New Orleans at that time was David Ferrie, an anti-Kennedy, anti-Castro, former Eastern Airlines pilot who was associated with the CIA and was a major player in the Kennedy saga in the Big Easy. He grew up in Cleveland, Ohio, attending Roman Catholic schools as a youngster. He started attending classes in a Catholic seminary but eventually dropped out. One of his passions was flying, and he got his pilot's license and moved to New Orleans to pursue his dream.

David Ferrie was a man of bizarre appearance, suffering from a rare skin disease called alopecia, a condition that left him hairless over his body. He wore a wig and false eyelashes, which made him look even more bizarre to passersby. He was also heavily involved in cancer research, trying to concoct homemade remedies that would cure the disease. He dabbled in a strange religious order called the Orthodox Old Catholic Church of North America, was a closet member of the New Orleans gay community, and headed a squadron of the local Civil Air Patrol in the city. One of his students was a young Lee Harvey Oswald.

When he arrived in New Orleans, he got a job as a pilot for Eastern Airlines and served with distinction before the company

David Ferrie with pilot's cap, circa 1959.

found out that he was a blatant homosexual. He was then fired. Somehow he managed to connect himself with mob boss Carlos Marcello and did legal work for him. Another man Ferrie was connected with was Guy Banister who often times employed Ferrie in his anti-Castro crusade in the city. Ferrie worked out of Banister's office at 544 Camp Street, which was the unofficial home of the various right-wing, anti-Castro, and US intelligence agents in the city (as well as Lee Oswald). (It is believed he flew a number of covert missions into Cuba in the early 1960s, supplying guns and ammunition to the anti-Castro underground.)

On the day of Kennedy's death, Ferrie was accused of making a long distance car trip with a number of friends to Houston, Texas. Ferrie told New Orleans DA Jim Garrison that he went to Houston to go ice skating. It has been alleged that the reason Ferrie went to Houston was to act as the getaway pilot for the conspirators, including Oswald, who was to have been taken to Mexico and eliminated. Another interesting fact concerning Ferrie's activities is that prior to the JFK murder, he deposited $7,000 into his bank account. Up to that point, Ferrie was living hand to mouth and it is still unclear where the money came from.

Upon his return to New Orleans, he was picked up in the investigation of the assassination of the president by DA Jim Garrison. Garrison was able to link Ferrie to Banister, Clay Shaw, a prominent businessman in the city (Shaw was later tried and found not guilty as a conspirator in the JFK assassination), and other anti-Castro Cubans in the city. Shaw, it later turned out, was a contract agent for the CIA and was on their payroll for some time. Garrison turned Ferrie over to the FBI who found no hard evidence linking him to the president's death. He was subsequently released.

While doing research at the National Archives, this writer found a rather interesting document linking Ferrie, Shaw (using an alias) and Lee Oswald. What I found was a flight plan dated April 8, 1963, along with follow up documentation. The flight plan is an ordinary one, with the type of plane being operated, its destination, and approximate flight time. But where this differs from a regular scheduled flight, say from Newark Airport, is the "Captain" of the plane (a Cessna 37) by the name of David Ferrie.

The names of the three passengers on board the flight's manifest were Diaz, Lambert and "Hidell." But there's more. Among the follow up material that goes with the flight plan is an affidavit by a former prisoner in the US penitentiary in Atlanta, Georgia (dated December 5, 1967) by the name of Edward Julius Grinus, stating that the "Lambert" listed on the plane's manifest is an alias used by Clay Shaw.

If the Grinus allegation is correct, we now have another alias used by Clay Shaw, besides the "Clay Bertrand" he is known to have used. Even more important is the name "Hidell" listed with "Lambert" and Diaz. If this document is authentic, it definitely links Lee Harvey Oswald and Clay Shaw (along with David Ferrie) for the first time.

The reason that Jim Garrison took an interest in David Ferrie was the fact that both Oswald and Ferrie had been seen together in the summer of 1963 in the city. Ferrie denied to Garrison any knowledge of Oswald but the fact that Oswald was in Ferrie's Civil Air Patrol unit makes that statement false. Garrison was going to use Ferrie as an important witness in the trial against Clay Shaw who was charged with being a conspirator in the president's death, but Ferrie died in mysterious circumstances on February 22, 1967 of a supposed "brain hemorrhage" in his apartment. When the coroner team went to Ferrie's apartment they found two suicide notes (who writes two suicide notes?), along with white mice that Ferrie was using in his cancer research, and a map of Cuba. Part of one suicide

David Ferrie with Oswald in a New Orleans Civil Air Patrol group photo in 1955.

note says, "To leave this life is, for me, a sweet prospect. I find nothing in it that is desirable and on the other hand, everything that is loathsome." And "when you read this I will be quite dead and no answer will be possible."

Another person to link Oswald and Ferrie was a New Orleans resident named Perry Russo. He said that he attended a party at Ferrie's apartment in September 1963. In attendance were Russo, Ferrie, Shaw (using the name Clay Bertrand), and a man who introduced himself as "Leon Oswald." During the party, the talk among the men turned to the assassination of the president.

According to Russo, "Ferrie took the initiative in the conversation, pacing back and forth as he talked. He said an assassination attempt would have to involve diversionary tactics... there would have to be a minimum of three people involved. Two of the persons would shoot diversionary shots and the third would shoot the good shot. You would have to create a triangulation of crossfire. If there were three people, one of them would have to be sacrificed."[17]

Jim Garrison said of David Ferrie, "I don't feel personally guilty about Ferrie's death, but I do feel terribly sorry for the waste of another human being. In a deeper sense, though, David Ferrie died on November 22, 1963. From that moment on, he couldn't save himself, and I couldn't save him."

17 Benson, Michael, *Who's Who In the JFK Assassination: An A-Z Encyclopedia,* Carol Publishing Co., New York, 1993, Page 136.

Chapter 9
The Hoover-Ruby Memo

On November 24, 1963, just two days after the president's assassination, with Lee Harvey Oswald now dead by the hands of a Dallas nightclub owner named Jack Ruby, FBI Director J. Edgar Hoover wrote a memo detailing the steady stream of events that had taken place over the past two days. Hoover opined on a number of topics, i\e.g., the murder of Oswald, the background of Jack Ruby, and the events surrounding Oswald in Mexico City.

In the first paragraph of Hoover's memo, he did not mince words regarding the death of Oswald and what it would mean for any future investigation. He began by saying that:

> There is nothing further on the Oswald case except that he is dead. Last night we received a call in our Dallas office from a man talking in a calm voice and saying he was a member of a committee organized to kill Oswald.
>
> We at once notified the Chief of Police and he assured us Oswald would be given sufficient protection. This morning we called the Chief of Police again warning of the possibility of some effort against Oswald and he again assured us adequate protection would be given. However, this was not done.

Hoover then went on to write about the transfer of Oswald from the Dallas Police Department to a waiting car that would take him to another location and the subsequent shooting of the suspect by Ruby. He wrote about Ruby by saying,

> He runs two nightclubs in Dallas and has a reputation of being a homosexual. Immediately after the shooting, he [Oswald] was moved to Parkland Hospital [the same place where the president died] and died about 45 minutes ago. We had an agent at the hospital in the hope that he might make some kind of a confession before he died but he did

not do so.

Ruby says no one was associated with him and denies having made the telephone call to our Dallas office last night. He says he bought the gun about three years ago and that he guessed his grief over the killing of the president made him insane. That was a pretty smart move on his part because it might lay the foundation for a plea of insanity later.

If Hoover knew at that time about Ruby's ties to organized crime, he decided not to reveal it.

Hoover then went on to rant about the Chief of Police, Jesse Curry and his staff for the bungling and talking out of line that Hoover found irritating. Hoover wrote:

> I dispatched to Dallas one of my top assistants in the hope that he might stop the Chief of Police and his staff from doing so dammed much talking on television. They did not really have a case against Oswald until we gave them our information. We traced the weapon, we identified the handwriting, we identified the fingerprints on the brown bag. We were able to identify the bullets as coming from that gun (Oswald's rifle). All the Dallas Police had was three witnesses who tentatively identified him as the man who shot the policeman (Officer J.D. Tippit whom Oswald was supposed to have killed as he made his way to the Texas Theater where he was ultimately captured) and boarded a bus to go home shortly after the President was killed. He got on a bus to go home to get a shirt and the bus conductor identified him as the man who boarded the bus.

The FBI chief then talked about Oswald's choice of a lawyer to represent him at a trial. The lawyer in question was a man named John Abt. "Oswald had been saying he wanted John Abt as his lawyer and Abt, with only that kind of evidence, could have turned the case around, I'm afraid. All the talking down there might have required a change of venue on the basis that Oswald could not have gotten a fair trial in Dallas. If they keep on talking, perhaps the same will be true of Ruby."

Jack Ruby posing with three of the strippers at his Dallas club.

It is evident from the remarks from Hoover regarding a fair trial for Oswald that it was something he was worried about, if Oswald had lived. Right from the beginning, after Oswald's arrest, there were many different versions of what happened in Dealey Plaza that day. There were reports by various, credible witnesses of shots being fired from the grassy knoll near where the president's motorcade passed. There were witnesses who took pictures of the fatal headshot that the president received near the grassy knoll that could have indicated a shot (or shots) coming from that area. No one actually saw Oswald fire the shots from the Texas School Book Depository, although one person who was on the floor below said he heard the sound of cartridges hitting the floor above. Then there was the year's-long controversy regarding the so-called "magic bullet" which struck both Kennedy and Texas governor John Connelly and the damage that was inflicted on both men from one bullet. Despite Hoover's allegations that the FBI identified Oswald's fingerprints on the alleged murder weapon, in fact, there was no fingerprint that belonged to Oswald when the FBI traced it after the assassination. Another discrepancy that Hoover talked about was that there was conflicting testimony by witnesses regarding who actually killed DPD officer Tippit. Some people in the area said Oswald did it, while others said he did not. There was even speculation going around that Oswald was at the Texas Theater, where he was captured, to meet people who were going to aid him in his escape from Dallas. Any good criminal attorney at that time, who weighed all the available evidence, may have had a good case in defending Oswald at trial. He did not have an attorney with him at questioning, and there were no notes taken during his interrogation by local and federal law enforcement officials; we only have the recollection of the people who were his questioners. Another questionable incident that the Dallas Police were responsible for guarding Oswald was when they paraded him in front of a large number of press people where Oswald held an impromptu press conference. He denied killing anyone and said the most famous words of his short life: that he was just "a patsy."

The Hoover memo goes on to rail against both Chief Curry and Captain Fritz of the Homicide Squad. He said that Curry could not control Captain Fritz:

> ...who is giving much information to the press. Since we now think it involves the criminal code on a conspiracy charge under Section 241, we want them to shut up. Furthermore, I have ordered the evidence be secured by the Police Department. We sent most of the evidence back to them. We still have the bullets that were fired and will keep them.

Hoover then made the most important statement regarding Oswald and the aftermath of the assassination in his memo. It reads as follows:

> The thing I am concerned about, and so is Mr. Katzenbach, is having something issued so we can convince the public that Oswald is the real assassin. Mr. Katzenbach thinks the President might appoint a Presidential Commission of three outstanding citizens to make a determination. I countered with a suggestion that we make an investigative report to the Attorney General with pictures, laboratory work, etc. Then the Attorney General can make the report to the President

and the President can decide whether to make it public. I felt this was better because there are several aspects which would complicate our foreign relations. For instance, Oswald made a phone call to the Cuban Embassy in Mexico City which we intercepted. It was only about a visa, however. He also wrote a letter to the Soviet Embassy here in Washington, which we intercepted, read, and resealed. This letter referred to the fact that the FBI had questioned his activities on the Fair Play for Cuba Committee and also asked about extension of his wife's visa. That letter from Oswald was addressed to the man in the Soviet Embassy who is in charge of assassination and similar activities on the part of the Soviet government. To have that drawn into a public hearing would muddy the waters internationally. To use all that would reveal our failure to carry out international courtesy laws. And since this had nothing to do with proof that Oswald committed the murder, I made the suggestion to Mr. Katzenbach that instead of a Presidential Commission, we do it with a Justice Department report based on an FBI report.[18]

The three man commission that Katzenbach wanted turned out to be the Warren Commission that President Johnson appointed on November 29, 1963, made up of a number of distinguished Americans, including Allen Dulles who was the CIA Director under JFK and who was fired by the president after the Bay of Pigs invasion of Cuba. As a commissioner, Dulles failed to report the CIA-Mafia plots to kill Castro, something the commission members would have been interested to learn about.

The reason that Hoover wanted to keep the probe into Kennedy's death in-house was to keep the FBI's failures in protecting the president from coming out in the open. For example, the FBI interviewed Oswald when he returned from Russia, as well as his wife Marina. FBI agent James Hosty interviewed Marina at her suburban Dallas home and she told Lee about it. Lee got into a tizzy over Hosty's visit and went to the Dallas office of the FBI to complain. After Hosty's second visit to Marina, Lee went to the FBI office and asked to see Agent Hosty. Hosty was out and Lee left a

18 RIF No. 180-10110-10104: Oswald, Lee, Murder By Ruby, 11/24/63.

message for him with the receptionist. Lee was told that the message would be given to Hosty upon his return. What the note contained is still a mystery. Researchers have postulated that the note contained a warning that JFK would be killed, the story being that Oswald was some sort of Bureau informant. Then a strange thing happened. After the assassination, the note that Lee had left for Hosty was ordered destroyed by higher-ups in the Bureau. Nancy Fenner, the receptionist at the FBI that Lee gave the note to, said she saw part of it and that it said, "Let this be a warning. I will blow up the FBI and the Dallas Police Department if you don't stop bothering my wife."

Hosty's recollection was different. He said that the note read as follows: "If you have anything you want to learn about me, come talk to me directly. If you don't cease bothering my wife, I will take appropriate action and report this to the proper authorities."[19]

The person in the FBI who told Hosty to destroy the note was Gordon Shanklin, the Agent in Charge. Shanklin called Hosty into his office after Oswald was killed and ordered him to destroy the note. Shanklin is supposed to have told Hosty, "Oswald's dead now. There can be no trial—get rid of this." Hosty then tore up the note in front of his boss but Shanklin wasn't through. He further said, "No. Get it out of here. I don't even want it in this office. Get rid of it." Hosty then took the note to the bathroom and flushed it down the toilet.

Years later, Shanklin denied the incident ever took place. Shanklin's denial was contradicted by William Sullivan, the Assistant Director of the FBI at the time of the assassination. Sullivan said, "Shanklin had often discussed an internal problem over a message from Oswald."

When the congressional investigative committee looking into the Kennedy-King assassinations looked into the destruction of the Hosty note they made a scathing report on it. In 1979, "it regarded the incident of the note as a serious impeachment of Shanklin's and Hosty's credibility. The Committee noted further the speculative nature of its findings about the note incident. Because the note had been destroyed, it was not possible to establish with confidence what its contents were."

Hosty later had a lot to say regarding the entire note incident. He said in 1978 of Congress' Assassination Committee, " I am the

19 Summers, Anthony, *Conspiracy,* 1980, Page 395-6.

one they are afraid is going to drop bombs-if they are going to try to contain this like the Senate Intelligence Committee and the Warren Commission, they don't want me there."

The last part of the Hoover memo regards the civil rights of Oswald that might have been violated while he was briefly in jail. Hoover said is this regard:

> Oswald having been killed today after warnings to the Dallas Police Department, was inexcusable. It will allow, I am afraid, a lot of civil rights people to raise a lot of hell because he was handcuffed and had no weapon. There are bound to be some elements of our society who will holler their heads off that his civil rights were violated — which they were.

This is an astonishing admission by Hoover, whose agents in Dallas were constantly keeping him abreast of the interrogation of Oswald and what he was telling the authorities. For someone who desperately wanted Oswald to be found guilty of killing the president, this was a statement that Hoover knew should never be

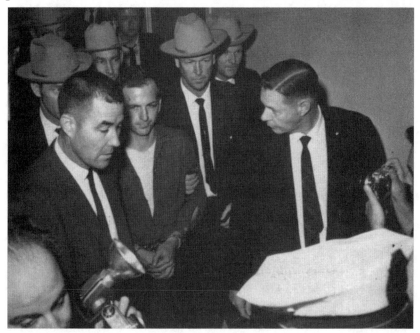

Oswald in the custody of the police moments before he was shot by Jack Ruby.

made public, lest the conspiracy theory of a plot to kill Kennedy would dominate the news.

He finished by writing a few words on the background of Jack Ruby which left out a lot of information on Ruby's background: "We have no information on Ruby that is firm, although there are some rumors of underworld activity in Chicago. Of his two night clubs, one is a strip tease joint and the other is a liquor place."

Hoover ignored the large amount of evidence linking Jack Ruby to a host of American mobsters, dating back to his youth in Chicago. While in Dallas, Jack made friends with both the local police and certain members of the Mafia, mostly from Chicago. Dallas Police Officers would frequently come to his Carousel Club, watch the strippers do their thing, have a few drinks, and schmooze with Ruby. Ruby also met a man who was closely associated with the mob, and its considerable ties to Cuba, Lewis McWillie. McWillie would later become Ruby's best friend and introduce him to the illegal gun running activities in Cuba. Ruby's reputation in Dallas had been noticed by the Federal Bureau of Narcotics, and in 1956, Ruby became an undercover informer for them as a "contact for a large narcotics set-up operating between Mexico, Texas and the East." He also served briefly as an informer for the FBI, but supplied little significant information.

Ruby's considerable Cuban connections on behalf of the American mob actually began in 1958, while the Cuban dictator Batista was still in power. Before Castro took power in Havana, the American mob was supplying him with small arms and ammunition to fight his revolutionary battle against Batista. The mob was having it both ways, still loyal to Batista who was allowing them to continue their lucrative casino business in Cuba, while seeing the writing on the wall as far as how long the hated Batista was to remain in power. Ruby served in the gunrunning organization of crime boss Norman Rothman. Rothman served Tampa mob boss Santos Trafficante, and managed the popular San Souci Casino in Havana which was run by Trafficante.

In the months following the Kennedy assassination, a report by a woman named Mary Thompson linked Ruby to the Rothman crime syndicate arms smuggling operation. She said that a relative of hers had traveled to the Florida Keys in June 1958 and was introduced to a man named Jack. He was the owner of a nightclub in Dallas, and was a member of the "syndicate," another name for the mob. Jack Ruby, it seems, was running guns to Cuba.

The HSCA investigated Ruby's mob connections and wrote, "The committee also deemed it likely that Ruby at least met various organized crime figures in Cuba, possibly including some who had been detained by the Cuban government."

While Ruby was in Cuba there were persistent rumors that he met with mob boss Santos Trafficante who was then in a Cuban jail. According to the HSCA report, "The committee developed circumstantial evidence that makes a meeting between Ruby and Trafficante a distinct possibility, but was not sufficient to form a final conclusion as to whether or not such a meeting took place."

Despite the Warren Commission's (and Hoover's statement on Ruby) pronouncements that Jack Ruby was not part of any organized conspiracy to kill President Kennedy, was not in prior contact with Lee Oswald (that too has been disputed) before he shot him in the basement of the DPD, and did not have any ties to organized crime in the United States, the documents that have been released on Ruby over the past decade now seem to refute those conclusions. As we have seen, Jack Ruby was closely tied in with certain top members of the mob in the United States and their plots to ship arms to Cuba. The Warren Commission, in its haste to close up shop, did not want to know about Ruby's unsavory background and refused to look into it. Of the three principal players in the Kennedy assassination drama, Jack Ruby still remains a puzzle.

The Hoover memo regarding Oswald, Ruby, the activities of the Dallas Police Department and its top brass, and the rush to convict Oswald of the president's murder, shows just how important it was on Hoover's behalf to close the case down and not let any exculpatory evidence on Oswald's behalf come to light.

Chapter 10
RFK and Operation Mongoose

One of the most intriguing questions in the Kennedy administration's efforts to oust Fidel Castro is what role Attorney General Robert Kennedy had in the plots. A partial answer to that query can now be answered due to the decades-long release of hundreds of files from the National Archives on what Robert Kennedy's role was in what was dubbed Operation Mongoose. What they reveal is a dominant role by RFK regarding the CIA and, to a lesser extent, the use of the mob in the Castro hits.

To the knowledgeable reader, Robert Kennedy's participation in the early CIA-Mafia plots are well known. What is not so well known is the extent that Bobby played in the CIA's planning to bring down Castro. While serving as Attorney General in his brother's cabinet, Robert Kennedy was put in charge of the attempts to kill Castro. To that effect, the CIA made a secret plan with certain members of the American mob. A book by author Ronald Goldfarb called *Perfect Villians, Imperfect Heros* gives the reader new information on that front.

Author Ronald Goldfarb says that he was told by Samuel Halpern, a top CIA officer, that RFK ordered the Agency to appoint an officer to meet with certain members of the Mafia to keep track of the old mob contacts left over in Cuba. This officer traveled to Canada as well as US locations in his clandestine meetings.

The man Goldfarb was referring to was Charles Ford, a CIA operative who worked in Bill Harvey's Task Force W. Ford worked in the Office of Training/Deputy Directorate for Administration and was a trusted member of the team. The name of Charles Ford would come up later when both Richard Helms and Sam Halpern testified before the HSCA. They spun a fascinating story concerning Ford and Robert Kennedy. According to the two CIA bigwigs, Robert Kennedy asked the CIA to supply him with a trusted agent who would be RFK's secret liaison with the mob to see if their old networks that had been closed down when Castro took over could be resurrected. Charles Ford was chosen to serve as RFK's secret intermediary with certain mob figures.

As told in *The Dark Side of Camelot* by Seymour Hersh, Ford was supposed to have traveled to cities in both the United States and Canada where he met clandestinely with mob figures to discuss their Cuban plans in post-Castro Havana. In an interview with Seymour Hersh, Sam Halpern said of the RFK-Ford relationship, "Charlie saw Kennedy in his office and of course talked to him on the phone quite regularly. Charlie was a good officer, and Bobby was his case officer. Charlie never reported that kind of information to me. He may not have reported it to anybody. He was Bobby's man. Nobody's going to touch him."

Hersh said that Ford made at least two trips to destinations on behalf of RFK per month to such places as San Francisco, Chicago, and Canada. Upon his return from these trips, Ford never turned over any of his information to Task Force W, which was running the Cuban ops.

In his work for the CIA, Ford went by the alias "Rocky Siscalini," as well as "Charles Fiscalini." He joined the CIA in 1952 and later was assigned to Task Force W. The documents in the Ford file state: "Mr. Ford was then assigned to Task Force W and was to travel to New York on 31 March 1962 to meet with an unidentified attorney who had contacted Mr. Robert Kennedy, the Attorney General, concerning assistance for Cuban prisoners."

In February 1963, he was still using his aliases and was utilized in the continental United States for operational purposes in pursuit of the mission of the Special Affairs Staff. By July 1963, Ford's use of his alias was no longer necessary and he had been reassigned to CIA headquarters.

In his testimony before the HSCA, Mr. Ford put to rest the allegations made by Seymour Hersh regarding his being the point man between RFK and the mob:

This is probably the appropriate point to underline my conviction that the main, if not the only, point of concern to the investigators is whether I was directed to sally forth and initiate contact with members of the underworld in the US and who directed me to do so. Their interest is even more pointedly focused on whether I had anything to do with the

Rosselli, Giancana, et al operations. Once again, I explained that my job was broader than this by a long shot, and that I was never directed to initiate in establishing contacts with the underworld. I said that several, probably no more than five or six of the people with whom I dealt with were somewhat "shady" characters, in some cases with recorded run-ins with law enforcement agencies.

Charles Ford is deceased, but his story that he had no secret relationship with RFK and the mob sets the record straight, and leaves out any preconception that RFK used Ford as his secret representative with the mob.

Bobby was the point man in the Agency's covert activities against the Castro regime, running roughshod over the CIA in its plotting against Castro. The Church Committee began its investigation into the Kennedy brothers' knowledge of the Castro plots by trying to link the president to the early CIA use of Sam Giancana and Johnny Rosselli. Giancana and Rosselli, two men who were then being investigated by Attorney General Robert Kennedy, were also working for the CIA in its early attempts on Castro. The cut-out in the early Rosselli-Giancana, CIA-Mafia plots was Robert Mahue, a former FBI and CIA agent who had close ties to both organizations even after his "retirement." The use of Mahue in the CIA-Mafia plots is a long, complicated story, but suffice it to say that Robert Kennedy, via various sources including Hoover's FBI, was well aware of the early Castro plots.

In April 1962, RFK was briefed on the CIA-Mafia connection of an Agency covert activity involving the bugging of the Las Vegas hotel room of singer Phyllis McGuire (one of the then popular McGuire sisters singing act).

What is of particular interest is that the CIA, in the persons of Sheffield Edwards and Lawrence Houston, met with RFK on May 7, 1962 and informed him of the wiretapping case that involved the mob, the CIA, and the initial plots to kill Castro. According to the IG's Report, Edwards "briefed Kennedy all the way." This is the first incident that we know of in which Robert Kennedy learned of the CIA-mob plots to kill Castro. It can be argued that Robert Kennedy, being so close to his bother, the president of the United

States, must have told JFK of this news. The men were so close in all respects, both personally and politically, that he wouldn't have let this type of very important information go by the wayside.

But RFK's briefing by the two CIA men left him in a quandary. Kennedy told his intimates that this presented a major problem for him as Attorney General due to his ongoing federal investigation Giancana and his fellow mobsters. He further said that he could not proceed with the wiretapping case against Mahue. Then Kennedy is quoted as saying, "I trust that if you [the CIA] ever have to do business with organized crime again—with gangsters—you will let the Attorney General know before you do it."

But what Bobby did not say to his CIA colleagues was *not* to have anything further to do with mobsters. Instead, he only said that he wanted to be kept informed if they had any further meetings with his old enemies. RFK was a man whose vendetta against organized crime in the United States began in the late 1950s when his brother, then Senator John Kennedy, was a member of a Senate panel investigating the mob. He was the committee's legal counsel. Why would he not bang his fist on the table, scream at the top of his lungs, and say *no more*! The CIA was now in alliance with the same members of organized crime that the Justice Department was raking over the coals. Did it matter that much of the enemy—the mob—and the CIA were working toward the same end—the murder of Fidel Castro? The enemy of my enemy is my friend. Did that ages-old saying stop RFK from continuing on his years-on-end struggle against the bad guys? Or did Robert Kennedy see a plan to use his old foes to bring down his new one? And did it really matter when it came to the reality of power politics, circa 1962? This was the way the game was played and Robert Kennedy was the consummate player.

After his meeting with Edwards and Houston, RFK assumed (incorrectly) that he would be given further briefings by the Agency if they did more covert work with the mob. But right after his May 7, 1962 summary of "Phase One"—that of the relationship with the gambling syndicate—"Phase 2" under Bill Harvey was already underway. On April 8, Harvey had been introduced to Rosselli and later that month Tony Varona and his men had been given lethal pills to kill Castro. But Robert Kennedy was not told that the plans to kill Castro were reactivated and that the Agency continued to use the mob in its deadly business.

The files show that Robert Kennedy got a briefing from the CIA (date not provided on the document) called "Briefing for Mr. Robert Kennedy," which was a detailed version of just what plans the CIA had for an invasion of Cuba, if and when the order was given.

The paper begins by saying:

> Basically, the policy reflected in this paper establishes that the militia will support State and CIA as necessary during the preparatory phase of Operation Mongoose in terms of supplies, transportation, personnel and bases. It also establishes the point that the military believe the continued existence of the Castro Communist regime is incompatible with the minimum security requirements of the United States and the entire Western Hemisphere. It further makes the point that the military could intervene overtly in Cuba without serious offense to national or world opinion if: a) We moved in response to a humanitarian requirement to restore order in Cuba, b) if we announced incident to going in; that we were moving in to restore order and hold free elections; and that we would withdraw from Cuba as soon as the new government advised that they had the capability to maintain order without further assistance from OAS nations; c) If the operation was conducted as quickly as possible and with sufficient force so that the Communist Bloc's ability to take effective counter-measures was reduced to the minimum. We feel very strongly that without damage to their international position and simply by making the decision to do so, the Soviets can take a page from our book and establish an overseas military base or bases in Cuba. This would greatly increase our national vulnerability and our defense costs as forces would have to be developed or shifted to meet this threat from the south. It would also provide the Communists with a secure base for espionage, sabotage and subversion throughout the entire Western Hemisphere.
>
> The Soviets have an option on which they can foreclose at any time. They can make the decision to establish military

bases in Cuba at their will and pleasure and if they exercise this option, we would likely be unable to remove them without initiating World War III. Consequently, we feel that it is mandatory that [we] face the facts squarely whether we can rid Cuba of Communism by covert support of Cubans within Cuba; and it is equally mandatory, for logistics and planning purposes, that we definitely intend to use military force, if covert means fail.

We also feel strongly that the United States should intervene to preserve Cuban nationals identified as being essential to the establishment of a friendly Cuban government if they are in danger of being exterminated by a widespread Hungarian type blood purge.[20]

The memo given to RFK then goes on to say how long it would take for the US to prepare for an invasion of Cuba should the order be given. It suggests that given 18 days we could respond:

...with sufficient strength to be clearly beyond Cuban capability to resist, to induce early capitulation of their units and to avoid needless loss of life.

A secondery plan can e activated from a condition of no warning in five days, although this plan involves a degree of risk by a piecemeal commitment of forces. CINCLANTAT is planning to reduce these reaction times through prepositioning of forces and materiel. This planning effort should soon provide us a basis for decision concerning the extent we wish to go in prepositioning without endangering security and the element of surprise to an unacceptable degree.

We feel that there is an alarming lack of appreciation that time is running out, that we cannot let this operation drag on for an indefinite number of years, hoping to develop a massive resistance capability within Cuba. We are concerned that the new proposal de-emphasizes the time factor by waiting until July before a decision is made as to what to do next. This would permit the Soviets additional time to foreclose on the options open to them, viz., entry of Cuba

20 RIF No. 202-10001-10171: "Briefing for Mr. Robert Kennedy," no date.

into the Warsaw Pact, and or the establishment of Soviet bases in Cuba [this is what happened in the Cuban Missile Crisis of October 1962]. Either one of these actions would add new dimensions to our problem, and postpone positive action indefinitely and not preclude for the foreseeable future the elimination of the Communist regime.

The memo for RFK then went to say what would happen if more covert means were needed to foment revolutionary action inside Cuba.

In the event that the coming months may disprove the feasibility of initiating an internal revolt in Cuba, it is suggested that Phase II might be sparked with the execution of a Cover and Deception plan. Normal training of US forces would be the primary cover; the deception would be concurrent efforts to convince the Communist Cuban government that we were in fact invading Cuba. This course of action could provide adequate provocation for US intervention depending, of course on Cuban rashness in their reaction.

The American military were hoping not to have to initiate any of these measures if the Cuban government saw reason. The document says, "If successful, we might not have to engage in the more difficult and dangerous game of developing pretexts although we should include this requirement as a final resort to assure successful initiation of Phase II."

The record is full of Kennedy administration officials' testimony of who knew what regarding the Castro plots:

[Richard] Helms said that although he did not know whether a Castro assassination would have been morally acceptable to Robert Kennedy, Helms believed that the president's brother would not have been unhappy to see Castro go. And Helms stated that Robert Kennedy never told him that a Castro assassination was ruled out. However, Helms further testified that although RFK was constantly in touch with him and their exchanges were marked by detailed, factual and highly specific discussions on anti-Castro operations. Robert Kennedy never raised the subject of a Castro hit and never instructed Helms to assassinate Castro. Helms further stated that he had no knowledge that RFK "was ever asked to specifically approve an assassination plot.

The documents that have been released in the past two decades show that Defense Secretary Robert McNamara urged that Castro be removed even if it meant killing him.

The members of a group who met on an almost daily basis to oversee Mongoose were Bobby Kennedy, General Edward Lansdale, who would become Mongoose's unofficial general in charge, General Maxwell Taylor, presidential advisor McGeorge Bundy, Roswell Gilpatrick, Arthur Schlesinger Jr., Richard Goodwin, and military men such as Secretary of Defense Robert McNamara, and General Lyman Lemnitzer of the Joint Chiefs of Staff.

On January 19, 1962 the "Special Group as they were called, met in Robert Kennedy's Department of Justice office to discuss Operation Mongoose. Bobby urged its members to "spare no time, effort or manpower, toward the overthrow of Castro's regime." Another prominent member of the Special Group was the new CIA Director, John McCone.

On August 23, 1962, JFK advisor McGeorge Bundy issued NSAM 181, ordered by the president, to implement a full course covert operation and propaganda war to topple the Castro regime. The CIA now set up its covert operation's headquarters in Miami, Florida and called it JMWAVE. Soon, JMWAVE would include the most elaborate paramilitary operation since the creation of the CIA in 1947. Working out of an abandoned site on the University of Miami complex, JMWAVE took on a life of its own. Some 400 CIA agents, their subagents and others, began plotting the demise of Castro.

Heading up JMWAVE was William Harvey whose name has previously appeared in this book. Harvey was disliked by both Kennedy brothers, but they saw in him the one man capable of getting rid of Castro. JMWAVE soon had its own air force, navy, foot soldiers, radio communications apparatus, banking operation, etc. Soon, Harvey was sending teams of agents into Cuba to sabotage sugarcane fields, attack Russian and Cuban ships in port and create as much havoc as possible. The flipside of JMWAVE was the secret CIA-Mafia plots to topple Castro.

What is still uncertain, and is the matter of much debate among historians, is to what extent JFK knew about Operation Mongoose and in particular, the CIA-Mafia plots to kill Castro. It seems logical that if Bobby Kennedy, the president's brother, and most confidential advisor, was put in charge of the Castro plots, then the president must surely have known.

A document released via the JFK Records Act some years ago on Operation Mongoose dated November 5, 1962, sums up the Kennedy administration's attitude toward Castro:

> Looking back to the origins of Mongoose, one finds the AG [Attorney General] and Mr. McNamara seeking primarily to remove the political stain left on the President by the Bay of Pigs failure. Both the AG and the Secretary of Defense felt it necessary for political reasons that some action with respect to Cuba to ensure the president's future. In a nutshell, they were out to dump Castro or make him cooperate.

What the new documents reveal concerning Robert Kennedy's participation in his brother's plans to overthrow the Castro regime is a man in almost total control of the plots to either kill or remove Castro from power. Both Kennedys were obsessed with getting revenge against Castro after the Bay of Pigs invasion. Until all the remaining CIA documents that are still being kept secret by the US government are released, all we have to go by regarding Bobby Kennedy's role in Operation Mongoose.

Chapter 11
Johnny Rosselli and Cuba

We return to Cuba once again, this time concentrating on Johnny Rosselli, one of the three men the CIA looked to in order to arrange a hit on Cuba's Fidel Castro. The documentation on Rosselli is large and his participation in the Cuba plots was well known to both the CIA and the FBI while the events were going on. Rosselli was at home in both the world of organized crime and among some of the most influential officers at the CIA.

He was born by the name of Filippo Sacco in Estera, Italy and came to the United States in 1931 with his mother. They settled in Boston where young Filippo decided he'd rather live life on the streets with its dangerous consequences than go to school. After his father died suddenly, his mother remarried and his new stepfather turned him to his lifelong career in crime.

By the 1930s, Rosselli teamed up with the most notorious criminal in Chicago, Al Capone, and eventually moved to Hollywood where he took over the mob's interests in that city. He was able to extort millions of dollars from the major movie studios and was the

A young Johnny Rosselli in these mug shots.

man to see among the criminal element in southern California. He was even able to produce a crime film called *He Walked By Night* that was a minor success. He soon was admitted to one of the most famous nightclubs in Hollywood, the Friars. Rosselli was immersed in the Friars Club throughout his life and he was convicted in a card cheating scandal there in 1969 and was sentenced to five years in jail.

Soon though, Rosselli would change his address and move to the mobsters' new haven, Havana, Cuba. By the 1950s, Havana rivaled Las Vegas as the number one playboy paradise of the Western Hemisphere. Only 90 miles from Florida, Havana, under the dictator Batista, was a flourishing atmosphere where the American mob raked in millions of dollars from the vast casino industry that lured vacationers from all over the globe. Meyer Lansky was the mob's number one man in Havana during that time and Rosselli shortly became a fan of his. Huge hotels like the Nacional, the Capri, the Havana Hilton, and the Hotel Commodoro were run by such mobsters as Lansky, Moe Dalitz, Charlie "the Blade" Tourine and Lucky Luciano. The dictator of Cuba, Batista, got his share of the hefty profits which enabled him to continue in power, thus, he let the mob run the gambling tables unmolested.

Rosselli represented the interests of Santo Trafficante Jr., the mob boss of Tampa, Florida. Rosselli, over time, would become a

Johnny Rosselli with actress Jeanne Harmen at a Hollywood premiere.

confidant of Batista. He also befriended such Hollywood actors such as George Raft, whose gambling interests led him to Havana during the late 1950s.

While he was in Cuba, Rosselli began his covert association with a number of CIA personnel such as David Atlee Phillips and David Sanchez Morales (both names were later mentioned many times in the aftermath of the Kennedy assassination).

When it was finally decided by the Eisenhower administration (in its final year) that Castro had to go, a set of events were put in motion that would lead to a years-long US obsession to get rid of Castro. The men running the covert Castro plots were Richard Bissell and Sheffield Edwards. These men handed over the job of contacting certain Mafia figures to Jim O'Connell, the CIA's security chief. O'Connell, in turn, called his old friend, former FBI officer now an influential private detective, Robert Maheu. Maheu contacted his old friend, Johnny Rosselli, and told him that certain persons were interested in getting rid of Castro. Would Rosselli be interested? Rosselli, knowing Maheu's intelligence background, immediately realized that the certain individuals were CIA officers and agreed to meet with them.

In late July/early August 1960, Maheu and Rosselli met for lunch in Los Angles at the Brown Derby restaurant. They had a long conversation regarding the current situation in Cuba and Rosselli asked for confirmation of what Maheu was telling him. Another meeting took place in Los Angeles between the two men to discuss further details but nothing was said about just how the hit on Castro would be carried out.

On September 14, 1960, Rosselli, Maheu and Jim O'Connell had a covert meeting in New York City in which a figure of $150,000 was offered to kill Castro. Rosselli said he didn't want to get paid but would instead give his friends the name of another Mafia figure who had more contacts than he did, "Sam Gold." Sam Gold was none other than Sam Giancana, the mob boss of Chicago and the successor to Al Capone.

In describing the newly formed CIA-Mafia connection to Allen Dulles, then head of the Agency, information went from A to B to C. "A" was Maheu, "B" was Rosselli, and "C" was the mob's principal man in Cuba.

In the next to the last week of September 1960, O'Connell and Maheu traveled to Miami where Rosselli introduced Maheu to "Sam Gold" in a meeting at the posh Fontainebleau Hotel. In that meeting, it was decided that a man named "Joe" would be the courier from the mob who would handle the assassination attempt on Castro. "Joe," it turned out, was Santo Trafficante Jr.

According to the newly released documents on the Rosselli chronology, a number of steps were taken concerning Rosselli and his role in the Cuba plots:

> Between Sept. 25 and the Bay of Pigs, a series of recruitments, meetings, and arrangements were made. The following is an outline of events that is not necessarily in chronological order.
>
> Meeting where Maheu is introduced to Trafficante, Meeting where Maheu is introduced to Giancana. Giancana was, according to Rosselli, to only be a "back up man." Rosselli states Giancana had nothing to do with the actual operation. Trafficante was used, according to Rosselli, as a "translator."
>
> Meeting with O'Connell, Maheu, Rosselli, and two Admirals to discuss the Cuban Project.
>
> Rosselli, in his contact with the Cubans, "invents" the cover story that he represents some Wall Street business interests who want to see Castro eliminated. Rosselli trusts Cubans he has recruited because they are part of the Bay of Pigs operation.
>
> First attempt at assassination involved the use of pills. Maheu and Rosselli met with Cuban #1 and #2. Maheu opened up his briefcase and gave the pills with instructions for their use to Cuban #1. Maheu also had $10,000 he gave the Cubans for doing the project. Rosselli did not know of the money. Rosselli states he received no remuneration for his work on the project. In fact, he paid out $800.00 for gas for a speed boat to deliver two or three man parties for guerilla raids into Cuba.
>
> Prior to Bay of Pigs there was no discussion of using guns to assassinate Castro.

Rosselli's cover name was "John Ralston."

At different times, Cuban #1, #2, or #3 would propose different projects. These would range from using plastic explosives to booby trap Castro's desk. Rosselli would relay these on to Maheu, who in turn, would contact the CIA. Most projects were vetoed, but the CIA did supply a short wave radio to their people in Havana.

Eventually, Rosselli felt the project had failed. There was no specific point when it was announced. But, at some time Rosselli assumed the project, for whatever reason, had not succeeded.[1]

The CIA had been watching Rosselli's activities with a keen eye even after the failure of the Bay of Pigs and the shutdown of the Cuba project. They knew Rosselli was a loose cannon who might go off at any moment, revealing the Castro assassination plots. This information was spelled out in a CIA memo dated Feb. 15, 1972 for the Executive Director-Comptroller, subject, John Rosselli.

The memo's salient points are the following.

Initially Rosselli was unwitting of government interest, but as time went on, he suspected that the US Government was involved and specifically the CIA. Rosselli is presently serving a prison sentence for conspiracy in a Federal penitentiary in Seattle, Washington and awaits deportation upon completion of his current sentence. This Agency was aware that Rosselli intended to expose his participation in the plot should we not intervene on his behalf. The DCI decided to ignore his threats and take a calculated risk as to the consequences that may occur with the disclosure of his story. This was subsequently done by Rosselli or someone on his behalf furnishing Jack Anderson details of the incident. Individuals who were aware of this project were Messrs. Dulles, Bissell, Col. J.C. King and Sheffield Edwards.

In an undated report to the Attorney General, the story of Rosselli's participation in the Cuban plots is discussed. It seems

---

1 RIF No. 157-10014-10236: Rosselli: Chronology of Events.

that after the failed Bay of Pigs invasion of Cuba, Rosselli's name was still in the loop. For all intents and purposes the operation was discontinued and cancelled after the ill-fated Bay of Pigs invasion in April 1961, but Rosselli had not been completely cut off, as he periodically indicated he was in a position to be of assistance:

> It appears Rosselli has since that time, nevertheless, used his prior connections with CIA to his best advantage. For example, in May 1966, when contacted by agents of this Bureau in connection with our current investigation of his activities he refused to talk and immediately flew to Washington, D.C. and consulted with Colonel Sheffield Edwards, who is now retired from CIA. Colonel Edwards in turn, advised CIA, which told us. Mr. Howard Osborne, the present Director of Security, CIA, freely had admitted to us that Rosselli has CIA in an unusually vulnerable position and that he would have no qualms about embarrassing CIA if it served his own interests. In furnishing this information, Mr. Osborne asked that it be held within this Bureau on a strictly need-to-know basis.
>
> In light of the above information furnished us by CIA and former Attorney General Kennedy, it appears that data which came to our attention in October 1960, possibly pertains to the captioned matter. At that time a source close to Giancana advised that during a conversation with several friends Giancana stated that Fidel Castro was to be done away with very shortly. Giancana reportedly assured those present that Castro's assassination would occur in November, 1960, and that he had already met with the assassin-to-be on three occasions, the last meeting having taken place on a boat docked at the Fontainebleau Hotel, Miami Beach, Florida. Reportedly, Giancana claimed that everything had been perfected for the killing and the "assassin" had arranged with a girl, not further identified, to drop a "pill" in Castro's drink or food.

Events moved quickly after the Bay of Pigs invasion that directly affected Rosselli. According to the declassified documents, Rosselli felt "sorry for the poor bastards left on the beach." Rosselli felt indirectly responsible for their deaths since he had encouraged many of them to participate in the invasion." Weeks after the invasion, Rosselli met with O'Connell and Harvey in Miami. O'Connell told Rosselli that Harvey was now in charge of the Cuban project and that Rosselli was to cease all contact with both Maheu and Giancana. "Further, Harvey stated that the government was still interested in using Rosselli for intelligence-gathering operations. Rosselli would report information from the Cubans to Harvey about personalities and events in Cuba. Rosselli would also relay on to his Cuban contacts requests for specific information from the CIA."

To recap Roselli's direct involvement in the Cuban project, in late February-March 1961, Rosselli passed the poison pills that the CIA's Technical Services Department had made for the first attempt on Castro's life. He gave them to Trafficante, who in turn, gave them to his contact in Cuba, Juan Orta. Orta had lost his position in the Castro government and therefore, could not make the assassination attempt.

Johnny Rosselli.

97

But the Rosselli attempts on Castro were not over. In the time period March-April 1961, Rosselli told Jim O'Connell that Trafficante had another contact in Cuba who would be willing to undertake a second attempt on Castro. That man was Manuel "Tony" Varona, the head of the exile group called the Democratic Revolutionary Front.

According to the CIA's IG's Report, William Harvey took over "phase two" of the operation and Rosselli's participation, along with that of Giancana and Trafficante, lessened. Said the report:

> Rosselli remained a prominent figure in the operation, but working directly with the Cuban exile community and directly on behalf of the CIA. Rosselli was essential to the second phase as a contact with Varona, who presumably still believed he was being supported by US businessmen who had a financial stake in Cuba. Rosselli needed Giancana and Trafficante in the first phase as a means of establishing contacts in Cuba. He did not need them in a second phase because he had Varona. However, it would be naïve to assume that Rosselli did not take the precaution of informing higher-ups in the syndicate that he was working in a territory considered to be the private domain of someone else in the syndicate.

In May 1962, an arrangement was made between Harvey and Rosselli in which the two men would be kept informed on any new developments. Harvey would call Rosselli at the Friars Club in California via pay phone at 1600 hours California time. Rosselli would then return Harvey's call at the latter's home that night.

In June 1962, Rosselli passed word along to Harvey that Varona sent a hit squad to kill Castro (three men would take part in the job) but no further details were provided.

It was during this time period, the summer-spring of 1962, that Rosselli would become an active member of the CIA's JMWAVE station in Florida. He was at the office every day, taking part in the agency's plans to send covert teams into Cuba, meeting with agents and going along on their forays. What would the ordinary members of the CIA have thought if they knew that working alongside them was one of the top members of organized crime in the United States?

But the CIA was not the only party interested in Rosselli. In the summer of 1963, Rosselli came to Washington and was a house guest of William Harvey and his wife. One night the three of them were out dining in Washington and were followed secretly by FBI agents. It seems that Hoover's FBI had placed Rosselli under surveillance due to his underworld past. The next day, William Harvey told Sam Papich of the FBI that Rosselli was finishing an assignment for the CIA. Papich then reminded Harvey that the FBI wanted to know whenever the CIA had an operational role with any member of organized crime. Papich further said that he would have to inform Hoover. This incident proved to be the last time Harvey and Rosselli would have a face-to-face meeting. As far as Harvey was concerned, the CIA and the mob were out of business in the

Johnny Rosselli, the Silver Fox, in his older days.

99

matter of assassinating Castro.

But Rosselli's involvement in the continuing saga of the US government versus Fidel Castro was not yet ended.

A few years after the Kennedy assassination, Johnny Rosselli made a move that would later prove fatal. He approached his lawyer and friend, Edward Morgan, a high priced Washington attorney and power broker, with some rather explosive news. He told Morgan of his close association with the CIA, and more importantly, of the Agency-Mafia links to kill Castro. Morgan called his powerful friend and Washington journalist, Jack Anderson. Anderson in turn, gave the news to his associate, Drew Pearson. Pearson was on good terms with former Chief Justice Earl Warren who, in 1964, chaired the Warren Commission's investigation into the Kennedy assassination. Pearson met with Warren and told him of Rosselli's incredible story. Pearson asked Warren to meet with Morgan but the former Chief Justice declined.

Rosselli now gave Anderson-Pearson another part of the Castro story, one that was most striking. He said that three Cuban hit men were sent to kill Castro but were captured and "turned" by the Cubans against the United States. After Castro learned of the attempt on his life, he cooked up a counterplot to kill JFK.

Jack Anderson then published his blockbuster story of Rosselli's association with the CIA and its efforts with the mob to kill Castro. He called Rosselli:

> A dapper, hawk-faced man with a thatch of white hair. He has been disciplined all his life to keep his mouth shut. His Mafia partner, Sam Giancana, was slain before Senate investigators could serve him with a subpoena. So here is Rosselli's own account of a real-life "Mission Impossible" — the attempt to kill Castro. It is a story of cash payments, poison pellets, high-powered rifles and powerboat dashes into Cuba.

In 1976, Rosselli met for questioning before the Senate panel headed by Idaho Senator Frank Church and Pennsylvania Senator Richard Schweiker that was looking into the Kennedy assassination. When questioned by the panel, Rosselli said that while he personally believed Castro had a hand in killing the president, he did not have solid proof. He also denied having spoken to Edward Morgan regarding the Castro hit-team story, and was circumspect when asked whether or not he had any dealings with Jack Ruby, the Dallas nightclub owner who shot Oswald.

Johnny Rosselli's demise came on July 28, 1976. That morning, he drove his car to a nearby marina and went out on a boat with certain unidentified men. While out fishing, these unidentified men killed Rosselli, dumped his body in an old oil drum, and set it adrift in the ocean. A few days later, the rusting drum carrying Rosselli's decomposed body washed ashore.

Who killed Rosselli and why? One of the prime candidates was Santos Trafficante of Tampa. Certainly the manner of Rosselli's death was a clear mafia hit. Florida police came up with a possible assassin, Sam Cagnina. He was a soldier in Santo Trafficante's organization and there were reports that certain people overheard Cagnina taking responsibility for the Rosselli hit.

While it is not possible to pin the crime on any one person, one can postulate on the theories. Was Rosselli killed because of his testimony before the Church Committee regarding the Kennedy assassination and his revelation about Castro and the retaliation theory? Could it be a coincidence that Sam Giancana was murdered in his home shortly before he was summoned to testify before the same Church Committee that Rosselli talked to? Rosselli testified before the committee three times, his last testimony coming three months before his death. Juan Ojeda, a member of the Miami homicide team that investigated Rosselli's death had this to say regarding the mobster's slaying: "If Cubans had killed Rosselli, they would have shot him down in the street or blown him up in his car to make a point, not stuffed him in a barrel and thrown him in the bay." When Rosselli testified before the Senate committee, he was asked by a staff member named Michael Epstein if he had any facts regarding his allegation about the Castro hit theory. Rosselli responded by saying that he had "no facts."

Did the CIA have Rosselli killed? His friend Joseph Breen, who was his partner in a gift shop at the Frontier Hotel in Las Vegas, said that the CIA would not have had Rosselli killed because Rosselli talked with Bill Harvey numerous times regarding the Castro plots over the years and that "the agency would have no reason to kill him."

According to the *New York Times*, one high-ranking, unnamed Mafia figure said of the Rosselli death:

> "When you're called before a committee like that, you have to go to your people and ask them what to do. Rosselli not only did not come to us he went before the committee and shot his mouth off all over the place." The Mafia figure said that shortly after Rosselli's first appearance before the Senate committee on June 24, 1975, his murder was approved by the commission of bosses that sets policy for the 26 Mafia families in the country. They decided he would just go on talking every time he was pressured, and he had to be hit.[2]

The same *New York Times* article said: "This explanation was confirmed in its essential points by Frank Bompensiero, the Mafia boss of San Diego, before he was shot to death outside his home on February 10, apparently because the Mafia found out he had been giving information to the Federal Bureau of Investigation."

However Rosselli died, he was a major figure in the CIA-mob hits on Castro and was even talked about as being one of the persons directly responsible for the assassination of the president.

---

2 Gage, Nicholas, "Mafia Said to Have Slain Rosselli Because of His Senate Testimony," New York Times, Feb. 25, 1977.

Chapter 12
"El Mexicano"

One of the most interesting documents that came out of the October 2017 release was a short page containing the cover name of "El Mexicano," or the Mexican. That in itself is not that interesting but what caught the eye of the reader was the following sentence, "Rene Carballo calls Bringuier, states he thinks head of training camp at Ponchatrain was "El Mexicano" & the same accompanied LHO [Lee Harvey Oswald] to Mexico City." This is indeed interesting because Lee Oswald supposedly did not have any company when he went to Mexico City in September-October 1963 in order to get a visa to go back to Cuba and then on to Russia, once again.

What makes this more interesting is the fact that the CIA had an undercover training base outside New Orleans in the summer of 1963 at which its members were taking guerilla training for another invasion of Cuba. Both the FBI and the CIA were well aware of what was going on in these camps and turned a blind eye to the activities. It was rumored that Lee Oswald was seen in one of these camps at various times. David Ferrie and Guy Banister were also at these various camps, overseeing the training of the men.

The real name of "El Mexicano" was Francisco "Rodriguez Tamayo. He used the alias Nicholas Diaz and his Agency file number was 201-293114. He was born in 1932 in Puerto Rico and it is not known when he went to Cuba, but he served in Castro's rebel army with the rank of Captain. He left for the United States in June 1959 and settled in Miami.

The FBI was very interested in Francisco Tamayo as of 1963 and it was reported that of July 1963, "El Mexicano" was a paid Castro agent and that he had been associating with Pedro Diaz Lanz.

In 1968, Rodriguez Tamayo was suspected of being involved in an assassination plot in Venezuela (target unknown). [3]

This is all very interesting as, if this is right, then we have a Castro assassin accompanying Lee Oswald to a CIA sponsored training camp outside of New Orleans, as well as going with him to Mexico

3 Educationforum.7266-el-mexicabi.

City. Unfortunately, the record as far as "El Mexicano" is concerned is still under wraps so we do not have any more information with which to complete this very interesting story.

Let's, for a minute, go into the training camps that were established outside of New Orleans during that time.

The Schlumberger Corporation was a French-owned arms and munitions company which was directly linked to the CIA in its secret war against Castro. The ostensible job of the company was to supply explosives and geological measuring devices to companies for use in blasting projects. In the early 1960s, the company was a supporter of the violent OAS French faction that was struggling to overthrow the French government and assassinate President Charles de Gaulle. As part of the CIA's covert efforts to support the OAS, it secretly supplied arms such as anti-personnel mines to the Schlumberger Company.

According to newly released documents, the CIA's Domestic Contact Services Division, "has discreet and continuing contact with the main Schlumberger office in Houston, and branch offices in Minneapolis and elsewhere."

One of their supply depots was in the town of Houma, Louisiana not too far from New Orleans. Once the OAS failed in its efforts to get rid of de Gaulle, the CIA made an effort to take back the unused military supplies.

Enter now two of the names that would crop up in the aftermath of the Kennedy assassination, David Ferrie and Guy Banister. According to participants in the mission, the Houma ammunition was retrieved and taken back to New Orleans where it was divided up between Ferrie and Banister. These munition's were then to be taken to Florida and given to the anti-Castro exile groups. Some of the munitions stored at Houma were also to be sent to countries such as Guatemala and the French West Indies where the CIA was training anti-Castro soldiers.

In Gus Russo's book *Live By the Sword,* he relates the story of Guy Banister traveling with high ranking officials of the Justice Department carrying a "Letter of Marque," an official paper that gives license to a person who is going to commit a crime (Letters of Marque were used mainly in the early 19th century by American presidents). The Letter of Marque stated, "You are hereby directed to seize ammunition or arms, the property of a foreign government that are illegally located within the United States, using any and all means to do so." According to Jack Martin, a private detective who worked out of Guy Banister's office, the letter was signed by Robert Kennedy.

The transfer of the illegal arms took place over a three month period in 1961, under the watchful eye of both the CIA and the FBI.

"It was a CIA operation," says Frank Hernandez, attorney for Sergio Arcacha Smith, a leading member of the anti-Castro directorate in the US. Frank Hernandez. "It was set up so that Schulumberger could report it (the weapons transfer) as a robbery, and be reimbursed by their insurance company. They went in at midnight and the material was waiting for them on a loading dock. We later verified that the CIA indeed reimbursed the insurance company."

The Houma arms raid was to play a part in yet another FBI operation located in the same area. On July 31, 1963, a number of FBI agents raided an exile training base on the shores of Lake Ponchartrain near New Orleans which was owned and operated by an anti-Castro mob bigwig, William McLaney. The feds confiscated a large cache of arms and ammunition, including a ton of dynamite, bomb casings, fuses, napalm and other lethal material. Many of these munitions were destined for shipment to Cuba, and it is believed that some of this material had originally been in the shipment confiscated by Guy Banister two years earlier.

In effect, the Schlumberger arms depot was a CIA front company, used by the anti-Castro guerillas, where shipments of arms were stored for transfer to Cuba. Involved at this facility were two men deeply connected to the Kennedy assassination, David Ferrie and Guy Banister. There were also rumors that Lee Harvey Oswald was seen in and around the Houma facility and the one owned by William McLaney during this time. If the El Mexicano story is true, Oswald was at one of these training camps, but we still don't know which one.

The William McLaney-Schlumberger operation was just one that had ties to the exiles training in the swamps around New Orleans. Another organization that took part in these operations was the MDC, also called the Christian Democratic Movement, which was one of the most important of the underground organizations that once flourished in Cuba. Once Castro took power, the leadership of the MDC, headed by its military chief, Laureano Batista Falla, ended its alliance with Castro and began its fight against him. Shortly after Castro proclaimed his pro-Communist leanings, Falla took his organization, along with his highly trained fighters, to Miami to join the cause.

One of the places in the United States where the MDC took root was New Orleans in the summer of 1963. New Orleans at that time was second only to Miami and its adjoining territory in its opposition to Castro, and hundreds of anti-Castro recruits joined the group to train in the desolate swamps and rivers near that city. Once settled in New Orleans, the MDC used a covert name to hide its true purpose: Maritima BAM, a supposed lumber company. Aiding the MDC with finances and military support was Manuel Artime's group. Falla had ties to various soldiers of fortune who, in turn, had their own links to various right wing groups in the United States that were also anti-Castro. One of them, a man named David Raggio, agreed to provide the MDC with approximately $10,000 per month for supplies and military equipment. There weren't too many men training at the site in New Orleans, maybe a dozen at the most, but they made enough noise to arouse the ire of the locals who called the police, and they called the feds. The FBI know all about Falla's MDC operation/training camp but turned a blind eye.

But all was not going smoothly in the New Orleans group. Among the anti-Castro partisans was one man who turned out to be an undercover agent for the Cuban services, Fernando Fernandez. Fernandez, it turned out, had sent a letter to the Cuban Ambassador to Mexico telling him of the exiles' plans to take part in attacks on Cuban targets. The letter was intercepted and Fernandez was put under detention. When the other members of the MDC found out about Fernandez's treachery, he was tortured and sent packing.

What little information we have on "El Mexicano" says that he was associating with Pedro Diaz Lanz. We have a large amount of information on Lanz that fills in some of the blanks in the story of the anti-Castro front in the United States, of which the CIA was well aware.

Pedro Diaz Lanz was one of the most popular and influential

of the anti-Castro leaders. His brother, Marcos Diaz Lanz, was the Inspector General of the Revolutionary Air Force until both men defected to the United States in the summer of 1959. The Diaz Lanz brothers were also aligned with Ricardo Lorie Valla who was a member of the 26th July Movement. The CIA report says, "The Diaz Lanz brothers broke with Lorie, who appeared to have been the most mature member of the group, for reasons which are not at all clear."

In July 1959, Diaz Lanz broke from the other anti-Castro organizations then based in the United States. He said that the followers of Rolando Masferrer, Justo Luis Pozo, the former Mayor of Havana, Nunez Portundo and the other exile leaders were not acceptable to the Counter-revolution against Castro. On the other side however, Diaz Lanz said he was willing, under certain conditions, to support Portundo if the latter broke relations with Trujillo of the Dominican Republic. There were reports that he tried to obtain $50,000 from associates of Pedraza in Miami. "If this attempt actually was made, it seems to indicate at last a willingness on the part of Diaz-Lanz to work with Pedraza, something he had hitherto steadfastly refused to consider."

In January 1963, the Justice Department received information from an informer who was knowledgeable in anti-Castro affairs that Pedro Diaz Lanz, his brother Marcos, and another man named Carlos Manuel Delgado Gonzalez, left the Miami Basin on the 22nd of that month, enroute to Cuba. Their trip lasted four days, and their mission included picking up arms for their cause. After the weapons were delivered they spent some time at Cay Sal Bank in the Bahama chain. En route to Cuba, their boat was spotted by Cuban ships that tried to intercept them. The Diaz Lanz brothers thought better of having a confrontation with the torpedo boats and left the area. When they were approaching Miami in international waters, they spotted two Russian ships and decided not to attack them because they were outgunned. A person named Manuel who was on board the ship later told the FBI that someone on Cay Sal betrayed them to the Cubans, "but that a United States Coast Guard plane helped them by flying low over the Cuban Government torpedo launches which had the effect of scaring off the torpedo launches and facilitating the escape of Diaz Lanz's boat."

Another informant said that on February 9, 1963, Gerry Hemming contacted Marcos Diaz Lanz asking if his brother could deliver some arms to him. Marcos said he would relay the message. On February 11, Frank Sturgis, a friend of Pedro's "complained that Diaz Lanz is inactive, and if he has any arms, he will not make them available to anyone who is capable of putting these arms to good use in Cuba against Communism. T-3 (the informant) said that Hemming was unable to obtain any arms from Diaz Lanz.

In September 1963, the FBI received a report from its source concerning anti-JFK propaganda that was written by Pedro Diaz Lanz. The source wrote that the paper written by Lanz was "to the effect that Kennedy and most of his administration are communists, and are betraying Cuba and the Cubans, as well as the citizens of the United States. This paper was shown to Frank Sturgis who told me that Diaz Lanz had edited it in cooperation with two American girls, not known to him by name."

Another man who was associated with the New Orleans training camps was Victor Espinosa Hernandez. He was a young man who had ties with many people, as well as groups, both in the United States and Europe, who were actively planning an assassination plot against Castro and his top aides. He was also well connected with Rolando Cubela, a.k.a. "AMLASH" a CIA-sponsored Cuban doctor who was preparing his own plot to kill Castro.

Victor Espinoza Hernandez was born in Cuba and came from a wealthy family whose businesses included farming and the petroleum industry. He went to the University of Havana for only one year before dropping out, and worked for the anti-Batista cadre inside Cuba. In 1955 he left Cuba for the United States where he enrolled at LSU (Louisiana State University).

Upon the death of his grandfather, Victor returned to Cuba to manage the family business. He came into contact with many of the mob figures who were then engaged in the lucrative casino business in Havana, including Mike McLaney and Norman Rothman.

He joined a group that took part in an assassination attempt against members of the Batista government. One of his co-conspirators was the aforementioned Rolando Cubela.

After Castro took power, he took refuge in the United States, living both in Miami and New York. He was recruited to become a member of the team of exiles that were planning the invasion of the Bay of Pigs and took military training in Guatemala and at a camp outside of New Orleans. He participated in several covert missions inside Cuba but did not specify what these missions were.

In August 1963, the FBI interviewed two men, named Rich Lauchli and Ralph Folkers, who gave them information regarding the activities of Victor Hernandez. Folkers identified Hernandez, in a picture, as the person who rented a U-Haul trailer at Collinsville, Illinois on July 11, 1963 destined for New Orleans. Lauchli orally admitted selling 2,400 pounds of dynamite in July 1963 to one who resembles Hernandez. Lauchli claims Victor did not say why he wanted the dynamite or where he obtained money to buy the same. Lauchli suspected dynamite was to be used against Castro.

Documents available from the HSCA investigation show that the FBI and the CIA had interviews with Espinosa on an ongoing basis.

An FBI document dated July 2, 1965 tells of a debriefing session by Bureau agents with Espinosa. William Doyle of the CIA informed the FBI on June 4, 1965 that Harold Swenson had come from Washington, D.C. to interview Espinosa. Also in attendance at the meeting was Special Agent Francis J. O'Brien. Said the document:

> After ESPINOSA departed the NYO, Swenson advised that 98 percent of the information furnished regarding the alleged assassination plots by Espinosa was accurate, and that the only reservation CIA had was that they disliked the two individuals who had contacted Espinosa concerning the plot and considered the contacts Espinosa, Alberto Blanco, a.k.a. "El Lobo," and Jorge Robeno, a.k.a. "Mago," to be individuals of questionable reputation.

In 1965, Espinosa traveled to France and Spain to meet clandestinely with members of the anti-Castro cause. While in Paris, "he was in contact with individuals involved in a plot to assassinate Fidel Castro and leading Cuban Government Personalities." One of the men he met while in Paris was Rolando Cubela or AMLASH. He also met with Alberto Blanco for a ten day period. Blanco worked for the Cuban Foreign Ministry and was in Paris to make a tour of the Cuban Embassy in France. Contrary to what the documents say, Espinosa expressed the opinion that he (Blanco) had no prior knowledge of the plot (described below) and went to Paris on the urging of Cubela, who had been a lifelong friend of his. He also stated that involved in the plot was Major Juan Almeida Bosque. According to CIA files, Bosque was then serving as the First Deputy Minister of the Cuban Revolutionary Armed Forces.

Espinosa advised that the plot calls for the assassination of Fidel Castro, Raul Castro, Ernesto "Che" Guevara and Ramiro Valdes. The assassination of these individuals is to take place in public so that everyone can see that the leaders have been killed. The plotters hope to seize the radio station and call for American help. The target date for the murder attempt was July 26, 1965, which was to coincide with the July 26 celebration in Havana.

The information that Espinosa gave to the CIA regarding the plots to kill the leaders of the Cuban government were so sensitive that they were "restricted to the White House and the Attorney General."

Intertwined with the activities of El Mexicano, Victor Espinosa and Pedro Diaz Lanz was a separate CIA training facility on the outskirts of New Orleans which was run by the CIA, the aforementioned JMMOVE. This operation was referred as the Belle Chasse Louisiana Ammunition Dump which operated from February to April 1961, and provided underwater training for Cuban exiles involved in the Bay of Pigs landing. JMMOVE was different from the MDC camp which has been written about in this chapter.

The initial mission of the base was to train 30 men— that increased to 149 men during its short history. Repots confirm that JMMOVE was the only Agency sponsored training camp. States that the MDC camp was 15 miles away from New Orleans, right after long bridge at entrance to Louisiana, with millionaires funding camp. In a taped interview, Carlos Quigora told Jim Garrison in 1967 that

Victor Paneque y Batista was in charge of a CIA training camp conducted for Cubans from Miami in Lacombe, La.[4]

So, what do we now know about "El Mexicano" and how he fits into the Kennedy narrative? He was born in Puerto Rico in 1962, was a person of interest to the FBI and had been associated with Pedro Diaz Lanz at his military training base outside of New Orleans. He was supposed to have accompanied Lee Harvey Oswald to the same training base and performed whatever tasks they were there for. He also accompanied Lee Harvey Oswald to Mexico City in late September-October 1963. Why did El Mexicano accompany Oswald to Mexico City and what did they do there? Did anyone fund their trip? Did anyone give them instructions during their trip to Mexico City and who might this have been? Did Oswald and El Mexicano meet with persons unknown while they were south of the border? Oswald was supposed to have taken his trip to Mexico City alone, as we've been told all these years. Are we now to believe that he had company for some reason that we still don't know? There's more to the story, but we still aren't in possession of all the facts.

---

4 Mary Ferrell Foundation website, "Cryptonym: JMMOVE."

Chapter 13
Bobby and Marilyn Monroe

On the night of August 5, 1962, an ambulance was called to the Los Angeles home of actress Marilyn Monroe, one of the nation's most well-known movie stars and sex icons. There have been conflicting rumors about what happened to Marilyn Monroe and the circumstances surrounding her untimely death at age thirty-six. Unknown to the public at the time of her death was that Monroe was having an affair with President Kennedy whom she had met when Kennedy was running for the Democratic presidential nomination in 1960. It was also rumored that she had some sort of an affair with Robert Kennedy, the president's brother and the Attorney General of the United States.

Some of the theories surrounding Monroe's death lead to the Mafia which was supposed to have bugged her home in order to get blackmail material on Robert Kennedy to thwart his longstanding war on the Mafia in the United States, i.e., Santos Trafficante, Jimmy Hoffa and Carlos Marcello. Another theory is that the Kennedys, either Bobby or the president himself, ordered that Monroe be silenced because she was about to reveal her relationship with the president (and/or Bobby), and that would have ruined the presidency. One of the stories says that Marilyn was going to tell the world some of the juiciest pieces of information that she'd gotten from either Bobby or the president, involving the plans to kill Fidel Castro of Cuba. Among the interesting facts about Marilyn's death is that she had a diary that she kept in her home regarding her relationship with friends and colleagues. The diary is supposed to have revealed her affair with the president as well as her other secrets. The person who told of Marilyn's diary was her friend Jean Carmen in whom she confided many of her secrets. A person who worked in the LA corner's office, Lionel Grandison, said that the diary arrived at the corner's office after her death, was put in a safe, but then went missing.

Documents that were released via the National Archives in October 2017 reveal an interest by the FBI in a book that was to be published regarding allegations of an affair between Robert Kennedy and Miss Monroe.

On April 2, 1976 the HSCA (House Select Committee on Assassinations) wrote a letter to the Justice Department, "requesting all FBI materials pertaining to communications between FBI Director Hoover and Attorney General Robert Kennedy with respect to the publication of a book about Marilyn Monroe by Frank Capell."

On July 14, 1976, the FBI, in the person of William Sullivan, who was a top-ranking Bureau executive, wrote a memo to an R.W. Smith under the subject heading "Frank Capell Information Concerning Internal Security."

> Memo, Baumgardner to Sullivan, 7/7/64, stated New York Office advised that a new book by Frank A. Capell entitled *The Strange Death of Marilyn Monroe*, which alleges that Attorney General Robert F. Kennedy had an intimate relationship with Miss Monroe, would be ready for sale about 7/10/64.

Under the heading "Kennedy's Friendship with Miss Monroe Well Known" the memo goes on to say:

> "[T]he New York Office has now furnished us with a copy of this 70-page book. The book claims that Miss Monroe's involvement with Kennedy was well known to her friends and reporters in the Hollywood area, but was never publicized. It is alleged that there are person-to-person telephone calls, living witnesses, tape recordings and certain writings to attest the closeness of their friendship."

The author suggests that Miss Monroe was led to believe his intentions were serious, and that Kennedy had promised to divorce his wife and marry her. When he failed to do so, the book charges, she threatened to expose their relationship which would have ruined his presidential aspirations. It was then that Kennedy decided to "take drastic action."

According to the book, Kennedy used the "Communist Conspiracy" which is expert in the scientific elimination of its enemies to dispose of Miss Monroe by making her murder appear to be a suicide. This could have been achieved without great difficulty, the author points out, because her personal physician, Dr. Hyman Engelberg, was a communist.[5]

The above-mentioned memo went right up the chain of command in the FBI to men like Belmont, Mohr, Evans, De Loach, Sullivan and Smith.

The FBI had gotten a copy of the book and read it closely. They wrote at one point, "It should be noted that the allegation concerning the Attorney General and Miss Monroe has been circulated in the past and has been branded as utterly false."

Under the title "References to Director and FBI" it states at one point:

There are several references in the book to the Director and/or the FBI. On page 49, it is stated that under the direction of Bobby Kennedy the FBI has been frustrated as never before.

On Page 69, it is said Mr. Hoover does not share Kennedy's opinion that the Communist Party USA, is a windmill virtually powerless to harm the United States.

On Page 70, reference is made to an anonymous letter quoted in a column of Walter Winchell datelined May 25, 1964, at Hollywood, California, which told of a 23-year old Beverly Hills blonde who has been "terrorized for months by the same person who caused Marilyn Monroe's death. You can check this with FBI Special Agent in Charge, Mr. Grapp in LA. Her initials are MJ."

Our Los Angeles Office reported that "MJ" was Mary Lou Jones, a would-be actress of no talent, who is apparently mentally disturbed. Miss Jones complained to the Beverly Hills Police Department that she was being followed and harassed by unidentified men, but her allegations were completely unsubstantiated by the police.

The memo notes that Monroe's doctor, Hyman Engelberg was the subject of a Security Matter investigation after his cooperative

5 RIF No. 157-10014-10205: Monroe, Marilyn, Kennedy, Robert.

Rare photo of Marilyn Monroe with Bobby Kennedy.

interview with agents in the Bureau's LA Office. "At that time Dr. Engelberg admitted membership in the Communist Party from 1939 to 1948."

In order to alert Robert Kennedy about the upcoming book by Frank Capell, the FBI sent a memo to him dated July 7, 1964, telling him what was in the book. The memo was sent by J. Edgar Hoover who must have taken great joy in knowing about Capell's book. For years, Hoover had great animosity for the Kennedy family, dating back to the time when Jack and Bobby's father, Joseph P. Kennedy, was Ambassador to Great Britain during World War II. Hoover well knew all about the Kennedys' secret lives, including all the extramarital affairs both Jack and his father had over the years. Hoover had files on all the Kennedy brothers in his safe, waiting for an opportune time to reveal them. One of these files contained information on a Swedish beauty named Inga Arvad, with whom Jack Kennedy had an affair with during World War II, before he was shipped off to the Pacific and had his encounter with the Japanese navy onboard his torpedo boat, *PT 109*, that made him famous across the country. There were rumors that Arvad was a Nazi spy, as well as being a journalist who met with Hitler in Berlin in the late 1930s while she was there covering the Olympics. The FBI had a file on Arvad, and Hoover was not reluctant to use it if he had to.

The memo of July 8, 1964 to RFK is detailed in its scope regarding Capell's book and what was in it. Here are some of the most interesting details of the memo:

> According to Mr. Capell, his book will make reference to your alleged friendship with the late Miss Marilyn Monroe. Mr. Capell stated he will indicate in his book that you and Miss Monroe were intimate and that you were in Miss Monroe's apartment at the time of her death.
>
> In recent years Capell has published "The Herald of Freedom," an anticommunist newsletter of an expose type, which names names and organizations. In the past several months he has been interviewed by Agents of our New York Office concerning numerous allegations he has made against a number of prominent individuals. Much of the information furnished by Mr. Capell has been of a very questionable nature and not subject to corroboration. He has consistently refused to reveal the alleged sources of his information.

Hoover then told his agents in the New York City FBI office to "follow the matter very closely. Furnish two copies of the book to the Bureau promptly upon its publication in order that the Attorney General may be kept advised."

The top officials of the FBI did a lot of digging into the allegations made by Frank Capell, and noted in the memo dated July 7, 1964 to Sullivan regarding the allegation that Kennedy was present at the time of Monroe's death, "The above allegation concerning the Attorney General has been previously circulated and has been branded as false as the Attorney General was actually in San Francisco with his wife at the time Marilyn Monroe committed suicide."

The FBI also had strong reservations regarding the veracity of anything that Frank Capell had to say. They wrote, "Inasmuch as Capell is the source of this information and his information has been extremely questionable, it is not believed that any action should be taken to determine the identity of the doctor who signed Monroe's death certificate."

The contents of the FBI's memo were sent to Robert Kennedy

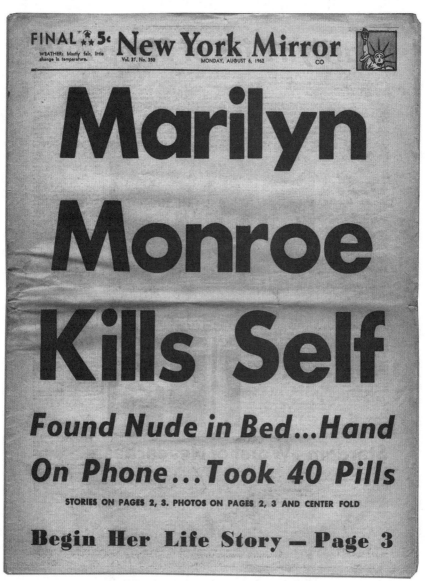

Front page news of Marilyn Monroe's tragc death.

for his files and in order to keep him informed of the Bureau's investigation into the Capell affair.

At one point in their frequent memos regarding the author and his new book, the FBI stated, "It is noted that Capell appeared very emotional and aggressive when he was advised of this book and was unable to state the exact purpose for having written it."

In the fifty-plus years since the death of Miss Monroe, there have been scores of books and articles written on the and countless theories of what really happened to America's sex queen on the day of her death.

One of these pundits was Milo Sperigilo, who, in 1982, was the director of the 76-year-old Nick Harris detective agency in Van Nuys, California. He says that Monroe's diary may have held the key to what she was thinking about in the days before her death. At that time he told reporters, "We know it [the diary] exists. I got a call from a New York attorney who told me his client had the book, but would turn it over only to a living blood relative of Miss Monroe's." According to Sperigilo, the missing diary details those affairs and also contains information about a CIA plot to kill Cuban dictator Fidel Castro.[6]

"Miss Monroe was murdered to keep her from talking about her relationship with the Kennedy brothers, the CIA plot and her association with San Diego Mafia figures," Sperigilo said.

Robert Slatzer, a writer as well as a close friend of Monroe's, said that Monroe had been angry over Robert Kennedy's attempts to break off their secret relationship and was angry because she could not get a hold of him at his Justice Department office. Monroe was alleged to have told Slatzer that if, "[Robert Kennedy] keeps avoiding me, I might just call a press conference and tell them about it, and my future plans." Slatzer claims that Robert Kennedy visited Monroe the day before her death.

Another person who had knowledge of the events on the day Monroe died was Jack Clemmons, an LA Police Department homicide investigator who was the first policeman to show up at Monroe's home right after the emergency call was made regarding her death. Clemmons said later, "She was murdered by needle injection by someone she knew and probably trusted. This was

6 Yates, Ronald, "Mystery still lingers on Marilyn Monroe," *Chicago Tribune*, August 6, 1982.

the cover-up crime of the century—a matter of the LA Police Department and other officials here protecting a famous political family of the East who had good reasons to shut Monroe's mouth."

The "Kennedy did it" conspiracy in the death of Marilyn Monroe is not a new one and it was given new life in a book by Jay Margolis, an investigative reporter, and Richard Buskin called *Case Closed*. Their book, which came out in 2014, places the blame for her murder on Robert Kennedy, Peter Lawford, and Dr. Ralph Greenson, her psychiatrist who was responsible for injecting a fatal dose of pentobarbital into her heart. Another witness to the event was supposed to have been the ambulance driver, James Hall. The aforementioned three men were at her Brentwood home on the night of August 5, 1962, pleading with Marilyn to give them the diary that held the hidden secrets of her affairs with both Jack and Bobby. The authors say that later that night, Bobby came back to Monroe's home with a bodyguard from the Los Angeles Police Department who injected her with a powerful sedative. Then, two LAPD "Gangster Squad" officers held her down, took off her clothes, and gave her an enema that contained a large number of Nembutal pills as well as seventeen chloral hydrates. They then departed the home, and later that night, Monroe's maid, Eunice Murray, found her seemingly dead. Mrs. Murry called an ambulance and when it arrived at her home, Monroe was barely alive. The paramedics put her on a breathing device and took her to the hospital. Dr. Greenson was there the whole time and he told the attendant to take her off the breathing machine, and when no one was looking, he injected some fatal substance into her heart, causing her death.[7]

This is just one of the many theories surrounding the death of Marilyn Monroe that cannot be verified to an absolute extent.

Non-conspiracy theorists say that Monroe was deeply depressed at the time of her death (she had once before tried to commit suicide), and that she accidentally overdosed while taking pills.

The Marilyn Monroe death, like so many other tragic losses that have been the staple of our lives over the past 50 years and more, will be debated as long as people are interested in learning the truth.

The story posed by Frank Capell was so shocking in its content and its possible ramifications for the political future of Robert

7 No author. "Bobby Kennedy ordered murder of Marilyn Monroe, new book claims," *Al Arabiya News*, May 17, 2014.

Kennedy, that the FBI were compelled to warn Kennedy about the contents of the book. The story that author Capell spun was fodder for the likes of J. Edgar Hoover, who saw possible blackmail against Robert Kennedy whom he disliked as much as the president. Whatever leverage Hoover could get over the Kennedy family he'd keep secret, but release it, if and when the time came. No one knows what Robert Kennedy's reaction was when he was presented with the contents of Capell's forthcoming book, but it couldn't have been positive. The warning to the Attorney General by Hoover was obvious: play ball with me or face the consequences.

Marilyn Monroe with Clark Gable on the set of her last movie, *The Misfits*.

Chapter 14
The Tale of Frank Sturgis

Before the Watergate burglary, in which a number of men were arrested in the offices of Democratic National Chairman Larry O'Brien, few people had ever heard the name of Frank Sturgis. Sturgis was part of the group that performed in the first act of what was to be the downfall of President Richard Nixon. Sturgis served a prison term and gained fame for his actions. But, years before, Sturgis was heavily involved in the plots to overthrow Fidel Castro, first working as an ally to Castro, and later, when it became obvious that Castro was turning Communist, for the CIA.

He was born Frank Angelo Fiorini in Norfolk, Virginia. After the separation of his parents, his mother married Frank Anthony Sturgis. The family lived for a time in the suburbs of Philadelphia where young Frank took on his stepfather's name (it is interesting to note that one of E. Howard Hunt's characters in his spy novels was a man named Sturgis).

Right after Pearl Harbor, Frank joined the Marines and saw action in some of the most bloody places of the war: Iwo Jima, Guadalcanal, and Okinawa. Frank was a commando and learned the art of killing. After contracting malaria in service, he was given a discharge in 1945 after a brief hospitalization.

After the war ended, he worked as a plainclothes cop in Norfolk, joined the Army for a two-year stint, and was then sent to Germany.

Sturgis became attached to the Cuban cause after going to Miami in the early 1950s, where he met Carlos Prio who was the former Cuban President. Frank Sturgis left for Cuba and eventually teamed up with Castro before his successful revolution that toppled Batista. Castro appointed Sturgis the Air Force's Director of Security. While in Castro's good graces, Sturgis met and befriended Pedro Diaz Lanz who was chief of the Air Force. Sturgis also served for a time as Castro's security chief for the casinos in Havana. Almost one year after Castro took power in Havana, Sturgis ad Diaz Lanz fled to the safety of the United States.

The CIA knew of Sturgis's Cuban connection and made its first contact with him in 1958 while he was still working for Castro. While there was no actual job offer by the CIA to Sturgis, he worked hand in glove with the Agency during its whirlwind efforts to kill Castro. He flew various missions with other anti-Castro exiles, oftentimes dropping leaflets over Cuba.

After one of his leaflet drop flights, the Federal Aviation Agency revoked his pilot's certificate (May, 1960). He was a member of Gerry Hemmings's Intercontinental Penetration Force, and came to know a number of top-ranking CIA men and others who were operating out of Miami. One of the men Sturgis met and worked with was E. Howard Hunt. Today, there is still a debate over when the two men met for the first time (Hunt's character "Sturgis" is in one of his earlier books). Andrew St. George said that in an interview he had with Sturgis for *True* magazine in August, 1974, Sturgis said he met Hunt in 1961, at the time of the Bay of Pigs invasion. He met Bernard Barker, Hunt's friend and fellow Watergate burglar, at the same time. In later years, Sturgis denied making that statement.

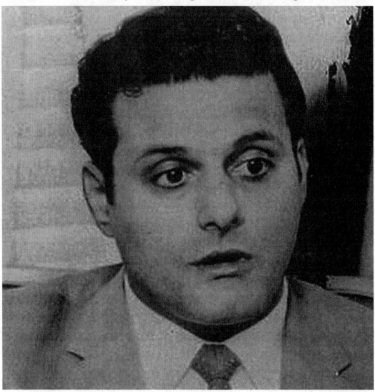

Frank Sturgis.

122

One official document on Sturgis stated the following:

On January 29, 1960, the United States Department of State decreed that the subject (Sturgis) had expatriated himself from the United States citizenship by his acceptance in March 1959, of an appointment as liaison officer in the Cuban Air Force. This decree was appealed and FIORINI's United States citizenship was subsequently restored.

In 1961, the subject formed an organization called the International Anti-Communist Brigade (IACB), described as an organization opposed to Communism and the CASTRO regime in Cuba.

The various intelligence agencies of the United States at that time were well aware of what Sturgis was up to and they had a large paper trail on him. What got their attention was an article in the May 14, 1961 edition of the *Miami Herald*'s Parade magazine which carried a front page photograph and an article on Fiorini's anti-Castro activities which was written by the noted columnist Jack Anderson.

The pertinent parts of the article are as follows:

As of September, 1961, Dr. ORLANDO BOSCH, who is identified as the leader of the MIRR, advised during interview that he had permitted Fiorini to go on a MIRR raid against Cuba in February 1961. BOSCH stated this raiding party traveled by boat and had failed to land in Cuba, and he was dissatisfied with FIORINI's performance and described the latter as a soldier of fortune and publicity seeker.

In the ensuing years, FIORINI has been reported through numerous sources and by his announcements as a participant in plans for several Cuban revolutionary adventures, one of which resulted in a military type action against the CASTRO forces.

A confidential source, who has furnished reliable information in the past and who has been closely associated with FIORINI through the years, advised as of May 1964, that the IACB was a paper organization, that is consisting of

FIORIN, but otherwise having no membership or source of funds, and that FIORINI himself is a soldier of fortune.

As of June 1964, FIORINI was reported in contact with Dr. Orlando Bosch of the MIRR in connection with plans for an air-raid against Cuba. Such an attempted raid did occur on June 19, 1964, when Cuban forces shot down a single engine aircraft which departed from West Palm Beach, Florida, and which had contained three Cubans who were affiliated with Dr. Orlando Bosch.

Orlando Bosch, who has been referenced in the above mentioned documents, was a terrorist leader bar none during that time period. For years, he and his terrorist group called MIRR wreaked havoc on the regime of Fidel Castro inside Cuba, and any pro-Castro organization or individuals anywhere they could be found.

Bosch's ties to the anti-Castro underground date back to the early 1960s, when he joined forces with such anti-Castro groups as the Christian Democratic Movement (MDC), the Cuban Revolutionary Council, DRE, and the 30th of November Movement. Bosch was at one time a pediatrician, but found throwing bombs far more important than healing children. Before the Bay of Pigs invasion in April 1961, Bosch's MIRR took part in various attacks against Cuban military installations. Bosch made an alliance with various soldier-of-fortune types in the anti-Castro movement such as Frank Sturgis and Gerry Hemming, who formed anti-Communist, anti-Castro groups. In the early 1960s, he worked with the CIA which quickly cut off funding for Bosch because he was much too violent, even for the Agency. It was during this time period that Bosch printed an anti-Castro pamphlet called "The Tragedy of Cuba," and accused the Kennedy administration of selling out the anti-Castro cause.

By 1963, Bosch and his mercenary allies such as Sturgis, Hemming, Alex Rorke, and others, were firebombing the Shell and Esso oil refineries in Cuba, and attacking MIG bases and sugar mills, among other Cuban targets. It was later reported that Bosch got his funding from Texas millionaire and right-wing fanatic H.L. Hunt (Hunt's name also came up in connection to the Kennedy assassination).

By 1968, Bosch's luck had run out and he was captured while trying to shell a Polish freighter in Miami harbor. He was sentenced to ten years but was pardoned in 1972. By the middle 1970s, he was arrested in Venezuela but the United States government failed to have him extradited back home. Back on the streets, Bosch began eliminating a number of men who were instrumental in sending him to jail.

By the late 1970s, he was in Chile, linking up with the dreaded Chilean security service, DNA, once again carrying out bombings in various parts of the world, including the United States. His power and influence waned with the US government's decision to end its efforts to remove Castro from power.

Bosch's eventual downfall came when he associated himself with a noted terrorist named Louis Posada Carriles. His extreme actions spanned two decades, from the 1960s to the 1970s and beyond, carrying out violent, deadly plans to kill Fidel Castro, as well as targeting commercial airliners. He was a veteran of the Bay of Pigs invasion, as well as being a CIA operative with his own code name. Over the years, the United States government charged Posada with drug smuggling, a blot on the record of a man who was associated with the CIA.

On October 6, 1976, a Cubana Airlines plane fell from the sky into the Caribbean Sea, resulting in the deaths of 73 people on board. Among the dead were members of the Cuban national fencing team who were returning to Cuba after a competition in Venezuela. This act of air piracy would be the precursor to the rash of commercial airline attacks that began during the decade of the 1970s, mostly taking place in the Middle East against US air carriers.

In the middle of October 1976, the CIA received a detailed and comprehensive report from one of its sources in Venezuela who had knowledge of this deadly attack. The informer said that in September 1976, Orlando Bosch was in Venezuela under the protection of that nation's president, Carlos Andres Perez. Assisting Bosch during his stay in Venezuela was Orlando Garcia who served as Venezuela's Security and Intelligence Chief. Upon his arrival in that nation, Bosch was met at the airport by Garcia and Louis Posada.

During a party hosted by some prominent exiles, Bosch made a rather chilling statement. According to the Venezuelan source:

Also during the evening Bosch made the statement that now our organization has come out of the Letelier job looking good, we are going to try something else. Bosch did not name the organization nor did he expand on his meaning. (Field Commentary): The Letelier mentioned above is probably former Chilean Foreign Minister Orlando Letelier, who was assassinated in the United States on 21 September.

A few days following the fund-raising dinner, Posada was overheard to say that, "We are going to hit a Cuban plane," and that "Orlando has the details." Following the 6 October Cubana airline crash off the coast of Barbados, Bosch, Garcia, and Posada agreed that it would be best for Bosch to leave Venezuela. Therefore, on 9 October, Posada and Garcia escorted Bosch to the Columbia border where the latter crossed into Columbian territory.

This was the same Orlando Bosch whom Frank Sturgis worked with, years before in their mutual endeavors to kill Castro.

Among the documents related to Sturgis came information from his stepson, Ronald Edward Thompson, who was born on July 1, 1944 in Norfolk, Virginia. The youngman said that his mother had died while Fiorini was overseas during World War II and that Fiorini never assumed responsibility for him. Mr. Thompson said that he accompanied Sturgis to Mexico, along with another man named Donald Francis Roche on a sanctioned MIRR mission that was supported by Orlando Bosch. They traveled to Mexico in Sturgis's 1958 Cadillac in the beginning of April, 1967.

Thompson claimed to be present when explosives and detonators were hidden in the body of Fiorini's car at a Miami garage while Dr. Bosch and other Cuban associates of Dr. Bosch were present. Thompson stated that these explosives were to be placed on a ship at Tampico or Veracruz, Mexico. Thompson stated this sabotage was intended to be an anti-Castro action supported by the MIRR. He said that circumstances prevented execution of this sabotage and he described the location on the highway between Ciudad Mante and Ciudad Victoria where the explosives and the magnets to be used in attaching the explosives to the hull of a ship were buried. He also advised that Fiorini had received a $200 money order from Orlandi Bosch, sent by Bosch from Miami to Ciudad Mante.

As of July 5, 1967, a confidential source abroad advised that Mexican authorities had located the cache of explosives, detonators, and magnets on the highway between Mante and Victoria as had previously been described by Edward Thompson. This same source advised that a money order for $200.00 had been received by Frank Sturgis, Hotel Mante, Ciudad Mante, on April 13, 1967, sent by one Aldo Fernandez.

When interviewed on May 1, 1967, Frank Fiorini claimed that his trip to Mexico in April 1967, together with Donald Roche and his step-son Ronnie Thompson, was in the nature of a vacation trip. He stated he was acquainted with Dr. Orlando Bosch of the MIRR but denied he had seen Bosch in several months. He denied that he carried any explosives to Mexico in his 1958 Cadillac, which he used on the trip. He denied that Orlando Bosch had sent him money to Mexico but said a Cuban friend had sent him $100.00 from Miami.

The documents also reveal an allegation that Frank Sturgis "alleged that Jack Ruby had visited Cuba in 1959 and again in 1963, and had, in fact, met with Fidel Castro." This information was given to Jim Johnston who was a member of the Senate Select Committee staff. The one-page document has no reference point as to who wrote it, but we can surmise that it had either come from the CIA or the FBI. The next paragraph sums up the allegation.

Johnston told me that he remembered seeing this report and surrounding CIA and FBI memoranda in both Agency and Bureau files. As he recalls he also remembers them in the Warren Commission files. It was his recollection that included in this information was the fact that Frank Sturgis had made an allegation in early 1964 similar to the one made in the July 9 *Washington Star,* and that the FBI had in fact interviewed sources in the Miami Cuban Community including Sturgis, and had concluded that the information could not be substantiated. Johnston also indicated that the information he now possesses (which he believes to be of some relevance to the Oswald case) does not pertain in any way to Jack Ruby.[8]

The gist of the Ruby-Castro story appeared in the *Washington Star* under the headline "Ruby Met With Castro, Sturgis Says." The article says that Ruby met with Castro in Havana 10 weeks before the president's murder, and discussed removal of the president along with arms purchases for Cuba and smuggling of illicit drugs into the United States. The article goes on to say that Sturgis said in an interview that he "and other agents passed information on to various government agencies in early 1964, before the Warren Commission completed its hearings, but he is uncertain whether the information was ever made available to the commission."

The story further states:

> Sturgis said he had been assigned to investigate possible involvement of Cuban exiles in the Miami area in the Kennedy assassination. He said neither his investigation nor that of fellow agents turned up any Cuban exile ties with the shooting of Kennedy. He refused to say which agency he was working for, or who gave him the assignment. Records have indicated that he was working for the CIA at about that time.

Sturgis was linked up on one of the early Castro assassination attempts with a beautiful woman, a mistress of Castro, Marita Lorenz. After a torrid affair with Castro, Miss Lorenz grew tired of Castro's flings and decided to leave Cuba. According to her accounts, she became pregnant with Castro's child and was forced to have an abortion. After this horrible incident, she decided to work against her former lover. She met with Sturgis and he convinced her to work for the CIA. Her first mission was to go back to Havana and steal documents from Castro's safe. At the same time, Miss Lorenz

8 Received from Captain John Matheny, NSC Staff, in mid-July 1976.

Frank Sturgis in Cuba, 1958.

also met Alexander Rorke, a man who was also involved with the intelligence community and participated in numerous bombing raids into Cuba. It was Rorke, according to Lorenz, who asked her to go back into Cuba in an attempt to poison Castro. The CIA made up poison pills that Sturgis handed to Marita Lorenz. She put the pills into her cold cream jar and when she returned to Cuba, the pills had dissolved. After the incident she blamed Sturgis for going public, and in the 1970s her story was written for all the world to see by Paul Meskill in the *New York Daily News*.

Lorenz said that during her time in Miami with Frank Sturgis in the early 1960s, Sturgis was working with such agencies as the DEA, the CIA, and the US Customs Service in uncovering illegal arms sales.

In another bizarre tale, Marita Lorenz told of a plot that she was inadvertently part of that involved Sturgis. She said that in November of 1963, right before the president's trip to Dallas, she went in a two-car caravan from Miami to Dallas. Some of the people in the caravan were Frank Sturgis and Lee Harvey Oswald. According to Lorenz, a high-powered rifle was in the back of one of the cars, along with a scope and silencer.

Along on the ride was none other than Orlando Bosch. Once they arrived in Dallas, they got two rooms in a motel, and one night a man came to visit. That man was Jack Ruby. When Lorenz told Sturgis that she was getting very nervous about the entire matter, Sturgis said it was a mistake on his part to have brought her to Dallas and she returned to Miami. She later said that she had a feeling that the Dallas trip (if it ever took place) was to plan the killing of someone.

In the aftermath of the assassination of the president, and for many years to come, the name of Frank Sturgis as a possible assassin in the deed gained fame. The interest in Sturgis's activities gained momentum when a news account was printed in the Pompano Beach newspaper, the *Sun Sentinel,* written by James Buchanan. According to the writer, Sturgis told him that Oswald was in communication with certain members of the Cuban security forces prior to November 22, 1963. When asked for his reaction to the story, Sturgis said that he gave "offhand remarks" to Buchanan and said they were "guesses, speculation, and rumor."

A Department of Justice memo on Sturgis dated October 13, 1967, gives information on what the Justice Department was doing in its follow up on Sturgis's activities. They wrote, "Investigation relating to the subject is produced upon information that members of the Revolutionary Movement for Insurrection Recovery (MIRR) and the Cuban Nationalist Movement (CNM), both of which are organizations with members in Miami, Florida, who are engaged in anti-Castro activities, were in the process as of June 1967, of planning military type action against Cuban targets in Canada, in particular the Cuban Pavilion at Expo 67 in Montreal, Canada."[9]

Over time, it has been rumored that Sturgis was somehow involved with the CIA in some official capacity. A document on Sturgis's possible role in the Agency is spelled out in a one-page message whose pertinent part reads as follows:

> At the time of delivery to OGC, and with the concurrence of the Director of Security, it was pointed out that the document is unclassified and contains a statement by the originator, James Schlesinger, former DCI, that in his discussion with William Colby, Colby stated that "Sturgis has not been on the payroll for a number of years.

8 RIF No, 104-10221-10185.

It was pointed out to OGC that this statement is in direct conflict with prior Agency public releases concerning Sturgis to the effect that he has never been connected with the Agency in any way.[10]

According to the website Muckrock.com, the FBI file on Frank Sturgis, which is still classified, runs 75,000 pages, "almost twice the combined Watergate and Kennedy assassination FBI files. The file covers his paramilitary activities in Cuba, his ties to assassins and assassination plots, accusations about involvement in the Kennedy assassination and meeting Lee Harvey Oswald, his confirmed CIA employment, his involvement in the break-in of the Chilean embassy and more."

If and when the rest of the Kennedy-related files are released (they have been kept under wraps for three more years), we may then close the book on Frank Sturgis.

---

10 www.muckrock.com/news/archives/2016, Frank Sturgis.

Chapter 15
The Onassis-Maheu Connection

The JFK files that were released in October 2017 were not exclusively related to the Kennedy assassination and its related material. A number of files in the collection that were also released tell the story of different people and events that took place in the decades of the 1960s and 1970s. One of these stories now told will add to our knowledge of those turbulent times. This one is about a plot hatched at the highest levels of the American government which involved two shipping magnates of the day, Aristotle Onassis (who married Jackie Kennedy after her husband's assassination), and his arch-rival, Stavros Niarchos. It also involves Robert Maheu, a high-ranking political fixer in Washington who was deeply involved in the plots to kill Fidel Castro, and who worked for Howard Hughes. Also connected to the story were then Vice President Richard Nixon and Warren Burger, who would later become Chief Justice of the Supreme Court.

The gist of the story is that Robert Maheu was hired by Stavros Niarchos to damage the lucrative contract that Onassis had signed with the government of Saudi Arabia to transport oil across the globe. What eventually took place was a vast, undercover operation against Onassis that included wiretapping and a dirty tricks campaign with the tacit approval of the US government.

The documents released on the Maheu-Onassis connection are not that extensive but they do tell a very interesting story about Maheu and his high-level government connections.

The story begins in 1956 when an unnamed foreign leader came to the United States on a diplomatic mission. The leader was vacillating when it came to the game of Cold War politics, but it was rumored that he was in favor of the Soviets at that time. When this leader came to Washington for talks, he wanted to procure a number of women for his pleasure. A lawyer was tasked with arranging these trysts, and he got in touch with someone in the State Department to place the women at his disposal. The leader wanted "a Latin type, an American type and a Nordic type." The man at State said he

Robert Maheu.

would have nothing to do with the deal and begged off. The State Department man told the lawyer that he should contact Robert Maheu about making the arrangements for the foreign leader. Maheu was a former FBI agent who operated his own private investigation business in Washington. Maheu was a friend of a man named Scott McLeod, then the US Ambassador to Ireland. It is thought that the lawyer contacted McLeod for this purpose:

> Maheu agreed to obtain the women for the foreign leader. He contacted Inspector Robb of the New York P.D. and wanted Robb to arrange for him and the girls to stay at the Waldorf Astoria Hotel, in rooms not too distant from the leader and his party. Robb refused to involve the police in this affair.
>
> Maheu and the prostitutes subsequently stayed at the

> Belmont Plaza Hotel on Lexington Ave., across from the
> Waldorf Astoria where the leader and his party were staying.
> Maheu used the name of Jordan at the Belmont Plaza. When
> he received a call from one of the secretaries, he would send
> one of the girls over to the hotel where (blank) was living
> and she would be secretly passed into one of the rooms.[11]

The foreign leader then made a trip across the United States, making stops in Detroit, Los Angeles, and San Francisco. It seems that Robert Maheu and his entourage followed his client and, in the process, violated the White Slave Traffic Act which forbids transferring women across state lines for immoral purposes. This unsavory trip had the silent blessing of the US State Department and the episode quickly faded away.

The documents say that the CIA's Office of Security had used Maheu's services since the early 1950s. He was cleared by the Deputy Director/Plans at the CIA and used in various capacities during that time.

The two protagonists in the shipping intrigue that involved Maheu were Aristotle Onassis, a wealthy Greek shipping magnet and part owner of the Monte Carlo casino in Monaco, and Stavros Niarchos, who had been related to Onassis by marriage.

In April 1953, Stavros Niarchos was indicted by the Justice Department for a violation of the Ship Sales Act of 1946. The basis of the act arose after World War II, when the US government "sought to unload its supply of surplus military equipment. Niarchos was accused of circumventing provisions of the act in order to gain control of tankers forbidden from sale to foreigners." The law firm that Niarchos used was Mudge, Rose, Guthrie, and Alexander, the law firm that would eventually hire Richard Nixon.

While Niarchos was in legal limbo, Aristotle Onassis was the beneficiary of his brother-in-law's legal jeopardy. To his great profit, Onassis, on January 20, 1954, signed an agreement with Saudi Arabia called the "Jiddah Agreement."

> The contract permitted Onassis to establish and operate
> an Arabian maritime fleet that would be guaranteed the right
> to ship between 10 percent and 100 percent of all Arabian oil.

11 RIF No. 157-10004-10271: Operation Robert Maheu, October 13, 1957.

The new agreement that left Onassis with a monopoly on the distribution of the world's oil, was a major blow to the nations in the Middle East who controlled the oil flow, the International Petroleum Cartel (IPC). The Saudi's held the majority of the world's supply of oil under their sands and were in a position to help Onassis immensely. The other oil producers now faced bankruptcy if the Onassis deal held up.

Who was Stavros Niarchos and how did he become the tycoon he turned out to be?

He was the owner of 80 tankers, a man of mystery, and had a fortune estimated at $4 billion. He was born on July 3, 1909 in Greece (his parents were naturalized American citizens). As a young man he joined a company founded by his maternal uncles that imported grain from Argentina, which later bought old freighters during the depression years for $20,000 each. Thus, the Niarchos Empire was born.

He leased his ships to the Allies in 1941, and spent the rest of the war in the Greek Navy. He later served as the assistant Greek naval attaché in Washington, and after his ships were destroyed by the German navy, he collected a hefty profit of $2 million in insurance payouts. He then began buying up old Liberty and Victory surplus ships and T2 tankers that had been made during the war. He got into hot water when he formed a company with his American-born sister and began leasing the ships to a Panamanian company to avoid US taxes. The government sued him and he agreed to pay $12 million in fines, and gave up some of his ships.

Aristotle Onasiis.

135

As the years passed, Niarchos and Onassis began a tanker war that would rival all else. Each man built bigger and heavier ships to transport their oil and Onassis, in order to show up his rival, created Olympic Airways.

Aristotle Onassis was born in Smyrna, then part of Greece. As a young man he moved to Argentina where he made his first million in the 1920s by importing tobacco. He became an Argentine citizen and purchased an old tanker fleet at a bankruptcy auction. He soon had a number of his own ships which he sailed under what were called "Flags of Convenience." During World War II, his tankers carried supplies across the Atlantic. After the war he made his primary home in Monte Carlo, and on an island called Scorpios where he built his palatial home. Jim Hogan, in his book called *Spooks,* said of Onassis that:

> In a single stroke he became landlord and croupier to the dragomen and lords of high-society: deposed dictators, exiled kings, playboys, arms merchants, and international financiers. Becoming the man who owned the bank at Monte Carlo, he invited others to break him, knowing that it couldn't be done.[12]

The fued between Onassis and Niarchos would not only engulf both of them, but thrust Robert Maheu right into the middle of their fight.

In an "Eyes Only" document titled "Subject: Robert Maheu" dated June 7, 1966, the US government's official version of just what Maheu was up to is spelled out:

> The only significant association the Agency (CIA) had with Maheu during that period involved the struggle between two Greek industrial giants, Stavros Niarchos and Aristotle Onassis. Maheu had been retained as a trouble shooter for Niarchos. Onassis had just concluded a pact with King Saud which would allow him to control approximately 90 percent of the oil shipments out of Saudi Arabia. In consummating the deal, he allegedly employed every trick in the book. His

12 Hougan, Jim, *Spooks: The Haunting of America—The Private Use of Secret Agents,* William Morrow & Co., New York, 1978, Page 284.

achievements caused much consternation among the British, German, and American interests. Niarchos also realized as a result of this balance of power and influence weighted heavily in favor of Onassis in their own private battle. It was this mutual concern of the United States and Niarchos that set the stage for a joint venture. Niarchos supplied the money, personnel, and documents; the Agency furnished the communications, courier facilities, and direction in the form of our Commo channel, pouch system, and the NEA Division's expertise and guidance.

Mr. Maheu was contacted to determine whether the Committee ([Long Committee] had been in touch with him. He stated he was not aware of their interest in him. When the Taggert conversation was mentioned, he promptly replied that it must be the Onassis operation they were looking into. He recalled that he had Onassis's New York office "covered" sometime during that period. John Frank, a former staff employee, and then a private investigator, was engaged to arrange for the coverage. Maheu could only identify the technician by the name of Leon. Presumably, this coverage was done as a routine technique to keep Niarchos interests informed on Onassis's movements. This was not initiated at the request of any Agency component so far as our records indicate.

It is not believed that Maheu wants or expects us to front for him in the Onassis tap matter. As mentioned previously, to our knowledge, this was not Agency sponsored. However, if exploited, it would probably eventually lead to exposing our part in the Onassis/Niarchos feud. As it is a matter of court record, it could not be denied or buried. Even though the details might be protected by a declaration that it involved classified operational information, it would set up a field day for the press and critics of the Agency.

In 1958-59, Maheu was used by the FE Division in two sensitive operations targeted against Sukarno who was the President of Indonesia. Mr. Allen Dulles was aware and approved of these operations. Mr. Joseph Smith who was then Chief/PMI, is knowledgeable of the actions.

While none of our interests in Maheu's activities relate to wire-tapping, it is evident that the extensive and diversified use of him makes us vulnerable to exploitation should he be interrogated in depth regarding his actions.

Mr. Maheu is maintaining a cooperative attitude and has promised to do all in his power to protect the Agency from embarrassment or compromise.[13]

What this document was referencing was a wiretap that had been placed on the telephone of one of Onassis's shipping companies in New York City:

Payment for this was made by Onassis's brother in-law and rival Niarchos. Robert Maheu, a former FBI agent and then and now a private investigator, was hired by Niarchos to help break this Onassis threat. One of the measures used was to get the United States to put pressure on Saudi Arabia officially and another was to cause Onassis all the difficulty possible with the American law. Maheu made numerous trips to Europe and into Saudi Arabia. Indications were that Onassis had bought off several Saudi Arabia government officials. CIA, according to Maheu, was interested as were McLeod of State and the FBI. Maheu allegedly turned over his investigative reports to these agencies.

The wiretap in New York therefore was an investigative technique. Maheu always said it was quasi-governmental in view of the fact that the US government knew of the tap and gave tacit approval.

The information obtained was not startling but names of certain high governmental officials in the Saudi Arabian government were mentioned. All information obtained was delivered to a man nicknamed Amby who was manager of Niarchos' company Oceanic S.S. Co., in the East fifties between Park and Madison Avenues in New York City.

When the Grand Jury was investigating the foreign registration case they went into this wire-tapping situation closely and in fact contacted some of Maheu's employees. Maheu, I understand, went to someone in the US and Saudi

13 RIF No. 104-10122-10344.

Arabia and it was decided not to proceed further in this matter. It is understood that Maheu spoke to Walter Yagely of the Justice Department in reference to this and he rushed to the Grand Jury and told the Grand Jury to forget this.

We now bring into this extremely interesting and disturbing story, the full force of the Eisenhower administration in the person of the president himself, and his vice president, Richard Nixon.

Minutes of a National Security Council meeting dated July 1954, reveal the interest President Eisenhower took in the Onassis/Niarchos battle. According to the minutes, Ike asked whether it was not possible, with all the power of the United States, to "break" Onassis. The NSC decided to take "all appropriate measures" to wreck the deal.

Enter Richard Nixon, Vice President of the United States. It seems that Maheu and a colleague named John Gerrity were called into Nixon's office for a conversation. "Nixon came in," recalled Gerrity, "and gave us the whole Mission Impossible bit. I know you'll be careful, but you have to understand that while this is a national security matter of terrific importance, we can't acknowledge you in any way if anything should go wrong. I could tell that Nixon enjoyed saying it. He loved these kinds of operations."[14]

The plot against Onassis went into high gear with Maheu's agents, working out of offices in the National Republican Club, placing a phone tap at Onassis's New York headquarters, and started a smear campaign against him in the New York press. Maheu himself flew to Saudi Arabia and persuaded the King to tear up the contract he had made with Onassis regarding the transport of the world's oil supplies.

In his book about Nixon called *The Arrogance of Power,* Anthony Summers writes of a chilling episode that directly involved the Vice President in the Onassis matter. This was a statement Maheu made in 1992 and it goes like this. Nixon said the following, "If it turns out we have to kill the bastard, just don't do it on American soil." Maheu suggested that Nixon may have said that merely as something to say, something that sounded tough.

John Gerrity, who was in on the meeting with Maheu and Nixon,

---

14 Summers, Anthony, *The Arrogance of Power: The Secret World of Richard Nixon,* Viking Press, New York, 2000, Page 195-196.

said that he had met with then Assistant Attorney General Warren Burger, who would later become Chief Justice of the US Supreme Court, regarding the Onassis operation. Mr. Burger told Gerrity that he would take "judicial oversight" of any activities that Mr. Gerrity might take against Mr. Onassis.

Besides the dirty tricks operation targeting Onassis, the campaign against Onassis even included the bombing and strafing of one of Mr. Onassis's whaling ships by a Peruvian fighter plane.[15]

While at the Justice Department, Warren Burger approved a large lawsuit against Onassis which alleged that he illegally bought some surplus American ships. Onassis also faced criminal indictment in the case, but it was dropped later as part of a settlement. Burger later denied any charges that he took part in the Onassis scheme. At that time, Nixon would not comment on the allegations brought against him.

As mentioned in this chapter, Gerrity traveled to Rome in his anti-Onassis campaign. While in Rome, Getty had two CIA agents at his command. "I wasn't a CIA agent—the CIA was my agent," he said.

Talking about the incident, one of Maheu's associates said, "We were always being reminded that the CIA was behind the operation, that it was government work."

For his extensive efforts to discredit Onassis, it was estimated that Maheu was paid $187,000 by Niarchos. Maheu said the payment was "peanuts."

A few years later, Robert Maheu would again take up work for the CIA as the intermediary for the CIA in its efforts to kill Fidel Castro, making arrangements with certain American mobsters to eliminate the "beard."

The Onassis-Niarchos fued was one of the best-kept secrets of the era, a story that is now being seen in its full light.

---

15 "A Plot On Onassis Charged In Article," No author, August 3, 1978.

Chapter 16
John Paisley

Another non-Kennedy assassination document that was released in October 2017 dealt with a former CIA agent named John Paisley whose death in September 1978 on board his boat in the Chesapeake Bay is the stuff of a good spy novel. Before going into the details of what the CIA and the FBI were looking into vis a vis the circumstances of John Paisley's death, a little background information is required on who he was and what he did for the CIA. The reader should know that Paisley was connected to the counterintelligence division at CIA, and played a minor role in the Watergate affair with the "Plumbers," via the CIA's Office of Security.

September 24, 1978 dawned with a bright sky and a warm breeze that skipped over the Chesapeake Bay. On that bright day, John Arthur Paisley, a 55-year old former CIA officer, a man privy to the nation's highest secrets, left the mooring at Solomon's Island near the Patuxent shore of the Chesapeake Bay. Before leaving, Paisley asked the harbor master to leave the lights on at the dock as he would be back that night.

His ship, the 31-foot *Brillig,* named after a character in Lewis Carroll's book, *Through A Looking Glass*, set sail for a routine day at sea.

Paisley, an expert sailor, navigated the *Brillig* on the historic bay, past the nation's capital. All went well and between five and six p.m. he received a call via ship to shore radio from his old friend, Colonel William Wilson. Paisley told Wilson that he would be back after dark. That call from Col. Wilson proved to be the last time that anyone would hear from John Paisley.

The next day, September 25, the Coast Guard received a call from a pleasure boat that a sloop had been sighted adrift near Point Lookout on the bay. A cutter was sent out to investigate and upon arriving found a blood-soaked deck, a highly sophisticated radio transmitter, a nine-mm bullet, and an empty ship. Also discovered were numerous classified documents belonging to the CIA, including the name and phone number of David Young, the head of President Nixon's infamous "Plumbers" unit. Despite the paper trail, no body was found.

On October 1, 1978, the Coast Guard found the body of John Arthur Paisley near the same Solomon's Island mooring from which the *Brillig* set sail only a week before.

After the death of John Paisley was discovered, the nation's intelligence services went into action to find out just what happened to him. Was Paisley killed by some nefarious person or persons, or was his death a tragic accident?

According to the newly released documents, on December 1, 1978, a few months after the death of John Paisley, Senator Birch Bayh wrote a letter to William Webster who was then the Director of the FBI requesting any and all information the Bureau had on Paisley and his death. Senator Bayh wanted to see :

>...all copies of the fingerprint cards and fingerprint registration cards which were located examined and or prepared in connection with the Bureau's recent Paisley fingerprint identification work, including, of course, the final report which was prepared on this subject for the Maryland State Police. In addition, it would be helpful for us to have copies of all the relevant materials relating to any FBI policies or practices which may have accounted for the purging from FBI files of the John Paisley prints which had been submitted at the time of Mr. Paisley's application for employment by the CIA.

The documents on the Paisley case revealed that the FBI had "opened a kidnapping case" in connection with this matter (which was later found not to be true). Senator Bayh wrote, "If this information is accurate, I would appreciate your providing us with copies of any materials which reflect the predicate and authorization for initiating that inquiry, together with whatever information was developed as a result."

A new twist to the Paisley story is evident in the next paragraph. It reads as follows:

We have also been informed by the CIA that on September 28, 1978, the Agency informed the Bureau by memorandum that a Coast Guard official had advised CIA that (a) on the night of Mr. Paisley's disappearance a Soviet vessel was proceeding up Chesapeake Bay and (b) on the same night there was an unusual amount of communications traffic from the Soviet summer residence on the eastern shore of Chesapeake Bay. Any information which might have been developed by your Bureau with respect to these two allegations would also be helpful.

The documents say that after an investigation by the Bureau, no kidnapping case on the John Paisley matter was opened, "although the FBI considered his disappearance as a possible violation of the Federal Kidnapping Statute, Title 18, US Code, Section 1201 (b)."

The story of the disappearance of John Paisley now gets murkier according to the documents. Whether or not the story is believable is up to the reader to discern.

The story goes that the FBI received information from Walter Taylor who was the national editor of the *Washington Star* who said that his assistant editor received a phone call from a person who called himself Ghawzi Ullah, stating that they had kidnapped a CIA employee named John Paisley.

At approximately 10:00 a.m., Mr. Taylor received a second call from Ghawzi Ullah stating that John Paisley, a CIA agent had been seized by one of their commandos in the Chesapeake Bay area. He stated that Paisley was valuable to them for identification of "Zionist Agents" in other countries. Ghawzi Ullah made the following demands for the "Muslim Council of War in New York." 1) The release of all Muslim prisoners, 2) $1 million and, 3) that Henry Kissinger be turned over to them.He stated that the specific time and date would be called in later and that he wanted this action to be published and widely circulated.

He further stated that this was no joke; that it was not a game, and that it affected the fate of Islam.

The document then goes on to talk about a possible Russian ship in the bay:

> CIA letter to FBIHQ, dated September 28, 1978, disclosed that Lt. Cook, Portsmouth, Virginia, US Coast Guard Station, advised that on the evening of September 24, 1978, when John Paisley did not return to port, information was made available to him which disclosed that a Soviet vessel was proceeding up the Chesapeake Bay.
>
> Inquiries with Naval Investigative Service Headquarters and USCG Headquarters further disclosed that a Soviet vessel was not in the vicinity of John Paisley's boat. Information did disclose that two Polish vessels, the *General Stanislaw Popawaki* and *Francis Zubrzycki* were in the Bay area, and in all likelihood USCG initial information was referring to the *Francis Zubraycki*.
>
> Additionally, USCG information also indicated that there was an unusual amount of communications traffic from the Soviet summer residence on the Eastern Shore of the Chesapeake Bay. i.e., Pioneer Point.
>
> On October 3, 1978, USCG Headquarters furnished information that communications traffic from the Soviet establishment located at Pioneer Point is not targeted by USCG and that USCG only monitors shipping and boating frequencies as required by existing regulations.

The fact that the USCG believed that a Soviet ship was in the vicinity of John Paisley's *Brillig* was something that could be of some importance. After all, Paisley was a high-ranking Agency official who may or may not have been followed by the Soviets for whatever reason they might have had.

But that is not the end of the Paisley story. There were lots of permutations regarding the circumstances of his death that do not immediately meet the eye.

Paisley's body was taken to the Maryland State Medical Examiner's Office for an autopsy. The Medical Examiner, Dr. Russell Fisher, found that thae bullet had entered from the left ear (Paisley was right handed), the body was weighed down with two sets of diving belts, and was badly decomposed. Another baffling set of facts was that the body contained no blood or brain tissue, nor were any weapons or cartridges found on the boat. These facts posit the theory that Paisley was killed someplace else and then returned to the ship. Yet, despite these numerous inconsistencies, Dr. Fisher ruled the death a suicide.

Other interesting facts concerning the body are these:

Item: The body discovered by the USCG was four inches shorter and twenty-six pounds lighter than that of Paisley. Dr. Fisher listed Paisley's height as 5'11" when the medical records state him to be 5'7".

Item: The body wore size 30 shorts while Paisley's was a size 34."

Item: When Paisley's fingerprints (they were severed along with his hands after the body was found) were sent to the FBI for positive identification, it was found that Paisley's fingerprint file had been lost.

After the autopsy was finished, the body was sent to an Agency-approved funeral home where it was cremated. It is also interesting to note that no one who knew Paisley in life was allowed to view the body before cremation.

Who was John Paisley?

At the age of 25 in 1948, he went to Palestine as a radio operator for the United Nations. There, he was recruited by James Angleton into the CIA. He began his agency career working on Soviet strategic research, learned Russian, and was privy to one of the most highly classified secrets in the CIA: the methods of obtaining information on Russia's nuclear program.

Paisley helped to develop a variety of US reconnaissance and spy satellite systems, including the KH-11 capable of reading the license plates of vehicles from miles in space. But his most important duty at CIA HQ was to debrief two Soviet defectors, Yuri Nosenko and Nicholas Shadrin. As a technical advisor, he was also involved in early CIA mind control experiments with LSD and hypnotism in the 1950s.

After his retirement from the Agency in 1974, Paisley was offered a post as a $200 per day "consultant" to the CIA. As an advisor, he worked in a highly secret section named "Team

B" from August to December 1976. Team B's work included a determination of the United States' evaluation of Soviet forces and the nuclear capabilities of the old USS.R. Paisley had access to the highest codes and information about the United States and Soviet nuclear power even though one CIA officer called Paisley "a rather unimportant intelligence officer and analyst."

When the *Brillig* was found, it contained a highly technical radio which enabled Paisley to send and receive thousands of words a minute of top secret communications used by the CIA and the National Security Agency. Why, if Paisley was such a nonentity in the agency, was he allowed access to such highly valuable information?

Dick Russell, the author of the book *The Man Who Knew Too Much,* tells the story of Richard Case Nagell, a military intelligence officer from 1962 to 1963, with whom he was a friend over a long period of time. Nagell gave Russell many tips on the world of intelligence, as well as his direct knowledge of Lee Harvey Oswald. In October 1978, Nagell sent Russell a clipping from a newspaper regarding the death of John Paisley. Under the headline, Nagell wrote "Was he nash."

When the two men met for lunch, Russell asked Nagell what "nash" meant. Nagell replied that it was a Russian phrase meaning "ours and nobody else's." What Nagell was implying was that John Paisley was a Russian agent.

James Angleton took an active interest in the Paisley case because of the strange circumstances surrounding his death. According to Michael Holtzman, who wrote a book on Angleton:

"He suggested that if it had not been for some of the weights slipping off the body and consequently it's surfacing, Paisley's disappearance would have been written off as a presumed suicide. Because Paisley had obtained a crucial overview of Soviet developments. Angleton speculated that Paisley's knowledge would have been of great value to the KGB, and if they had obtained it they might also have had an incentive to hide his success by disposing of Paisley."[16]

---

16 Holtzman, Michael, *James Jesus Angleton, The CIA & the Craft of Counterintelligence,* Unknown Sponsor, 2008, Page 317.

The motive for Paisley's death is the stuff of fiction. For years, reports of a Soviet mole hidden inside the CIA had been widely investigated. Was Paisley a Russian mole, a trusted confidant of Agency directors and knowledgeable of their inner secrets? Or was he a CIA double agent, sent to penetrate the KGB? Was Paisley found out by the Russians, who had him killed? The answers to all these questions lie at the bottom of Chesapeake Bay, begging for a plausible solution, but unwilling to reveal their deadly secrets.

Chapter 17
LBJ and Covert Action

One of the newly released documents tells the story of a meeting between CIA Director John McCone and President Johnson in which all sorts of covert intelligence activities and personalities were discussed. The topics discussed ranged from Spain's dictator Francisco Franco to ex-President Dwight Eisenhower, and what Johnson really thought the role of the CIA was to be in the world of 1964.

The two men met on February 20, 1964, alone, without anyone else present for the meeting. The first topic concerned President Eisenhower. LBJ said that he had planned to meet with him to discuss certain topics "if he thought this would be constructive. He said he felt General Eisenhower might feel he was being high-pressured and that he intended merely to advise him of the plan to surface the OXCART and exchange formalities."

While there is no reference to just what OXCART was in the document, a little checking of the record sheds light on just what they were talking about. OXCART was the A-12 reconnaissance plane which was operated by the CIA and was the successor to the famous U-2 plane that was involved in so many Cold War operations. OXCART flew high-level reconnaissance missions over the USSR and began its operations in November 1965. It is possible that LBJ wanted to let the former president in on the secret development of OXCART as a matter of respect to the ex-president. OXCART was the father of the SR-71 Blackbird high-altitude spy plane.

McCone then told the president an interesting fact about current CIA activities in Mexico City.

> I told the president we had a very sensitive effective operation working in Mexico City [blank space] which involved telephone surveillance and was being done in a most careful manner with his knowledge and with the assistance of a few of his trusted officials. This had resulted in a very intimate relationship between or station chief [a whole paragraph blanked out].

It should be mentioned that the CIA had an ongoing surveillance operation going on in Mexico City only a year before in which it tapped the phones of both the Soviet Embassy and the Cuban Consulate when Lee Harvey Oswald was in that city in late September-early October 1963 trying to get a visa to go back to Russia via Cuba. The surveillance of Oswald in Mexico is still one of the unsolved areas in the whole Kennedy assassination story, relating to just what Oswald was up to when he went south of the border for those few weeks. It is possible that McCone was referring to the Mexico City CIA surveillance methods that were going on at that time.

McCone then went on to other interesting topics on the agenda that day.

> I told President Johnson that we continued our interrogation of Yuri Nosenko; our counterintelligence people were inclined to feel he was a plant but had not made up their minds. President said he thought he was probably legitimate and would give us some good information. I said I hoped this was true-that we were working closely with the FBI, however we could only conclude at the moment that the Soviet's performance and action were so different from any other defector case that our suspicions had been aroused. The President asked to be kept informed [there will be more about the Nosenko case later in this book]. [17]

The conversation then turned to Spain and its dictator Francisco Franco:

> The President then raised the question of Spain, suggesting that I might return to Spain to talk again to Franco. He said he was in a very difficult situation because of announcement of the cut-off of aid to Britain, France, and Yugoslavia which he did not know about until he read it in the paper, and that he was beside himself because he wanted to give aid of $31 million to Spain but had the greatest

17 RIF No. 177-10001-10445: NSF, John McCone Memorandum 6 Jan 64-2 April 64, Box 1.

difficulty in the justification. I told the President it was my impression from information gained from clandestine sources that Franco had made some moves to curtail trade with Cuba after my visit with him but that the Spanish companies were endeavoring to circumvent his orders by various surreptitious methods. The President asked that I study the matter carefully and speak to him about it next week.

The document now gets down to its most important part, what LBJ really thought about how the CIA conducted its covert action operations.

The President then said he wanted to do everything possible to get me out of the cloak and dagger business. That he was tired of a situation that had been built up that every time my name or CIA's name was mentioned, it was associated with a dirty trick. He asked if our economic studies had stood up and I said yes, that they had, and that they were reconfirmed and supported by an exhaustive article in TIME Magazine. The President seemed pleased at this, expressed satisfaction in CIA's operations but was most emphatic in his feelings that we should get away from the cloak and dagger image and expressed a determination to bring this about by statements he would make from time to time.[18]

The president's statement regarding cloak and dagger operations conducted by the CIA was most revealing. The historical record is not replete with LBJ's public statements regarding the use of covert activity by the CIA, but he was quoted as saying about its use of the mob to kill Castro, "the CIA was running a Mafic Inc. in the Caribbean."

President Johnson had the right to be worried about just what the CIA doing during that time. Over the years, the Agency had morphed from a purely intelligence collection agency to one that ran paramilitary operations/covert actions around the globe.

The role played by the CIA in the post-World War II era was

18 Ibid.

not that of the 1950s and early 1960s. President Truman signed the legislation via the National Security Act of 1947 that created the modern-day Central Intelligence Agency. The task of the CIA under Truman's tutelage was much different from what it became in the 21st century. Truman envisioned that the CIA would be a collection and evaluation agency that would provide the president information on foreign countries in order for the United States to formulate its foreign policy. Over the next decades however, as times changed, future presidents decided to use the Agency as more of a covert, paramilitary arm in order to fight the Cold War.

On December 22, 1963, long after Harry Truman left the White House and was in permanent retirement, he wrote an article in the *Washington Post* spelling out his discomfort over how the agency he created had changed, all for the wrong reasons.

As is the case with modern-day presidents, Harry Truman wrote that presidents needed to have all the best information available to them from a variety of sources. He said that information reaching the president's desk often times reflected the views of the writer or the government department that was supplying the data. He further stated that it was vital that the intelligence given to the president not be used to influence or lead a chief executive to make the wrong political decisions.

The former president, in his usual crusty, no-nonsense style, chastised the CIA on how it was being run, and where he believed it had deviated from its original mandate:

> For some time I have been disturbed by the way the CIA has been diverted from its original assignment. It has become an operational and at times a policy-making arm of the government. This has led to trouble and may have compounded our difficulties in several explosive areas. I never had any thought that when I set up the CIA that it would be injected into peacetime cloak and dagger operations. Some of the complications and embarrassment I think we have experienced are in part attributable to the fact that it is being interpreted as a symbol of sinister and mysterious foreign intrigue—and a subject for Cold War enemy propaganda.

We have grown up as a nation, respected for our free institutions and for our ability to maintain a free and open society. There is something about the way the CIA has been functioning that is causing a shadow over our historic position and I feel we need to correct it.

President Truman did say, however, that the first two directors of the CIA "were men of the highest character, patriotism, and integrity," but he also said that he could only assume the same about "all those who continue in charge." In a huge sea change for him, Truman wrote that the CIA's "operational duties" should be terminated. What the ex-president was really calling for was the abolition of the CIA as a fully functioning agency.

Truman wrote the article only nine days after the assassination of JFK and whether the president's murder led him to write the opinion piece (called "Limit CIA Role to Intelligence") is open to debate.

Truman's op-ed piece struck a nerve with certain people at the CIA including ex-Director, and Warren Commission member, Allen Dulles. Four months after Truman wrote the article, Dulles went to visit Truman at his home and tried to get him to retract his article. Truman said, "No dice." But four days later, in a formal memo for Lawrence Houston, the CIA's general counsel, Dulles fabricated a retraction. He claimed that Truman told him the *Washington Post* article was "all wrong," and that Truman "seemed quite astonished at it."

Truman went ballistic and, in a June 10, 1964 letter to *Look* magazine, Truman repeated his call for the CIA to be reorganized, saying that he never intended the CIA to get involved in "strange activities."[19]

In 1946, President Truman began the process of creating a new intelligence service for the United States with the creation of the Central Intelligence Groups, the predecessor of the CIA. President Truman appointed Rear Admiral Sidney Souers as its new head on January 22, 1946. In a ceremony at the White House which was not covered by the hordes of press that were always waiting for any tidbit of news, the president gave Souers his new marching orders, as well

19 After JFK was killed, former president Truman called for the abolition of CIA covert operations. JFKfacts. Org/December 22, 1963.

as a badge of his new office—a black cloak and wooden dagger. In a lighthearted proclamation, Truman gave them their mandate, "By virtue of the authority vested in me as Top Dog, I require and charge Fleet Admiral William Leahy and Rear Admiral Sidney Souers to receive and accept the vestments and appurtenances of their respective positions, namely as personal snooper and as director of centralized snooping."

Despite being handed the top intelligence job in the nation,

Lyndon Johnson and John Kennedy hated each other.

Admiral Souers told the president and his advisors that he would only stay in office six months and then go home. Those six months, however, were a heady time for the new director of the CIG, getting the infant agency in shape, and working out the many kinks that any new organization ran into.

Souers worked closely with President Truman's personal representative to the CIG, Admiral William Leahy. With the various military services vying with each other to lead America's new intelligence agency, the president created an organization entitled the National Intelligence Agency (NIA) which was tasked with the job of making intelligence activity. The members of the NIA were Secretary of State James Byrnes, Secretary of War Robert Patterson, Navy Secretary James Forrestal, and Admirals Souers and Leahy. From the beginning, the CIG and the NIA were under the mercy of the military services who were reluctant to divulge any information to a civilian agency. Their most important function was using what little information was provided to them the distribution of a daily intelligence summary, for the president. This is still done and is called the President's Daily Brief)

As promised, after his six months of service ended, Admiral Souers retried from government work and returned to the private sector. His time as the first director of the CIG/CIA was unremarkable in that he had little eaffect on the planning of the new agency, due in large part to the time restrictions he placed upon himself.

After a short stint in nongovernmental work, President Truman picked Souers, in May 1947, to be the intelligence director of the newly established Atomic Energy Department. He served only three years and returned to private life once again. He died on January 14, 1973.

President Truman's reservations regarding how the CIA was being run is a startling example of how a man of immense power can change his mind as time and events warrant. It's too bad that future presidents didn't feel the same way as old Harry did.

Chapter 18
Anti-Castro Leaders

After the successful revolution that ousted the corrupt regime of Batista by the forces of Fidel Castro in 1959, a large-scale anti-Castro movement began, mostly in the United States to which many thousands of Cubans fled after Castro seized power. These groups and their leaders were not monolithic in nature and they did not logically follow each other's motives and philosophy.

Not long after Castro took over in Havana, he began to change the Cuban democratic nation which he pledged his people, into a communist one aligned with the Soviet Union. Among the first of Castro's supporters to quit the cause was Major Pedro Diaz Lanz. Lanz was then Chief of Castro's Air Force (his story has been told in a previous chapter).

Another official who left the Castro government was Manuel Urrutia, who was Castro's hand-picked president. However, the most serious defection was that of Major Huber Matos, who was one of the top military leaders in Castro's armed forces. He was subsequently arrested, quickly tried and sentenced to twenty years in jail. Manuel Artime, who would later defect to the United States and form his own, militant anti-Castro force (MIRR) said of the time period, "I realized that I was a democratic infiltrator in a Communist government."

By the end of the Eisenhower administration, Castro had seized more than $700 million worth of US property inside Cuba. In March 1960, President Eisenhower gave the CIA instructions to organize an anti-Castro force to overthrow his regime. Exile training camps were formed in both the United States and Latin America (Nicaragua, as being the most important) Over 100,000 Cubans had fled Cuba and resettled in the United States. Almost all of these anti-Castro groups were being funded and organized by the CIA, with US government approval. The Cubans trusted the actions of the United States government totally, believing that the Eisenhower and Kennedy administrations had their best interests at heart (wrongly, it turned out).

The blind trust that the new anti-Castro groups had in the American government suffered a huge setback when the United States refused to allow full military support during the failed Bay of Pigs Invasion in April 1961. Their bitter feelings were summed up by Pepe San Roman, the military commander of the Bay of Pigs leaders, who said, "Most of the Cubans were there, because they knew the whole operation was going to be conducted by the Americans, not by me or anyone else. They did not trust me or anyone else. They just trusted the Americans. So they were going to fight because the US was backing them."

An important outcome of the Bay of Pigs failure was the shattering of confidence among anti-Castro exiles in the United States and JFK in particular. Despite the president's statement that he bore full responsibility for the invasion's failure, the leaders of the anti-Castro cause took it upon themselves to mount a no-holds-barred attempt to oust Castro.

Anti-Castro efforts such as leaflet drops over Cuba were initiated, as well as certain paramilitary operations mounted from Florida, as well as from a base in the Dominican Republic. The CIA was monitoring these efforts and wrote in a memo entitled, "Anti-Castro Activities in the United States":

> ...these efforts have been weakened, however, by rivalries between the more prominent exiles, for the leadership of any formal anti-Castro movement established, and their failure to agree on any program. Their activities also have been affected by the fact that most of the exiles were connected either actively or passively with the Batista regime... These rivalries plus Castro's followers' long training in revolutionary methods appear to have enabled Castro to learn the plans of the alliances thus far well before they are put into action. Nevertheless there has been and continues to be, a general recognition by most of the more prominent exiles that they must unite if they are to succeed in removing the present regime.

The documents released by the National Archives give the names and background information for some of these anti-Castro leaders. Among them are the following.

Ramon Donestevez Domingue:

Born in Cuba went to Caracas, Venezuela in 1959 and entered the US in 1962. Operated the International Machinery Corporation in Hialeah, Florida, which manufactured plastic boats. Made numerous, unauthorized trips to Cuba to bring out relatives and political prisoners. In 1965, he visited Cuba and allegedly talked with Castro. In September 1967, he was issued notice of prevention of departure by INS. May 1968, an unexploded bomb found at his business. July 1968 detained by INS and given deportation hearing. Paroled and restricted to land area of Dade County in March 1969. In 1973, plead guilty to extortion and put on probation. September 1974 he went to Cuba and detained on return. Given two year jail sentence. In December 1975, given seven year imprisonment for probation violation. Very controversial and many Cuban exiles felt he was pro-Castro or even an agent of Castro. Murdered on 13 April 1976 at his office. No Agency association.

Luciano Nieves Mestre:

Nieves was reportedly a Captain in the rebel army under Osmani Cienfuegos and subsequently arrested by the DSE in January 1963 for political reasons. He was released from prison in 1965 through the intervention of his brother, a high Cuban official. Nieves went to Madrid in April 1965 where he was introduced to a CIA officer. He came to the US in August 1965 and was again contacted by a CIA officer. The relationship was unsatisfactory as Nieves proved erratic and uncooperative and he provided fabricated information. In March 1966, Army indicated an interest in Nieves and was given an assessment of Nieves. Since the CIA no longer had an interest in Nieves, ASCI (Army) picked him and subsequently terminated him in March 1967.

Rolando Masferrer Rojas:

Former Cuban Senator who was considered ruthless. Arrived in US in January 1959 and over the years has engaged in a series of activities related to the overthrow of the Castro regime. Reportedly involved with Jose de la Torriente in the TORRIENTE plan. As of 1972, still considered himself to be a Socialist, and had been virulent critic of the US in the past. Killed by a bomb in Miami on 31 October 1975. No Agency affiliation.

His reputation as one of the most militant anti-Castro soldiers quickly got the attention of the Kennedy administration and at the time of the Bay of Pigs Invasion, he was put under government confinement in Miami's Jackson Memorial Hospital under guard. It seems that the Kennedy team did not want Masferrer running around stirring up more trouble than was necessary when the exiles stormed Castro's beaches. In the days preceding the Bay of Pigs Invasion, there was considerable talk in the American press about a possible American-led invasion of Cuba. President Kennedy went out of his way to deny any American involvement in any attack against Cuba, railed against the militant anti-Castro Cubans who were staging hit-and-run raids into Cuba, and named Rolando Masferrer as one of the men the United States did not want to see in power in a post Castro Cuba.

He later went to New York where he found a job at the newspaper *El Tiempo,* partly owned by Ruben Batista, the son of the former Cuban dictator, and Anastasio Somoza, the dictator of Nicaragua.

When Masferrer came to the United States he began organizing anti-Castro units in various cities in the country, including Miami and Los Angeles. By 1962, however, Masferrer had joined with the other militant anti-Castro groups, especially Antonio Veciana's powerful Alpha 66 which now took on the acronym SNFE/Alpha 66.

But Masferrer had more than an interest in writing for *El Tiempo*. By the mid-1960s, he set his considerable sights on the island of Haiti, then ruled by the dictator Papa Doc Duvalier. He got it in his head that with the right amount of money and men, Haiti would be ripe for the picking. He, of course, would lead the revolution, with Cuba his next stop. Masferrer traveled the streets of Little Havana in Miami, where a huge anti-Castro population now lived. He managed to take in hundreds of thousands of dollars for his anti-Castro cause and set out to assemble a rebel army. But what he did not plan on was that when CBS television got wind of his plans they would decide to tag along. The network decided to spend $200,000 for the rights to film Masferrer's little rebel army's invasion of Haiti. The only thing that Masferrer had to do in return was assure that his invasion would succeed.

In time, CBS sent cameramen down to film Masferrer's training and his remarks were soon broadcast all over South Florida. It seems that Masferrer told his vast audience that his first bullet would be directed at Papa Doc and that he was ready to do the deed himself. Masferrer's threat was passed on to the FBI and then to the CIA, which then decided to keep a close watch on Masferrer and his group.

What began as a private scheme to liberate Haiti (as a stepping stone to retake Cuba) turned into Project Nassau, a full-fledged campaign that took on a life of its own.

Manuel Artime Buesa:

ARTIME was one of the leaders of the MRR, a democratic Catholic oriented anti-Batista reform movement which allied itself with the Castro forces in overthrowing Batista. ARTIME was de facto chief of the agricultural reform program in Oriente Province after Batista's fall. ARTIME became disillusioned with Castro, departed Cuba and became one of the leaders of the Bay of Pigs invasion force. He was captured, imprisoned and returned in the prisoner exchange in 1962. From June 1963 to April 1965, CIA supported ARTIME and the MRR operations against Cuba which can be broadly characterized as harassment, sabotage and psychological warfare at a cost of approximately $ seven million. Following that, CIA supported psychological warfare operations such as radio broadcasts and the publication of anti-Castro periodicals. This continued until ARTIME was terminated in January 1967. Since that time

159

there has been no official CIA relationship with ARTIME although there have been occasional unofficial contacts between CIA officers and ARTIME. These contacts were not of operational significance. During the mid-east war ARTIME offered DCI Colby the use of himself and his men in any capacity that would assist the Agency. ARTIME was last reported to be closely associated with Nicaraguan president, General Anastasio Somoza, in the export-import business. He is believed to be residing in Managua.

Manuel Artime had his own CIA cryptonym, AMBIDDY-1, and he participated in various,, anti-Castro operations with the full knowledge of the Agency. According to CIA documents on Artime, he became a person of interest to the CIA in 1959 and was used by the Agency's Western Hemisphere Division as relating to Cuban operations from 1959 to 1963.

From June 1963 through April 1965, Artime conducted paramilitary (Project AMWORLD) against Cuba under the political banner of his exiled group, MRR. The Project expenses during this period were approximately $7 million. The support was terminated effective 1 May 1965 but support for political operations was restored in June 1965 at the rate of $15,000 per month. This was scaled down to $5,000 a month in September 1965, to about $3,000 a month in June 1966, and termination on 31 December 1966. Artime accepted this termination gracefully in a meeting on 13 January 1967. That ended the formal operational relationship with Artime, although he maintained informal contact with CIA, most recently with Robert Shaw when Shaw was [redacted].

Chapter 19
Cuban Exile Attempts on Castro

It seems that the CIA-Mafia alliance was not the only venue for possible actions regarding the overthrow of the Castro government. In documents released via the JFK Records Act, various unnamed Cuban exiles offered their services to the CIA for large cash amounts. While the names of these people are not supplied in the documents, it provides a look into their associates and how they expected the CIA to pay them for their work.

The memo regarding this event was dated June 10, 1964, from the Director of Central Intelligence, the subject being: "Plans of Cuban Exiles to Assassinate Selected Cuban Government Leaders." The recipient was David Belin, a counsel to the Warren Commission. Other high-level officials who received this document ranged from Robert Kennedy to the Director of the Defense Intelligence Agency and the president's Special Advisor for National Security Affairs.

The first contact came on March 2, 1964, from an unnamed person who had a plan, in its early stages, to kill Castro. The man said his contacts offering the plot were a businessman, who owned a number of ships, as well as someone who was legally allowed to place slot machines in gambling halls. This man had a partner who was a former policeman from St. Louis. They had associates in the criminal underworld who were willing to go along with their plan. These mob figures were willing to ante up $150,000 "no advance funds were requested" to kill Castro. Their only stipulation to the CIA was, "If the mission cannot be accomplished, or if the plan is unsuccessful, an amount not to exceed $10,000 would be paid for the travel and living expenses of five men involved in the mission." The intermediary turned down the offer, saying "that an approach might be made to someone who had much more money."

Another secret approach took place on March 3, 1964 from a Cuban exile who was the owner and operator of a merchant vessel. "Among the persons attending the meeting were the co-owner of a shipping firm and two of his employees, friendly competitors in the Caribbean area." The ship owner said he was in contact with an "unidentified group which would be willing to assassinate selected Cuban officials for cash; specifically, the ship owner's group is interested in assassinating Fidel Castro, Raul Castro, and Ernest 'Che' Guevara."

After a discussion with the unidentified Americans regarding the assassination offer, "it was thought that the amount of $150,000 for the assassination of Fidel Castro, plus $5,000 expense money, payable in advance, was too high and [blank] felt that this situation was just another attempt to swindle patriotic Cuban exiles. In a subsequent meeting, a counter offer of $100,000 for the Castro hit, as well as $2,500 for expenses, to be paid in advance was offered."

It seems that on March 15, an accommodation in principle by all unnamed persons was agreed upon. An amount of $100,000 was to be paid for the Castro hit, Raul Castro was worth $20,000, "Che" Guevara was agreed as another $20,000, and $2,500 was agreed upon for expenses. The proposed hits were to take place within a 90-day period, and the money would only be paid when it was verified that the Cuban officers were dead.

In April 1964, a wealthy Cuban exile agreed to pay the up-front costs only if his name was not publically revealed. On April 25, the unnamed ship owner said he had contacted his men on the island and that "their other man" would be heading for Cuba shortly. The Cuban exile then said, "We hope to have some good news for you between 20 and 25 May." The documents then say that the ship owner flew to Miami where he transferred the $100,000 to a safe deposit box in that city which was to be held jointly by him and a confidant of the wealthy Cuban exile.

The ship owner made it clear that he did not want his true identity to be revealed because the Mafia was involved in the scheme. He did state however, that his main accomplice was a police officer who worked in the St. Louis, Missouri Vice Squad. This man was at retirement age and had excellent contacts with the mob. The "other man" mentioned in the affair was then in Spain. "The ship owner knows that he could be indicted for conspiracy and that if there is any treachery on his part (blank) and his associates would not hesitate to sink his ship."

In May, this "other person" said that his boss had a firm plan underway to kill Fidel Castro for $150,000 that the US government

162

Fidel Castro.

would provide. The documents ends by saying, "the other person indicated that he believes that a quick change for the better in the Cuban situation can be brought about only by the physical elimination of Fidel Castro and that his elimination is well worth $150,000."[20]

The CIA's Inspector General's Report on the plans to kill Castro, which was finally declassified in the mid-1990s, had this to say regarding these early attempts on Castro's life

Prior to August 1960: All of the identifiable schemes prior to about August 1960, with one possible exception, were aimed only at discrediting Castro personally by influencing his behavior or by altering his appearance.[21]

One of the men who took a front-row seat in the Cuban government during these tumultuous times was Fabian Escalante who was then the Division General of the Cuban Ministry of Interior

20 RIF No. 157-10005-10202.
21 *CIA Targets Fidel: The Secret Assassination Report*, Ocean Press, 1996.

unit that was responsible for countering the CIA's efforts against Cuba. Today, Mr. Escalante has retired his warrior's uniform and is now writing about these times.

Over the years, Mr. Escalante has opined on aspects of the Kennedy assassination he was privy to via his high position in the Cuban intelligence services. While he said he had no inside knowledge about who killed JFK, he did say "that Cuban exiles recruited by the CIA had planned to kill Kennedy twice in November 1963, because they felt the US president had done too little to topple the government on the Caribbean island. They had the capability, the means and the intent. How was this meant to turn out? To assassinate Kennedy, launch a furious campaign against Cuba, blaming it for the assassination, which they did, then kill Fidel Castro a few days later, on December 12, and invade Cuba."[22]

Mr. Escalante said that one person he believed knew quite a lot about the Kennedy assassination was Luis Posada Carriles, whose name has been mentioned in this book. "He has a life insurance policy, which is what he knows about the Kennedy plot," Escalante said. "He and Orlando Bosch were in the thick of the Kennedy plot. Remember, both he and Posada were part of this terrorist mechanism set up in New Orleans, which is where the plot was hatched, to assassinate Kennedy." (What Escalante was referring to were the roles played by Guy Banister, David Ferrie, and Clay Shaw whose activities were looked into by New Orleans DA Jim Garrison. Posada Carriles died on May 23, 2018).

Mr. Escalante told reporter Martin Roberts of Reuters in an interview that he once worked at the Q Section of Cuban intelligence in 1961, which had 50 case officers to thwart the efforts of the so-called JMWAVE CIA base in Florida assigned to conduct sabotage operations in Cuba with a $100 million budget and 4,000 agents. He wrote that there were 634 attempts on Fidel's life between 1959 and 2000, including 168 plots that might have succeeded.

The former Cuban spy says that one of the first attempts on Castro's life was scheduled to be perpetrated in 1958 by Eutimio Rojas, who was a traitor to the Batista regime. Rojas was bribed by Batista's army to kill Castro while he slept in his mountain hideaway in the Sierra Maestra mountains. When the appointed time came for

22 Roberts, Martin, "Cuban ex-intelligence chief recalls JFK assassination," Reuters, July 12, 2010.

Rojas to kill Castro, he got cold feet.

Another attempt was made by an American named Allan Robert Nye on February 2, 1959. Nye was associated with a number of mob-related people, members of the so-called "gambling Ssyndicate" who owned a large share of the casinos and hotels in Havana. His assignment was to kill Castro near the grounds of the presidential palace using a rifle with a telescopic sight. While waiting for Castro to arrive, Nye was arrested by Cuban police.

Robert Nye had been recruited by the FBI to infiltrate Cuban exiles groups who were then working against the brutal ruler of Cuba, Flugencio Batista. The FBI planted a false story with the emigres saying that Robert Ney had been thrown out of the Cuban Air Force for conspiring with the anti-Batista forces.

Nye was asked to contact Efrain Hernandez who was the Cuban consul in Miami. Hernandez's job was to keep watch on the large anti-Batista groups in that city. He also told Nye that he had a secret operation that Nye was going to be asked to carry out but would not say anything further at that time. He did hint that the job would pay him $50,000 when it was done.

Nye arrived in Cuba on November 12, 1958 and was taken by Cuban officials to the Comodoro Hotel. Ney was met by two top Batista officers, Carlos Tabernilla and Orlando Piedra. Tabernilla was the former chief of the air force, while Piedra was then head of the secret police. Sitting over drinks at the bar, both men told the astonished Nye that their plan called for Nye to kill Fidel Castro, the hot-headed revolutionary leader who was causing so much political trouble for Batista.

The plan called for Nye to join Castro's forces in the mountains and offer his services as a pilot who would bomb Batista's military facilities around the island. Nye coordinated his infiltration scheme with Col. Manuel Garcia Caceres, a military officer in charge of the post at Holguin in the northern part of Holguin Province. Carrying a 38-caliber revolver and a Remington 30-06 rifle with a telescopic sight, Ney successfully entered Castro's area of operations in December where he offered his services. To his dismay, his proposal to join the rebels was turned down and Neye was put in a camp that contained wounded soldiers. Nye believed it was only a matter of time before he would be allowed to meet with Castro, collect his guns, and take on the assignment given to him.

Nye's plans came crashing down in front of him when, on January 1, 1959, Castro's men forced Batista to resign his presidency and flee Cuba. Nye was transferred to Havana where his story would be looked into in further detail. In their investigation, Cuban officers found out that Nye had checked into the Comodoro under the alias of "G. Collins," not the name he originally gave to Castro's forces. Under further questioning, Nye's story about wanting to help the Cuban cause was permanently eroded and he was placed under arrest. He stayed in custody until April 1959 when he was expelled

Ernesto "Che" Guevara and Fidel Castro in Cuba, 1961.

from Cuba.

General Escalante writes that he reviewed thousands of pages of Cuban military reports and could document as many as 612 attempts on Castro's life from 1959-1993.

While the CIA-Mafia plots to kill Castro have been given the most play by historians, the first CIA sanctioned attempts on the Cuban leadership took place in July 1960 with the full authorization of the CIA.

This previously little-known attempt is documented in the US Senate Select Committee on Intelligence report and is listed under the heading "Proposal to Sabotage Flight."

On July 18, 1960, the CIA received word from a Cuban airline pilot who volunteered his services to eliminate the Cuban leaders. The name of the Cuban pilot is not released but he said that he was scheduled to fly to Prague, Czechoslovakia on July 21, 1960 where he was to bring Raul Castro back to Cuba. The pilot told his CIA case officers that he was willing to inform the CIA of the activities of Raul Castro, as well as any pertinent information that he could get on Czech affairs. At no time in their initial meeting was the word "assassinate" mentioned.

The CIA station in Havana reported this information to Langley headquarters on July 20. The CIA duty officer said he gave the report to Tracy Barnes, who was deputy to Richard Bissell who was DDP (Deputy Director, Plans), as well as J.C. King, the chief of the Western Hemisphere Division at CIA. The duty officer testified about the chain of command, saying, he would have read the cable to Barnes before sending it because Barnes "was the man to whom we went... for our authority and for work connected with the Cuba Project."

On the morning of July 21, a cable from CIA headquarters to the Havana station was sent regarding this proposal. It read, "Possible removal top three leaders is receiving serious consideration at HQS." It questioned if the pilot was willing to take the risk of "arranging an accident during return trip," and also directed the Havana personnel to "at discretion contact subject [pilot)] to determine willingness to cooperate and his suggestion on details." The case officer described the exchange of ideas as "quite a departure from the conventional activities we'd been asked to handle." In testimony to Congress years later, the case officer said he remembered the incident 15 years later. He said that when he first saw the cable he "swallowed hard."

The case officer had a hurried meeting with the pilot on the way to the airport for the trip to Prague at which time, details of the operation were quickly discussed. The word "assassinate" was never mentioned but he "made it clear that the CIA contemplated an "accident to neutralize this leader's [Raoul's] influence. Upon the request of the pilot, in the case of his death his son would be given a college education, he agreed to take a "calculated risk" in planning an accident somewhere along the route. They discussed the possible burnout of an engine or a water ditching three hours from Cuba.

Now, events began to take on an ominous turn. When the case officer got back to the station he was told "Do not pursue ref. Would like to drop matter."

The pilot had left and could not be contacted. The CIA held its breath as events seemed to be spiraling out of control. Luckily, the pilot had no chance to cause an "accident," and he returned to Havana without further incident.

The Senate Committee wrote that the cable requesting the operation be dropped was signed by Tracy Barnes. The case officer said that he had heard Allan Dulles had countermanded the cable authorizing the possible assassination attempt on Raul Castro.

CIA involvement in these first attempts on the lives of the Cuban leadership was soon to be formalized in a major covert operation between the mob and the Agency to "whack the beard." This would soon morph into a major CIA-Defense Department mission called Operation Mongoose, which has been described thoughout these chapters.

Chapter 20
The Golitsyn Secrets

One of the most interesting of the newly released JFK documents concerns one of the biggest spy cases of the Cold War years, that of the defection to the west of Yuri Nosenko, a high-ranking KGB officer who first made contact with the CIA in 1962 while he was in Geneva, Switzerland in his capacity as chief of security for the Soviet delegation to the disarmament talks then going on in that city.

His defection began three months after the assassination of President Kennedy, and what he told the CIA was nothing but astounding. He told the CIA that he worked for the Seventh Department of the KGB, an agency whose job it was to oversee all visiting Americans who came to Moscow as tourists. At the time that Nosenko was monitoring the few Americans to set foot on Russian soil, his branch was keeping an eye on a recent American defector, a former Marine radioman named Lee Harvey Oswald.

The Oswald case would come back to haunt both the CIA and the FBI, and would fuel the ever-growing feud between James Angleton and J. Edgar Hoover. They had two different views on Nosenko and the information he brought with him.

As the Nosenko interrogations were going on in earnest, he dropped a major bombshell that made James Angleton even more distrustful of him. Nosenko said that while he was in Moscow, he had seen the KGB file on Lee Oswald, the alleged assassin of President Kennedy. Under further questioning, Nosenko said that there was no connection between the Russians and the assassination of the president. Nosenko said that the Russians had no interest whatsoever in a loner like Oswald and the only reason they allowed him to stay in the country was his attempt at suicide.

Despite the fact that the Warren Commission decided that there was no conspiracy, foreign or domestic, in the Kennedy assassination, James Angleton was convinced that Oswald was a "dispatched agent," sent to the US to absolve the Russians of guilt in any plot to kill Kennedy. Furthermore, Angleton believed that Oswald was groomed as an assassin by the KGB during his three-year stint in the Soviet Union, that he was sent to the United States

169

to kill Kennedy, and lastly, that the Nosenko mission was meant to excise any possible involvement by the Soviets in the president's death. The real culprit in the whole, sordid mess was none other than Yuri Nosenko.

But now, the whole affair gets messier. In the documents being referred to, it becomes clear that the CIA, while interrogating Nosenko, was talking to another Soviet defector named Anatoly Golitsyn, who, like Nosenko, would send the CIA into a tailspin.

In the annals of the CIA, the most contentious defector to come to the West was a topflight Soviet intelligence officer named Anatoly Golitsyn. When Golitsyn first contacted Western intelligence in 1961, no one in either the American CIA, or the British SIS would have believed the hornet's nest they were about to enter. For the defection of Golitsyn to the West began a decades-long search for a top Soviet "mole" inside both the CIA and the British intelligence service, a witch hunt that would tear the CIA apart and ruin the careers of many decent men.

Golitsyn had a long career in Soviet intelligence. Joining the KGB in 1951, he began his long vocation as an agent of the First Chief Directorate's Anglo-American Division. In the mid-1950s, he served in Vienna, a top city for spies in continental Europe. It was in that posting that he got into a fight with the KGB resident in charge of operational matters. At the time of his original contact with CIA officer Frank Friberg in Germany, Golitsyn was serving as a Major in the KGB's First Chief Directorate, which was responsible for foreign operations on NATO and its military command.

At CIA headquarters, the men in the Soviet Russia Division pulled out all the stops to find out who Golitsyn was and if he could be trusted. The first bit of information came from Peter Deriabin, a KGB officer who had defected to the United States. In their research, the CIA had found out that Deriabin was not happy with his life in the Soviet Union and thus, was a possible target of recruitment, which turned out to be correct.

Friberg got permission from Washington to bring Golitsyn in, and after a long and tiring voyage from Frankfurt, West Germany to London, and a one-night stopover in Bermuda, they finally arrived in New York. With his CIA escorts in tow, Golitsyn and his family were put up in a CIA safe house for debriefing. He was given the code name AE/LADLE. For the CIA and Golitsyn, it was just the beginning of a long and frustrating dance of conflicting egos.

In the winter of 1962, the CIA moved Golitsyn to a safe house near the Choptank River in Maryland for the long debriefing process. During his interrogation, Golitsyn began to spill the beans on a number of Soviet penetrations of US and allied intelligence services. He began by saying that the Soviets had a number of highly placed moles inside the French intelligence agency, SDECE. He went so far as to describe an assassination plot on the life of Phillippe de Vosjoli, the French liaison to the CIA.

This information was given to President Kennedy who passed it along to French President Charles de Gaulle. Golitsyn surprised the CIA even further when he said that the KGB was using its French spies in the United States to mount a clandestine operation to gain information on US missile sites.

As his interrogations continued, his questioners asked him about the possibility that the Soviet Union had penetrated the CIA, a query that had the deepest consequences if answered in the affirmative. Golitsyn, to everyone's surprise, said yes, but he could not give any further details, nor could he provide any names. Friberg said of Golitsyn's news regarding a potential mole inside the CIA, "That's all he had, there was no meat on the lead. Golitsyn didn't know anything more himself."

Golitsyn was able to give the US the names of three other Russians agents, a Canadian diplomat, and Hugh Hambelton, a Canadian teacher. As far as any Soviets in the CIA were concerned, the only vague hint that Golitsyn gave was the name of a suspected mole called SASHA, a man who formerly worked in Berlin and was of Slavic heritage. He said that this person's last name began with the letter K and probably ended in "sky."

As time went on, Golitsyn began to show paranoid characteristics, telling different versions of stories he had earlier spun, which now did not make sense. He also demanded to have a face-to-face meeting with President Kennedy. He was allowed to see Robert Kennedy instead. He also asked for a secret slush fund of $1.5 million for his own use that would be used in the overthrow of the Soviet government.

The document that was released from the National Archives in

2017 was a detailed memo from the FBI regarding the Nosenko case and Anatoly Golitsyn. It is an important document from which I will quote at length.

The memo was dated May 11, 1964, with the subject heading "Yuri Nosenko, Espionage-Russia":

> Nosenko is the Soviet KGB officer who defected to CIA in Switzerland in early February, 1964. CIA is convinced he is a plant and has been intensively interviewing him for five weeks, but as of Friday, May 8th, had not been successful in breaking him.
>
> On May 8th, during our discussion with representatives of CIA, Mr. Peter Wright and Harry Stone of MI-5 had future plans concerning Nosenko were discussed with CIA initially felt subject would break during their interrogation, they also recognized the possibility that he might not and as of May 8th were inclined to believe that they might not be successful in breaking him based on current information.
>
> CIA and MI-5 have been of the firm belief that both Nosenko and Yuri Krotkov, a Soviet journalist who defected to the British in 1963, are part of an over-all Soviet deception program as Krotkov and Nosenko have furnished very similar information. Mr. Wright advised that MI-5 believes that Krotkov can be interrogated and broken and therefore current plans are for an intensive interview of him. In view of the fact Nosenko is being interviewed by CIA in this country, CIA and MI-5 currently plan to bring Krotkov to the United States where he will be interrogated and if broken, his information then utilized in further interrogation of Nosenko.
>
> The CIA representatives and Mr. Wright remain absolutely firm in their conclusion that both Nosenko and Krotkov are plants. In connection with the continuing interview of Nosenko, CIA advised that they contemplated using Soviet defector Anatoly Golitsyn to a very large extent. They did not state that they would utilize Golitsyn for actual interviews, but did say he would be furnished all information concerning Nosenko and his analysis would

be the basis for further action against Nosenko. In this connection, CIA stated that at the present time, no information developed by the FBI is made available to Golitsyn without specific Bureau authority. They stated that with regard to Nosenko's information, they would like to secure Bureau permission to make the results of our investigation (based on Nosenko's information), available to Golitsyn for his review and analysis. They feel that this will be necessary for successful handling of the Nosenko interrogation. They also advised that in the forthcoming interview of Krotkov they would like to have similar permission from the Bureau for any investigation we have conducted based on Krotkov's information, but it is noted that Krotkov had very little information concerning activities in the United States and had no information concerning any Americans supposedly cooperating with the Soviets.

Observations: Both CIA and the British remain absolutely convinced that both Nosenko and Krotkov are Soviet plants. If this is so, then the Soviets are well aware of what information they have furnished to us. It is believed in view of this that we should accede to CIA's request and permit them to make available to Golitsyn for his analysis the information we have developed by our investigation based on Nosenko's information, with the understanding that the information will be paraphrased and Golitsyn will not see any actual FBI reports or communications. It would appear we could lose little from this and if we did not agree and CIA is not successful in their interview of Nosenko and Krotkov, they could always claim that they might have been successful had the Bureau permitted use of the results of our investigation.

Recommendation: If you approve, we will advise CIA if they feel it is necessary and desirable we will interpose no objection to their furnishing the results of our investigation in the Nosenko and Krotkov matters in paraphrased form to Golitsyn for his analysis and use in the interrogations.

What we see from this document is the fact that the American intelligence services were taking a huge risk is allowing Golitsyn to see the interviews being conducted with Yuri Nosenko, even though Golitsyn's bona fides were still being questioned by many in US intelligence community. If Golitsyn proved to be a Russian plant, then many US secrets could be compromised and the Soviets could have a huge windfall of US classified information.

The other interesting fact in all this is the trust the US gave to its British allies in the Nosenko-Golitsyn affair. The author had not heard about the British operative Harry Stone before, but that cannot be said of the other participant in the drama, Peter Wright. Peter Wright was a controversial British intelligence officer during the Cold War years who set off a firestorm when he published a highly controversial book called *Spycatcher,* which revealed the innermost workings of British intelligence and embarrassed the British government, which successful banned the book from being published in the UK. It was eventually released to a world-wide audience when it was published in Australia.

Peter Wright began working for MI-5 in September 1955, and worked in the counterintelligence service in British intelligence, looking for moles. In time, Wright became a confidant of James Angleton, the head of counterintelligence for the CIA; both men believed that their respective agencies had been infiltrated by Russian moles.

One of the men Wright suspected of being a Soviet mole inside British intelligence was Roger Hollis who became head of MI-5, thus being one of the most powerful men in British intelligence at that time. Over time, a detailed investigation regarding the possibility that Hollis was a Russian mole was mounted but no clear evidence was found to back up Wright's (and others,) allegations against him.

In looking back at what powerful information Anatoly Golitsyn provided to the CIA, and Angleton in particular, it is not too much to ask if these messages were on the level. After all, Golitsyn told Angleton that another Soviet agent would soon come to discredit him. Yuri Nosenko arrived one year later. He also discredited Soviet agents called Top Hat and Fedora, as well as Oleg Penkovsky, who some writers of 20th century intelligence called "The Spy Who Saved the World." By describing the division of the KGB into "inner" and "outer" organizations, Golitsyn made the CIA question all the countermoves it took against the Russians during this time. Was Golitsyn sent ahead of Nosenko to soften up the CIA, and initiate inside Langley a mole hunt for bad spies who didn't exist?

It was now the FBI's turn to interrogate Golitsyn and they went at it full bore. The US government set Golitsyn up in New York City and paid him a handsome salary of $200,000 for his help.

Unlike Angleton, J. Edgar Hoover did not believe anything that came out of Golitsyn's mouth. Hoover was astonished when the defector asked for US files on Soviet operations. Despite the FBI's distrust of Golitsyn, a secret meeting between the top brass of the FBI and the Russian was arranged. In 1962, a number of FBI counterintelligence specialists met with Golitsyn at the Mayflower Hotel in Washington. In the end, nothing of substance came from the meeting.

During these meetings Golitsyn told the Bureau that there were a number of unidentified communist spies inside the FBI. Since he did not have the names of these alleged moles, Hoover chose not to believe him. Hoover also held to the view that Angleton was being taken in by Golitsyn's notion of a "Monster Plot," wherein Soviet moles were infesting the West's intelligence services.

For all the tug-of-war statements between the agencies regarding the bona fides of Golitsyn, the FBI had as one its main jobs the role of investigating moles inside the CIA and of getting access to any defector, real or fake, who came calling. For the CIA's part, it did not want any FBI agents looking into its sensitive counterintelligence functions, even if it meant creating deep divisions between the two agencies. Golitsyn was just the first of the defectors in the 1960s, who would create a split in the US intelligence community.

What this document shows is how paranoid the CIA was when Nosenko came calling, and that it had no idea just what can of worms had been created by his defection to the United States.

175

Chapter 21
Operation Tilt

One of the most interesting missions in the secret war against Castro was the so-called "Bayo-Pawley Affair," or as the CIA termed it, "Operation Tilt."

"Operation Tilt" was not a purely CIA affair, but was closely watched and aided by the Agency. The mission involved a former US Ambassador and anti-Castro financier, the editors of *Life* magazine who helped to finance the mission, and a number of soldier-of-fortune types who were never heard from again.

The principals in this affair were Eddie Bayo (whose real name was Eddie Perez), William Pawley (a World War II air legend who organized the Flying Tigers air unit, along with General Claire Chennault), and John Martino, an anti-Castro organizer an expert in electronics and surveillance agent with close ties to the mob.

Operation Tilt was designed to see if it was possible to bring out of Cuba four Soviet military officers who had allegedly defected from their missile unit. These men were to supposed to have knowledge that the Soviets had disregarded the terms that ended the Cuban Missile Crisis and knew the whereabouts of missiles that were still hidden in Cuba.

Working independently of the CIA, William Pawley offered the use of his yacht, the *Flying Tiger*, to ferry invaders into Cuba to bring back these Russian officers. The mission was funded by *Life* magazine, whick only asked to be given exclusive rights to print the story and use the photos taken on the mission. Eddie Bayo was to lead the group of soldiers of fortune, rendezvous with the Russian officers, and bring them back to the United States. For all their well laid plans, the mission turned out to be a disaster in the making.

Operation Tilt was not a formal CIA operation but it did use certain CIA land and sea assets. In a document released under the JFK Records Act, the CIA wrote,

> Operation Tilt was not KUBARK [code name for the CIA]controlled, but it did utilize QUDALE as KUBARK's window into the operation. Operation Tilt involved a

strange cast of characters and this resulted in the operation following patterns of implementation which are not typical of KUBARK-controlled operations.

The raiders were infiltrated into Cuba on June 9, 1963. According to their plan, they were to bring the Russians out the next day. When they did not show up at the pre-arranged rendezvous area by June 13, the search for them was called off. The Miami CIA station continued to receive bits and pieces of information concerning the mission. What they did receive is outlined as follows.

Ten men were on the infiltration team, none of whom returned. One of the men was Luis Cantin. CIA records say that he was a port pilot who had considerable knowledge of Oriente Province in Cuba. A CIA agent met with Cantin's son in Miami on July 21, 1963. They told the son that his father had gone to Cuba in June 1963 on an "operational assignment." It was further stated that the CIA had not heard from the elder Cantin and he was presumed dead. The only thing that the CIA came away with from the interview with Cantin's family was that they still had no concrete information regarding what had gone on inside Cuba, but that "at least one member of the infiltration group had not returned to Miami or communicated with his family as of 24 August 1963."

On August 26, 1963, a CIA officer designated AMCRAG-1, met in Miami with Mrs. Laudelima Perez, the wife of Eduardo Perez, aka "Eddie Bayo." Mrs. Perez hoped that AMCRAG-1 would have knowledge of her husband's whereabouts. AMCRAG-1 said that a man named Benito Quevedo might have some information regarding her spouse. She asked him to contact Quevedo and see what he had to say. Mrs. Perez said that her husband had gone into Cuba on some mission that involved John Martino. She also said that her husband had never spoken to her about the possibilities of him staying in Cuba for a long period of time, but that some unforeseen development made him change his mind.

The CIA, after reading AMCRAG-1's report, was still uncertain as to what had really happened to the infiltration team.

On September 21, 1963, the CIA reported additional information regarding Operation Tilt. John Martino had contacted a man named

Irving Cadick on September 12 saying that he had gotten a letter dated August 28, 1963 from Victor Garcia. Garcia said that Eddie Bayo and his men had been in a firefight in Cuba and had killed a number of militia men, as well as some Russian officers in Oriente Province. (The CIA later said it could not verify that such an incident happened.) Perez said that he lost two men in the fight and that he was expecting supplies to be delivered to him by a Cuban named Angel Luis Castillo Cabrera. After considering the matter further, both John Martino and Cadick realized that they could not send and men to help Bayo.

Despite not having operational control over the mission, the CIA did know one thing for certain—that Bayo/Perez was still alive in Cuba in August 1963.

In further discussions with his contacts in the Cuban community in Miami, AMCRAG-1 was able to determine that he had no real knowledge or the status of Bayo/Perez or his men inside Cuba.

In January 1964, Mrs. Perez had another interview with a CIA source regarding her husband. She said that her Cuban contacts told her that her husband was hiding in the hills of Oriente Province. JMWAVE (the CIA's Miami station) could not verify the report.

In reading the documents regarding Operation Tilt, it is obvious that there were two different versions, that of the crew and that of the CIA, regarding what transpired. For example, the infiltration team did not pay much attention to the fact that the CIA's plan called for them to be picked up at a range of 25 nautical miles at sea after the mission was completed. The raiders did not inform KUBARK (the code name for the CIA) of their plans to make an overland trip across Cuba. It seems that both groups were not aware, on purpose or not, of what the other was planning. Bayo told the Agency three times that they should not wait for them beyond 1800 hours (6:00 p.m.) on the Tuesday of their supposed return, because if they were not at the rendezvous point at that time, they were probably going to stay in Cuba.

In the end, Pawley, Martino and others in the group returned safely to Miami on the evening of June 12 via a PBY Flying Boat. The CIA after-action report says,

We feel KUBARKERS [CIA men] on vessels and PBY

did excellent job and without their participation do not believe [operation] could possibly have been launched. Mr. Pawley stated completely satisfied WAVE support.

Chadick got impression from discussions with team leaders that perhaps team did not really plan to come out. Team very interested in briefings on infiltration but showed little interest in briefings on exfiltration. Showed no interest in discussing possible pick up on shore if in trouble.

John Martino was one of the most interesting men in the plots to oust Castro from power and had a lot to say regarding the assassination of JFK. It is worth giving the reader a full discussion of who he was and what he was up to during that time.

John Martino was born in Atlantic City, New Jersey on August 3, 1911 and lived in that city for many years. Martino's name has been linked to the CIA-Mafia plots to kill Castro and he was reported to have given a reporter information linking Lee Harvey Oswald to the Cuban government in the murder of JFK.

Martino once worked for mob boss Meyer Lansky as an electronics expert and surveillance agent. He was responsible for the operations of electronically-controlled gambling machines in the casinos in Havana, whereby the floor manager could watch the players via a small television camera and oversee the entire gambling operation. In 1959, Martino arrived in Cuba where he took over the race track called Oriental Park where he upgraded the track's electronic operations. He was the author of a book on Cuba called *I Was Castro's Prisoner,* which was an account of his three-year imprisonment in Cuban jails prior to the Bay of Pigs Invasion. Martino's co-author was Nathaniel Weyl who was released in November 1963.

When he arrived in Cuba with his 13-year-old son, Martino was stopped by Cuban immigration authorities and charged with having flown into Cuba in his own plane that they said he had hidden in a remote airfield near Havana. The Cuban police said he was being charged with "counter-revolutionary" activities such as gunrunning, burning of sugar fields, and taking people out of the country. His son was let go but Martino was put in solitary confinement before being put on trial. He was found guilty and put in prison. He was given a 30-year sentence but served only 30 months. He was released on October 2, 1962, in exchange for some spies from a South American country. After his release, according to government documents, Martino was "closely associated with people from Guatemala and worked for the CIA." After returning to the US he worked for H.L. Hunt and other Texas oilmen who were anti-Castro and funded the various anti-Castro organizations that were so prominent in various parts of the country.

After the assassination of President Kennedy, the FBI received information that Martino may have had some knowledge of Lee Harvey Oswald and his possible Cuban ties. He was interviewed by the FBI on November 29, 1963. According to FBI records on Martino, he told the agents that a source in the Miami area, whom he would not disclose, told him that Oswald had traveled to Mexico City and from there to Cuba. Oswald was supposed to have come back to the US via the same route. Martino could not verify this information other than that his sources were various refugees from Cuba.

The FBI report said that Martino's inference that Oswald was financed by the Cubans was his own, and that no genuine proof was available. He also said that Oswald was financed by the Fair Play For Cuba Committee that had close ties to the Cuban government. The documents go on to say that Martino was being sponsored in his travels across the country denouncing the Castro regime by the ultra-right wing John Birch Society. At the end of the document the writer says, "It is not deemed feasible to re-interview Martino at this time."

In the JFK Files, there is a memo dated August 29, 1977 from Ken Klein and Cliff Fenton of the HSCA staff regarding Martino's allegations as to Oswald and his possible Cuban connections. Martino revealed the following information concerning the president's death.

JFK was killed because he betrayed Cubans by giving the Free Havana speech at Miami Stadium withdrawing support from the Bay of Pigs invasion. RFK was killed for the same reason as the go-between who negotiated with the Cubans for JFK.

Oswald thought he was working for pro-Castro Cubans, but in fact, was working for anti-Castro Cubans. Oswald's murder of Dallas Policeman J.D. Tippitt was not part of the plan. Oswald was acting as part of the post-assassination plan when he entered the Texas Theatre after the assassination but did not know that he would be killed there. The assassins knew the motorcade route long before November 22, 1963.

On January 20, 1964, Martino gave an interview with reporter Kay Pittman of the *Press-Scimitar,* a daily paper in Memphis, Tennessee. In the article, Pittman said that Martino had been in Mexico City and had left from a secret airport in Yucatan for Cuba and was there the week of October 4, 1963. Miss Pittman said that Martino said that he did not have firsthand information regarding these Oswald allegations but that he got this story from his sources in the Cuban underground.

In reaction to this story, Martino said that he was "grossly misquoted" by Miss Pittman regarding his Oswald-Cuba story.

It now seems obvious that Martino's Oswald-as-a-Cuban-associate story was certainly disinformation on his (or others,) behalf to shift the blame to Castro for the assassination of JFK.

After the assassination, Martino was questioned by the FBI regarding any information he might have on the president's death. He told the agents that his source was a man named Oscar Ortiz, a member of an unnamed anti-Castro group. The Bureau never found out who this "Ortiz" man was.

In the December 1994 issue of *Vanity Fair,* author and reporter Anthony Summers wrote a long piece on the Kennedy assassination including information regarding John Martino. Summers wrote that Martino was a close friend of mob boss Santo Trafficante, the same man who was hired by the CIA to kill Castro. Summers found John Martino's wife Florence, then 80, living in Miami Beach, Florida. She told Summers that prior to the assassination, her husband told her, "they're going to kill Kennedy when he gets to Texas." She said that after the news of JFK's death, her husband went white and was constantly on the phone that day. Mrs. Martino also said that John told her that there was another Cuban man in the Texas Theater who was allowed to escape, while Oswald was arrested by DPD officers.

John also told her that one of the men came to their home two months prior to the Kennedy killing with another man who was involved in the crime. Florence Martino died shortly thereafter.

Further information on Martino's links to the assassination came from reporter John Cummings, who worked in the 1970s for the New York newspaper *Newsday*. After the assassination Cummings contacted his sources in the anti-Castro community including Martino. Martino spilled his guts to Cummings, telling him that there had been "two guns [in the assassination], two people involved."

Shortly before his death in 1975, Martino again met with Cummings and talked further about the assassination. He said he was part of the assassination but did not pull the trigger. He was used for "delivering money, facilitating things."

He further told Cummings a most revealing story. He said that several weeks before the assassination he met with Oswald in Miami. He said that an FBI agent named Connors asked him to come to a dock on Biscayne Bay where he was introduced by Connors to Oswald. Martino said that Oswald looked like he didn't know what was going on and the real reason he wanted to introduce him to Oswald was because they were both anti-Castro in their politics. Martino said that he was under the impression that Oswald was an agent Connors was running. Author Summers said that he was able to trace down an ex-FBI agent by the name of James O'Connor who said that Martino's name rang a bell but that he had never met Lee Oswald.

That same year, Martino talked with his friend and business partner Fred Classen regarding the assassination. He said that Oswald was not the hit man and that the Cubans "put him together."

John Martino died in 1975.

The Bayo/Pawley Affair (along with the information on the assassination provided by John Martino), remains one of the lingering mysteries in the CIA's long war against Castro, even after all these years.

Chapter 22
Castro and Kennedy

From day one after the assassination of President Kennedy, rumors began to swirl regarding a possible role of Cuba and Fidel Castro in the president's murder. When the alleged assassin's background was made public, the American people began to get glimpses of Lee Oswald's pro-Cuban orientation and his alleged ties to the Cuban government. It was revealed that Oswald was in New Orleans in the summer of 1963, supposedly working with the Fair Play for Cuba Committee, a pro-Castro organization, handing out pamphlets on the streets of that city. It also turned out that while Oswald was playing his pro-Castro game, he was working on the sidelines with some nasty, anti-Castro men such as Guy Banister and David Ferrie, whose stories have been revealed in earlier chapters of this book.

In the decades since the assassination, researchers have been studying the "Cuba did it" theory as part of the legitimate assassination inquiry. What role, if any, did Castro play, or have advanced knowledge of, in the events that unfolded in Dallas? Fidel Castro was a bright man, despite his unkempt appearance and loudmouth style. Castro knew of the many attempts on his life and, at one time, made a public speech accusing the US of trying to assassinate him and vowing retribution in response. All of this talk was heard in Washington by the Kennedy White House and put away for another day.

So, it was not surprising that after the president's death, Fidel Castro made his first public comment on the president's murder, giving his own account of the terrible deed.

A document dated November 29, 1963 from the National Security Agency entitled "Castro Speaks on President Kennedy's Assassination," said the following:

> Fidel stated that Events are demonstrating the sinister plot behind the assassination of Kennedy. Contradictions show that Oswald was made the culprit by the police or was prepared to commit the act with promise of escape, and was assigned activities so as to have responsibility fall on or be

insinuated against those whom the perpetrators wished. It is clear that United States reactionaries tried to make Cuba and the world the victims of their criminal designs, even at the price of assassinating their own president. They sent Oswald to Mexico to request a transit visa to Cuba for later travel to the USSR. Imagine the president's assassin just returning from the USSR and passing through Cuba. The visa to the USSR he could have been requested from the nearest European country and he would not have to come to Cuba to later go to the USSR, which is much farther.[1]

What is clear from this document is that Castro had a thorough knowledge of what Oswald was doing prior to the assassination, and his mysterious trip to Mexico City in late September-early October 1963, two months before he allegedly killed JFK. He also hinted in his speech about the possibility of others in America being involved in the assassination, and the possible use of Oswald as an unwitting participant in the event.

The reason that Castro and the Cuban government knew so much about Oswald prior to November 22, 1963 was his mysterious trip to Mexico City that has been referenced much in this work. According to the Warren Commission Report, Oswald went to Mexico City in order to get a visa from the Soviet Embassy to return to Russia. According to the Warren Commission, Oswald was eager to get back to the Soviet Union as he was entirely frustrated as to what his life in America had become.

One of the many mysterious people with CIA connections who was in Mexico City at the same time Oswald was, was a man named William Gaudet. Gaudet said he was the editor of a small newspaper based in Costa Rica called *Latin American Traveler*. In reality, Gaudet had been employed by the CIA for over twenty years. Gaudet had known Guy Banister in New Orleans and had seen Oswald pass out FPCC flyers in the city. Gaudet is now deceased, but before his death he said he thought Oswald was a "patsy," but refused to say why he was in Mexico City at the same time Oswald was there.

One of the first things that Oswald did upon his arrival in Mexico City was to make his way to the Cuban Consulate. There, he showed off his "leftist" credentials: his FPCC card, letters received from the

1 RIF No. 144-10001-10096: Castro Speaks on President Kennedy's Assassination.

American Communist party, a picture of him being arrested in New Orleans after his "fight" with Carlos Bringuier, and a now disputed membership card for the American Communist Party (it was never proved that Oswald ever belonged to the Communist Party of the US). When he asked for a visa to travel to Russia he was told that he had to go to the Russian Embassy. There, he was told he'd have to wait for months in order to get his visa. It was at this time that Oswald is supposed to have made a warning that he would "kill Kennedy" in retaliation for his not being allowed back into the Soviet Union.

But here the story became mired in mystery. Was it the real Oswald who came to both the Soviet Embassy and the Cuban Consulate? The answer to that question seems to be *no*.

The first person to cast doubt on the real Lee Oswald as being the man who came to the Cuban Consulate was Sylvia Duran, who worked there and who spent the most time with him. Years after the assassination, Duran said, after seeing pictures of the real Oswald, that the man she saw was *not* the real Oswald.

But the most telling piece of evidence that there was an Oswald imposter in Mexico City is the photo of an "Unidentified Man" that the CIA took of a person that the Agency said was the real Oswald. This man, whose picture has been known for years, is still a mystery and what, if any, his relationship was to Oswald and the assassination is still in doubt.

The origins of the unidentified man in the photograph goes back to November 23, 1963, when the FBI, after getting it from the CIA, showed it to Marguerite Oswald, Lee Oswald's mother. This photograph was supposed to have been the real Lee Oswald but it was clearly not. This man was beefy, with broad shoulders and a receding hairline and older than the 24-year-old Oswald. When she testified before the Warren Commission, Mrs. Oswald said the man in the photo was Jack Ruby (another lie).

An important document referencing the activities of Oswald in Mexico City, and important Cuban facts about other topics is the so called "Scelso Document," prepared by John Whitten (writing under the name John Scelso) whose real name has only recently been revealed. Whitten was tasked by the Agency to write its own report on the assassination, one that the Warren

The photo of an unidentified man in Mexico said to be Oswald.

Commission was not given. The WC was not given the photo of the unidentified man by the CIA because it concerned a covert intelligence mission in Mexico City that it wanted to keep secret.

Soon, what action the CIA should take in informing the Warren Commission about this problem spread to the top of the covert branch. On March 1, 1964, Ray Rocca, a highly placed CIA officer wrote an internal memorandum to Richard Helms stating, "we have a problem here for your determination." The "problem" was what to do about the photo of a man the CIA said was the presidential assassin, but was clearly not. If, as many people suspected, this man was part of some covert operation hinted at by Whitten in Mexico City at the time of the Oswald visit, was he in fact a part of the assassination conspiracy? Was he in fact linked with Oswald in a possible framing of the ex-Marine?

But what neither Castro nor the American public knew at the time was that the Kennedy administration was initiating a secret, two-track policy towards Cuba with the ultimate goal of re-establishing good ties between the countries which had been broken by the Eisenhower administration after Castro seized power in Havana in 1959.

After the end of the Cuban Missile Crisis, the Kennedy administration conducted a two-track policy as far as Cuba was concerned. On one hand, Operation Mongoose was "officially" ended, but separate exile raids against targets in Cuba continued. With Cuban exile leader Manuel Artime's commandos heading for the safety of Nicaragua, where they could mount their clandestine raids against Cuba, the Kennedy administration, on March 30, 1963, announced that it was going to take whatever measures were necessary to stop the exile raids originating from US territory. Robert Kennedy's Justice Department quickly stepped up FBI undercover surveillance on the secret training camps run by anti-Castro groups, such as Alpha-66, in such places as the Florida Everglades and outside of New Orleans (where David Ferrie and Guy Banister were training).

One of the Kennedy administration's first secret contacts with the Soviet Union after the crisis took place on September 30, 1963, when JFK sent his Press Secretary, Pierre Salinger, to meet covertly with a Russian named Colonel G.V. Karpovich. Karpovich was a KGB officer who was attached to the Soviet Embassy in Washington. Soviet Premier Nikita Khrushchev himself had approved of this secret contact, hoping to bypass the normal diplomatic channels that might stifle important contacts between the two countries. While it was hoped that his back channel negotiations would lead to increasing contact, it did not significantly materialize.

In another diplomatic move to lessen Soviet-American tensions, JFK sent US Ambassador Averell Harriman to Moscow on April 23, 1963, where he had several meetings with Prime Minister Khrushchev. Among the topics covered were Cuba and other important items. Another prominent American to visit Khrushchev was Norman Cousins, the editor of the *Saturday Review*. Upon his return to the US, Cousins met with JFK and told him that the Russian leader wanted to have a new start with the American president. Also in April, Fidel Castro arrived in Moscow and met with Khrushchev. Before leaving for home, Castro had an interview with American journalist Lisa Howard. Castro told Howard that he was ready to reach a rapprochement with the United States.

But while this was going on, the Kennedy administration was mounting a second, large -scale covert war against the Castro regime. Operation Mongoose had been revived in a smaller form, but was still run by the CIA. Why the Kennedy administration was using the carrot and the stick is open to speculation but one can assume that they wanted it both ways. The next year was an election year and Kennedy did not want to be accused of losing Cuba like President Truman had been accused of "losing China" after World War II. But he also wanted to placate the doves who wanted to see an easing of tensions with Cuba, especially after the Missile Crisis of 1962.

At the same time that the secret war against Castro was going on, Track Two was being developed. A June 6, 1963 meeting between CIA Director John McCone, William Bundy, Vice President Johnson, and Lyman Kilpatrick regarding Mongoose produced the following information:

> On June 6, 1963, the SGA discussed "various possibilities of establishing channels of communication with CASTRO. All members of the group agree that this is a useful endeavor. Mr. Bundy cautioned that of course CASTRO should not be made privy to any US positions while Mr. McCone emphasized the necessity of keeping any such approach entirely secret.

A memo about a later meeting between Bundy, Johnson, Vance, and McCone regarding Mongoose planning says,

> On November 6, 1963, Bundy told the SG that "It has come to the attention of the White House that Castro would like to have a talk designed to bring about some arrangement with the US. To hear what Castro has to say and to know on what he might wish to negotiate would be of some use to the US. After discussion, it was decided by the SG members not to try to reach a firm decision at this time (as to an emissary to talk with Castro) but to study the problem for several days and attack it again.
>
> November 6, 1963, higher authority (President Kennedy) disapproved all Cuban operations scheduled to be run before November 12. Two operations dated November 8 and 10 are

therefore disapproved.

In September 1963, the administration received tentative feelers from Castro wanting to know if the Kennedy administration would be willing to enter into secret talks. Both JFK and RFK were interested and privately asked William Atwood, a former editor of *Life* magazine to act on their behalf. At the time, Atwood was part of the US delegation to the U.N., having formerly been US Ambassador to Guinea for two years. In a September 18 memo to the State Department, Atwood argued that it would be wrong to permanently isolate Castro, and that that might lead him further into the Soviet orbit. He also stated that his contacts told him that Castro was disillusioned with Russia and wanted more freedom to run his own country. Atwood asked JFK if he could put out feelers to the Cuban Ambassador to the U.N., Carlos Lechuga. He also asked JFK whether he could visit Cuba and if he could persuade Lechuga to gain an invitation for him. The president gave his permission and soon a chance encounter took place. The writer, Lisa Howard, who had interviewed Castro in the spring, hosted a dinner party at her home. Among those attending the party were William Atwood and Carlos Lechuga.

The day after the Howard party, Atwood reported to the White House where he met with both Kennedy brothers. While nothing of real substance took place, Robert Kennedy thought Atwood's contacts with Castro were "worth pursuing." William Bundy told Atwood that the president himself was in favor of "pushing towards an opening toward Cuba to take Castro out of the Soviet fold and perhaps wiping out the Bay of Pigs and maybe getting back to normal."

Lisa Howard's covert contacts with top-ranking Cubans continued and she had a good discussion with Dr. Rene Vallejo, Castro's friend and private doctor. On October 31, Vallejo told Howard that Castro was ready for a meeting with a high-ranking American diplomat. JFK was informed, and he told Atwood to go to Cuba.

Newly released documents tell the two sides to the question of cooperation between Castro and Kennedy and are interesting reading. Some of the highlights are as follows:

April 11, 1963: Memorandum for Mr. Bundy. Subject: Cuba Policy.

We are all concerned about solving our Cuba problem, but so far, we have been looking seriously at only one side of the coin—ways to hurt Castro by varying degrees of covert [action] and nastiness. We have not yet looked seriously at the other side of the coin-quietly enticing Castro over to us.

If the current approach turned out to be feasible and, in turn, successful, the benefits would be substantial. In the short run, we would probably be able to neutralize at least two of our main worries about Castro—the reintroduction of offensive missiles and Cuban subversion. In the long run, we would be able to work on eliminating Castro at our leisure and from a good vantage point.

While the practical obstacles to this sort of approach may be immense, they may not be insuperable. Two such obstacles are the domestic political situation and Castro's reluctance to be enticed.

Domestic Problem—If the American people can be shown that the offensive missile threat and the subversive threat are under control, that the Russian presence in Cuba is reduced and that Castro is much more a nationalist than a Communist, the selling job necessary for a careful, quiet policy turn-around may not be impossible.

Castro's Reluctance to be Enticed—This may be an easier nut to crack now than it once would have been. Castro may have received, from our point of view, some very valuable education over the past couple years. Hopefully, he has learned that the Russians are not as tough and reliable as he thought they were and that we are a lot tougher and nastier than he thought we were; also hopefully, he is scared. Our present nasty policy is probably a necessary prelude to a sweet approach. The more we can (1) scare Castro and (2) demonstrate to him that the Bloc is either unwilling or unable to fill his security and economic requirements, the more amenable Castro probably will be to a new approach. In this regard, perhaps the worst thing we can do is to let our nasty policy ease off without a particular objective in sight.

I understand that, in the near future, the President will be looking at some more violent solutions to the Cuban problem. It might be interesting if, at roughly the same time, he could have a look at a feasibility study on a policy-turn-around. Do you think this timing for such a study is right? Or do you think it is still premature?

It is not known just what the "more violent solutions" were. Might they have been a new assassination plot against Castro or his inner circle, or some type of American-led invasion of Cuba? We will never know.

The recently released documents provide more light on this interesting time period whern the Kennedy administration was trying to mend ties with Castro. In a May 1, 1963 document titled "Interview of US Newswoman with Fidel Castro indicating possible interest in Rapprochement with the United States" these steps are spelled out. On April 30, 1963, Lisa Howard had an interview with several leading Cuban figures including Fidel Castro, Ernesto "Che" Guevara, Vilma Espin de Castro, Raul Garcia, and Rene Vallejo. Here are the most important parts of the document:

It appears that Fidel Castro is looking for a way to reach a rapprochement with the Unites States Government, probably because he is aware that Cuba is in a state of economic chaos. The October blockade hurt the Cuban economy. Lisa Howard believes that Castro talked about this matter with her because she is known as a progressive and she talked with him in frank, blunt, honest terms; Castro has little opportunity to hear this type of conversation. Castro indicated that if a rapprochement was wanted President John F. Kennedy would have to make the first move. In response to the statement that Castro would probably have to make the first move, Castro asked what the US wanted from him. When a return to the original aims of the revolution was suggested, Fidel said that perhaps, he, President Kennedy and Premier Nikita Khrushchev should discuss this. Lisa Howard said that she thought it was a more likely topic for

Castro to discuss with President Kennedy. Castro said that he doubted that President Kennedy would talk with him without Khrushchev present. When Howard pressed Castro for further information on how a rapprochement could be achieved he said that steps were already being taken. Pressed further, he said he considered the US limitation on exile raids to be a proper step toward accommodation. It is Lisa Howard's opinion that Castro wants to pursue the discussion of rapprochement with a proper progressive spokesman. Based on her discussions with the following persons, Lisa Howard feels that Guevara, Raul Castro, and Vilma Espin oppose any idea of rapprochement; Roa and Vallejo favor these discussions.

Castro asked Howard, who had previously interviewed Khrushchev for an appraisal of him. When Howard said that Khrushchev was a shrewd politician who would break and dispose of Castro when the Soviets no longer needed him, Castro made no comment. Lisa Howard had no insight or advance notice of Castro's travel to Moscow.

Castro is in complete control in Cuba. No major decision is made without him. Neither Guevara nor Raul Castro would be able to rule Cuba if Fidel were assassinated.

In discussions with Castro about terror and secret police methods Lisa Howard received the impression that he was not completely aware of the extent to which terror has gripped Cuba.

While discussing a possible rapprochement Castro asked for a full assessments of President and Mrs. Kennedy, and Robert Kennedy, and wanted to know if Adlai Stevenson had power in the US and if his voice was heard in President Kennedy's councils. Castro commented that James Donovan was a good man; it was Lisa Howard's impression that Donovan had a platform from which he could launch political discussions on the philosophy of revolution. [James Donovan was a New York lawyer who was the intermediary between the US and the Soviet Union in the release of the captured U-2 pilot Francis Gary Powers and captured Russian spy Rudolf Able.]

Lisa Howard said that she was willing to undertake further

discussions with Castro concerning a possible rapprochement. Other possibile candidates whom she suggested were Edwin Martin, Adlai Stevenson, and Luis Munoz Marin. She also mentioned Donovan but was not quite certain that he was progressive enough. Lisa Howard is willing to arrange a meeting for any US Government spokesman with Castro through Vallejo, who will be the point of contact.

While these secret backchannel meetings were going on, it seems that Castro still had another side of him that he wanted to put forward. On September 7, Castro had a meeting with reporter Daniel Harker of the Associated Press at the Brazilian Embassy and gave a three-hour interview. In that meeting, Castro issued the following warning to the United States:

> We are prepared to fight them and answer in kind. United States leaders should think that if they are aiding terrorist plans to eliminate Cuban leaders, they themselves will not be safe.

Conspiracy theorists involved in the Cuban connection to the Kennedy assassination point to this statement as the rational for Castro being behind the president's death. This statement has other, important implications as well. Did Castro know of the CIA-Mafia plots to kill him? Was he privy to the Kennedy administration's "Operation Mongoose" and the ZR/RIFLE program? Did Castro have a double agent in the Cuban exile community feeding him sensitive information? And could that double agent have been Santo Trafficante Jr.? It seems reasonable, from all the facts, that to all of these questions the answer is yes. Except for the most critical question: Did Castro order the assassination of President Kennedy? The answer to that query, based on the historical record, is no. If it was proven beyond a reasonable doubt that Castro was behind the assassination, Cuba would have been invaded by the US and the Castro government toppled. This writer believes that Castro truly wanted a political accommodation with the United States in November 1963 and was working to that end.

Chapter 23
The Adventures of Alexander Rorke

To the casual reader interested in the Cuban connection to the Kennedy assassination, the name of Alexander Rorke may not mean much. But in his own way, Rorke remains a man of mystery, associated with the CIA and the Anti-Communist Penetration Force headed by Gerry Patrick Hemming and Frank Sturgis. He died in a plane crash that has still to be explained.

The documents released under the JFK Records Act shed new light on the activities of Alexander Rorke and the roles the various US intelligence agencies had in his covert activities.

Rorke was a rabid anti-communist in the early 1960s, a commando who took part in various covert raids into Cuba, he may have been on one at the time of his disappearance in the fall of 1963, age 37. He was married to the daughter of one of the most well known New York restaurateurs, Sherman Billingsley, owner of the Stork Club that catered to well-connected patrons, including the political and business elite of that city. Rorke was associated with the anti-Castro group MIRR, and took part in raids in Cuba with the MIRR's military chief, Major Evelio Duque. On one particular raid, the two men took off for Cuba on Rorke's ship, the *Violynn III*. Their target was a Soviet ship at anchor off the Cuban coast.

Alexander Rorke and infant daughter, 1962.

Instead, they were caught by the small navy of the Bahamas that had been tipped off by the FBI. They were taken into custody at the small island of Norman's Cay in the Bahamas and eventually released.

Rorke also participated in attacks against two of the largest refineries in Cuba, the Shell and Esso facilities. In the violent mercenary world with which Rorke was associated, one of his partners was Orlando Bosch, a man wanted by various countries for acts of terrorism, mostly against Cuban targets.

Rorke, however, is the subject of much debate in connection with early assassination plots against Castro and his possible link to the JFK death. The theory regarding Rorke says that Rorke, a friend of Frank Sturgis, was supposed to have recruited Marita Lorenz, the aforementioned beautiful young woman who met Fidel Castro and soon became his lover. After a while, young Miss Lorenz became disenchanted with Fidel and agreed to work with the CIA to kill him. Rorke took on Marita Lorenz as a CIA participant in the Castro plots in the summer of 1960, saying, "You could knock him off. It would save everybody a lot of trouble." For Lorenz, it would prove more trouble than she ever thought.

Rorke's name was well known by the US Justice Department and the FBI which had been keeping an ever-watchful eye on various anti-Castro groups and persons who were constantly attacking Cuban facilities. In September 1963, Rorke was called to the US customs headquarters where he was told in no uncertain terms that his actions were in violation of the neutrality acts of the United States; he was told to stop his forays. He did nothing of the sort.

President Kennedy's attempts to rein in the mercenaries did not go over well with them, and hatred among the soldiers of fortune for the Kennedy administration's Cuba policies ran rampant.

Rorke's association with the CIA during that time was a well-known fact and was given credence by author and journalist, and CIA associate, Andrew St. George. St. George said that Rorke was associated with Johnny Abes, the intelligence chief in the government of Rapahel Trujillo, the dictator of Nicaragua.

In the book *Coup D'eat in America* by author Allan Weberman, there is a long quote from Frank Sturgis concerning his old friend, Alexander Rorke. This reads in part:

He was a freelance photographer and reporter involved in many different Latin American intrigues. Alex participated in a number of operations that went into Cuba, also into Mexico. I sat with Rorke where his plane was parked at the Opalocka Airport which is close by here, the day he made is ill-fated trip. And I will get the names of everybody that knew about the trip and so forth, that the FBI investigated. I believe even the CIA investigated that.

What was the "trip" that Sturgis was talking about?

On September 24, 1963, the same day that the alleged presidential assassin Lee Oswald arrived in Mexico City, Rorke and his partner, Geoffrey Sullivan, left Miami in a rented twin-engine Beechcraft going to Honduras. That same day the men arrived in Merida, Mexico. On September 27, they arrived in Mexico City where they stayed for four days. On October 1, they flew back to Merida and later went on to the Mexican holiday city of Cozumel. According to FBI records, there was a third man on board the plane but his identity has never been verified. After leaving Cozumel the plane and the pilots were never seen again. It has been suggested that they were on a bombing mission over Cuba at the time of their disappearance but that cannot not be confirmed.

Official documents released by the FAA said that the plane went down in a storm Hurricane Flora, which battered the Caribbean. But the hurricane did not reach Cuba at the time that Rorke and Sullivan were in the area.

In early October, a search party consisting of Gerry Hemming, Frank Sturgis and a number of their fellows took off in a DC-3 to look for the missing men. A $25,000 reward was offered for any information by Rorke's father. Hemming later told the author Gaeton Fonzi that the men were on a bombing mission in Cuba when their plane went missing. Hemming also said the third person with Rorke and Sullivan was a Cuban named "Rafael Molina" who was to be sent into Cuba by the exiles to monitor Castro's movements for later attempts on his life. The Miami Police Department's Intelligence Division got a report from the US Secret Service that Molina was a suspect in a planned assassination attempt to be carried out on JFK when he went to visit his family at the Palm Beach home.

What happened to Rorke and Sullivan? Many theories have been bandied about in the ensuing five decades. Was Rorke's plane shot down by the Cuban Air Force? Was Rorke killed on the orders of Orlando Bosch for reasons that we still do not know? Until further documents on Rorke and Sullivan are released by the US government, another mystery will linger in limbo.

With the passage of time, we now have more information concerning the activities of Alexander Rorke via documents declassified from the HSCA (House Select Committee on Assassinations).

A one-page FBI memo dated January 28, 1964 reveals just how much interest the Bureau had in the Rorke-Sullivan disappearance. The memo reads as follows:

> Page 2, Paragraph 2, of San Antonio enclosure contains information concerning "Edwards". Miami sources do not know any such Edwards, but state the circumstances indicate Edwards is possibly Alexander Rorke, Jr.
>
> For the information of San Antonio, Rorke, 37 years old is a free-lance photographer and newspaperman, and reportedly made several leaflet dropping flights over Havana, Cuba. On September 24, 1963, Rorke and pilot Geoffrey Sullivan, in a rented Beechcraft Travelaire Airplane, Registration N6795T, left Florida, filed a flight plan for Belize, British Honduras, and were never heard from again. On October 2, 1963, a private search mission of nine persons in a DC-3 aircraft flew to Central America to look for Rorke. On October 5, 1963, the party returned, without success. Charles Collier of Dallas, Texas, paid for the mission, and was aboard this DC-3. Collier represented the insurance company which had insured the Beechcraft airplane flown by Rorke.
>
> Miami associated and friends of Rorke now believe he is dead, and possibly went down at sea in the airplane.[2]

The US Justice Department, the FBI, and the FAA all had an on

---

2 RIF No. 124-90019-10298: Alexander Rorke, Floyd Park, Jr.

going interest in the activities of Alexander Rorke and his partner, Geoffrey Sullivan. Their main focus was the raid that Rorke made against two of the largest refineries in Cuba, a raid which Rorke denied making in his interviews with federal authorities. Rorke was interviewed in New York on May 27, 1963 by FBI agents regarding this mission over Cuba, and what they got were conflicting answers. Rorke denied that he and Sullivan had made the sortie over Cuba in their Beechcraft plane. He said that the only proof the FBI needed to see was that the Beechcraft took off from West Palm Beach Airport, was refueled in Jacksonville, Florida, and then proceeded to Washington, DC. He said that the "burden of proof rests with the government."

According to FBI files:

> Rorke said he was going to stick by his story that he left from vicinity of Miami by boat and picked up a PBY at sea and returned to boat at sea after flight over Havana, and then proceeded to Jacksonville, Fla. where he boarded the Beechcraft plane and proceeded to Washington where he arrived on April twenty-six.
>
> Rorke was fined one thousand dollars by US Customs Service for his illegal flight over Cuba, as well as a hefty twenty six thousand dollars imposed on them by the F.A.A. Rorke expressed great dissatisfaction with present administration (Kennedy) and believes that Justice Department is out to "get him." Rorke also expressed in vehement terms concerning past dealings with US Customs and CIA.

On May 21, 1963, the CIA wrote a short memo regarding the bona fides of Rorke's so called raid into Cuba. The report was actually prepared by an unnamed US Army representative who had knowledge of the affair. The gist of the report is that the Cuban government did not have any notification of the bombing raid until Rorke made his public comments. The Army representative said that if the Cuban government had known about the raid they would have made it front-page news, and there would have been public demonstrations in the streets of Havana.

The Rorke affair made its way up the political chain of command in Washington and landed on the desk of Deputy Attorney General Nicholas Katzenbach who was briefed on the incident by Alan Belmont, Hoover's Assistant Director. The memo to Katzenbach reaffirmed Rorke's denial of the flight over Cuba. The Deputy A.G. was told that Rorke's plane was located in Meriden, Connecticut, and it was being examined by the FAA to determine if it was safe to fly. Geoffrey Sullivan, it was advised, refused to talk with members of the FAA. It was reported that Sullivan's air certificate had expired and he was being temporarily grounded until the matter was cleared up.

Mr. Katzenbach was further advised by the FBI that they were not holding Alexander Rorke:

> Mr. Katzenbach specifically stated that he is in full agreement and has, as a matter of fact, advised that it is his feeling that no restrictions should be placed on Rorke. The possibility of the Department desiring to issue a Grand Jury Subpoena for Rorke was mentioned to Mr. Katzenbach. He stated that in his opinion such action is not warranted at this time but could be considered by the Department at some later date after more information has been developed.

Katzenbach also determined that Rorke did not violate any FAA rules requiring that a flight plan be filed if a plane flew south of Key West, Florida. This seems odd, until one digs deeper. The Department of Justice under Attorney General Robert Kennedy, was well aware of all the anti-Castro operations being conducted during Operation Mongoose and by the various anti-Castro groups in Florida. It is not a leap of faith that RFK might have been aware of Alexander Rorke and Geoffrey Sullivan's activities long before Nick Katzenbach was notified by the FBI.

The FBI field office in New Haven, Connecticut, interviewed Geoffrey Sullivan and he denied having taken part in the raid inside Cuba. Sullivan told the FBI that he and Rorke had purchased the Beechcraft plane in 1962 for $13,000. He said that he first met Rorke in 1960 and they became friends. He said that Rorke contacted him in the winter of 1963 because he wanted Sullivan to fly him to Florida. They left Meriden, Connecticut airport on either April 23 or 24, 1963 on a trip that would take them to LaGuardia Airport in New York and Myrtle Beach, South Carolina, before they finally landied at West Palm Beach's Butler Aviation Terminal one day later. They then took a car to Bal Harbor, Florida and stayed at the Kennelworth Hotel.

Sullivan then said that he, Rorke, and another unnamed man went back to West Palm Beach on April 25 and took off at 9:00 p.m. Their route took them to Jacksonville, Florida enroute to Washington, DC, their final destination. At Washington, their passenger got out, and they returned to Meriden.

According to an FBI memo about the raid dated April 29, 1963, from Alan Belmont to Courtney Evans, "He ([Sullivan] vehemently denied having taken part in any way in such an incident," noting, that he "would not have the guts."

The documents in this case of the Rorke-Sullivan disappearance attracted the attention of three well-known adventurers of the time, all anti-Castro fighters, Gerald Patrick Hemming, Frank Sturgis, and William Johnson. According to a US Justice Department document dated March 12, 1964, the three men said they had a conversation with Rorke two days before his plane vanished on September 24, 1963. Their discussions centered on a proposed trip "for Central America, where they talked up a plan with Rorke:"

> Fiorini [Sturgis] and Johnson said they were working out a plan with Rorke, wherein they were to go to some Central American country and conduct an aerial operation against Cuba. The three were going to participate in this mission outside the United States, so as not to violate US neutrality laws.

According to Hemming, they tried to get financing for the trip, but having failed to do so, Rorke made the trip himself. Hemming and Fiorini said they were going to try to locate Sullivan and Rorke by themselves.

After the disappearance of Sullivan and Rorke, William H. Rorke Sr., the uncle of Alexander Rorke, arrived in Miami seeking information about his missing nephew. He had a notice put in the local press offering $25,000 for any information on the whereabouts of the two men. Hemming tried to get money from William Rorke to fund his rescue mission but nothing materialized. Hemming though, did say, "There are two unidentified Americans in jail in Cuba. These two Americans were recently turned over to the Cuban Government by some Central American government." Hemming said this was secret information, and implied that these two Americans are Rorke and Sullivan.

MMT-1, a source for the FBI, explained that Hemming made up the story and it was designed to obtain money from Rorke, Sr. by deceit. MMT-1 also said that Sturgis and Johnson were devising a plan to swindle large sums of money from Rorke Sr. This new information, while it does not solve the central question of what happened to Rorke and Sullivan, underscores the interest the American government took in their disappearance.

Note: For those people interested in getting a good background of Alexander Rorke and his gunrunning activities, go to RIF# 124-90019-10339 for an article by John Raymond in the *Boston Traveler* newspaper.

Chapter 24
The CIA's Miami Station

As mentioned numerous times in this tome, the CIA's JM/WAVE Station was responsible for running the covert war against Fidel Castro. We need not go into all the details, as they have been recorded throughout this narrative. However, the writer discovered documents relating to how the CIA's Miami Station conducted its covert activities regarding their Cuban underground contacts, and further, how the station reacted to the assassination of the president.

Theodore Shackley was the CIA Station Chief during this highly volatile period, beginning in mid-April 1962 until his transfer in the spring of 1965. He was responsible for overseeing the daily conduct of the JM/WAVE station and its communications with Washington. As per his instructions, the station sent daily SITRE's (Situation Reports) to Washington which described in detail all the operations that went on in any given day. For the SITRE, CIA officers attached to JM/WAVE would contact their informants in the Cuban community to ascertain what was going on.

The documents report that Shackley initiated a number of procedures outlining how JM/WAVE used their Cuban contacts to ferret out information. The most important were as follows:

> a. Query resident agents in Cuba who had WT (Wireless Transmitters) commo with our Station or a combination of W/T to the agent and telephonic response from the agent to a cutout in the Miami Cuban community.
> b. Use of singleton Cuban exile support agents and the AMOT intelligence service in Miami to communicate with lists of on-island contacts by phone or with lists of Cuban exiles in the US who were irregular sources of information.

One of the first times the Miami Station pulled in all their resources involved the activities of Rolando Masferrer when he left his New Jersey home, enroute to Florida. Masferrer was once an ally of Castro and held a position in the Cuban Senate from the province of Santiago in Oriente Province. However, when Castro gained the upper hand in Cuba, Masferrer turned against him and even ordered his private soldiers into the field to hunt Castro down. In retaliation, Castro put a "hit" on him and Masferrer, or "El Tigre" (the Tiger), wound up on the side of the United States in its war against his former friend.

It was reported to the station that Masferrer was coming to Florida with a number of his men for an unspecified action against Cuba that was in violation of the Neutrality Act. CIA sources were instructed to "hit the streets" in Miami to find out what Masferrer and his men were up to.

From the fall of 1962 to the time of JFK's death (after the Cuban Missile Crisis), the Station was on high alert for various possible incidents involving the travels of President Kennedy, as well as other possible exile operations.

On one occasion, JM/WAVE officers pulled out all the stops to query their sources "because President Kennedy was traveling about in the USA and Headquarters and internal USG security agencies wanted to be alerted to the presence of known dangerous Cuban exile activities in the area the President was to visit and wished to learn of any conspiracies being hatched in the Cuban exile community or in Cuba to exploit or interfere with the President's movement."

Miami Station officers were also put on full alert for other highly charged dangers, including: a possible Cuban or Cuban exile act when the Pope visited New York City; possible ongoing exile raids into Cuba in violation of the Neutrality Act; the locations of automatic weapons, explosives and ships which were being assembled by exiles in preparation for raids into Cuba.

The documents also describe how the Miami Station reacted in the aftermath of the president's death. CIA agent Warren Frank, who was one of the top JM/WAVE officers at the time of the president's death, ordered all his agents to hit the streets and find out what they could learn regarding any Cuban connection to the Dallas tragedy.

The writer of the memo says:

> I do not recall whether Mr. Shackley was on Station that day, but I recall that Mr. Anthony Sforza, AMOT case officer, told me later that he had received specific

instructions from Shackley about how the AMOT service was to go about aiding in the investigation. I also recall quite clearly that there was communications from Hqs to our station about the need to query our assets. There was also some communication from the FBI and other agencies to our Station asking for information about possible Cuban involvement in the Kennedy murder.

He further states that he called one of his contacts in the Miami area, as well as another agent who was then living in Cuba, and also called "01," to find out about any possible Cuban angle to the assassination. This agent queried his other contacts in Miami whom he called AMPAN-22, AMGABE-1, and AMBLEAK-1 to provide further information.

He wanted information on any exile who disappeared prior to Kennedy's murder, who was missing under "suspicious circumstances." He also wanted to be informed if any of these agents had been contacted during the fall of 1963 for assistance in getting large amounts of funds, weapons, or cars. He contacted AMING-3 and AMBLEAK-1, saying, "Give me a list of all Cuban exiles or Cubano-Americans you consider to be capable of orchestrating the murder of President Kennedy in order to precipitate an armed conflict between Cuba and the USA."

He further asked AMBLEAK-1 to furnish him with a list of the richest Cubans in exile, Cubans possessing sufficient personal wealth and the possible inclination to bankroll the murder of President Kennedy.

The document goes on to say that the agent went to Mexico City several weeks after the president's death to speak with his principal agent whom he called "01." "01" worked inside Cuba for the CIA and traveled to the Mexican capital for the meeting. "01" said that on the night of November 22, 1963, he saw Osmani Cienfuegos, a prominent Cuban leader, arrive at the home of an unidentified American who lived in Cuba. This American worked as a technician who built audio-surveillance equipment for the Cuban intelligence service. The reason Cienfuegos visited this unnamed American was "because he was one of the few American sources the Cuban government could talk to in Cuba about what was going on in the

USA as a result of Kennedy's murder."

The writer of the memo said that of all the officers at the Miami Station, it was Ted Shackley who had the most knowledge of the station's investigation of the Kennedy murder. He ends the memo by stating, "I do not recall anyone ever seeking information on security matters in the USA which was not related to Cuban exiles and their activities with respect to Cuba."

With this intriguing memo, we now have better knowledge of how the JM/WAVE station conducted its almost unlimited resources in both the anti-Castro cause, and the aftermath of the Kennedy assassination.

Note: The date of this document is 22 March 1977 and the title reads "1963-1964 Miami Station Action to Aid USG Investigation of the Murder of John F. Kennedy."

Who was Ted Shackley and how did he fit into the mosaic of the Miami Station and the plots to kill Castro? Theodore Shackley was born in Massachusetts, and served in the US Army from 1945 to 1947. He graduated from the University of Maryland in 1951 and was immediately hired by the new CIA. During the time that he was in the Agency, Shackley reentered the Army and left with the rank of lieutenant.

His first important post upon joining the CIA came in the early 1960s when he was given the most sensitive job of station chief of JMWAVE. At age 34, Shackley was a former station chief in Laos and Vietnam, two of the most important Southeast Asian countries in which the CIA had a major presence.

He took over his duties at JM/WAVE in February 1962 and hired as his deputy station chief Gordon Campbell. Campbell's primary responsibility was to oversee the agency's maritime operations through which clandestine boat attacks against Cuba were carried out. As in other large corporations, position had its privileges. Shackley drove the most expensive car, a Cadillac.

Another person who worked closely with Shackley was William Harvey who was head of Task Force W, another prime mover in Operation Mongoose.

But not all CIA personnel enjoyed Shackley's good graces, among them CIA officer Thomas Clines who asked to be transferred from the program saying that he did not believe that the Agency was going about getting rid of Castro properly. In the end though, Clines was persuaded to stay on.

Under Shackley's leadership, a large number of agent teams were successfully infiltrated into Cuba where clandestine intelligence collection and reconnaissance began. Others who worked clandestinely for the CIA in Operation Mongoose were friendly diplomats in Western embassies who agreed to help after being asked by Shackley. Information on Cuban political and military developments were funneled directly to the CIA and passed on to Shackley. One of his most important intelligence successes was winning over the sister of Fidel Castro, Juana Castro. Juana Castro turned against her brother's authoritarian regime and made contacts with certain members of Shackley's underground movement in Havana.

As Operation Mongoose got going, Robert Kennedy became a major player. He came down to the Miami Station on numerous occasions and immediately got into a running feud with William Harvey over the extent of the agency's Cuban operations.

Shackley ran a tight ship, as far as the day to day operations of JM/WAVE was concerned. Besides insisting that he approve all clandestine agent operations into and out of Cuba, he was a stickler when it came to approving or disapproving expenditures for these operations. He made many side trips back to Langley headquarters to brief the top men at CIA concerning the progress of Operation Mongoose.

When it was noted that Castro's agents had infiltrated the large Cuban community in Miami, and possibly the exiles themselves, Shackley ordered his own CIA officers to deliver guns and equipment directly to their people in Cuba, instead of using third parties. This cut the theft of equipment and the potential loss of agents.

But for Shackley and Operation Mongoose, things radically changed after the Cuban Missile Crisis of 1962. With the crisis over, JFK pledged, as part of the final settlement, that there would be no American invasion of Cuba. Operation Mongoose was shut down and the administration began to get tough with the various militant exile groups and their constant attacks on Cuba. Scores of exiles were arrested by the FBI after returning from forays into Cuba. At the JM/WAVE base, William Harvey was forced out and was replaced by a Kennedy friend, Desmond Fitzgerald.

Fitzgerald and Shackley got on well and a new phase of the CIA's efforts to overthrow Castro came into being. Task Force W was now put into the Special Affairs Staff whose job it was to make "noise" against Castro. The JM/WAVE station resumed its "boom and bang" operations inside of Cuba but they turned out to be mere pinpricks rather than any serious military attacks.

Much to Shackley's dismay, the administration set up training camps in various Latin American countries such as Costa Rica and Nicaragua where the exiles trained. Now, his JM/WAVE station was not in charge, and the exiles went off on their own in their attacks on Cuban soil.

By the fall of 1963, CIA and exile raids were continuing inside Cuba, hitting oil refineries and sugar plants, attacking the occasional military site and making a nuisance of themselves, as far as Castro was concerned. Desmond Fitzgerald was working with the CIA's number one agent inside Cuba, Rolando Cubela, a.k.a. AMLASH, in the Castro assassination plots.

On November 22, 1963, President Kennedy was killed in Dallas and all CIA operations against Cuba came to a halt. After the assassination, Shackley ordered his agents in Cuba to find out if they had any information regarding the death in Dallas. He primarily wanted to find out if any of his Cuban contacts had left Miami just prior to or just after November 22. None had.

In December 1963, Shackley was ordered to send ammunition to a few select agents inside Cuba, but in early 1964 the new president, Lyndon Johnson, cut off any further covert operations.

In later years, Shackley became associated with the rogue CIA agent Edwin Wilson and a number of ex-CIA and military men in the Iran-Contra scandal that almost cost Ronald Reagan his presidency. Nicknamed the "Blond Ghost," Ted Shackely retired from the Agency in 1979.

Chapter 25
The Jack Anderson Story

As we have seen, there were a number of groups and individuals who were working independently from the US government in their efforts to bring down the Castro regime. Other attempts were ongoing during this time period mostly from rabid, anti-Castro Cubans. One of these attempts was given wide publicity by the noted newspaper columnist Jack Anderson, who had a nation-wide following due to his syndicated column.

In the 1960s, Jack Anderson was not the powerhouse investigative reporter that he was to become in later years. At that time he worked as a partner of one of the giants of the journalistic field, Drew Pearson. The men wrote a well-known column called *Washington Merry-Go-Round* which was read by the powerbrokers of the time. Anderson's claim to fame in the aftermath of the Kennedy assassination occurred in 1967 at the time of the trial of Clay Shaw, who was brought up on charges of murdering JFK by New Orleans DA Jim Garrison. But it was Anderson's connections with some of the most powerful mob bosses in the United States, the same people who were secretly involved in the CIA-Mafia plots to kill Castro, that propelled him into the frenzy of the JFK assassination debate.

On January 30, 1977, Anderson wrote a column called *"CIA Tied to False Oswald Story."* This powerful article tantalized the American public when he wrote that one of his sources, a man known as "Mr. X," alleged that a CIA agent tried to link Lee Harvey Oswald to Cuban intelligence in Mexico.

After the assassination of the president, rumors swirled around the corridors of power in Washington that Oswald, who himself had been gunned down by night clubowner Jack Ruby on November 24, 1963, was part of a conspiracy to kill the president led by Fidel Castro of Cuba. If word got out that Castro had masterminded the Kennedy assassination, the lust for war in America would be hard to keep under wraps.

Years later, after he left office, President Lyndon Johnson voiced his own doubts about whether or not Castro was involved in his

Jack Anderson in 1972.

predecessor's death.

But there was one other major piece of news in the Anderson column that day that went unnoticed in the frenzy of the alleged Oswald-Cuban connection. Anderson wrote of the activities of "Mr. X" and this man's contact with a CIA officer in Havana before the severing of diplomatic relations with Castro's government.

On January 21, 1977, one day after the Anderson article appeared, the CIA's Deputy Director for Operations, wrote a letter analyzing Anderson's allegations. He wrote,

> Mr. X had helped to organize bank accounts to embezzle Cuban government funds to finance anti-Castro causes. Mr. X was reportedly recruited by a Morris Bishop [CIA contact] to plan an attempt on Castro's life. The plan was to fire a bazooka from a nearby apartment building while Castro was delivering one of his marathon speeches. According to the Anderson column the plot was discovered by Castro's police and Mr. X escaped to Miami. The Anderson column ends with the report that Mr. X worked for the CIA until

1975 for expenses, but was paid $253,000 in cash by Morris Bishop when he was terminated."[3]

The CIA memo says that the person identified as "Mr. X" by Anderson is Antonio Veciana Blanch, an assistant bank manager and past president of a public accountants association in Havana. He first contacted the CIA in Havana in December 1960 and asked the COS (name blanked out) to help in an assassination plot against Castro. Veciana asked for visas for ten relatives of the four men assigned to kill Castro, and also requested four M1 rifles with adapters for grenades, plus eight grenades. The COS did not encourage Veciana and subsequently checked with an Embassy officer who reported that Veciana had made similar, "wild-eyes" proposals to him. On 23, November 1961, the *Miami News* published a report of an unsuccessful attempt to assassinate Castro and Cuban President Osvaldo Dorticos on 5 October in Havana, but the bazooka the assassin was using failed to fire.[4]

Antonio Veciana was one of the most important of all the anti-Castro exile leaders, having founded the militant group that operated at the behest of the CIA for over a decade. His name was also prominent in the aftermath of the Kennedy assassination, as he had been in close contact with his CIA case officer, one, "Maurice Bishop," or "Morris Bishop," as reported in the Anderson article. Maurice or Morris Bishop, oversaw all of Alpha-66's operations, and may have known the president's alleged assassin, Lee Harvey Oswald.

The CIA's 201 file on Antonio Veciana reads like a good novel, full of covert activities and vital information on him that the Agency found useful.

In 1960, Veciana was the President of the Association of Public Accountants, and from 1957 to 1960 was employed as a CPA and manager of Banco Financerio in Havana, which was owned by another exile leader, Julio Lobo. The CIA files state that on December 7, 1960, Veciana made contact with the Agency's COS Havana station with a friend, Justo Carrillo Hernandez,s to inform the of a plot against Fidel Castro. The file states that Veciana had spoken to an unnamed State Department political officer concerning this

3 RIF No. 104-10065-10120;. "CIA Tied to False Oswald Story" by Jack Anderson
4 Ibid.

information. On October 7, Veciana entered the US at Key West, via small boat, carrying a passport but no visa. He was allowed to stay in the country, and was given a lot of money in refugee assistance.

In December 1960, the CIA and Veciana had become mutually acquainted, and a relationship began. During that time, the CIA's JM/WAVE station in Miami agreed to use him on sabotage raids into Cuba. (At this time, Veciana's wife and children were still living in Cuba. His wife later came to the US.)

The files report that by 1962, Veciana and a friend named Emelio Fuentes went to Puerto Rico to garner funds from forty people for the anti-Castro cause. Veciana's pitch was a demand, rather than a request for funds with interference reprisals against any who failed to fulfill his duty. He said that he needed to do this outside of US control. He said that the group was in contact with a man named "Joe" (possibly Santo Trafficante Jr.—Joe the courier) and that his group was going to confide in the CIA and were taking precautions to avoid CIA penetration.

On July 23, 1962, Veciana met with CIA agent Harry Real who was an officer of the New York Contact Division. Veciana said he needed CIA help but under no circumstances would he ask the CIA to become identified with his group. He told Real that he had up to $50,000 in the bank and "wanted someone in the Agency sufficiently highly placed to make a commitment."

By August 1962, Veciana had arrived in Key West after making fundraising trips to New York and Chicago where he got $64,000 which was placed in a bank in Puerto Rico. An FBI informant said that Veciana made contact with three men, already in Cuba, who would aid his movement, Vincente Noble, Guillermo Ruiz, and Bernardo Paradela. The files say that both Noble and Ruiz were "cold blooded killers."

In September 1962, Veciana held a meeting of Alpha-66 members in San Juan, P.R. that was attended by 200 Cuban exile recruits. In October, according to the files, Veciana was trying to obtain two boats from an unknown source in Texas. His group was now centered in Puerto Rico, and also operated out of the small islands in the Bahamas.

In August 1962, Veciana told the Cuban Affairs officer in Miami that Orestes Guillermo Ruiz Perez, who was married to one of his cousins, "was dissatisfied with the Castro regime and receptive to recruitment." The files on Ruiz say that he lived in the US illegally in 1957, and was assigned to the Cuban Embassy in Mexico City in September 1963 as a diplomat. "DGI (Cuban intelligence) activities was to penetrate counter-revolutionary groups. He flew from Mexico City to Havana on 22 November, 1963." This was the day of the president's assassination. Also note that it was said that an unidentified man flew from Mexico City to Havana on that same day (see the chapter on the Cubana Airline incident).

Veciana's 201 file now skips to 4 January 1974. A report from the US Attorney's New York Office, makes mention of the fact that Veciana and another man, Ariel Powers, were involved in "the unlawful importing of cocaine and other narcotics."

His 201 file ends with this remark, "Veciana has allegedly been involved in several assassination attempts against Fidel Castro, which, for one reason or another, never came off. They were not connected with the Agency."

The most controversial aspect of Antonio Veciana's relationship with the CIA and the Kennedy assassination concerns his case officer, a man known only as "Maurice Bishop." It has been alleged that Bishop was Veciana's handler at the CIA for over a decade, deciding where and when his Alpha-66 group would make its attacks against Cuban targets. It is reported that Bishop and Veciana met a total of 100 times over the years on CIA-Cuban business. Veciana was supposed to have met Bishop in Havana; Bishop, was carrying a forged Belgian passport, which allowed him easy entry and exit from Cuba in 1960.

It is not known if Bishop was working at the CIA's JM/WAVE station but Veciana's group got its logistical and Agency leadership there. One of Alpha-66's attacks against Cuba came in 1961 when they connected with another exile organization run by Luis Toroella. This was a bazooka attempt on Castro when the leader was to appear at a Havana sports stadium. Due to tight security, the attack was canceled.

The most debatable aspect of the entire Veciana story came when he told the House Select Committee on Assassinations that in September 1963, while he and Bishop were meeting in Dallas on Agency business, Bishop met a man who later turned out to be Lee Harvey Oswald. No one knows if it was the real Lee Oswald whom

Bishop met that day, or a possible Oswald double—note that there were numerous Oswald sightings in Dallas in the period right up to the assassination. The HSCA was never able to finally decide who the real "Maurice Bishop" was. It has been speculated that he might have been CIA agent David Atlee Phillips who was well connected with the CIA's Cuba and Mexico City operations at the time of the Kennedy administration's war against Castro.

Writing about any possible CIA knowledge of the true identity of "Maurice Bishop." the Agency said, "There is no indication in the file that any Agency officer in contact with Veciana used an alias Morris Bishop. There is no Morris Bishop listed in true names in the DDO rolls. There was never any contractual relationship with Veciana and he was not paid CIA funds."

In Veciana's memoir called *Trained to Kill: The Inside Story of CIA Plots Against Castro, Kennedy, and Che,* he minces no words on the lack of credibility that he saw in the actions and testimony of David Phillips as it related to Cuba. Both David Phillips and Veciana testified before the HSCA committee regarding what they knew about the Castro plots. Writing in his book, Veciana said, "Yet, Phillips, who had been involved with Cuba throughout much if not most of his career, claimed not to know about a single anti-Castro plot."

Writing about his relation to the Cuba plots in his book called *The Night Watch*, Phillips expanded on what he knew (or didn't want to reveal) about his participation in the Castro schemes:

I have often been asked how it was possible that I did not know the Castro assassination schemes. The question is usually predicated on the assumption that when I became chief of Cuban operations and then head of all Latin American affairs someone would've told me, or I would've read about the endeavors and documents in my safe. The fact is that those few CIA officers did not discuss their participation even with senior officers in the chain of command at the time of the plots. And highly sensitive papers are not retained in a division's chief's office. Which sounds plausible, except I knew the truth.[5]

5 Veciana, Antonio, with Harrison, Carlos, *Trained to Kill: The Inside Story of CIA Plots Against, Castro, Kennedy, and Che,* Skyhorse Publishing, New York, 2017, Page 191-192.

In his book, Veciana wrote this regarding David Phillips: "For my own reasons at the time, I chose not to expose Phillips's lies. I never told Fonzi [Gaeton Fonzi, an expert member of the committee looking into the Castro-Kennedy assassination ties] that Phillips was Bishop. And I didn't identify Phillips when I was asked about Bishop's identity under oath by the committee."

CIA documents say, "There has been no Agency relationship with Veciana." However, that flies in the face of other, known facts surrounding Veciana and his Alpha-66 organization. On July 23, 1962, Veciana met with the abovementioned CIA officer Harry Real. "Veciana asked Real to arrange a meeting with a senior CIA officer to discuss Alpha 66's plans to assassinate Castro and to request CIA's assistance (US $100,000: 10,000 Cuban pesos: 48 hand grenades). There is no indication that this request was ever acted upon by CIA."

Veciana was not a man to hold things back if it would aid Alpha-66's cause. According to Veciana, "Bishop" gave the orders instructing his group to attack Cuban and Soviet ships. At one point, Veciana held a press conference in Washington in which he told the assembled reporters of his group's military actions against Cuban targets.

In April 1966, the CIA had another interview with Veciana, again in its New York City office. The meeting was arranged by an unnamed retired naval officer who knew Veciana. At the meeting, Veciana told the CIA about the latest intelligence coming out of Cuba and that the only solution to the problem then going on in Cuba was the assassination of Castro. The CIA officer told Veciana that the Agency was not able to give him any assistance in overthrowing Castro but that they would accept any information he might be able to provide. Veciana then told the CIA officer that his roommate, Felix Zabala who was a Cuban refugee, had good contacts in Cuba. The CIA document says that the only reason Veciana gave them the name of Felix Zabala was to get the Agency to provide money for Alpha-66. Veciana asked for $50,000 in seed money. The CIA officer told Veciana that he "would look into the Zabala matter and would probably arrange for Zabala to be contacted in Puerto Rico."

In an interesting document the writer found among those released in 2018, is a letter from the FBI which related to Jack Anderson, the man who started the entire Mr. X-Antonio Veciana story. The memo was dated March 22, 1972 from W. R. Wannall to Mr. E.S. Miller and entitled "Subject: Jack Anderson White House Inquiry."

The memo reads as follows:

Early this afternoon, John W. Dean III, Counsel to the President, asked to see Supervisor [blanked out] and advised that "Newsweek" magazine is preparing a cover story concerning Jack Anderson and his leg man [blank]. Dean advised that this story is going to paint Anderson as "the all-American boy." Dean asked that the Bureau furnish him with any information available in its files relating to Anderson or [blank] which the White House could use through unidentified channels to get across a more balanced picture of Anderson. After checking, Dean was advised that we had previously furnished him all pertinent material we have concerning Anderson in connection with the Senate Judiciary Committee hearings in regard to the nomination of Kleindienst, that we are checking Bureau files concerning [blank] and will advise him of the results of this check.

Action: Crime Records Division is reviewing files concerning [blank] and will prepare a suitable memorandum for approval for transmittal by liaison to Dean.

For whatever reason, the Nixon White House was interested in the journalistic actions of Jack Anderson and what he might write about them in the future.

When Jack Anderson first wrote about Antonio Veciana and Mr. X, he did not know what a can of worms he was about to release. The public was soon to learn about Veciana's covert role in the Castro plots, as well as his relationship to the elusive Morris Bishop, whomever he might be. Veciana's story is just one of many in the 1960s saga regarding the CIA plots to assassinate Fidel Castro and the Cubans' covert role with the CIA during this heady time in our nation's history.

215

Chapter 26
Project JMMOVE

Earlier in this book, the author mentioned the case of a secret CIA base which was operating outside of New Orleans, Louisiana in the prelude to the ill-fated Bay of Pigs invasion of Cuba. The training camps were run entirely by the CIA with the tacit approval of the local law enforcement authorities. One of the main supply bases was in the town of Houma, Louisiana not too far from downtown New Orleans. Two of the men who trained in these camps were connected, one way or another to the assassination of President Kennedy, David Ferrie and Guy Banister. In the background of the Kennedy assassination, there were reports that the alleged presidential assassin, Lee Harvey Oswald, also might have been at one of these training camps.

In the documents released via the National Archives, we now have more information regarding a particular training camp run by the CIA outside of New Orleans and the events that took place at that facility. They tell of the cooperation between the CIA and the various local and other federal governmental agencies who aided the boys from Langley in their covert training. The code name for this operation was JMMOVE.

The information on Project JMMOVE was written on May 1, 1975 in a Memorandum for the Record Subject: Alleged Illegal Domestic Activities CIARDS Extract. The copy of this record came from the Gerald R. Ford Library collection, although the originator of the memo is not mentioned.

The beginning of the memo reads as follows:

> For the Director of Security:" Office of Security file number 536198 captioned "Belle Chasse Louisiana Ammunition Depot," sub-captioned "Project JMMOVE," was established in late 1967/early 1968 in response to requirements from DDP/CI/R&A for information concerning Agency activities in and about New Orleans, Louisiana, relative to Cuban training for the Bay of Pigs.

The DDP/CI/R&A inquiry was prompted by inquiries into the assassination of President John F. Kennedy conducted by the New Orleans District Attorney, Jim Garrison. Material drawn together at the time of the Garrison inquiry included a 7 June 1961 memorandum for the Chief, WH/4, sent [blank] captioned "Report of Base JMMOVE prepared by [blank] Chief of Base, JMMOVE covering the activities of JMMOVE in support of JMMATE. Included in this report by Chair of Base [blank] are the following pertinent comments:

JMMOVE was the cryptonym designating the Agency training base established at the US Naval Ammunition Depot at Belle Chasse, Louisiana, during the period 12 February 1961, through 12 April 1961. This Base located eight miles from the city of New Orleans, had been inactive for five years.

The initial mission assigned to the Base was to hold, condition and conduct limited training for thirty men organized into small infiltration teams, and to prepare these teams for operational employment. On activation of the Base, the mission was immediately expanded to include the reception and training of 149 men for organization into small guerilla warfare teams; reorganization and training of the 149 men, training of raider teams, development of necessary support facilities.

Under Objectives, Chief of Base included: Maintain maximum external security in such a fashion as to deny knowledge of the activities of the Base to the local populace. In addition, holding, training and movements of trainees had to be accomplished in such a fashion as to deny to trainees identification of the Base, i.e., the Belle Chasse Naval Ammunition Depot.

Develop effective liaison arrangements. This included liaison with US Border Patrol, New Orleans, if we so desired, to arrange that the Border Patrol pick up and detain trainees in our behalf. Immigration and Naturalization Office, New Orleans to establish procedures whereby this office would assist it if we had any disposal or detention cases.

Under base and operational security, Strickler listed, the following steps were taken to maintain maximum cover and security, the removal of agitators, defectors, or suspected Castro agents to safe-houses and/or the sheriff's jail.[6]

The document now goes on to explain the level of cooperation that the CIA got from the various local and federal law enforcement authorities in the region pertaining to what was going on at the JMMOVE facility. By and large, the local law enforcement agencies complied without question with the CIA's request for security as far as what was going on in the training camps. A detailed narrative of these actions are as follows:

This activity involved establishing and maintaining liaison with Superintendent and Assistant Superintendent of the Louisiana State Police; FBI; Superintendent of the New Orleans Police Department; Plaquimines Parish Sheriff's Office and deputies, whose cooperation and assistance proved invaluable in handling back movements of trainees, movement of ammunition and high explosives, to and from the base. The Sheriff of Plaquemines Parish, at my request, made available a holding facility which consisted of an entire jail and jailer at Port Sulphur, La., for the incarceration and retention of hard-core or troublesome trainees who threatened to leave the base. The jail was also utilized to hold a Spanish Captain of one of the cargo ships which had been loaded at the Braithwaite Dock on the Mississippi River with fuel, ammunition, high explosives and other equipment for the invasion [Bay of Pigs]. The Captain jumped ship for the purpose of returning to Havana to join his wife, who was pregnant. Through the cooperation of the INS, the Border Patrol, with whom liaison had previously been established, the Captain was apprehended, and with the assistance of the Plaquemines Parish deputies, the Captain was confined in the jail at Port Sulphur until after the invasion. He was then removed from jail and flown to New York City, where he was granted a thirty-day extension by INS to await the

6 RIF No. 178-10004-19424: Alleged Illegal Domestic Activities CIARDS Extract—1 May 1975.

arrival of his wife and newborn son, before proceeding to his home in Spain. Additional liaison was established with the Navy, Coast Guard, Armed Forces Police Detachment in New Orleans, all of whom provided support during the operation.

The document now tells the story of various people and events that were directly involved in Project JMMOVE.

The relevant narrative begins by saying, "Volume 16, Office of Security file number 219000 concerns Project SEAL, containing information concerning Office of Security operational support of the DEP relative to the Bay of Pigs invasion." The file contains a copy of a memorandum dated 12 May 1961, captioned "JMMOVE" directed to the Chief, WH/4 Security, reporting on activities at JMMOVE from 14 February 1961 to 21 April 1961. The following are verbatim extracts from this memorandum:

> During the latter part of February 1961, liaison was established with the Plaquemine Parish Sheriff's Office, Ports La Hague, Louisiana and Deputy Sheriff's [blank] regarding the JMMOVE activity and the nationality of the trainees. Sheriff [blank] was questioned regarding the possibility of utilizing jail in the event it became necessary to incarcerate one or more of the trainees at some future date. He immediately advised that he had a jail at Port Sulphur, Louisiana, which he would make available if the need should arise. He explained that the jailer [blank] would afford privacy since few prisoners were placed there. It was also agreed that there would be no records maintained if trainees were incarcerated and that members of his staff would deny that such trainees had ever been incarcerated in the event of future inquiries by representatives of the news media.
>
> Subsequently, it was necessary to incarcerate three trainees and the former Captain of the S.S. Houston at the above jail. This matter will be treated in detail later in this report.
>
> During the JMMOVE activity, members of the Sheriff's

Office were most helpful, especially, Officers [blank] in assisting with the handling and jailing of the above individuals; providing escorts for trainee and cargo moves from JMMOVE to the NAS or vice versa; conducting periodic patrols to the front and rear gates of JMMOVE to keep fishermen and poachers out of the base and reporting local gossip regarding speculation as to the type of activity conducted within the base.

The memo now goes into detail regarding the activities of a ship's captain who came under the radar of the members of the JMMOVE station and what happened to him. The tale is briefly referenced in the first document quoted in this chapter. It is an interesting story, to say the least.

Around March 16, 1961, members of the Immigration and Naturalization Service in New Orleans were briefed by members of the JMMOVE station in the apprehension and detaining of the Captain of the S.S. *Houston*, who was put in jail at Port Sulphur, until after the ill-fated invasion of the target area:

At 1500 hours on 28 March 1961, Mr. Frank Lowe, Logistics representative, in charge of loading ammunition on vessels at the Braithwaite Docks, telephonically advised the reporting agent that a crew member from the *Lake Charles* and the Captain from the S.S. *Houston* had jumped ship after the vessels had loaded and anchored downstream in the Mississippi River. The individuals were identified as [blank] approximately 44 years old, a former American who had renounced his US citizenship and who is now a naturalized citizen of Cuba, and one, [blank] Captain of the S.S. *Houston*, approximately 39 years old and of Spanish origin.

It seems that the Captain of the S.S. *Houston* was granted political asylum by the INS at New Orleans and had left that city by bus at 1000 hours on 28 March 1961, enroute to Miami, Florida.

According to Mr. Lowe, Captain [blank] left the S.S.

Houston on 28 March 1961, after which he reported to his employer, Hansen & Tidemann, Inc., with offices in New Orleans. He refused to return to the vessel. The captain insisted that his reason for leaving was the fact that his wife was pregnant and expecting to give birth to a child in approximately 10 days. He was afraid the birth would be by caesarean section and he was concerned for her safety. He wanted to return to Cuba at the earliest possible date.

It was reported that in view of the Captain's knowledge of the cargo on board the S.S. *Houston* and his probable knowledge of the use for which the cargo was intended, he would create a serious security hazard if he was released, and especially, if he should return to Cuba. It was decided that there were three possible ways of handling the matter. First, to release him and permit him to remain in the area running the risk that he might contact his wife and/or return to Cuba. This was ruled out on security grounds. Second, to force him aboard the vessel and place him under the custody of the Captain replacing him. This was believed too risky since it was feared the crew would be more loyal to him than to his replacement. Furthermore, if he should regain command of the vessel, he might divert the craft to Cuba. Third, to detain him until after the invasion." It was decided to put the captain in jail.

Now things began to go faster for the unlucky captain. On March 28, 1961, he was taken into the custody of Deputies from the Plaquemine Parish Sheriff's Office and transported to "a spot near the Naval Air Station at Belle Chasse, Louisiana, where he was handcuffed and transferred to the rear of the panel truck." He was guarded by an MP and taken to the jail at Port Sulphur, La., and put in jail on March 29, 1961. As mentioned in this chapter, he was subsequently sent to New York and then on to Spain.

US Border Patrol personnel were given a briefing by members of the JMMOVE team about what they were doing in the area (but not who was actually running the operation).

The narrative says, "Subsequently, the Border Patrol was very helpful in forcing fourteen crew members who had threatened to jump ship to stay aboard the *Caribe* after it had loaded at the Braithwaite Docks. Also, they assisted by taking into custody and holding Captain [blank] of the S.S *Houston*, until JMMOVE security representatives could assume custody."

Another member of the JMMOVE team was LCDR. James Phillips, M.D. (US Naval Station, Algiers, Louisiana), who treated some of the men who were wounded while training. He even made a trip to the jail at Port Sulphur to "examine trainees who were in detention there." (These people were not named.)

So, it seems that the CIA was running a covert training base near New Orleans before the Bay of Pigs invasion of Cuba, code named JMMOVE. While the available documents do not say the names of the trainees (and they probably never will), we now have a better idea as to just what went on there at that time, and the lengths the CIA went to cover its tracks prior to the Bay of Pigs.

Chapter 27
The Somoza Plan

The government of Nicaragua, led by Luis Somoza and his brother Anastasio, played a large role in the pre-Bay of Pigs planning, and its territory was used by the ill-fated Brigade 2506 in preparation for the attack on Castro's Cuba. Two years after the disaster of the Bay of Pigs, Louis Somoza would use his country as the staging area in yet another attempt to overthrow the Castro regime.

In April 1961, the Cuban exiles who would invade Cuba at the Bay of Pigs, assembled on the shoreline of Nicaragua in preparation for their departure. Waiting to see them off was General Luis Somoza, the leader of Nicaragua, a staunch American ally in the Caribbean. Like an aging potentate who sought the limelight, Somoza said to the waiting men, "Bring me a couple hairs from Castro's beard." The men he was sending off did not bring back anything from Castro's beard, and he felt the sting of defeat as much as the men left on Cuban shores.

Nicaragua had been a focal point in the pre-Bay of Pigs planning. When Castro's forces began to pin down the members of Brigade 2506, plans for a second strike to relieve the men at the beachhead went into effect. It was agreed that Nicaraguan pilots would fly their P-51 Mustangs to the battle zone. As the pilots and planes were made ready for combat, the unexpected news reached them that the sortie was to be canceled. With no air cover above their heads, the last remaining survivors of Brigade 2506 gave up their heroic fight and were quickly captured by Castro's forces.

Itching for another chance to mend the mistakes of the Bay of Pigs, Somoza, in 1963, began talks with leading exile leaders to mount another attack to liberate Cuba from Castro's clutches.

During that year, General Somoza met with Manuel Artime to make plans for anther invasion of Cuba. Artime was a confidant of the Kennedy brothers and was one of a few men who met with Senator John Kennedy during the 1960 US presidential election campaign. He was a leader of the Cuban counter-revolutionary group called MIRR, Movement for the Recovery of the Revolution. Artime and Tony Varona (who would play an important role in the later CIA-Mafia plots) were the top leaders in the anti-Castro cause.

During their secret meetings, Artime and Somoza made a deal whereby the exiles would once again conspire to stage an invasion to topple Castro.

Somoza put in a call to the president of Costa Rica, Francisco Orlich, who agreed to let the exiles use his country as a training base. Two military bases were set up in Costa Rica on land that was owned by a friend of President Orlich's brother. A naval facility in Nicaragua called Monkey Point was used as a staging area where outdated torpedo boats were docked in readiness for any attack on Cuba. Funds came from the United States through intermediary banks with over a half million dollars winding up in the coffers of the exiles. One check for the amount of $450,000 was deposited in an exile account to be used for "modern military equipment" on November 19, 1963, three days before JFK's assassination.

In November 1963, as final preparations for the second invasion of Cuba were taking place, Somoza said to his aides, "In November strong blows will begin against Cuban Prime Minister Fidel Castro by groups we are training." On November 15, 1963, about 300 men belonging to the MIRR left their training facilities based in the United States (in Virginia and North Carolina) enroute to Costa Rica. The commander of the group was Pepe San Roman, a confidant of Robert Kennedy.

According to documents under the aegis of the JFK Records Act, the Kennedy administration, in August 1963, already had a good idea into what the Somoza regime was up to. In an August 9, 1963 memo from McGeorge Bundy, the Special Assistant to the President entitled "Luis Somoza's Involvement in Cuban Exile Operations," he points out what steps Somoza was already undertaking.

Bundy told the president that the US had learned that Somoza was planning commando raids, guerilla warfare and acts of sabotage mounting in scope and intensity, culminating in a general uprising. Hardly concealed is his conviction that such an uprising would give the United States government little choice but to intervene militarily on the side of the insurgents, especially should Soviet troops be committed to quell the uprising.

The document reveals the names of three Cuban leaders who had contact with Somoza regarding the use of Nicaraguan bases for actions against Castro: former Cuban President Carlos Prio Socarras, former Prime Minister Jorge Garcia Montes, and former Ambassador to Washington, Guillermo Belt.

Bundy said that he had doubts that the Somoza regime could ultimately hide the scope of the military buildup then commencing in Nicaragua due to the overt nature of the beast.

The memo said that the United States considered these exile plans would probably come to naught and that only certain actions described below would contain the situation:

> a. Artime to forgo raids and externally based actions and to concentrate on resistance within Cuba.
>
> b. While leaving elements of his operational mechanism in Nicaragua and not breaking with Luis Somoza, Artime to shift the use of the more limited facilities Costa Rica has to offer.
>
> c. If additional pressures be needed, it should be remembered that ex-Ambassador Whelan, who is considered to enjoy the trust of the Somoza brothers, could be asked to help in tempering their zeal.
>
> d. We can, as a very last resort, drop a hint to Castro through nonofficial but authoritative channels that he should not be taken in by the "Somoza Plan," designed to provoke him into retaliatory acts and thereby to call forth a military invasion of Cuba.

The last paragraph shows just how delicate the Kennedy administration saw exile plans against Castro to be in the context of the overall military/political situation in the Caribbean at that time.

The above-mentioned McGeorge Bundy was President Kennedy's National Security Advisor during JFK's thousand days in the White House, a close friend and confidant, who advised the president on many foreign policy areas including Cuba. Before coming to Washington to work for the new Kennedy administration, Bundy was a dean at Harvard University (JFK's alma mater), and, in David Halberstram's coinage of the time, one of the "best and brightest." McGeorge Bundy's brother, William Bundy, was also a powerhouse in the Washington establishment and the president often times got the two of them mixed up. He would sometimes call McGeorge Bundy, "George" or better still, "McBundy."

After the Bay of Pigs invasion the administration turned its attention to getting rid of Castro via the CIA-lead Operation Mongoose. Bundy, along with other trusted members of Kennedy's cabinet and advisors, made up a new organization called The Standing Group which would meet to go over policy on Cuba.

Bundy advised the president to make some sort of accommodation with Castro and by the summer and fall of 1963, the administration was on a "two-track" course of both exile raids and possible peace feelers towards Castro. On November 19, 1963, Bundy was informed by William Atwood, President Kennedy's special backchannel to Castro, that the administration would be in touch with Castro's representatives after the president's upcoming trip to Dallas.

In his testimony before the Senate Committee investigating the Castro plots in the 1970s, Bundy said that the Kennedy White House discussed many options regarding what would happen if Castro was no longer there. "Clearly," said Bundy, "one of the possibilities would be Castro being removed from power by means (including assassination) but without going further with the notion of assassination itself." It is also noteworthy that right after President Kennedy's assassination, Robert Kennedy called Bundy at the White House to change the combination locks on the late president's safe. That he did.

The Kennedy administration was keeping a close watch on Somoza's activities regarding new exile raids and had various informants bring back information on just what the general was saying.

Somoza told his confidants that the Kennedy administration had given him "the green light" to conduct raids against Cuba, and that he had discussions with both RFK and JFK regarding these missions. He said that Kennedy brothers asked him to take four Brigade leaders to Nicaragua, and said that JFK asked him to represent him in discussions with the other leaders of Latin American countries.

He said that he had assurances from members of the US government that they would not stop him from using Nicaraguan territory as a staging area for the new Cuban invasion. He was said "to have found that there are no obstacles, despite the fact that the United States Government did not tell me anything concretely."

The Somoza plan for a second invasion of Cuba in November 1963, we now know, was just a part of a larger US invasion of Cuba that was scheduled for that time. Whether or not it would have gone ahead as planned was ultimately moot; it was scrapped with the president's death.[7]

As early as June 1959, the American government was taking an active interest in what was going on in Latin America and with Luis Somoza in particular. They wondered what threat Cuba might pose to Nicaragua. In a memo dated June 16, 1959 via an NSC Briefing, the following was discussed:

> We have reports from [blank] that arms and men from Venezuela arriving in Cuban Isle of Pines for transfer to Nicaragua. There is some Cuban army buildup on the Isle of Pines possibly to support action against Nicaragua (or the Dominican Republic), but more likely in response to rumors of counterrevolutionary plotting against Cuba. [blank] told US Ambassador in San Jose 10 June that Castro had, in fact, promised aid to Nicaraguan revolt and that all is lost to Communist in Nicaragua unless Somoza leave now." 1) Soviet lecturer in Moscow on 17 May said "among ourselves, Raul Castro is a Communist, 2) Nicaraguan exiles in Cuba, Venezuela and some in other places are Communist-led, 3) We have reports that Nicaraguan exiles in El Salvador and Guatemala moving to Honduras for new invasion effort. Over the long run, Somoza regime is bucking climate of opinion in Caribbean area that its days are numbered-that it is dictatorship and all dictators on way out. This line, nurtured by persons like Figueres and Betancourt as well as by Communists, probably in part responsible for decided coolness to Nicaraguan position in OAS. In fact, President Luis Somoza, who succeeded his father in 1956 and was

---

7 RIF No. 176-10019-10167.

subsequently elected in his own right, has tried to liberalize his regime. 1) Until 30 May, when civil rights were suspended in anticipation of revolt, there was complete freedom of press and assembly, 2) Businessmen's hostility to regime due largely to current economic downturn and to government's tax program which favored lower classes, 3) Somoza has promised free elections at the end of his term in 1963 and that his successor will not be family member; in effort counteract opposition line that "Somoza dynasty" will continue after 1963 under General Somoza, president's brother and military chief. 4) Whatever Somoza does, however, he still handicapped by Somoza name—a symbol of dictatorship—and by wide resentment over tremendous wealth built up by family over past 25 years.

Luis Somoza died on April 13, 1967, another dictator whom the United States worked with during that era.

Chapter 28
New Insights into the 1960 Campaign

The 1960 presidential campaign between Senator John F. Kennedy and Vice President Richard Nixon has been written about in detail since that era-shifting event, fifty-eight years ago. The election of John F. Kennedy was a monumental shift in the political dynamic in the United States at that time. Kennedy was replacing President Dwight Eisenhower who had served in the Oval Office for eight years. As we look back at Eisenhower's time in office, on the surface we can say that he did not do much as president. But that was not true. Ike, a hero of World War II, the man who brought victory to the Allied cause over Nazi Germany, reshaped the United States in ways that, with the hindsight of history, we can see were important. He built the interstate highway system, faced down the Soviets in the Middle East in Lebanon, and brought a feeling of safety and calm to the nation.

But under the surface, the people of the United States were looking for more; they wanted new leadership in the challenging decade of the 1960s that was just around the corner.

Both John F. Kennedy and Richard Nixon were World War II veterans; both served in the Navy. While Nixon had an undistinguished wartime record, that could not be said of Jack Kennedy. Kennedy's call to fame came when his PT-109 boat was rammed and sunk by a Japanese ship in the Solomon Islands on August 1, 1942. In the aftermath of the tragedy, Lt. Kennedy somehow managed to swim with his surviving men to safety on a nearby island, and they were finally rescued after a number of days on their isolated refuge.

Kennedy's exploits were given top news coverage in the United States and he was now a genuine war hero.

In 1946, a reluctant JFK ran in a Congressional a primary in Boston and at age 29, he beat a field of 10 candidates and came in first. He appealed to women who had lost sons in the war, and with his father's considerable money, won the election. He didn't particularly like being a member of the House, finding it boring, not did not really like his colleagues and he was basically interested in his own political future. After two undistinguished terms in the House, Kennedy decided to challenge then Senator Henry Cabot Lodge of Massachusetts for the senate in 1952.

1952 was a presidential election year and Dwight Eisenhower, who was running on the Republican ticket, and seemed like a shoe-in for election. Congressman Kennedy was taking a huge risk in running in that environment but with a well-healed campaign that was run by his brother Robert Kennedy, he got the upset. Kenneth O'Donnell, a friend of Kennedy's who would later serve in his administration, said of Kennedy's victory, "If Bobby had not arrived on the scene and taken charge when he did, Jack Kennedy most certainly would have lost the election." While in the Senate, Jack Kennedy wrote a book called *Profiles in Courage* that won him the Pulitzer Prize. There was some talk in certain circles that Kennedy did not actually write the book and it was later learned that his speech writer, Ted Sorensen, helped him (Sorensen would later serve in JFK's administration).

With Kennedy's newfound fame, his name was being mentioned in the upcoming 1956 presidential election as a possible candidate for Vice President. Despite the advice coming from his powerful father, Ambassador Joseph P. Kennedy, that he not put his hat in the ring, Kennedy decided the opposite and made it known that he was interested in the nomination. It was believed that if the Democratic nominee, Adlai Stevenson lost by a landslide that Jack's political career would be ruined. Kennedy took the chance nevertheless and in the end, Stevenson was defeated by President Eisenhower.

Kennedy won re-election in 1958 and then set his sights on the 1960 presidential election with the White House in mind. He announced his candidacy for president in Washington on January 2, 1960 by saying:

> I believe the Democratic Party has an historic function to perform in the winning of the 1960 election, comparable to its role in 1932. I intend to do my utmost to see that that victory is won. For 18 years, I have been in the service of the United States, first as a naval officer in the Pacific during World War II and for the past 14 years as a member of the

Congress. In the last 20 years, I have traveled in nearly every continent and country—from Leningrad to Saigon, from Bucharest to Lima. From all of this, I have developed an image of America as fulfilling a noble and historic role as the defender of freedom in a time of maximum peril—and of the American people as confident, courageous and perservering. It is with this image that I begin this campaign.

Once again Jack Kennedy chose his brother Robert to be his campaign manager, just as he was in Jack's earlier races. Kennedy had one huge distraction facing him as he entered the race—his Catholic religion. No Catholic had ever been elected president in the nation's history and Kennedy was bucking a huge trend in that regard. But Kennedy faced the issue head-on and addressed the matter directly. He spoke to a group of Protestant Ministers in Houston where he addressed the separation of church and state by saying, "I am not the Catholic candidate for president, I am the Democratic candidate for president."

He entered as many presidential primaries as he could (there were a lot less of them in 1960 than there are now). In West Virginia, he was challenged by his old foe, Minnesota Senator Hubert Humphrey (Humphrey would lose the election to JFK in the 1960 primaries but would win the 1968 Democratic nomination and lose once again to Richard Nixon). Kennedy's other rivals were Senator Lyndon Johnson from Texas, Stuart Symington and Adlai Stevenson. Kennedy won the primaries in West Virginia (where his religion took center stage), Wisconsin and Indiana.

He eventually won the Democratic nomination in 1960 and accepted the nomination at its convention in Los Angeles that summer. In a surprise move, Kennedy chose his rival, Senator Lyndon Johnson, as his vice presidential running mate, catching most of his advisors off guard. It was a controversial pick to be sure, but in the end it worked out politically as Johnson was able to lure a number of southern states into the Democratic column in the November election.

Kennedy now faced his old rival, Vice President Richard Nixon ,in the election and in a hard fought campaign, won the election by the barest of margins: 118, 550 votes nationwide, out of 68 million cast.

With the release of many new archives from the Kennedy Library, which can be found on-line at a site called "Paperless archives.com," historians now have a much better understanding of certain events that took place during and after the 1960 election, regarding information from Russian Premier Nikita Khrushchev about the 1960 election, as well as information about the West Virginia Election Law Matters.

The first item we'll discuss is dated May 24, 1961 and is a memo that was sent from the American Embassy in Moscow on a meeting that was held with Soviet Premier Nikita Khrushchev ahead of the Kennedy-Khrushchev meeting in Vienna, which turned out to be one of the most contentious meetings of the Kennedy era. The memo mentions Khrushchev's claim that he did not want to do anything before the US presidential election that might swing the vote to Vice President Nixon, and his dislike of Nixon. Here is what the memo says:

Following are minor and supplemental items of my conversation with Khrushchev last night.

K mentioned we had pressed him for release RB-46 fliers. He had deliberately not done so until after election as earlier release would have been exploited by Nixon and in his opinion might have changed outcome. Said frankly did not like Nixon and thought President Kennedy much higher caliber. Said Lodge had told him relations would be even better under Nixon than under Eisenhower.

K mentioned Laos only in passing stating hope we would be able reach agreement. No mention of Congo.

K said that if Vienna went well and relations improved hoped would be possible invite Kennedy to visit Soviet Union next year though clearly atmosphere not right for invitation this year.

K pointed out they had abolished foreign bases and settled Austrian problem. They were satisfied Austrian solution. He mentioned he had traveled extensively throughout Austria in 1946 incognito in Generals uniform.

Discussing Division of Germany, mentioned his brother

had supported Whites in Soviet Civil War and I gathered had been killed at that time.

The most interesting thing about this State Department memo is the fact that Khrushchev liked Kennedy over Nixon and did not want to do anything to help Nixon win the election. The other interesting part is the invitation for Kennedy to come to Moscow in 1962 for a visit. That, of course did not happen because of the 1962 Cuban Missile Crisis and other U.S-Soviet disputes like the building of the Berlin Wall that separated the two Germanys. Also going on at the same time was the Kennedy administration's secret plan to topple Castro called Operation Mongoose. No one knows what the relationship between Moscow and Washington would have been if Kennedy had lived. JFK started the ball rolling when he proposed a nuclear test ban treaty with the Soviets that limited nuclear testing in the atmosphere (the Congress passed the bill).

The other important document that this writer had never seen before was in reference to Kennedy's primary campaign in West Virginia that got the attention of the FBI. The West Virginia primary was of considerable importance to Kennedy's race for the White House and there were persistent rumors of money and other favors being handed out to the voters in that state. In the end, Kennedy won the primary and that started him off on his eventual win at the national convention in Los Angeles.

The memo was dated July 5, 1960 from C.A. Evans to a Mr. Rosen entitled "West Virginia Election Law Matters." It said:

Robert Kennedy, former Chief Counsel of the McClellan Committee and brother of Senator Kennedy, telephoned. He advised that Jack Anderson, associate of Drew Pearson, had called Senator Kennedy's office at about 1:45 p.m. today. Anderson talked with one of the Senator's assistants. Anderson is reported to have stated that Drew Pearson had received information that the FBI had conducted an extensive investigation with reference to Senator Kennedy's campaign in West Virginia; that a voluminous FBI report which contained an extensive amount of information concerning Senator Kennedy was being delivered to the

Department today.

Bob Kennedy asked for his own information whether there was any truth to what Anderson said. Kennedy was informed that the FBI had not conducted any investigation of Senator Kennedy in this regard. Bob Kennedy said this was most reassuring and he was aware of our policy of informing reliable Government officials should any request for investigation be made and he knew his brother had never been advised of any FBI investigation.

Bob Kennedy continues to be most enthusiastic and optimistic in his brother's possibility of obtaining the Democratic nomination.

As a matter of background, the allegation publically made with reference to vote on the part of the Kennedy forces in the West Virginia primary did not involve a violation of Federal law. The investigation which we did conduct in West Virginia at the request of the Department concerned the illegal moving of a polling place and was not concerned with Senator Kenney's campaign in any way.

One more interesting nugget from the files is a comment that Khrushchev made about Richard Nixon. "In a 1965 oral history interview conducted by the JFK Presidential Library, Kennedy press secretary Pierre Salinger recounted a meeting with Khrushchev. Salinger says the Soviet leader said, "Mr. Nixon reminds me of a herring salesman who would sell spoiled herring as the real thing." (I guess, Mr. K. was a good judge of character.)

These two memos, the one regarding Nikita Khrushchev's interest in the US presidential election and his interest in having Kennedy elected, as well as the previous unreported FBI investigation of the Kennedy primary campaign in West Virginia, add new insight into the Kennedy era.

Chapter 29
Howard Hunt's JFK Assassination Probe

When the Watergate affair first broke, and after Howard Hunt was arrested along with the other burglars, columnist Dick Russell, then working for the *Village Voice,* interviewed White House advisor Chuck Colson concerning the Nixon/Haldeman June 23, 1972 tape. Russell asked Colson if he thought that Hunt knew anything about the Kennedy assassination. Colson replied, "I doubt it. I really do. I don't think Hunt had anything to do with that."

E. Howard Hunt may not have had "anything to do with that," as Colson said, but information which was found in the Archives via the JFK Records Act indicates that Hunt was, at the very least, quite interested in the assassination of President Kennedy. This information further indicates that a secret report about the roles of Cuba and Fidel Castro was prepared by Hunt and his future Watergate burglar associates—and was, in fact, circulated to Charles Colson and the Nixon circle as well as officials within the CIA. With this information, and other long-obscure Watergate data, a picture seems to be emerging which places the secret Hunt report on the Kennedy assassination at the heart of the feverish cover-up activities of the Nixon circle in the immediate days following the Watergate break-in of June 17, 1972. Beyond that, as will be shown, it appears that several mysterious pieces of information regarding the Kennedy assassination may well have been a central topic of the earliest Watergate cover-up discussions held by Nixon as his men—taped discussions that were permeated not only by the strange references to Hunt, Helms, and "the Cuba thing," but also by various "gaps" of which the 18-minute erasure is the best known. The following information was obtained under the title "E. Howard Hunt's Missing Report on the Kennedy Assassination/Sturgis." From Mike Ewing, HSCA Agency File No. 015106 found in the National Archives.

With the death of Howard Hunt a number of years ago, any information that he had on the Kennedy assassination went to the grave with him (except for his "confession" that was revealed), but his silence over the years only added to the mystery of what he may

Howard Hunt (left) arriving in court, 1973.

or may not have known about the events in Dealey Plaza.

Hunt served as Acting Chief of Station for the CIA in Mexico City in August and September 1963, the exact time that Lee Harvey Oswald is supposed to have been in the city trying to get a passport back to Russia. The CIA took a photograph of a man it said was Oswald coming out of the Russian and Cuban embassies, but this mysterious man certainly was not Oswald. It is inconceivable that Hunt, if he was working in the Mexico City CIA station, did not know about the mysterious comings and goings at the Cuban Consulate and the Soviet Embassy concerning either Oswald involving an imposter.

Hunt alluded to certain CIA activities relating to Dallas and Mexico City that went on during that time. It was revealed in Hunt's 1974 autobiography *Undercover:*

> ...that the CIA did in fact use Dallas as a "backstop" location for changing the identities of CIA agents operating in Mexico City. Hunt told of a CIA break-in at a Communist Embassy that he had coordinated during one of his tours of duty in Mexico City. Before dawn the entry team had flown from Mexico City to Dallas, where they changed identities and flew to Washington.

Hunt always denied that he was in Mexico City at the time that

Oswald was there. Hunt's record at the CIA had been a closely-kept secret and prompted this observation. A Justice Department official who once was denied access to a partial set of requested Hunt CIA records, has remarked, "They treat those Hunt files like they were the Hope Diamond. It's just incredible."

The authors of a 35-page report were very aware of possible links between Watergate affair and the Kennedy assassination, and wrote: "In tracing the genesis of a possible connection between the Watergate and aspects of the Kennedy assassination, the period immediately following the Watergate break-in is crucial, for it is there that the story begins to take shape."

As the Watergate affair began to break in earnest, Charles Colson, the White House counsel and the man who had brought Hunt into the Plumbers Unit, confirmed to John Dean Hunt's links to the Nixon White House. It seems that Hunt had kept a secret safe in his office at the Old Executive Office Building, room 338. Hunt's safe was drilled open on June 19 by the Secret Service and its contents removed. What was found in the safe were a clip of live ammunition, a gun, a holster, secret files on the Plumbers operation regarding Daniel Ellsberg, files concerning Ted Kennedy's Chappaquidick incident, and forged State Department cables concerning the death of President Diem of South Vietnam. But what was missing, and now reported in the document called "E. Howard Hunt's Missing Report on the Kennedy Assassination/Sturgis," is information on another Plumbers probe into the Kennedy assassination.

The story begins with an April 1974 NBC interview with Watergate burglar Bernard Barker by newsmen Robert Rogers and Edwin Newman. "Barker told of a secret assignment that he and fellow Watergate burglar Frank Sturgis had conducted for their important White House friend and patron, Mr. Hunt." Unfortunately, Barker garbled a key point in the interview, mistakenly referring to "the death of Bobby Kennedy," rather than the death of John Kennedy, which was the actual subject of the Barker/Sturgis assignment for Hunt.

This is a partial account of the interview:

Rogers (NBC): And in Miami we learned that Hunt and Barker conducted at least one interview—the results of which supposedly went to the CIA.

Barker: Mr. Sturgis said to me that he had some information about some lady that had been at the home of the Castro family at the time of the death of Bobby Kennedy and that she was telling some very strange stories or very interesting stories, as he put it. I spoke to the lady in Spanish and brought her—took her—to Mr. Hunt. Mr. Hunt personally examined her, in the sense that he questioned her, and he took it down on tapes. Mr. Hunt told me that he would be turning this information over to the old agency.

This information was given to the Ervin Committee then looking into the Watergate affair and stayed buried until the files were opened via the JFK Records Act.

The report speculates that Hunt was trying to tie the Cubans to the Kennedy assassination or "perhaps the more likely explanation behind Hunt's decision to probe the Cuban woman's information about Castro and the Kennedy assassination, is that he was ordered to do so by superiors."

The next part of the story is an interview that Hunt gave in November 1975 with two reporters from the *Providence Journal*, Jack White and Randall Richard. The two reporters questioned Hunt on his possible involvement in the Kennedy assassination, and while Hunt hotly denied that he had anything to do with the Dallas tragedy, he added more information on the then secret probe of the

Howard Hunt at a congressional hearing, 1973.

assassination. Hunt said that one of the burglars at the Watergate complex, Eugenio Martinez, was also involved in the secret Kennedy probe in addition to Frank Sturgis and Bernard Barker. While this was going on, Martinez was still working for the CIA on a retainer basis. Hunt told the newsmen that the interview of the Cuban woman took place in the Ambassador Hotel in Miami, sometime between July 1971 and June 1972, and that Martinez helped translate the woman's story.

Hunt said that the lady was in the Castro household when the news of JFK's death reached him. Castro was shocked and saddened by Kennedy's loss because, "Castro had counted upon John Kennedy to reestablish diplomatic relations, and there had been some sort of understanding."

Further in the interview, Hunt told the reporters that he had sent the secret report to the CIA, and also a copy to Charles Colson. While Hunt did not say who he sent the report to at the Agency, it was most likely, according to the document, CIA Director Richard Helms, who was a good friend of Hunt's.

Hunt said that he kept a copy of the JFK probe for himself and put it in his safe at the White House. But what happened to the secret Hunt report that was supposed to be in the safe? Hunt told the two reporters that he believed that it disappeared on June 19th when John Ehrlichman and John Dean gave it to Patrick Gray of the FBI.

But in the ensuing decades after the Watergate affair, the three most important people in the story—Colson, Dean and Ehrlichman—have refused to speak about what happened to Hunt's secret Plumbers investigation of JFK's death.

Before leaving the White House after being fired, Hunt told Colson that his safe contained sensitive material:

> Before I left the White House for the last time, I stopped by Colson's office, not to see him but to inform Mrs. Hall, whom I knew held the combination to my safe, that it contained sensitive material. I simply told her, "I just want you to know that the safe is loaded."

It seems obvious that Colson knew of the "sensitive" materials in Hunt's safe. So, why the silence all these years?

The Ewing story revealed in the released documents goes on to say:

> As scrambled as the testimony is at this point, a couple of things are clear. The Hunt report relating to the Kennedy assassination is missing. No copy of it has ever surfaced, nor have the tapes that Hunt, Barker, Martinez, and Sturgis made during the probe ever been found.
>
> The possibility that this secret Hunt report was either hidden or destroyed following their opening of his safe on June 19 is obviously strong. Not only did Gray burn "politically sensitive" Hunt documents that he received from Ehrlichman and Dean, Eirchliman and Dean themselves had discussed much the same "game plan" shortly after Hunt's safe was drilled open.

John Dean told the Ervin Committee of an Ehrlichman plan for handling the secret papers in Hunt's safe:

> He told me to shred the documents and "deep six" the briefcase. I asked him what he meant by "deep six." He leaned back in his chair and said, "You drive across the river on your way home at night, don't you?" I said yes. He said, "Well, when you cross over the bridge on your way home, just toss the briefcase into the river."

The Ewing narrative sums up their feelings on what had taken place at that particular moment by saying, "The last thing in the world the Nixon men needed at that point was a secret report on the Kennedy assassination coming out of Hunt's safe—written and produced by Hunt and his burglar friends Barker, Martinez, and Sturgis."

Now, however, the story gets more involved. It concerns one of the Watergate burglars, Frank Sturgis, and possible links he may have had with Lee Oswald.

By June 19, the FBI had sent over a large amount of material it had gathered in the initial Watergate investigation and background material on the men who were arrested. A large amount of information concerned Frank Sturgis, a one-time soldier of fortune, a gunrunner to Cuba, a one-time Castro supporter, and a man with close ties to organized crime in the United States. Part of this report was an article on Sturgis that appeared in the Pompano Beach, Florida *Sun Sentinel* dated November 25-26, 1963 which stated that Frank Fiorini, Head of the Anti-Communist Brigade, said that Lee Oswald had telephone conversations with the Cuban Government G-2 during November 1962.

The article was written by a friend of Sturgis', Jim Buchanan, who at one point was a member of Sturgis's Anti-Communist Brigade which was based in Florida. The FBI report said that upon reading the article, Sturgis said that Buchanan had "misquoted him."

"With his background," the narrative continues, "perhaps it was inevitable that Frank Sturgis would be the one who triggered the secret Hunt probe into the Kennedy assassination, and the very strange stories he had heard about Castro's reaction to it."

In the Bureau's files was another article written by Buchanan concerning Sturgis and Oswald:

> Oswald also tried to infiltrate several other major organizations in Miami, including the Anti-Communist International Brigade, which is headed by Major Frank Fiorini. Fiorini said his outfit turned down Oswald's application because they could not find out anything about his background.

This article concerning Sturgis's possible meeting with Oswald in Miami corresponds to previous statements by Gerry Hemming in which he alleges that he had seen Oswald in the Miami area.

The authors of the Ewing report were deeply troubled about who, in the Nixon administration, ordered the secret Hunt report on the Kennedy assassination to be written in the first place. They were so troubled and intrigued by all they had learned that they wrote this important paragraph summing up their feelings:

> However, a few reasonable inferences (one hesitates to use the word conclusions) can be drawn from this sequence of events. Indeed, E. Howard Hunt's recent brief disclosure

to the two *Providence Journal* reporters of what he and three of his future Watergate burglar associates were up to, may in fact open up a whole new area of Watergate.

After going over all the facts regarding the Hunt safe probe, the writers of the report turned their attention to who might have ordered the inquest in the first place. "Yet with Hunt now disclosing that he sent the secret report to both Charles Colson at the White House and also someone (possibly Director Richard Helms) at the CIA, it would seem likely that either one — or both — of these parties were behind the Hunt probe."

They discussed in the report Richard Helms' continuing interest in the Kennedy assassination inquiry. They noted that the CIA gave the Warren Commission scant cooperation in its investigation of the president's murder, as well as the fact that Helms took an active interest in the investigation of the president's death that was being conducted by Jim Garrison, the District Attorney of New Orleans. In later years, it would be learned that Clay Shaw, who was indicted by Garrison in the JFK killing, had been a CIA agent years earlier and that Helms was actively working on Shaw's behalf.

On August 22, 1973, during a news conference, President Nixon himself made a curious statement on the Kennedy assassination that left reporters in the room wondering what he was talking about. While commenting on a reporter's question concerning the disclosure that Nixon had approved a domestic spying operation called the Houston Plan, President Nixon made the following statement:

> I understand the height of the wiretaps was when Robert Kennedy was Attorney General in 1963. I don't criticize him, however. But if he had 10 more and as a result of wiretaps had been able to discover the Oswald plan it would have been worth it.

Nixon continued to speculate on the Oswald matter:

> I said if 10 more wiretaps could have found the conspiracy, if it was a conspiracy, or the individual, then it

would have been worth it. As far as I'm concerned, I'm no expert on that assassination than anybody else, but my point is that wiretaps in the national security area were very high in the Kennedy administration for a very good reason.

What did President Nixon really mean by his comments on Robert Kennedy's wiretaps and any Oswald connection? It is obvious that the president had an ongoing interest in the background of the Kennedy assassination, knew about the plots to kill Fidel Castro (actually ran them in the Eisenhower administration) and was paranoid about facing Senator Edward Kennedy in the 1972 presidential election contest.

The Ewing report also reveals information on one of the members of President Nixon's Plumbers unit, New York police detective John Caulfield, and his investigation of the Kennedy assassination. As a member of the NYPD's Bureau of Special Services, Caulfield, in late 1963, investigated the activities of the DRE, the militant anti-Castro group that was planning the second invasion of Cuba in the last week of November 1963. Caulfield reported that several members of the DRE were arrested in New York for protesting against the Kennedy administration's actions taken against anti-Castro exile groups. This Caulfield information was given to the Warren Commission, who found it interesting to say the least. Also, at the same time that Caulfield was looking into the actions of the DRE, the FBI was investigating Frank Sturgis and his apparent knowledge of Lee Oswald's possible Cuban activities. The Senate report fails to clarify what role, if any, Caulfield played in the Hunt-JFK probe.

So what do we have here? Howard Hunt's safe was drilled open on June 19, 1972 and its contents removed, minus the Kennedy report. The next day, President Nixon met with H.R. Haldeman presumably to discuss the Watergate affair and possibly the contents of Hunt's safe. Nixon aide Gordon Strachan said that on the same day, Haldeman ordered various confidential files belonging to him be destroyed. Nixon then phoned John Mitchell to talk about Watergate matters but this call was not recorded. Did the conversation that was never recorded have anything to do with the Hunt investigation? We will probably never know.

The Ewing narrative sums up the Hunt-Kennedy probe by saying:

> Whether E. Howard Hunt's report on the Kennedy assassination can yet be found—or whether the circumstances surrounding his and his strange burglar associates' probe of the Dallas murder can be cleared up—can only be hoped for at this time. Until the whole area becomes the subject of renewed questioning and investigation, one is left with the inevitable suspicion that the "smoking gun" of Watergate may indeed date back in some direct or indirect way to another smoking gun that fired the bullet that tore off the upper third of President Kennedy's head.

Chapter 30
Victor Espinosa Hernandez

The name of Victor Espinosa Hernandez has recently come to the attention of JFK researchers from documents released by the HSCA and other forms from the federal government. He was a young man who had ties with many people, as well as groups, both in the United States and Europe, who were actively planning an assassination plot against Fidel Castro and his top aides. He was also well connected with Rolando Cubela, a.k.a. "AMLASH," a CIA-sponsored Cuban doctor who was preparing his own plot to kill Castro.

As we have mentioned, Victor Espinosa Hernandez was born in Cuba and came from a wealthy family involved in farming and the petroleum industry. He went to the University of Havana for only one year before dropping out, and worked for the anti-Batista cadre inside Cuba. In 1955 he left Cuba for the United States where he enrolled at Louisiana State University. The Louisiana connection to the Kennedy assassination has been well documented. A number of people connected with the plots to kill Castro and Kennedy began their operations in New Orleans, including such people as David Ferrie, Clay Shaw, Guy Banister and Lee Harvey Oswald, who was born in New Orleans and spent the summer of 1963 there, plying his trade as a possible double agent.

Upon the death of his grandfather, Victor returned to Cuba to manage the family business. He came into contact with many of the mob figures who were then engaged in the lucrative casino business in Havana, including Mike McClaney and Norman "Roughhouse" Rothman.

He joined a group that took part in an assassination attempt against members of the Batista government. One of his co-conspirators was Rolando Cubela.

After Castro took power, Victor took refuge in the United States, living both in Miami and New York. He was recruited to become a member of the team that were planning the invasion at the Bay of Pigs and took military training in Guatemala and at a camp outside

245

of New Orleans. He participated in several covert missions inside Cuba.

In August 1963, the FBI interviewed two men who gave them information regarding the activities of Victor Hernandez. They identified Hernandez as the person who rented a U-Hall trailer in Illinois destined for New Orleans. They admitted selling 2400 pounds of dynamite in July 1963 to Victor.

It is clear from documents available via the HSCA investigation that the FBI and the CIA had interviews with Espinosa on an ongoing basis.

An F.B.I document dated July 2, 1965 tells of a debriefing session with Espinosa. William Doyle of the CIA informed the FBI on June 4, 1965 that Harold Swenson had come from Washington, DC to interview Espinosa.

> After Espinosa departed the NYO, Swenson advised that 98 percent of the information furnished regarding the alleged assassination plots by ESPINOSA was accurate, and that the only reservation CIA had was that they disliked the two individuals who had contacted ESPINOSA concerning the plot and considered the contacts of ESPINOSA, ALBERTO BLANCO, a.k.a. "El Lobo", and JORGE ROBENO, a.k.a, "Mago," to be individuals of questionable reputation.

Shortly after that meeting, Blanco and Robeno left for Europe, with Robeno heading for Madrid, while Blanco went to Paris. A few days later, Espinosa contacted the New York office of the CIA, telling them that he heard from Robeno and Blanco regarding possible CIA assistance in their plans against Castro. On June 25, 1965, CIA agent William Doyle contacted Harold Swenson asking for his assistance in this matter. Swenson told Doyle that he should inform Espinosa:

> ...this is a very difficult and far reaching question in which CIA could not definitely commit itself. Espinosa was to be advised that all the information furnished by him regarding the alleged plot to assassinate leading Cuban Government figures had been passed on in Washington,

D.C.to the proper authorities, and that for the time being, CIA could not give any definite answer to Espinosa and his friends who were involved in this plot.

Espinosa told the CIA that he was disappointed in their lack of support and also said that in his opinion, "Robeno and Blanco would probably attempt to kill Castro themselves. He also mentioned another man who would take matters into his own hands when it came to the plots against Castro. That man was Rolando Cubela. Espinosa told the CIA that he knew that Cubela had met with Manuel Artime in Rome. According to a report on the subject:

> This meeting between ARTIME and CUBELA was arranged in order for CUBELA to take some "piece of equipment" back to Havana with him. Espinosa stated that he knew that CUBELA took the piece of equipment to Havana and that he had received this equipment from ARTIME. ESPINOSA said that he reasoned that if this equipment belonged to ARTIME, ARTIME had gotten it in the first place from the CIA and that it was given to CUBELA either with or without CIA's approval but in all events CIA certainly knows what this piece of equipment was which CUBELA got from ARTIME.

Agent Swenson confirmed that Artime had met with Cubela in Rome, and that the piece of equipment he took with him was "some type of radio in order to maintain contact with individuals involved in the plot inside and outside Cuba."

In 1965, Espinosa traveled to France and Spain to meet clandestinely with members of the anti-Castro cause. While in Paris, "he was in contact with individuals in a plot to assassinate Fidel Castro and leading Cuban Government Personalities." One of the men he met while in Paris was Rolando Cubela. He also met with Alberto Blanco for a ten-day period. Blanco worked for the Cuban Foreign Ministry and was in Paris to make a tour of the Cuban Embassy. Contrary to what the documents say, Espinosa expressed the opinion that "He [Blanco] had no prior knowledge of this plot and went to Paris on the urging of Cubela, who has been a life-long friend of his. He also stated that involved in the plot was Major Juan Almeida Bosque."

According to CIA files, Bosque was then serving as the First Deputy Minister of the Cuban Revolutionary Armed Forces:

> Espinosa advised that the plot called for the assassination of Fidel Castro, Raul Castro, Ernesto "Che" Guevara and Ramon Valdes. The assassination of these individuals is to take place in public so that everyone can see that the leaders have been killed. The plotters hope to seize the radio station and call for American help.

The targeted date for the murder attempt was July 26, 1965, which was to coincide with the July 26th celebration in Havana.

The information that Espinosa gave to the CIA regarding the plots to kill the leaders of the Cuban government was so sensitive that it was "restricted to the White House and the attorney General."

There is a long memo concerning the activities of Victor Hernandez from Hal Swenson to John Hart which provides a lot of background information. The Agency gave Hernandez the code name AMHINT-2 (he also went by the nickname "Papucho"). In the section called Source, the writer of the memo identified "Victor Espinosa Hernandez, a PM trainee who was terminated on 20 March 1961 as a malcontent."

Detailed in the area called Supplemental Data, this is what Espinozsa told his listener that day:

> I do not have a high regard for the CIA or for most of the exiled Cubans but I am against the Castro regime for which reason I have become involved in these matters about which I must be sure the CIA is informed. I contacted the INS and the FBI because through them I could ensure contact with a responsible CIA officer.
>
> I was a good friend of Rolando Cubela. We conspired together against BATISTA supporters and we planned assassinations of Batista supporters. We carried out the killing of one of the SIN chiefs, Rico Gafan, successfully. A lot of the things the anti-Batista students did were not

effective but we did more than talk and this old assassination is proof that people like Rolando and myself act.

After Castro took over I left Cuba and engaged in anti-Castro activities. I got shot in the process, I was betrayed by some of the Cuban exiles when I was going to bomb Cuba, I saw how the CIA bungled and I became bitter. I was bitter about Rolando too. I thought that he had turned communist, I sent him a message, a long time ago, telling him that he was a traitor and no friend of mine. That was when a Pan American stewardess whom he liked came to me with a message from him about how he was still a friend of mine and things were not like they seemed. I got mad and told her to tell him off for me and I showed her the bullet wound in my leg that I had because I was fighting Castro and those with him like Rolando. Afterwards I did not hear from Rolando until just a little while ago.

It was in May when I got a letter from an old friend, Luis Fernandez, He had written to me before to let me know that he is working for the CIA in Paris. This letter in May was pretty confusing but Luis made it clear that there was something very important, that it involved Rolando Cubela, that Rolando wanted me to go to Paris on an urgent matter, and that another friend, Luis Trasencos, knew something about it. The letter said that the CIA knew about this and that Luis Fernandez thought maybe the CIA already had told me to go to Paris, although he was not sure.

I decided to go to Paris because of the mention of Rolando. The CIA had taken my old Cuban passport when I was in training in Guatemala and never returned it. Also, because I got caught when I tried to bomb Cuba, the INS had warned me not to travel outside the US saying I could go to jail for five years and I could not get a reentry permit and all that. However, I checked with an INS officer who knew me. He said that probably the INS was not so interested in me anymore and I probably could get a reentry. Because the letter was so pressing in my travelling at once, I decided not to go through a lot of red tape. I went to Florida to see my brother, Rene. He arranged through some friends whom

I don't know to get me a false Cuban passport. I bought a ticket and left for Paris without having any trouble. I am not sure about the dates and the sequence of travel because everything was so hurried. I went to London as well as to Paris and I tried to go to Spain but had to turn back. Anyway, I remember the important things.

At Paris, I telephoned Luis Trasencos who invited me to lunch in his apartment. When I got there I found Alberto Blanco, "El Loco," whom I have known since early 1959 and whom I considered a traitor. I called Luis aside to tell him this but Luis explained that Blanco was instructed by Rolando Cubela to see me, that Loco and Rolando are against Castro, and that my seeing Loco was the reason that it was so urgent for me to come to Paris.

Rolando Cubela had been in Paris a couple of months earlier and, according to El Loco, had left a letter instructing El Loco to get word to me personally and asking that I get in touch with the CIA on the highest level. El Loco did not have the letter with him but I believe it. I know that Cubans are liars and exaggerate and are insecure and all that is wrong about them but I know what is good about them and how to check on things. So I crossed questioned El Loco and others until I was sure that they told me the truth. What I am telling you is what I found out from El Loco, confirmed later through Robeno, and confirmed in part through questioning others who know parts of the story but not all of it.

Rolando Cubela plans to kill Fidel and Raul Castro and other key men in the regime. Rolando has a house at Veradero Beach adjacent to the house of Fidel, so it is easy for Rolando to get Fidel anytime. The idea is not just to kill Fidel but to change everything in Cuba so Rolando has the cooperation of other people whose names I do not know but except for El Loco and El Mago Robeno and ALMEIDA. Rolando is very security conscious so he does not want people involved to know any more than is necessary. You must understand the danger to these people. What I can tell you now is that El Loco has his faults and so does Robeno, but both worship Rolando and are trustworthy insofar as he is concerned.

Some of the CIA people are untrustworthy. This is what bothers Rolando Cubela and El Loco and El Mago and me too. This is why Rolando wants me to get his message through. He wants an answer fast. The message is that Cubela and the others with him are able to kill Fidel and others in the regime, but they need some help and they need to know whether the CIA and the US Government are with them and willing to support them or not. This is important because Rolando says that he cannot delay more than three or four months. That is the maximum. Cuban security forces would find out and arrest everyone if there is more delay.

El Loco and El Mago said that on 5 or 6 June someone is passing through Madrid en route from Prague to Havana and that this person could carry the answer to El Mago but I suppose I can fly to Madrid to give it in person and, if you want, one of you can accompany me. I myself suspect that Rolando will move earlier than in two or three months. I believe that 26 July is a good date because all the chief targets will be assembled so it will be easier to get them all fast, but Rolando did not send me this as his plan.

El Loco and El Mago have access to any Cuban Embassy in Europe and these embassies are engaged in contacts with communists and in subversion. The same applies to embassies in Africa. El Loco and El Mago could have been giving you valuable information all along. Yet your people play security games and do not use people like this. Instead, you use unreliable and risky people.

Rolando will send someone to see you if you agree to support him. Among other things, Rolando will need some money, Cuban not American, or some gold or something because some people have to be bought. Also he might need help getting out. Anyway, he needs to know your stand.[8]

What we have here is Victor Espinosa Hernandez spilling his guts to the CIA regarding his efforts, along with others, to eliminate the leaders of the Cuban government by whatever means possible.

8 RIF No. 104-10169-10253: CIA Ops and Plot to Kill Fidel Castro, Raul Castro and other key figures of the Present Regime in Cuba.

He enlisted the aid of Rolando Cubela, aka, AMLASH, in whom the Agency put its highest trust to carry out the deed. The AMLASH plot was one of the most sensitive covert actions taken by the CIA in its efforts to kill Castro, and has many repercussions that will be covered in later chapters of this book.

Another man Espinosa worked with was Juan Almeida Bosque, to whom the CIA turned in its efforts to overthrow the Cuban government in a project called AMWORLD which has been much written about.

Victor Espinosa Hernandez was one of the many people who took matters into their own hands in order to free Cuba from the grip of the Castro brothers. It was only many decades later with the death of Fidel Castro that his (and many others,) dreams were finally realized.

Chapter 31
Richard Goodwin & Latin America

Richard Goodwin was a speechwriter for John Kennedy when he ran against Richard Nixon in the presidential campaign of 1960. Goodwin was called upon in the latter stages of the 1960 campaign to write a speech attacking the Eisenhower administration's lack of effort to oust Castro from power. The speech was released without Kennedy's approval, yet it made headlines throughout the country. Nixon attacked Kennedy for being reckless regarding US actions against Cuba. But what the country did not know was that the Vice President was running the administration's secret effort to get rid of Castro.

When Kennedy was elected, he gave Richard Goodwin a large role in the administration's efforts to remove Castro from power. Goodwin was informally assigned to work with Robert Kennedy who oversaw the US government's anti-Castro policies. Newly released CIA documents show that Goodwin wrote many important internal memos regarding the Kennedy administration's Cuban policy. One memo dated November 1, 1961 reads as follows:

> I believe that a commando operation for Cuba, as discussed with you by the Attorney General, is the only effective way to handle an all out attack on the Cuban problem. The beauty of the operation over the next few months is that we cannot lose. If the best happens, we will unseat Castro. If not, we will emerge with a stronger underground, better propaganda and a far clearer idea of the dimensions of the problems which affect us. I believe that the Attorney General would be the most effective commander of such an operation. Either I or someone else should be assigned to him as Deputy for this activity, since he obviously will not be able to devote full time to it. His role should be told to only a few people at the very top with most of the contract work in carrying out his decisions left to this deputy [Goodwin].

A November 2, 1961 Goodwin memo to JFK and RFK makes his role in the Castro plots more evident. Goodwin outlined a plan in which the CIA would lend a top-flight counterinsurgency expert to work with the Cuba Group. He outlined a five-point plan of operations against Castro including, "intelligence collection and evaluation, guerilla and underground operations, propaganda, economic warfare and diplomatic relations."

He suggested that writer Tad Szulc, who worked for the *New York Times,* would be a good candidate for propaganda purposes. Tad Szulc was on good terms with President Kennedy and his brother Robert and often times discussed the situation in Cuba with both of them.

In later years, Goodwin would say that in regard to Cuba, Robert Kennedy did nothing that his brother, the president, did not tell him to do.

After the president's murder, despite his objections, Goodwin worked for President Lyndon Johnson as a speechwriter, the same job he did for JFK.

A memo that was written on May 27, 1975 described a meeting which took place at Goodwin's residence in Washington at 1536 32nd St. NW. Entitled "Intelligence Activities in Latin America,"

Richard Goodwin (left) and a staffer with LBJ in the 1960s.

which was submitted by Gregory Treverton. Mr. Goodwin talked extensively on his knowledge of all things that were going on in that part of the world.

The participants in the meeting were members of the Senate Select Committee: David Aaron, Rick Inderfurth, and Greg Treverton.

The memo begins as follows:

> During the 1960 Presidential campaign, Goodwin did foreign policy work for John Kennedy, especially in Latin America. After the election he moved to the White House to handle Latin America. During that period he spoke with the President about a Latin American matter on the average of once a day. Goodwin left the White House in the fall of 1962, becoming Deputy Assistant Secretary of State for Inter-American Affairs under, first, Robert Woodward and then Edwin Martin. After working for the Peace Corps, Goodwin was brought back to the White House by President Johnson, in the spring of 1964, after the Panama crisis. At that time, however, he did not specialize on Latin America, instead writing speeches for Johnson. He left the Administration late in 1965.

The next topic in the memo dealt with the area of assassinations which was then being looked at by the CIA in its Castro plots.

> Assassinations: In general, Goodwin had not heard much specific talk of assassinations, although it would not have surprised him if it had gone on. He mentioned one specific instance in which he had heard talk of assassinating Castro. After the Bay of Pigs, a Cuban Task Force was established, first chaired by Paul Nitze and then by Goodwin in his capacity as White House Staff Officer. At a meeting of the Task Force, held at the State Department, McNamara suggested "getting rid of Castro," someone from the CIA, perhaps Bissell, then asked if McNamara meant "Executive Action." McNamara responded that he did and stressed his interest in the idea. However, Goodwin did not bring

the topic up later in the meeting after McNamara left. To Goodwin, the idea was not reasonable even apart from moral objections, for the Bay of Pigs had shown that Cuba was politically stable; Castro would merely have been replaced with Raul or with Che Guevara, both worse than Castro. Somewhat later, Goodwin sat in on an interview Tad Szulc had with Kennedy in which the President pledged not to kill Castro. Szulc reported that pledge in an article in *Esquire*. When he finished his period as Chairman of the Cuba Task Force, Goodwin wrote a memo recommending that the United States let Castro alone; anything the United States did to him could only buttress his position in Latin America.

During his time at the State Department, Goodwin met every week or so with J.C. King, Chief of the Western Hemisphere Division of the CIA, and King never mentioned a plan to assassinate Castro. Nor did Robert Kennedy ever mention such a plan to Goodwin when Goodwin worked for Kennedy, in 1966 and 1967.

Goodwin did believe, however, that the United States was involved, at least indirectly, in the successful plot on Trujillo's life. During the Eisenhower administration, the United States had severed diplomatic relations with Trujillo and attempted to isolate the Dominican Republic. There were frequent reports that Trujillo was about to be assassinated, but the assassination never came off. In fact, the government was surprised when it occurred. Henry Dearborn, the American Consul in Santo Domingo, had been charged with staying in contact with anti-Trujillo forces. Prior to the assassination, he had transferred some weapons, presumably handguns, to those forces. Goodwin suspected that the President probably did not know of the gun transfer, but he said that the assassination and the US role with respect to it would have come as no surprise to the President. He doubted that the CIA even would have had to clear the transfer, although a general policy of that sort might have been passed by the Special Group.

Goodwin reported no other mention of assassinations. In fact, he said he once heard a CIA man say that assassination was a bad idea because once started, it never ended. However, an agent in the field might regard killings of one sort or another as within his mission in supporting one political faction over another. And of course someone might have gotten carried away. It was clear from the Bay of Pigs that the CIA sometimes acted without, or even against, instructions (e.g. by bringing Batista followers into the Bay of Pigs invasion team). In general, Latin American work seemed to attract the worst personnel in all Washington agencies including the CIA.[9]

The next topic on the agenda concerned CIA activities in Brazil:

Goodwin knew little of CIA activities in Brazil. The United States had strongly backed Quadros and never liked Goulart. In the period before 1964, the US gave political support to anti-Goulart factions: followers of Kubit and even to the Furtado in the Brazilian northeast [there is a long deleted section after this sentence]. On the military side, Walters was brought from Rome to keep a contact with the Brazilian military. How much further Walter's activities might have extended, Goodwin did not know.

Chile was next on the agenda, and while Chile would not play a large part in its relations with the United States under the Kennedy administration, it would be a large ingredient in US relations during the Nixon administration when the US took covert steps to oust the legitimate government of President Salvador Allende.

CIA Activities in Chile:
The Kennedy administration decided that left wing democratic forces in Latin America were the only means of combating communist influence and promoting development in the region. That decision was applied to Chile, and the US switched its support from the conservative Alessandri. Goodwin sat in on meetings of the Special Group only rarely, only if Latin America were the subject

9 RIF No. 157-10002-10083: Intelligence Activities in Latin America, 5-27-75.

of the meeting. As he remembered it, the proposals that came to the Special Group were general statements, policy papers, not descriptions of recipients of support or conduits. In line with the policy, support was given to left democratic political elements. The US certainly provided assistance to the Christian Democrats, but Goodwin did not know how much. He contested, however, the assertion that the Chilean election was the most intensely watched election in Washington since the 1948 Italian campaign. From his vantage point in the White House it did not seem so.

Changes during the Johnson Administration:

Johnson cared less about Latin America than had Kennedy—Johnson was interested only in Mexico—and so knew less about covert actions in the region. Thomas Mann was left to run Latin American policy, although, the President did become active in the two crisis—Panama and the Dominican Republic. Goodwin saw a sharp change in United States' policy under Mann. Mann supported the military and conservative elements in Latin American societies, and American support for left democratic reform ended. Goodwin professed himself puzzled by Johnson's assertion that he had discovered a "murder incorporated" in the Caribbean. The only specific instance Johnson ever cited was Trujillo, yet Johnson had known about the Trujillo assassination from the very beginning and so could hardly have "discovered" it after the became President.

Covert Operations and Counterinsurgency:

When asked about the ethos surrounding covert actions during the Kennedy Administration, Goodwin responded that the major emphasis was counterinsurgency, not covert action. There was certainly no reluctance to use covert action, but no one believed that American objectives could be secured through it. Counterinsurgency was something different. A good deal of money was spent training police through AID, much more was spent through the Pentagon equipping Latin American militaries, and there was as well some CIA activity. At that point, the US really believed that the communists could not get elected to power and

Richard Goodwin in the 1980s.

that the threat was subversion. Paramilitary operations were considered by the Special Group (counterinsurgency). Latin American matters was considered a kind of training ground for Southeast Asia. Goodwin believed that in sum US counterinsurgency efforts made little difference to the course of events in Latin America. Cuba could not in any case provide support to guerilla movements in South America without substantial support from the Soviet Union, and the guerilla movements that began had little indigenous support.

In response to a question about NSAM's, Goodwin noted that these came out of the Bundy shop, which had little formal staff. Goodwin often wrote these documents. They were both general and, on occasion, specific, indicating groups to be supported and the like. Kennedy wanted to know the details of American activities in Latin America.

Goodwin Suggestions:

Goodwin believed it impossible to control the activities of intelligence organizations without becoming involved in their day-to-day operations. What is required is an active Congressional committee, on the model of the early Joint

259

Atomic Energy Committee, with an active staff. One the President is permitted both to decide what is a major operation, and thus needs to be communicated to Congress, and who to tell, the game is over. Confidence in men will not do; institutional checks are required.

With respect to people to be interviewed, Goodwin mentioned that the Station Chief in Mexico functioned as a kind of regional sub-director. He also thought we might talk with the FBI person in Puerto Rico, with Arthur Schlesinger, and with Tad Szulc. In response to a question, Goodwin indicated that Nixon had been interested in the Bay of Pigs through Cushman. He thought that Douglas Dillon might know of that.

Richard Goodwin, one of the "wiz-kids" whom JFK brought with him into the White House to staff his New Frontier, died in May 2018 at age 86. He was married to presidential historian and author Doris Kearns Goodwin.

Chapter 32
The Riddle of Che

The charismatic leader of the Cuban revolution, Ernesto "Che" Guevara is one of the non-Kennedy related topics that were covered via the release of documents in the last two years, along with those released from the private research organization, the National Security Archive which documents the entire Cold War period. The legend of Che is one that still resonates all these years after his death on October 9, 1967 in Bolivia. He is still a cult figure for thousands of his followers as a revolutionary who fought for the independence of his country and, like Fidel and Raul, was targeted for assassination by the United States.

Che Guevara was born on June 14, 1928 in Rosario, Argentina. He was central figure in the Cuban revolution that began with the overthrow of the hated Batista government by a young and brash Fidel Castro in the mountains of Cuba. He was the eldest son of five children from a middle-class family of Spanish descent and leftist political beliefs. He entered medical school and graduated in 1953. After getting his medical degree, Che traveled across South America where he witnessed the widespread poverty that was the common theme among the majority of the people he met. Seeing the horrible conditions that these people endured, his believed that the only way to break the cycle of poverty was armed revolution against the existing order. During his sojourn across South America, he wrote a journal called *The Motorcycle Diaries: Notes on a Latin American Journey.*

Returning home to Argentina he witnessed the overthrow of the Arbenz government in Guatemala in which the United States took an active part via the CIA. The ouster of Arbenz was the catalyst that drove Guevara into the camp of like-minded individuals who believed in armed revolution. It was then that he linked up with Fidel Castro in Cuba and it was there that his legend began.

Guevara made it to Cuba where he teamed up with Castro and his small band or revolutionaries, then hiding out in Oriente Province. In December 1956, about 81 men, including Fidel, were spotted by Batista's forces and in a fierce firefight, almost all the men were killed. Guevara was one of the lucky ones to escape. They regrouped to fight another day.

Over time, the rebels consolidated their position, making allies of the locals in Cuba who hated Batista and agreed to join the rebel cause. Soon, guns and ammunition were coming in and Castro's forces made hit-and-run raids against Batista's forces. Che served as the doctor for the revolution, treating the wounded and working as Fidel's most trusted lieutenant. However, "the complex Guevara, though trained as a healer, also, on occasion, acted as the executioner (or ordered the execution) of suspected traitors and deserters."

"After Castro's victorious troops entered Havana on January 8, 1959, Guevara served for several months at La Cabana prison, where he oversaw the executions of individuals deemed to be enemies of the revolution." He then became a Cuban citizen, and took a high position in the new government, spouting his Marxist theories which soon took root, taking direct aim at the United States as being evil incarnate in the world. He took jobs as the chief of the Industrial Department of the National Institute of Agrarian Reform, the president of the National Bank of Cuba, and minister of Industry.

Che found time to write a book on his new revolutionary theory called *Guerilla War,* 1961, in which he spelled out his vision of

Ernesto "Che" Guevara in Cuba, 1958.

revolution throughout Latin America, following in the Cuban model.

Over time, though, Che became disenchanted with the Soviet Union and its policies towards Cuba, and felt betrayed after the Cuban Missile Crisis of 1962 when the Soviet Union dismantled its nuclear missiles and returned them home.

As his views changed, he grew disillusioned with the Cuban Revolution and in April 1965, he dropped out of sight and turned to a new arena of conflict: the Congo. At this time, he resigned his positions with the Cuban government and renounced his Cuban citizenship. After the Congo fiasco, he somehow made it to Bolivia where he took up arms against that nation. He led a group of revolutionaries in the region of Santa Cruz, and after a number of military successes, he found himself on the run from the Bolivian army, a man desperate to get out of the precarious situation he found himself in.

On October 8, 1967, his armed group was almost wiped out by a highly trained unit of the Bolivian army that was advised by members of the CIA. Guevara was wounded in the attack, was captured and shot. "Before his body disappeared to be securely buried, his hands were cut off, they were preserved so that his fingerprints could be used to confirm his identity.[10]

The newly released documents give a broader survey of the CIA's role in his capture, along with information on the relationship between the Cuban regime of Fidel Castro and the Soviet Union during this time.

The CIA had been monitoring Che's activities in Cuba and his hot, revolutionary pronouncements since he joined Fidel's band of brothers. A memorandum dated October 18, 1965 called "The Fall of Che Guevara and the Changing Face of the Cuba Revolution" is a case in point:

Summary. 1) Fidel Castro's willingness to drop Ernest "Che" Guevara confirms the shift in Cuban policies that has been under way for about the past year. Guevara's fall from power apparently resulted from his persistent opposition to the practical policies recommended by the Soviet Union. His views on Cuba's economic development and foreign

---

10 :Che Guevara: Biography, Facts, Fidel Castro, & Death." Britannica.com.

policy—reflecting his general opposition to Soviet advice—both seem to have played a role.

2) Guevara, who has been considered Cuba's most militant revolutionary spokesman, disapproved of Castro's alignment with the USSR in the Sino-Soviet dispute and of his willingness to diminish Cuba's role as a catalyst and supporter of revolutions in Latin America and Africa. This side of the controversy has been amply treated elsewhere.

3) While he was in favor with Fidel Castro, Che Guevara was one of the most important architects of the Cuban economy. He retained this role for some time, even after his industrialization plan had been proven wrong and some of his other policies were being challenged. Not until July 1964, when President Dorticos became the Minister of Economy and the Director of the State Planning Board, did Guevara's position really begin to weaken. Since that time Fidel Castro has devoted most of his energy to Cuban internal matters, and to finding remedies for the disastrous effects of the regime's early policies—largely those engineered by Guevara.

4) From the outset Guevara had encouraged the rapid nationalization and centralization of the economy, and by the spring of 1961, the Cuban economy was almost entirely state owned. Although he was not a trained economist, Guevara convinced Castro against the objections of Carlos Rafael Rodrigues and others, that accelerated industrialization was necessary. He maintained that a diversification of agricultural production and increased investment in industry was required to end dependence on sugar and Cuba's "economic enslavement" by the US By the time Guevara and Castro admitted in late 1963, that the industrialization plan must be scaled down to reassign resources to sugar production, Guevara's policies had brought the economy to its lowest point since Castro came to power.

The US government was also watching how the Soviet Union acted with regarded to Cuba and its internal and external developments. One thing they watched closely was the activity of

Che Guevara.

A CIA Intelligence Information Cable of October 17, 1967 called "Background of Soviet Premier Aleksey Kosygin's Visit to Havana and Content of Discussions between Kosygin and Cuban Premier Fidel Castro" gives a good readout on their discussions about Guevara and the goings on in Latin America:

> In late 1966, [blanked out] ...Brezhnev strongly criticized the dispatch of Ernesto "Che" Guevara to Bolivia and Castro's activity in Latin America. During Kosygin's visit, Castro explained the basis of his revolutionary policy. Cuba evaluated the Kosygin visit as productive, although it was clear that divergent views continued to exist regarding revolutionary activity in Latin America.
>
> In the fall of 1966, Castro informed Brezhnev that Ernesto "Che" Guevara, with men and material furnished by Cuba, had gone to Bolivia to mount a revolution within that country. In June 1967, Brezhnev, in response to a question about Guevara, replied that he expressed his disappointment at the failure of Castro to give the Soviet Union advance notice concerning the dispatch of Guevara, and in strong terms criticized the decision of Castro to undertake guerilla activities in Bolivia or other Latin American countries. Brezhnev stated that such activities were harmful to the true interests of the communist cause and inquired as to "what right" Castro had to foment revolution in Latin America without appropriate coordination with the other "socialist" countries.
>
> It appears that Castro was irritated at Brezhnev [blank]. The Soviets decided that a visit to Cuba by one of the Soviet leaders was advisable. Plans for the visit had been completed before the Middle East crisis erupted in the spring of 1967. Subsequently, when it was decided that Premier Kosygin would visit the United States to address the United Nations General Assembly concerning the Middle East crisis, it was agreed that Kosygin would return to Moscow via Havana. The primary purpose of Kosygin's trip to Havana 26-30 June 1967 was to inform Castro concerning the Middle East

crisis, notably to explain Soviet policy regarding the crisis. A secondary but important reason for the trip was to discuss with Castro the subject of Cuban revolutionary activity in Latin America. Kosygin repeated the Soviet view that Castro was harming the communist cause through sponsorship of guerilla activity in Latin America and through providing support to various anti-government groups, which although they claimed to be "socialists" or communist, were engaged in disputes with the "legitimate" Latin American communist parties, i.e., those favored by the USSR.

In replying to Kosygin, Castro [redacted] ...stated that Che Guevara had gone to Bolivia in accordance with the same "right" as that under which Guevara had come to Cuba to aid Castro in the revolutionary struggle against Batista; the "right" of every Latin American to contribute to the liberation of his country and the entire continent of Latin America. Castro then said that he wished to explain the revolutionary tradition in Latin America, and went on to describe the feats of the leading Latin American "Liberators", notably Bolivar and San Martin.

Despite the open disagreement concerning revolutionary action, the discussions with Kosygin concerning economic and military aid from the Soviet Union to Cuba were held in an amicable atmosphere. The Soviets indicated that they were willing to continue to supply Cuba with considerable amounts of economic aid and that the military aid programs, especially those concerned with the modernization of the Cuban armed forces, would be continued.

After Kosygin's departure the Cuban leadership assessed the visit as having been a useful one. The Cuban leaders judged that they had clearly explained the Cuban revolutionary attitude to the Soviets, but that there had been no serious deterioration of relations between the two nations. The Cubans were especially pleased to see that although major disagreement existed in the political sector, relations in the economic and military had remained on a friendly and productive basis.

The story now turns to the last days of Che Guevara and of his final downfall.

The Soviet leaders were not the only ones interested in the comings and goings of Che Guevara in his last days. The boys at Langley headquarters too were following his actions in Bolivia with keen interest. Documents brought to life in the past few years show how he was killed and the reaction of the American government to that event. One report reads as follows:

> Bolivia: Cuban-supported guerillas have been nearly wiped out by recent army operations. For the past three weeks, the Bolivian Army has scored a number of successes against the guerillas. In the latest encounter at least seven guerillas were killed. One of these has been tentatively identified as Ernesto "Che" Guevara. The Bolivian Army believes that the remaining guerillas are surrounded and will soon be eliminated. The defeat of the guerillas will be a severe blow to Fidel Castro. Although in itself this is not likely to weaken Castro's determination to continue to foment armed rebellion in the hemisphere, it will dim the enthusiasm of many Latin American extremists who have been making plans along these lines.

The story of how Che met his demise is written in a CIA release called "Effects of Che Guevara's Death":

> The death of Ernesto "Che" Guevara at the hands of the Bolivian Army has dealt the Cuban sponsored guerilla movement in Latin America its sharpest blow to date. Documents seized over the past several months indicate that Guevara entered Bolivia in November 1966 and was still in the process of organizing and training a guerilla band when he was forced into combat with an army patrol the following March. Although the first series of contacts with Bolivian troops resulted in one-sided victories for the guerillas, the tide gradually turned, culminating in Guevara's capture on 8 October and his death the next day. Circumstances are still clouded but it is probable that Guevara, injured in the

fighting, was captured alive and later executed.

Fidel Castro admitted Guevara's presence in Bolivia on 15 October when he delivered a somber and emotional two-hour speech, conceding, "We have reached the conclusion that these news reports concerning the death of Major Ernesto Guevara are sadly true."

The remaining guerillas with Guevara's are under strong pressure from the Bolivian army, which is continuing its mop-up operations. The guerillas, now under the leadership of Guido Peredo, are few in number and are reportedly short of food and ammunition.

Castro apparently has written them off as an effective fighting force. In his speech he said: "There is no question that the guerilla movement in Bolivia is in a phase in which the survival of the guerillas depends basically on their own strength. So, it is a matter of survival rather than of military capability."

Castro has certainly been dealt a severe psychological reverse. Cuban involvement with the insurgents and Havana's known desire to make Bolivia an example of victorious armed struggle are well documented. Guevara's death will further dissipate the myth of guerilla invincibility and will dim the enthusiasm of others.

On October 12, 1967, the US State Department wrote a memo called "Guevara's Death—the Meaning for Latin America." The most relevant parts are the following:

The mystery of Guevara. Argentine-born Ernesto "Che" Guvara, Fidel Castro's right hand man and chief lieutenant in the Sierra Maestra, author of a book on guerilla tactitc, one-time president of Cuba's National Bank under Castro and later Minister of Industries, mysteriously disappeared in March 1965. Rumor said that he was ill, or that he had been put to death by Castro, or that he was in the Dominican Republic during its civil war or in Vietnam or in the Congo. In October 1965, Castro finally announced that Guevara had renounced his Cuban citizenship and set off to devote his services to the revolutionary cause in other lands. Rumors as to his whereabouts continued, but until recently there was no substantial evidence to prove even that he was still alive.

Guevara makes a strong comeback. The March 1965 disappearance of Guevara occurred during a period when Fidel Castro was toning down his emphaisis on violent revolution and trying to expose his differences with the traditional pro-Soviet communist parties in Latin America. But it was not long before Castro again began to favor openly the independent revolutionary theory which he and Guevara had developed based on their view of the Cuban revolution. Since the Tricontinental Conference in Havana in January 1966, Castro has advocated with increasing stridency the thesis which is set forth most clearly in a book entitled "Revolution Within the Revolution" by Castro's principal theoretical apologist, French Marxist intellectual Jules Regio Debray. Disgusted with the "peaceful path-to-power, arguments of the Latin American old-line communist parties—especially the Venezulean CP—and their Soviet supporters, Fidel and Debray have asserted that Latin America is ripe for insurgency now and have specified that the rural guerilla movment rather than any urban-based communist party or other group must be the focal point and the headquarters of the insurgency.

Ernesto "Che" Guevara was many things to many people, a revolutionary, a Marxist theorist, and a champion of the poor, fighting against the ruling elite. He was a hero to many, despised by many more, (look how much the American government took an interest in his life, and now it helped hunt him down in the wilds of Bolivia). Chewas as large in death as he was in life.

Chapter 33
The Deposition of Gerry Hemming

On March 21, 1978, the HSCA provided a 5five-page summary of the deposition of soldier of fortune Gerry Patrick Hemming for the historical record. The subjects that Hemming covered in his deposition were "Anti-Castro activities, Frank Sturgis, the CIA, and Oswald, Lee, Post-Russian period, associates and relatives." The Hemming deposition took place one day in Miami, Florida where Hemming and his associates were waging a covert war against the regime of Fidel Castro, using any available method to get the job done. Hemming was a storyteller and would talk to anyone who'd listen. There were rumors over the years that Hemming was working for the CIA, the FBI, or some other US intelligence agency. This writer met Hemming by chance in the early 1990s in Washington at the headquarters of the Assassination Archives run by James Lesar. Hemming and his friend Howard Davis spoke to me about all sorts of adventures he took part in, and I later did an interview with him for my magazine *Back Channels*. He was an interesting character to say the least, and over the years he made appearances at various JFK assassination conferences that were held each year in different parts of the country. Before going into the context of his deposition, a little background of Hemming is in order.

In the late 1950s, Gerry Hemming was part of an anti-Castro group in Florida called the Intercontinental Penetration Force, a.k.a. Interpen. Their unofficial headquarters was a rooming house operated by a spry, elderly lady named Neli Hamilton. It was from here that they planned their secret war against Castro

As a young man, Gerry joined the Marines in 1954, after enlisting while still under age. He took basic training at Jacksonville, Florida and later was selected to work as an air controller. He served on duty stations in Kansas, California, and Hawaii. While never actually serving with the ONI (Office of Naval Intelligence), he was approached by them shortly before his discharge. "They were interested in what I was doing with Castro in Cuba, supplying them with weapons. They wanted to get some information about security violations at Guantanamo where some time previously some naval and marine personnel were captured by Raul Castro," he said. Hemming said that at this time some of the Americans at the base were supplying guns and ammo to the rebels.

While in the Marines, Hemming wanted to join the ROTC program because he wanted engage in the Special Forces training program but he was not successful. He left the Marines in1958 and enrolled in the officer's candidate preparatory school for the Naval Academy where he stayed for a short period of time. "I decided that the Cuban thing was more in line with my warfare goals."

Hemming returned to California in October 1958 and worked at odd jobs like heavy labor. He left for Cuba via Miami in the latter part of February 1958 and immediately took up the Castro cause. CIA documents give the following reasons for his joining the rebel army:

A) A strong desire to experience the excitement and glamor of warfare, and particularly guerilla warfare, and the opportunity to gain experience in the field.

B) The opportunity to combine mentioned desire with identification with a "just" cause.

C) A desire to see for himself what was going on in Cuba, and possibly to carve a niche for himself from which he might be able to influence later developments.

Once in Cuba, Hemming, according to the CIA papers, met with Captain Johnny Mitchell, a US national who was serving in the Headquarters General Staff, Camp Columbia. It seems that Mitchell got along so well with Hemming that Mitchell gave him a pass for the base. There, Hemming talked to a number of Cuban military officers and told them that he had been in contact with the Cuban Consul's office in Los Angeles before coming to Cuba. It was there, at the new Cuban mission in Monterey Park, that Hemming was to have his first encounter with Lee Harvey Oswald.

A Cuban army officer named Camilo Cienfuegos took a liking to Hemming and appointed him to a new paratroop group he was forming. Hemming went into the unit as a Sergeant, having been turned down as an officer by another Cuban officer. Hemming stayed with this unit until December 1959, helping to train paratroops at

271

Gerry Patrick Hemming circa 1960.

the San Antonio de los Banos Air Force Base and later near San Jose de los Lajoas.

In December 1959, Hemming transferred to the Cuban Air Force and was stationed at the San Juan AFB where he flew patrols and helped train the militia. He was discharged from the Cuban Air Force in June 1960, flew to Mexico City and stayed there until the end of August. One month later he returned to the US via San Antonio, Texas.

Hemming had a long history of gunrunning and it was through this business that he met Lee Oswald. One day, as Hemming was plying his trade at the Cuban Consulate in Los Angeles in 1959, he was told by a Cuban "that there was an American looking for me. I went out and there was Oswald standing there. Oswald said he wanted to join the group. I was abrupt with him and ran him off."

The next morning Hemming found Oswald sitting in the ante-room. Hemming asked what Oswald was doing there. The Cubans thought Oswald was a friend of Hemming's because Oswald had asked to speak to "the American." According to Hemming, Oswald was still on active duty with the Marines and Hemming was livid that the Cubans would invite an American military man into the building. Hemming feared an "international incident" should Oswald be discovered. At that point, Hemming took Oswald aside and said, "What is it you want?," thinking that the young Marine was some sort of a plant. Oswald replied, "I want to go to Cuba and join the revolution."

According to Hemming, Oswald, who had never met him before,

began using military code words describing where he was stationed (LTA Base) and what kind of work he did, and knew of Hemming's military background. "Marines don't talk to civilians and use that slang. They would only say it to someone who they knew was a Marine. He's a snitch, or somebody sending me somebody and now he's going to tell me about me," said an incredulous Hemming. As they parted, Oswald said to Hemming, "I'll find you there [in Cuba]. I know how to find people."

While he was in Cuba working for the revolution, a very curious thing happened to Hemming. In an unusual move, Hemming was allowed entrance to the presidential palace, a place where most Americans were not allowed to go. While at the palace, Hemming was taken aside by one of the men he knew from the Cuban mission in Monterey Park. The man said, "Do you remember your gringo buddy, the rabbit? He was here at the palace." That man was Lee Oswald. (There have been no other confirmations over the years to verify this story of Oswald being in Cuba.)

By 1961, Hemming's activities via his Interpen group were being closely watched by both the CIA and the FBI. While Hemming had no actual connection to the CIA, and was not an active contact agent, he often led people to believe that he was working for the Company.

In June 1962, Hemming went to New Orleans to help the anti-Castro cause. There, he joined a group of men who were taking paramilitary training near Lake Pontchartrain. He later went to Florida to train anti-Castro men in the Everglades.

While in New Orleans, Hemming came to the attention of Jim Garrison who was looking into the New Orleans connection to the Kennedy assassination. One of Garrison's investigators, Stephen Jaffe, wrote a long memo to Garrison regarding Hemming and his associates in the city. The date of the memo is May 2, 1968, and is entitled "Gerry Patrick Hemming, Meeting at Press Conference of Loran Hall on May 2, 1968. Subsequent meeting at KJH Radio News, Los Angeles."

Stephen Jaffe attended a press conference in which Loran Hall was a panel member, along with Art Kevin. The other people in attendance were Gerry Hemming and his friend Roy Hargraves. Jaffe wrote that,

The two did not know of my affiliation with the office [Garrison] at that time and were talking primarily to Kevin in order to discredit Hall's remarks earlier.

Patrick [Hemming] stated that all of the people Hall knew in connection with soliciting funds, especially in Dallas, Texas, during 1963 were contacts which he, Patrick, had given Hall to make. Patrick further stated that Hall was lying when he said he'd partaken in raids inside of Cuba. Hargraves did not say much, rather just corroborated Patrick's comments.

Patrick alluded to his activities with the anti-Castro movement of 1963 and added he'd been present at numerous meetings where the project of possible assassination of President Kennedy was discussed. He said in this case a man like Hall would have never been allowed to partake in a true, professional plot because he was an unreliable, unstable, over-talkative person. Patrick stated that if discussion of possible assassination was made during any kind of a meeting it was dismissed as "wishful thinking," unless, if the people were serious, there was money placed on the table. That's when Patrick would take the "contract seriously," and he added he'd attended a few meetings where this occurred.

Patrick further stated that in St. Louis, Chicago, Miami, Dallas, and elsewhere, there were a lot of powerful elements who desired to get rid of President Kennedy.

Patrick said that he'd given most of his information to Garrison and that he thought that Mr. Garrison was on the "wrong track." He later repeated this thought in stronger language. He stated that he knew Oswald did not do it alone and he knew that the assassination of President Kennedy had been a highly planned professional execution performed by experts.

It was impossible to recall all that Patrick said because I could not tape his remarks or take notes without fear of his asking my name and the possibility that he would say something thereafter even to Kevin. I therefor excused myself so that Kevin could continue the conversation.

The memo continues, covering the following topics:

Patrick identified the heavy set man in the photograph which I had determined to be Charles Brehm from the DCA film, as a Cuban named "Molina."

Patrick gave information about Edward Anderson Collins, saying that this was a former member of Patrick's Raiders [Interpen], that Collins had bragged about being a member of a group which was organized to "wipe out Kennedy." Patrick had tracked down former friends of Collins. Patrick said that in September of 1963, Collins was in Dallas, Texas in contact with Lester Logue. He then dropped out of Patrick's Raiders saying that they, his group, was ready to proceed to kill Kennedy. In December of 1963, Collins died by drowning in 8 inches of water in a boating accident in Key Biscayne and is now buried in Richfield, Mississippi.

Patrick stated that Kiki Ferrer was a CIA instructor of some kind (not in the sense of guerilla training) like a coordinator of operations. Patrick definitely felt that Kiki was an agent of the CIA.

Patrick asked Kevin if the Garrison Investigation had run across the name of De Birely. Kevin did not know.

On May 4, 1963, Lawrence Howard Jr., telephoned me saying that he had talked with Patrick and had told him that I was in investigator for the office. This did not seem to surprise Patrick. I asked Howard to arrange a meeting with myself, Patrick and Steve Burton. Patrick agreed to the meeting through Howard for the date of May 7, 1968 at 8 PM. I will relate the results of that meeting in a future memorandum.

In December 1962, Hemming and his men were arrested by US Customs officers at Sombrero Cay after an abortive mission into Cuba to verify the withdrawal of the nuclear weapons after the missile crisis.

By 1967, Hemming had teamed up with New Orleans DA Jim Garrison in his investigation of the Kennedy assassination, and the New Orleans connection via David Ferrie, Clay Shaw, and Lee Oswald.

Here are the highlights of Hemming's deposition to the HSCA:

DPOB — 3/1/67 at Los Angeles, California.

He received training in the Marine Corps, primarily in air control.

He took free flights to other bases (including Atsugi four times), but never saw Oswald.

Upon leaving the Marines, he became involved in obtaining weapons for the Cuban rebels.

Before his separation from the service, Naval Intelligence became aware of his activities in weapons supplying, and attempted to recruit him.

While still in the Marines, he spent more than one weekend in Cuba contacting the 26th of July people.

As a teenager, he developed an interest in "irregular" guerilla warfare.

He went to Cuba in February 1959, and was approached by William Morgan and Col. Kail, to determine which way Camilo Ceinfuegos would go. Camilo Cenfuegos was Chief of the Army, and Hemming was a Major.

Hemming went to Cuba intending to watch a communist government develop. He, secretly, was never in favor of the Castro government.

He met Frank Fiorini (Sturgis), but did not trust him.

Upon leaving Cuba in September 1960, he stayed in Mexico City for two weeks and had contact with Sylvia Duran.

Upon returning to Miami, Hemming was aware of Sturgis, but thought it best to avoid him and did not work with him.

He was aware of Howard Hunt, but never worked with him.

Hemming believed Sturgis was working for Military Intelligence.

Hemming had nothing to do with the Bay of Pigs invasion.

In 1962 he applied to be employed by the CIA, but was turned down.

In late 1962, he and others were "running a training syllabus" at

No Name Key. Americans present were: Hemming, Howard Davis, Dick Watley, James Lewis, Ronald Ponce de Leon, Joe Gorman, Bill Seymour, Lawrence Dennis Harbor, Tom Duncan, Steve Wilson, and Justin Wilson. They had been associated with Felipe Vidal Santiago, who was on "a loose retainer" with both CIA and ONI. They were arrested by Cesar Diosdado.

After that arrest, Hemming returned to Los Angeles, and a female reporter who "was working for somebody" referred Loran Hall to him. That circumstance "blew his cover right off the bat."

On the trip back to Miami, Hemming met Robert Morris, who introduced him to Lester Logue. He warned Logue that Hall might be "working for somebody."

They proceeded to New Orleans, where Hemming met with Frank Bartes, Luis Rabel, and Larry Laborde, leaving Hall in the car.

Upon arriving in Florida, Hall attempted to establish contact with Santos Trafficante.

Hemming introduced Bayo to John Martino, and arranged for financing from a Haitian group. Once the money was secured, Sturgis showed up "from nowhere."

Martino told Hemming that the real purpose of the Bayo-Pawley raid was to kill Castro.

The Operation 40 group was the intended new government for Cuba—they were sponsored by Carlos Marcello and Leander Perez.

The Miami organized crime contacts were Mike McLaney and Norman Rothman. Howard Davis introduced them.

In May or June of 1962, at Luis Rabel's house, Hemming met Rabel, Frank Bartes, Larry Laborde, Guy Banister, and George de Morenschildt. There was an attache case filled with $100 bills. The purpose was to pay for assassinating Fidel Castro. Hemming declined because he thought Raul Castro would be even worse.

After leaving, he only returned to Cuba once.

He once heard a suggestion that Kennedy should be assassinated, using Lester Logue's group in Dallas, and the same group came to Miami and made a similar offer to Tony Questa and Alpha 66.

Hemming made an inspection trip in a plane outside of New Orleans to find a site for a training camp. He observed David Ferrie.

He was upset about the disappearance of Alex Rorke, and

Attorney Ellis Rubin (Sturgis's current lawyer) contracted him to do something about it.

On the day that JFK was to land in Miami, he was asked to be at the airport, armed, to help with problems. He advised he would be there unarmed.

He was home in Miami when the assassination occurred.

He phoned Logue and other people in Dallas, warning them to stay away from Loran Hall, since he "had his gun."

The Marita Lorenz story is false.

Hemming had the "impression" that Sturgis was in Dallas the week of the assassination.

Right after Castro took over in Cuba, Hemming was in the Cuban consulate in Monterey Park, California, and Oswald arrived. Oswald seemed to know a lot about Hemming's background, and Hemming was suspicious.

On another occasion he met Oswald, after his group had been arrested at No Name Key in December 1962. Oswald had been trying to infiltrate Hemming's group at the motel where they were being detained.

"Last year," while in Los Angeles, Lawrence Howard reminded Hemming of the incident with Oswald at the motel after the arrest. Hargraves and Ashman also saw Oswald.

Hemming met Jack Ruby, in September or October 1959, at William Morgan's house in Cuba. Ruby had sold inferior jeeps to the Cuban Air Force, and Hemming had a few choice words about them. They were filmed by Clete Roberts of Channel 13 in Los Angeles.

In late summer of 1963, Hemming first met Bernardo de Torres in a Military Intelligence office—thought he worked there.

He first me Marita Lorenz at Perez Jimenez home in 1962.

There is one final piece of the puzzle regarding Hemming and his story that he saw Oswald in Monterey Park California. Hemming later told author John Newman that upon seeing Oswald, he called James Angleton, the legendary spycatcher at the CIA who was responsible for all the CIA's counterintelligence operations and told him about Oswald. Hemming said that he told Angleton that he did not like being with him, and Oswald wanted to know whether it was

ONI (Office of Naval Intelligence) that put him on to Hemming. "Oswald was like a rabbit. I figured these guys were pulling snitches on me."

How Hemming, an ex-Marine who briefly worked for Castro, and was *not* on the CIA payroll, could have gotten in personal touch with James Angleton is highly questionable. One does not call CIA headquarters in Langley, Virginia and ask to speak to the head of the clandestine service unless they are highly placed in the Agency or has impeccable contacts on the inside. Hemming had neither.

The Hemming story regarding his meeting with Oswald would be resurrected with the account of Marita Lorenz and her allegations about a car trip that she took with Hemming and Sturgis to Dallas in November 1963 shortly before the Kennedy assassination, another story that cannot be backed up.

In the end, Hemming had more important things on his mind during those heady days of the Cold War, than a skinny Marine he thought was working for the Office of Naval Intelligence. Once in Florida, he organized an anti-Castro para-military group called the Intercontinental Penetration Force, a.k.a., "Interpen." Soon, Frank Sturgis would form his own paramilitary group called the "International Anti-Communist Brigade." Together, Hemming and Sturgis declared their own personal war against Fidel Castro.

Gerry Patrick Hemming died on January 28, 2008, age 71, near his home in Fayetteville, North Carolina. Whatever stories he failed to tell during his life went with him to the grave.

Chapter 34
The Death of Johnny Rosselli

The name of Johnny Rosselli has come up numerous times in this book regarding his association with the CIA's plans to kill Fidel Castro of Cuba.

Johnny Rosselli was one of three members of the mob whom the CIA made covert deals with in 1960 in its campaign to oust Fidel Castro (the other two were Santos Trafficante and Sam Giancana). Rosselli was at home in both the world of organized crime and among some of the most influential officers of the CIA.

As I related earlier in this text, Roselli was born in Italy and moved to America in 1911. When his father died, his mother remarried, and his stepfather nudged him further into the life of crime he had already espoused. By the 1930s he was affiliated with Al Capone and the Chicago crime syndicate. He moved to Los Angeles and extorted the film studios and became a fixture at the Friars Club. In the 1950s, he was a kingpin in Havana, where the Batista regime was becoming rich off its share of the profits of the mob casino business that attracted players from all over the world.

Meyer Lansky was the mob's number one man in Havana during that time and Rosselli shortly became a fan of the boss. This was the lucrative game that Johnny Rosselli entered, at his own risk, and soon he was immersed in the CIA's covert efforts to kill Castro, with consequences neither Rosselli nor the other two members of his team, Giancana and Trafficante, could ever have imagined.

Skip now almost sixteen years to 1976. John Kennedy has been dead for thirteen years and the Warren Commission has decided that JFK was killed by a lone nut, an ex-Marine named Lee Harvey Oswald. Furthermore, the CIA never told the commissioners about the plots to kill Castro involving the CIA and the mob, and the man who headed the Agency in the early 1960s when Kennedy was president, Allen Dulles, never informed his fellow members of that most important fact.

By now, Rosselli had given his story regarding his role in the Cuba assassination plots to the press, who eagerly printed his lurid tale of Caribbean mayhem and murder. Rosselli's story that he gave to reporters Jack Anderson and Drew Pearson was that a team of Cuban hit men were sent to kill Castro but were captured, and "turned" by the Cubans against the United States. After Castro learned of the attempt on his life, he cooked up a counterplot to kill JFK.

In 1976, Rosselli met for questioning by the Church Committee, the Senate panel looking into the Kennedy assassination. When questioned by the panel, Rosselli said that he personally believed that Castro had a hand in the killing of the president, but he did not have solid proof. He also denied having spoken to Edward Morgan regarding the anti-Castro hit team story, and was circumspect when asked whether or not he had any dealings with Jack Ruby, the Dallas nightclub owner who killed Lee Oswald.

Johnny Rosselli's demise came on July 28, 1976. That morning, he drove his car to a nearby marina and went out on a boat with certain unidentified men. While out fishing, these unidentified men killed Rosselli, dumped his body in an old oil drum, and set it adrift in the ocean. A few days later, the rusting drum carrying Rosselli's decomposing body, washed ashore.

Who killed Rosselli and why? One of the prime candidates was Santos Trafficante of Tampa, his co-conspirator in the Castro plots. Certainly Rosselli's death was a clear Mafia hit. Florida police came up with a possible assassin: Sam Cagnina. Cagnina was a soldier in Santo Trafficante's organization and there were reports that certain people overheard Cagnina taking responsibility for the Rosselli hit.

Reports that Santos Trafficante put out the order to kill Rosselli fly in the face of a few certain happenings before his death. The men had been in contact with each other at the time of the The Committee hearings and one can only imagine that they both discussed what was going on. Rosselli's family said that the men had met while they were in Miami on two occasions in January 1976, going to a restaurant that was run by Jose Quintana, who was the husband of one of Rosselli's nieces. "At that point in time, Rosselli already appeared twice in Washington, and would return for a third, crucial session devoted to the Kennedy assassination; his friendly relations with the ruthless don hardly fit the pattern of a man testifying in bold defiance of his boss."[11]

---

11 Rappleye, Charles, and Becker, Ed, *All American Mafioso: The Johnny Rosselli Story,* Doubleday, New York, 1991, Page 316.

In addition, Rosselli's attorney told authorities soon after his murder that he had arranged to conceal Trafficante's identity in his testimony, despite the fact that CIA personnel had already placed Trafficante's name in the record. David Bushong, who conducted intensive interviews with Rosselli separate from the committee hearings, contends that "no deal" was ever accepted in taking Rosselli's testimony. But Les Scherr was quite specific, and had no reason to deceive; Rosselli would not use Santos Trafficante's name, but would refer to him in testimony as "Mr. X."[12]

David Bushong also said this about Rosselli: "I didn't get anything from him that I didn't have corroborated or didn't have in existence before I talked with him. I'm positive that he didn't give me anything new about the plots, and he didn't give me anything new about Trafficante."

The HSCA, after going over the Church Committee's work three years later said, "The 1975 and 1978 testimony of Rosselli and Trafficante corroborated each other, but remain contrary to how the principals reported the facts in 1967."

In other words, the House committee reported Rosselli collaborated with Trafficante in an effort to "downplay his role." Yet, when interviewed in 1990, Bushong rejected the idea that Rosselli might have been playing a double game. "It was not reconnaissance by Rosselli. They [the Mafia] don't deal in subtleties like that. You're talking about dinosaurs here."

While it is not possible to pin the crime on any one person, one can postulate on the theories. Was Rosselli killed because of his testimony before the Church Committee regarding the Kennedy assassination and his revelations about Castro and the retaliation theory? Or did the Mafia silence Rosselli for some other reason? The jury on that one is still out.

The reported death of Johnny Rosselli must have sent shock waves across the bow of the US Intelligence agencies, including the FBI and the CIA. Both agencies had a thorough knowledge of what role he played in the Castro assassination attempts and they put out an all points bulletin to find out who was responsible for his killing.

Since Rosselli's killing took place in Dade County, Florida, the local authorities opened a case to try to find his murderers. That got the attention of the federal government, and on October 8, 1976, a

12 Ibid.

Santos Trafficante.

memo for the Director of Security from Charles Rivers, subject, "Dade County Request for Agency Assistance Regarding the Death of Johnny Rosselli" was initiated:

> The Dade County Sheriff's representatives requested all Agency information pertaining to several Cuban nationals. A review of Office of Security indices in this regard disclosed the following: Among the people whose interest sparked the Dade County authorities were the below mentioned people, a few of whom were well known to the government in its anti-Castro assassination plots.
>
> Ramon 'Donestevez Dominquez—Office of Security records were negative.
>
> Rolando Masferrer Rojas—Covert and overt security files were located regarding Rolando Masferrer, a Cuban citizen born 12 January 1918 in Holguin Cuba. Although limited national agency checks were conducted on subject

283

in January 1950, there is no indication that Masferrer was ever utilized by the Agency. He is a former Cuban senator and Cuban Communist Party member (expelled in 1945), a former commander for Batista's private army, and firmly anti-Castro. The two files contain numerous FBI reports regarding his activities in connection with an attempt to invade Cuba in 1960 and a subsequent effort to invade Haiti in 1967. Masferrer and 75 of his followers were arrested in January 1967 in Marathon, Florida, while preparing for the invasion of Haiti. A handwritten note in Masferrer's file revealed that he died in 1975 when his car was blown apart by a bomb in Florida. No further details regarding his death were contained in his subject files. Since Masferrer has never been affiliated with the Agency, despite his claims, it is believed that Dade County officials should be referred to the FBI for information regarding Masferrer.

Luciano Nieves—Office of Security files contain [blank] information regarding Luciano Nieves, date and place of birth 6 October 1933, Santa Clara, Cuba. Nieves was [redacted] on 4 February 1966 in Florida. It was developed that he was a Cuban national who had been arrested, tried, and sentenced to 20 years in Cuba for allegedly being involved in an anti-Castro plot. He was released in March 1965 after serving approximately 16 months of his sentence and went to Spain briefly where he was of interest to the [redacted]. In August 1965 he entered the United States and in November 1965 was contacted by Directorate of Operations (DDO) representatives. From November 1965 until approximately January 1966 he was of operational interest to the DDO.

Jose de La Torriente—Security files contain only sparse information provided by the Domestic Contact Service in 1970 showing that one Jose de La Torriente, not further identified, claimed to have worked for the CIA for many years. An attachment to a 1970 Domestic Contact Service memorandum containing details of Torriente's claimed association with the Agency was not contained in Office of Security files. It is believed that a decision to release information regarding Torriente would have to be deferred to the DDO.

Manuel Artime—Security records contain overt and covert files regarding Manuel Francisco Artime-Buesa. Artime Buesa is a former Agency operational asset utilized by the DDO during the approximate period 1959-1963. Any decision regarding the release of information regarding Artime Buesa or his present whereabouts should be deferred to the DDO.

AMLASH—Rolando Cubela (Secades). Agency cryptonym-AMLASH, is the subject of the Office of Security covert file 101 089. Cubela is a rather celebrated Cuban national and operational contact of the DDO mentioned throughout both of the Senate Select Committee assassination reports. Although Cubela is identified in the assassination reports as AMLASH and his identity has never been revealed by the Agency, his true identity has been surfaced in several recent news articles. All information on Cubela in the possession of the Office of Security would fall within the purview of the DDO, and it is believed that any decision to release information pertaining to Cubela should be deferred to the Latin America Division of the DDO. It should be noted that during their investigation, Senate Select Committee staffers reviewed Cubela's raw files from

Manuel Artime with President Kennedy, 1962.

both the DDO and the Office of Security.

Dade County Sheriff's Office representatives requested the "names of the three Cubans mentioned in the Rosselli testimony." It is believed that the response to this question should be deferred to the Senate Select Committee on Intelligence since the Office of Security does not have access to the Rosselli testimony.

Additionally, the Dade County Sheriff's Office representatives ask for all Agency information pertaining to several individuals of unknown citizenships, but believed to be US citizens. A review of the Office of Security indices in this regard disclosed the following:

Fred Black—Office of Security records revealed only newspaper clippings contained in the Robert G. Baker subject file showing that Fred Black Jr., a consultant with North American Aviation, was a close friend and business associate of "Bobby" G. Baker. Black was mentioned repeatedly in the news media coverage of Senate Investigations of Baker in the early 1960s. While Black's citizenship is undetermined, it is probable that he is a US citizen.

Edward Morgan—A covert security file was located regarding Edward Pierpont Morgan, date, and place of birth 28 May 1913, St. Louis, Missouri. Morgan, a US citizen and former FBI agent from 1941-1945, was granted a covert security clearance on 2 February 1951 for use as a "cut out" in connection with negotiations for the [redacted].

It is noted that while only the aforementioned subject file exists regarding Morgan, in his capacity, Morgan is mentioned sporadically in the Maheu, Harvey, and Rosselli files. In 1967, Maheu was interviewed and advised that he had briefed Morgan regarding the details of his involvement in the Agency-sponsored Castro assassination plots. Morgan's current association with Maheu, professionally and/or personal, is unknown. Morgan is currently practicing law in the District of Columbia law firm of Welch and Morgan.

Joseph Shimon—No Office of Security subject file exists regarding Joseph Shimon, aka Joseph Shiman.

However, he is mentioned in the Johnny Rosselli file as a personal friend of Rosselli. It is further noted in the Rosselli file that Shimon knew Maheu, but the nature and extent of their official/social relationship is unknown. Shimon is described as a former District of Columbia Metropolitan Police Department (MPD) inspector who was discharged from the D.C. MPD as a result of a conviction involving wiretapping activities.

To date, no decision has been made as to the type and form of response to be made to the Dade County Sheriff's Office request. Additionally a formal request to the Office of Security has not been received. Office of Security files have been searched and pertinent information reviewed. Pending a decision as to what form the response, if any, will take, it is recommended that the Office of Security files containing information pertinent to the request be retained in a readily available status and no further action be taken at this time.

From the information provided in the memo, it seemed to the Dade County officials that Johnny Rosselli had a lot of friends/enemies the feds wanted to talk to in relation to the circumstances surrounding his death.

The above-mentioned list is a Who's Who in the anti-Castro world (Masferrer, Nieves, de La Torrenente, Manuel Artime, and Rolando Cubela-AMLASH), the political world (Fred Black), the covert dealings of the CIA (Edward Morgan), and the police community (Joseph Shimon). Also, let's not forget the names of William Harvey and Robert Maheu who were involved in the Castro assassination plots.

For a poor, immigrant son from Italy, Johnny Rosselli had come a long way.

Senator Frank Church (left) of the Senate Church Committee.

Chapter 35
Richard Cain

Richard Cain, a.k.a. "Richard Scalzetti, is a relatively new name that has been added to the roster of people involved in the anti-Castro plots thanks to the work of his half-brother, Michael Cain, in his book called *The Life and Death of Richard Cain—Chicago Cop and Mafia Hitman,* as well as from a wealth of documents released via the National Archives over the past decades. Cain was a member of the Chicago Police Department, as well as a close associate of Chicago mob boss Sam Giancana. Some writers have tried to name Richard Cain as one of the shooters in Dealey Plaza on November 22, 1963, but that allegation has been discredited, most notably by his brother.

Richard Cain was an enigma. He was a man with little formal education, yet he became a high-ranking Chicago police official, as well as a hit man for the Chicago mob. During his life, he aided the anti-Castro cause in Chicago, meeting with a number of high-ranking anti-Castro Cubans, making several trips to Cuba on behalf of these people, and at the same time, offering his services to the CIA, who read his reports, yet did not want to formalize their relationship with him. Cain, in the company of an unidentified woman, was sent to Cuba to kill Castro. According to Cain's account, he made it into the office of Fidel Castro but was not able to hide the poison that he was going to use (his woman partner was caught and executed).

Richard Cain was born in Chicago on October 5, 1931. His parents divorced when he was between five and seven years old, and moved in and out of each other's homes on a steady basis. He said that he felt neglected as a child and did not have the proper rearing that other children had. At age 14, he left home. As a young man, he moved to different parts of the United States, doing odd jobs—dishwasher, pool hall hustler, bartender, living hand to mouth in rundown hotels and boarding houses. At age eighteen, he enlisted in the US Army and served from the years 1942 to 1950. After his military tour was over, he came back to Chicago to start a new life.

He was married at least four times, at one time to a professional singer. During the 1950 and 1960s, Cain moved around the world,

Richard Cain.

staying mostly in Chicago, but also Mexico and Argentina. In the mid-1950s Cain worked as a private investigator doing polygraph examinations. The name of his company was called Accurate Laboratories, but the business also went by other names. He performed such duties as wiretapping, political investigations and espionage for his clients. He said that some of his employers were the Republican Central Committee, the CIA, the Justice Department, Time Inc., and the Hugh Hefner Company (*Playboy Magazine*).

From May 16, 1956 until May 16, 1960, Cain worked for the CPD and rose to the rank of detective in February 1958. He resigned from the force in May 1960 because of an investigation that was started against him by the police. At the time of his arrest, he was working for the Police Sex Bureau Squad. He was accused of spying on City Commissioner Irvin Cohen, and was alleged to have been paid $1,700 by the State's Attorney's office.

Cain then moved to Mexico City where he got a job with Banco De Mexico, the Mexican Treasury Department, between 1960 and 1962. He taught his clients sabotage and espionage techniques. He said that he was deported from Mexico City "after a Bobby Kennedy man found out I had been wiretapping the Czechoslovakian Embassy there."

Despite his prior arrest by the Chicago Police Department,

Cain was allowed to resume his police work when, in 1962, he was appointed as the chief investigator for the Cook County Sheriff's Department, a job he held until 1964. His time at the Sheriff's Department was controversial, to say the least. He got good marks for his many drug arrests and his name was mentioned many times in the local press. He built a good reputation as a streetwise cop whose tactics sometimes went beyond the law. During this time period, Cain was accused by the State's Attorney's office of improperly issuing warrants in his investigations, with the result that many of the cases that he investigated did not result in convictions. He was convicted at trial but the verdict was later reversed. He was subsequently fired from the Sheriff's Office.

During his time on the force, Cain became the target of both the CIA and the FBI who compiled a large dossier on him, largely, for his work in the anti-Castro cause in Chicago.

The CIA began taking an interest in Cain in the early 1960s according to an article on Sam Giancana that was published in the *Chicago Tribune* dated December 28, 1973. In the fall of 1960, Cain made contact with the Domestic Contact Division of the CIA and gave them information on the activities of anti-Castro organizations in Chicago. In June 1961, Cain contacted a Mr. Lohmann of the CIA's Chicago Field Office. He said that he had been contacted by a man named "Mr. Kroupansky" who reportedly was negotiating with the president of Panama to investigate communism in Panama. Cain was to assist Kroupansky in this endeavor. In the summer of 1961, Cain and an unidentified CIA staffer met in Mexico City for "purpose unknown." In October 1961, Cain again contacted Mr. Lohmann and reported on his meetings with his contacts in Panama. At that meeting he offered his services to the CIA.

In April 1962, Cain, while living in Mexico, made an unannounced visit to CIA Station Chief Winston Scott and another man. He told them that he was the owner of an investigative agency in Mexico that trained members of the Mexican police and other government agents. "He was told by Messrs. Scott and [blank] that the US Ambassador did not approve of American citizens becoming involved in Mexican politics."

On June 4, 1962, "Cain was deported from Mexico for carrying a loaded revolver and brass knuckles, impersonating a Mexican

Government official, and violating his tourist permit by working."

On August 19, 1963, Cain met members of the CIA's Western Hemisphere Division at the Lake Shore Drive Athletic Club in Chicago. Cain said that he would like to work for the Agency in an overseas capacity. The CIA men countered by saying that they believed it would be better for Cain if he sought a position with the Cook County Sheriff's Office. Cain further told the CIA men that he was in contact with certain anti-Castro Cubans in the Chicago area. Cain agreed to help the CIA by providing them with information on Cuban activity in Chicago, especially that of Paulino Sierra, a Cuban exile leader. In August 1963, Cain reported to the CIA on information he picked up concerning the activities of members of the Cuban Student Directory, whose headquarters was located in Miami. He also reported on information that exile leader Miro Cordozo was interested in buying arms.

On September 12, 1963, Cain gave the CIA information on members of the DRE, who were planning to buy weapons for their organization. More on that later.

By May 1972, Cain moved again to Mexico City, possibly enroute to Latin America. CIA memos of the time say that Cain was "allegedly involved in illegal arms deals and on various occasions that he was working for the CIA."

On May 16, 1972, an FBI agent in Mexico City asked other US intelligence agencies for traces on Cain's activities. "According to the FBI an Eastern Airlines pilot had identified Cain as the skyjacker who forced him to fly to Honduras on 5 May, 1972." The memo ends by saying, "There is no indication that a clearance was ever granted for the use of Cain by the Agency or that he received any compensation from the Agency."

These documents reveal an Agency interest during the mid to late 1960s but, as noted above, the CIA interest in Cain dated back to the fall of 1960. On October 11, 1960, the CIA's Chicago office wrote a memo about a call they received from Cain concerning his interest in helping the CIA regarding Cuba. He reported on his meeting with the leader of the Chicago branch of the Counter Revolutionary Movement in Cuba. Cain said that this man arranged for him to be sent to Cuba ostensibly to take pictures of the members of this anti-Castro group. Cain said that he was going to Cuba in the employ of the *Chicago Daily News* and would be paid between $5,000 to $7,500 for his services. He said he would fly into Cuba from an airstrip either in Florida or Alabama and that arrangements had been made with certain elements of the Cuban Air Force to let his plane arrive safely. He said that these same groups would facilitate his departure from Cuba.

Cain asked his CIA contact if there was anything he could do for the Agency while he was in Cuba. The reply was:

> I went to great lengths to explain to him that there was absolutely nothing we would request of him and that since he was affiliated with the *Chicago Daily News* and also *Life Magazine* that it would prove embarrassing not only to himself but to these organizations if it were ever revealed that he would place himself in jeopardy by mentioning any contact with me.

His CIA contact however, did say that if Cain believed he had any worthwhile information that he thought the CIA would need, he should call. Making what would later prove to be a smart call, the agent ended by saying, "I am sure that we will hear more about Richard Cain."

As the anti-Castro crusade grew in the United States among the disgruntled Cuban exiles, Cain began to meet with these people on a regular basis. He gained entry via his mob connections, especially Sam Giancana who was heavily involved with the CIA-inspired plots to kill Castro. In September 1963, the CIA reported that Cain informed them that he had met with two men by the names of Mateo and Torres who were members of the DRE. Torres told Cain that he was the buyer for the DRE and wanted to purchase machine guns, .45 caliber pistols, 9mm submachine guns, bazookas, and other materials for up to 500 men. He said he was ready to spend up to $25,000 for these guns.

> Cain said that Torres told him that KUBARK [CIA] would stop the transaction if it learned of them." Cain was to meet with Torres and Mateo again, and Cain would try for a picture of Torres. After this meeting, Cain wants to get

out, but will be happy to introduce anyone to the pair. Cain speculated that Miro Cardona was in the dealings somehow.

The CIA told Cain to "get out of the picture as soon as possible, and to make no commitments. Apparently the DRE is an MD-controlled organization which, at times, seems to act independently of its monitor."

Today, researchers looking into the Kennedy assassination have tried to link Cain to the events in Dealey Plaza. A Brazilian journalist named Claudia Furiati wrote in her book *ZR RIFLE* that Cain was working with two mob hit men, Dave Yarras and Lenny Patrick, in the Kennedy assassination. In a book by Charles Giancana called *Double Cross,* it is alleged that Sam Giancana tasked Cain, Chuckie Nicoletti and a man nicknamed "Milwaukee Phil" as the men who actually killed the president.

What is known is that Cain operated a mob-run clearinghouse in Chicago to train exiles for anti-Castro activities. He was a courier and chauffeur for Sam Giancana and helped him with his mob business in the city while Giancana was living in forced exile in Mexico. He tried to get himself hired by the CIA for these activities but the Agency wanted nothing to do with him. Cain was also a close associate of Johnny Rosselli, who was working in partnership with Task Force W in its Cuban operations. He also worked as an informant with the FBI, under the direction of FBI agent William Roemer. Cain and Roemer would meet on a weekly basis whereby Cain would inform the FBI of the goings on in the Chicago Outfit. Roemer tolerated Cain's petty criminal activities, but warned him that if he crossed the line into violent activities, he would be arrested.

On May 22, 1967, the CIA's Director of Security received information on Cain from the FBI:

...which ties the Subject to the Mafia in Chicago; and he directed that the DCS ([Domestic Contact Service] be contacted for information as to whether or not they ever established contact with him, and if so, for what purpose. The DCS was also to be advised that, if they were in contact with him, it was suggested that they break it off.

Insight into the CIA's interest in Richard Cain can be found in a memo dated October 9, 1967 from M.D. Stevens to Chief, SRS regarding Cain's activities. Here are some of the most interesting parts of the memo:

Subject, it is obvious, had been a source of information regarding an alleged discussion of the assassination of President Kennedy at a secret meeting of the Fair Play for Cuba Committee held in Chicago in February 1963 under the direction of Richard Criley. He also was the source of information regarding the alleged attempted recruitment into the Communist Party of young Cubans in the Chicago area by one Guillermo Escobar, who according to the Chicago office "was one of Horace Speed's leads" obtained by Ralph Perez. The documents also indicated that in February 1964, Cain was the subject of a conversation initiated by Eldon Cohen, with a representative of the DCS Chicago office who believed his purpose was to learn whether or not Cain was in fact on a two-month's sick leave from the COOK County Sheriff's Office, as he was said to be on a political undercover assignment which COHEN inferred involved tapping the telephone of gubernatorial candidate Charles H. Percy and other political figures.

The first time CAIN came to the attention of the Security Office was when the Mexico Station requested traces on him. Their request stemmed from an unannounced visit he made to the Station, during which he stated that he had an investigative agency in Mexico with branches in Chicago and Los Angeles. He had also stated that his agency in Mexico was for the purpose of training Mexican Government agents in police methods, in investigative techniques, and in the use of the lie detector; and had added that he was investigating Communism in a certain unnamed Central American country.

The 1 September 1967 copy of *Life* magazine contains an article titled "Brazen Empire of Organized Crime," in which it is stated that Sam Giancana, head of the Chicago Cosa Nostra, is "still running things by remote control from a hide-out in Mexico where he poses as Riccardo Scalzetti.

The real Scalzetti, Giancana's erstwhile chauffer and courier, is more familiar to Chicagoans as Richard Cain, a well-known former Chicago policeman and more recently a private investigator.

Eldon Cohen who is mentioned in this memo as having evidenced an interest in Cain during the gubernatorial campaign of the now Senator (from Illinois) Charles H. Percy is now Percy's Executive Assistant. Cohen, who became employed by Percy in January 1964, following his resignation from CIA which was effective 31 December 1963, at the time he contacted a representative of the Chicago Office of DCS regarding Cain on 10 February 1964, did not indicate that he was employed by Percy. He said, rather, that he'd been asked by the "Percy for Governor" people to inquire as to Cain's status.

During the time that Cohen was a CIA employee (1949-1963), he was of concern to the Security Office, due principally to the activities and proclivities of his wife, Rita Heller Cohen, the former wife of Irving Roth. Cohen was the subject of an Employment Review Board case in 1956; and in 1956 was disqualified as a member of the Junior Career Development Program. It was then decided to put him in a job in FBIS in which he would not be exposed to highly sensitive material. At the time of his resignation, he was an I.O. Contact, GS-14, in the Chicago Office of the DD/OO Contact Division.

In January 1965, the DCS requested approval to contact Cohen on an ad hoc basis to participate in the briefing and debriefing of his employer, Senator Percy, who planned an extensive tour of the Far East. In June 1967, Mr. George Cary, Legislative Counsel requested a check on Cohen stating that there may be occasion to brief him from time to time. According to Mr. Cary, Cohen would be briefed generally on the build-up in Cuba but would not be exposed to operational information or exotic material.

There is attached a copy of the above referred to September articles in *Life Magazine*, in one of which Cain is described as the erstwhile chauffeur and courier of Sam

Giancana. The second of these articles makes reference to alleged friendly contacts of Jim Garrison, of the Oswald case, with henchmen of the Cosa Nostra in the Louisiana area.

During review of Cain's security file, I noted a message regarding him from Mexico City, on 25 April 1962, which mentioned a "Willard Andrews," reputable American businessman in Mexico, who obviously had contact with some kind with Cain, as well as with a CIA representative in Mexico to whom Andrews had commented that Cain claims to have been with OSS during WWII. In answer to this message that requested traces on Cain, Headquarters, in furnishing limited information obtained regarding him, advised that neither his claimed employment by OSS, nor a claim he made to have worked with Task Force W, could be substantiated. The Station was advised that he did have (or had) a legitimate detective laboratory in Chicago.

With reference to Willard Andrews, Security indices contain no record. I believe the individual referred to is Wyilys Andrews, a former OSS/CIA employee who has lived in Mexico for many years and has continued to have social contacts with representatives of this Agency in Mexico as well as with Agency employees from Headquarters who visit him from time to time. Andrews like Cain, was born in Chicago of parents who also were born in the general area of Chicago.

Over the past few years, new information has been revealed concerning an assassination plot on the life of JFK in Chicago in the summer of 1963 (another foiled plot was quashed in Tampa, Florida that same year). This information comes from the testimony of the first African-American Secret Service agent, Abraham Bolden, who was part of JFK's protection detail at the time of the assassination. The news of Bolden's accusations came in an article in the *New York Times* on December 6, 1967 called "Plot on Kennedy in Chicago Told." According to the article, Bolden told his attorney Mark Lane, an early Warren Commission critic, that "the agency had known before President Kennedy's assassination that an attempt to kill him had been planned."

At the time the article was written, Bolden was serving time in jail for "having conspired to sell official information in a counterfeiting case." Bolden told his attorneys that he had been sentenced to prison after the Warren Commission refused to hear his testimony regarding the Chicago assassination plot. Bolden said the real reason he was investigated by the feds was that he was going to publically tell of the lack of security among JFK's Secret Service detail while the president was on his fatal trip to Dallas. On November 26, 1963, four days after the assassination, the *Chicago American* published a piece on the assassination by Maggie Daly in her column called "Daly Diary," who "reported that the assassination of President Kennedy was planned at a meeting in Chicago's west side in the early part of February 1963 by a dissident Cuban group and that the FBI was investigating this group." Here is where the connection between Richard Cain and the president's assassination comes in.

On November 29, 1963, the Chicago office of the CIA wrote a lengthy memo on the Bolen accusations, as well as information concerning Cain and the president's death. The memo said that Cain, than employed by the Cook County Sheriff's Office, said that his department received information:

> ...that early in 1963 the Chicoms [Chinese Communists], took over the operations in the US for the Fair Play For Cuba Committee. In February 1963, a secret meeting of the Committee was held at 907 South Spaulding, Chicago, under the direction of Richard Criley, Secretary of the Chicago Chapter. At the meeting, the assassination of the President of the US was discussed.. Cain then added the information that Lee Oswald purchased the rifle that was used in the assassination of President Kennedy in March 1963. Cain then said that the Cook County Sheriff's Office had not established that Oswald was at the February meeting. However, they had strong suspicions that Oswald was in Chicago in April.

Cain alleged that he was instructed by Sheriff Ogilvie to look into the matter himself, and to ask the FBI "officially" for information on the Fair Play for Cuba Committee (Oswald was the lone member of the New Orleans chapter of the FPCC). The local FBI office bluntly told Sheriff Oglvie that the FBI had jurisdiction into the Kennedy case and that Cain should defer to them.

Richard Cain's violent end came on December 20, 1973 when he was having a meal at Rose's Sandwich Shop in Chicago with mobster Marshall Caifano. Dick Cain unexpectedly left the restaurant at around 12:30 p.m. He returned one hour later and found Caifano gone. Suddenly, two men wearing ski masks burst into the diner, and lined Cain up against the wall. He was shot point blank with a shotgun and died instantly. It is an irony that two of Dick Cain's best friends were men on the opposite side of the law: Sam Giancana and Bill Roemer.

Chapter 36
Were the Oswalds Agents?

From the day that ex-Marine Lee Harvey Oswald, fresh from his discharge from the service, arrived in Moscow for who knows what real reason, there have been longstanding rumors that he was on some kind of intelligence mission for either the CIA or the Office of Naval Intelligence. A point of contention is, just who was Marina Prusakova, the young Russian girl Oswald would meet and would marry after a six-week courtship? Was she just a pretty pharmacy worker in a local hospital in February 1959 who found the young American defector just too good to be true? Or was she something that she pretended not to be, someone who was asked to look into Oswald and find out what he was really doing in Russia?

Newly released documents paint a very different picture as far as the Russians were concerned when it came to both Lee and Marina. The documents discuss Oswald's time in the city of Minsk where he worked in a radio factory, met Marina, and had the time of his life as a foreigner in a strange land. But the story does not begin and end with the cold days and nights of Russia. It began in November 1958 when Oswald ended his overseas military tour of duty and returned to the United States where he was stationed at the Marine Air Control Squadron in El Toro, California, after a thirty-day leave.

In March 1959, Oswald took a series of high school level courses, and received a rating of "satisfactory." At that time, he also applied to the Albert Schweitzer College in Switzerland, for admission in the spring term. Why he chose to apply to the little known Albert Schweitzer college in the first place is a mystery in itself. How did he come to learn about the college; did someone else tell him of it? He could have easily applied to a lower ranked college in the United States and have been accepted, but instead, he applied to a foreign college that most people had never heard of. The application was approved by the college by letter dated June 19, 1959, and Oswald sent in his registration fee of $25.

Oswald was scheduled to serve in the Marines on active duty until 7 December 1959, but in August, he made a $40.00 payment to his mother, who said she needed the money. Soon thereafter, Oswald applied for a dependency discharge because he said his mother needed his financial help in order to survive. Within a quick, two-week period, his application for discharge was approved. His application for a quick separation was questioned by the persons involved but in the end, it was accepted.

On September 4, Oswald, while waiting to be processed out of the Marines, applied for a passport. His application stated that he planned to leave the United States on 21 September to attend the Albert Schweitzer College and the University of Turku in Finland, as well as travel to Cuba, the Dominican Republic, England, France, Germany, and Russia. He got his passport six days later (so much for heading home to take care of dear old mom).

Oswald got his hardship discharge on September 11, and arrived in Fort Worth, Texas on September 14 where his mother was then living. He gave her $100.00 and three days later, left for New Orleans bound for Europe.[1]

In New Orleans, where he'd spend the summer of 1963 doing all sorts of anti-Castro operations, he booked passage on the ship The SS *Marion Lykes,* set to sail on September 17, and paid $220.75. The ship sailed on September 20 and carried only four passengers, Oswald being one of them. Oswald embarked at Le Havre on October 8 and left for England that same day, arriving on October 9. He told English passport control officers that he planned to stay in England for one week before heading to Switzerland for college. That same day, he flew to Helsinki, Finland, and while he was in the city, he applied for a visa at the Russian Consulate on October 12. The visa was issued on October 14. He then took a train and arrived at the Finnish-Russian border at Vanikkala, and arrived in Moscow on October 16.

In its narrative of Oswald's trip to Russia, the Warren Commission noted the following holes in the tale:

Further questions arise from Oswald's obtaining a Soviet entry visa within only two days of having applied for it on 12 October, 1959. Normally at least a week would elapse between the time of a tourist's application and the issuance

1 Duffy, James, R., *Who Killed JFK? The Kennedy Assassination Cover-Up, The Web,* Shapolsky Books, New York, 1988, Pages 23-25.

of a visa. The minimum time was, if anything, all the more necessary, in addition to the processing of the visa application, lodgings were to be arranged through Soviet Intourist, as appears to have been the case with Oswald, inasmuch as he was met at the Moscow railroad station by an Intourist representative and taken to the Hotel Berlin.

The circumstances of Oswald's arrival in Moscow is further muddied by the following information

However, the Soviet Consul in Helsinki, Gregory Golub, was suspected by American intelligence of also being an officer in the Soviet KGB. Golub had once disclosed in a luncheon conversation that Moscow had given him authority to give Americans visas without prior approval from Moscow, and that "as long as he was convinced the American was 'all right,' he could give him a visa in a matter of minutes.

Now in Moscow, things began to build rather quickly for Oswald. He told his Intourist guide, Rima Shirkova, that he wanted to leave the US and become a Russian citizen. He was then taken to a new hotel, the Metropole, and in the meantime, wrote a letter to the Soviet Supreme Court asking that he be granted Russian citizenship. He was told on October 21 by the Passport and Visa Department that his visa had expired and he was to leave Moscow within two hours. Desperate that his hopes of finding a new life in Russia would be dashed, he slit his wrists in a suicide attempt and was taken to a local hospital where he was treated. He was released from the hospital on October 28.

While he waited for a decision from the Russians regarding his application for a visa (which was now being reconsidered), Oswald went to the American Embassy on October 31. He told the astonished consular officials that he wanted to "dissolve his American citizenship." He was interviewed by two US officials at the embassy, Richard Snyder and his assistant, John McVickar. Oswald took swipes against the US and its policies. Oswald also told Snyder and McVickar about his job in the Marines and hinted that he'd give the Russians whatever secret information he had. Snyder and McVickar tried to convince Oswald not to give up his citizenship and a hot debate between the three of them ensued. At one point, McVickar asked Oswald if he was willing to serve the Soviet nation. Oswald's answer, according to McVickar , "tended to extinguish any sympathy one may have felt for a confused and unhappy young man."

Counsel Snyder wrote this about his reflections when speaking with Oswald at the Embassy,

> Oswald offered the information that he had been a radar operator in the Marine Corps and that he had voluntarily stated to unnamed Russian officials that as a Soviet citizen he would make known to them such information concerning the Marine Corps and his specialty as he possessed. He intimated that he might know something of special interest.[2]

Oswald wrote of this encounter in his "diary" saying, "I leave Embassy, elated at this showdown, returning to my hotel I feel now my energies are not spent in vain. I'm sure Russians will accept me after this sign of my faith in them."

Once in Russia, Oswald was packed off to the city of Minsk where he worked in a radio factory, lived high on the hog and married a pretty Russian woman named Marina. Marina lived with her uncle, Ilya Prusakova, who worked at the Ministry of Internal Affairs (MVD). Marina worked at a pharmacy in a local hospital and in February 1959, she met Lee at the city dance hall. Six weeks later they were married (that was fast), and the next year the couple had a daughter.

His two and a half years in Russia are a huge mystery to this day and the debate lingers as to just what he was doing in Russia in the first place. Some people have speculated that Oswald was part of a covert US false defector program that was sending US intelligence operatives into Russia to gather information on the Soviet Union. In the eighteen months prior to 1960, two former Navy men, five Army personnel stationed in West Germany, and two employees of the National Security Agency changed sides. Joan Hallett, who was married to the Assistant Naval Attaché and worked as a receptionist in the embassy, told author Anthony Summers that Counsel Snyder

2 Newman, John, *Oswald and the CIA,* Carroll & Graf Publishers, New York, 1995, Pages 5-6.

and a security officer "took Oswald upstairs to the working floors, a secure area where the Ambassador and the political, economic, and military officers were. According to Hallett, Oswald came to the embassy several times in 1959."

If Oswald was just a low level defector, then why did the Navy change all the aircraft call signs, and radio and radar frequencies at the last base where Oswald was stationed? Did they fear that he would give away that information to the Soviets? After his "defection," the Navy did not conduct a "formal damage assessment" on what Oswald might have given up. This was done in the two previous cases where US military men defected to Russia.[3]

Is it possible that Oswald was used by the US government as an unwitting false defector to see how much the Soviets would debrief him and what information Oswald could bring back with him?

A former Chief Security Officer at the State Department, Otto Otepka, said that in 1963 his office was working on a program to study American defectors that included Oswald. Otepka said that in the months before the Kennedy assassination, the State Department did not know if Oswald "had been one of theirs."

When Oswald returned to the United States with Marina from Russia, he was not charged with desertion by the Navy. Why? By defecting to the Soviet Union, Oswald should have been considered a traitor but there was no disciplinary action taken against him. The Office of Naval Intelligence told the FBI that they had no intention of taking any further action against one of their own. Once back in Texas, the FBI opened a "security case" on him and found him to be "cold, arrogant, and difficult to interview." Since the FBI did not have any evidence that Oswald had given any secrets to the Soviet Union, they left him alone.

As has been noted in a previous chapter, it is very possible that Oswald was part of the REDSKIN program. The State Department listed Oswald as a "tourist" when he made out his application to go to Russia. In the late 1950s, there were at least 20 REDCAP agents sent to the Soviet Union, It is not out of the realm of possibility that Oswald was sent to the Soviet Union in order to find out as much as possible on the activities inside the country.

The newly released documents reveal an active interest by the

3 Summers, Anthony and Swan, Robin, *Lee Harvey Oswald: A Simple Defector?* www.wordpress.com, 11/19/ 2013.

CIA in both Lee and Marina Oswald, as well as what was going on in Minsk as far as a Russian intelligence school being run while Lee was living in the city.

One such query was based on an operation called GPFLOOR and was sent to Mr. Wigren. The one page note reads as follows:

> Mr. Paul Chretien called me at 1420 hours on 17 December presumably on the basis of some press query, asking "whether there is still a Soviet intelligence school in Minsk." I told him I'd never heard of one in the first place; had he? No, he hadn't. I then checked through Mary Kay Viering and got the following sole trace which I passed on to Chretien by phone, simply saying that there has been a report

A photo of a young Marina Oswald about the time she met Oswald.

of one back in 1947, source reliability unknown, but that if, as I suspected, his query concerned "spy schools" then there was none anywhere. Spies were trained individually—schools are for staff personnel, here and in the USSR. I discussed fabrications of this sort, and he seemed to understand fully.

Further information on the possible Minsk spy school came in a CIA memo dated February 15, 1990 called "Debriefing Report: KGB Higher School in Minsk." The memo is entitled "Lee Harvey Oswald and Wife Marina." This is the memo in full:

The source discussed the Lee Harvey Oswald case with former instructors at the Minsk KGB Higher School of Counterintelligence. Following his defection to the USSR, Oswald was resettled in Minsk, outside of Moscow. He was placed under full surveillance by the regional territorial KGB in Minsk. KGB officers from the Second Directorate of the White Russian KGB were in contact with Oswald and considered him an agent because he would provide them with some information on his past. Marina was also considered an agent.

Oswald resided very close to Victory Square and the KGB Higher School in Minsk. His apartment was very nice by Soviet standards. Oswald was also interrogated several times by KGB officers in Moscow. The source does not know what type of information Oswald provided to the KGB in Minsk or Moscow. Oswald fell into deep depression in the USSR. He was homesick and wanted to return to the United States. He eventually received Soviet permission to return to the United States with his wife Marina.

His KGB handlers did consider passing Oswald to the First Chief Directorate to be handled by a KGB residency in the United States. This proposal was ultimately rejected, however, because Oswald was considered too unstable. According to the source, the KGB did not handle Oswald in the United States and had no further contacts with him.

Marina was considered an agent, but she did not like to cooperate with the KGB. She was interested in Oswald, but even more interested in getting away from the Soviet Union and poverty.

The KGB instructors who told the source about Oswald were Colonel [blank] and Colonel [blank]. These individuals used to be members of the White Russian KGB. SCD officers [blank] and [blank] also told him about this operation. The stories were all consistent.

According to the source, each one of these officers told him that the KGB did not handle Oswald after his re-defection to the United States, and the KGB did not give any tasks to Oswald. They also said that the KGB never gave Oswald a task to kill President Kennedy.

The source said that rumors in the West suggesting the KGB was involved in Kennedy's assassination were absurd. According to the source, the KGB would never risk the scandal of assassinating a major world leader.

Debriefer's Comments: Needless to say, we will go back over his knowledge of Oswald in an effort to acquire additional information.[4]

This memo has the CIA inquiring about any possible links between Oswald and a spy school in Minsk. The fact that the writers of the memo also believed that Marina Oswald was an agent is very interesting to say the least.

Another long memo regarding whether or not Oswald was an agent is a CIA memo dated Feb. 21, 1992 from [blank] Acting Chief, Soviet/East European Division, subject: Soviet Volunteer Allegations Re Oswald Involvement in the Kennedy Assassination. Here are the most important parts of the document:

On 31 December 1991, a Soviet volunteer to [blank] Station, Boris Zhuravlev, claimed that Lee Harvey Oswald was in fact a Ukrainian KGB intel source (code named Velktor) who had additionally been a controlled agent of the KGB. Zhuravlev stated that Oswald had actively conspired with two former US presidents to assassinate former President Kennedy. Zhuravlev when pressed could not provide any additional information. This information was transmitted

4 RIF No. 104-10014-10068.

to Headquarters in a staff channel message with no LIMIT or RYBAT control. We have taken immediate steps to have this message removed from the message system to prevent further access to it.

As background, Zhuravlev is an un-vetted volunteer who waked in to [blank] station on 30 December claiming to be a former KGB officer with access to leads concerning Western agents of the KGB. The above information was obtained during the second meeting with him when the Station was attempting to obtain details on the alleged leads to which he

Lee Harvey Oswald handing out leaflets in New Orleans on August 16, 1963.

claimed access. When pressed to provide information, he had only one vague agent identification in Canada and para one above information. He was not able to provide any other leads despite claiming some twenty years of service in the KGB.

Based upon information received to date, we consider Zhuravlev to be a highly questionable source. [blank] describes him as being stressed out, shaking and in fairly rough physical state; he was considered to be of no value. He departed the Embassy without incident and no further contact is anticipated.

As regards para one allegations, we have substantive information from IJDECANTER which outlines Oswald and wife's KGB connections and emphatically denies any KGB involvement in dispatching Oswald to assassinate President Kennedy. We have no information from any Soviet intel source indicating that the KGB had contact with Oswald after he returned to the US or that he conspired with any other element in the assassination.

A one-page memo from a debriefing report dated February 15, 1990, gives some more information on Oswald. The debriefer's name was "George F" and others present were "Jim/FBI Washington HQs." The subject was "KGB Higher School in Minsk-Part 111." One important paragraph says:

One instructor discussed his involvement with Lee Harvey Oswald and how he ran Oswald. Debriefer's Comment: Source was not sure if it was a true story or just some talk. This instructor alleged that Marina was a plant and that Oswald was an agent. Source opined that it was a piece of cake for the KGB to run the Oswald operation in the Soviet Union. Source is also convinced that Marina had to be a plant of the KGB. The operation was organized by the KGB and Oswald fell in love with her. The instructors also indicated in their lectures that the KGB did not task Oswald to kill the President. (Note: Believe we should return to this topic again and discuss it with Source in more detail).

Source questioned KGB's rationale in running Oswald, an ex-Marine with very little access to information. Based on information available to Source at the School the KGB did in fact run Oswald.

A further government document called a Counterintelligence Information Report dated November 29, 1900, Subject: Marina and Lee Harvey Oswald, Source: A former KGB officer, offers more interesting information on the Oswalds and the KGB:

According to senior staff officers from the Minsk KGB Counterintelligence School and Department 1 (American targets) of the Second Chief Directorate (internal security and counterintelligence-SCD) Headquarters, ex-Marine, Lee Harvey Oswald was an agent of the KGB, and was one before he met his future wife, Marina. The Minsk KGB had recruited Marina as a "swallow" (Soviet female prostitute) for use in sexual entrapment operations. Marina was directed against Oswald, who fell in love with her, when he was living in Minsk. Headquarters Comment: It was unclear whether the local or regional KGB was involved.

The Minsk UKGB kept numerous files on Oswald which contained agent, surveillance, and monitoring reports as well as other information. Headquarters Comment: When source questioned the KGB's access to information, he was only assured that Oswald was run in Minsk as an agent). Yurshak, who held a low opinion of Oswald, stated that Oswald was a bit crazy and unpredictable. Oswald was never required to sign an agreement to cooperate, even though he was cooperating. Yurshak believed that Oswald knew he was in contact with the KGB.[5]

These documents provide a window into the CIA and its counterintelligence branch that painted a picture of both Lee and Marina as possible agents of the KGB. Of course, the Warren Commission did not know any of this information when it was writing its report and one can only imagine what their narrative would have been if they'd have been given this blockbuster news.

5 RIF No. 104-10014-10057.

Marina Oswald with her second husband, Dallas carpenter Kenneth Porter.

As for Marina Oswald, she became the widow of the man accused of killing the president of the United States. After the assassination, she was taken by the FBI and kept at the Inn of the Six Flags Hotel in protective custody. She was threatened with deportation but decided to cooperate with the Bureau and gave certain information to the Warren Commission, and said she believed her husband was the killer of the president.

In 1965, Marina married Dallas carpenter Kenneth Porter and lived with him in Richardson, Texas with her two daughters. She later had a son with him.

Over the years, Marina made contact with journalist Priscilla Johnson and a friendship was born. According to Johnson, she spent thirteen years researching her book called *Marina and Lee* that came out in 1977.

At first, Marina accepted the verdict of the Warren Commission but as the years passed, she began to change her mind. She began telling all who would listen that her views had changed regarding Lee and the murder the JFK. She now believed that her late husband might not have been the assassin after all, and in an interview she gave to the *Ladies Home Journal* in September 1988 she said, "I'm not saying that Lee is innocent, that he didn't know about the conspiracy or was not part of it, but I am saying he's not necessarily guilty of murder. At first, I thought that Jack Ruby (who killed Oswald two days after the assassination) was swayed by passion; all of America was grieving. But later, we found that he had connections with the underworld. Now, I think Lee was killed to keep his mouth shut." Marina added, "I believe he worked for the American government. He was taught the Russian language when he was in the military. Do you think that is usual, that an ordinary soldier is taught Russian? Also, he got in and out of Russia quite easily, and he got me out quite easily."

In April 1996, she wrote:

> At the time of the assassination of this great president whom I loved, I was mistaken by the "evidence" presented to me by government authorities and I assisted in the conviction of Lee Harvey Oswald as the assassin. From the new information now available, I am now convinced that he was an FBI informant and believe that he did not kill President Kennedy.[6]

She never addressed the allegations made by the CIA in the above-mentioned documents that both she and Lee were some sort of agents for Russia.

---

6 American History/ The Assassination of JFK-Marina Oswald: Biography, Spartacus-educational.com/JFK.

Chapter 37
Watergate and the CIA

On the night of June 17, 1972, five well-dressed men in suits with walky-talkies and electronic equipment were arrested at the headquarters of the Democratic National Committee (DNC) located at 2650 Virginia Avenue NW in Washington, DC. Police were called to the Watergate building after a security guard noticed that a piece of tape had been put over the lock of a door at the offices of Lawrence O' Brien, the DNC's Chairman. The five men arrested were Eugenio Martinez, Virgilo Gonzalez, Frank Sturgis, Bernard Baker, and James McCord. Also taken into custody (at a later time) were G. Gordon Liddy and Howard Hunt. Both Hunt and Liddy had extensive ties to both the CIA and the FBI.

What started out as a routine break-in turned out to be the tip of a very large iceberg that finally toppled the presidency of Richard Nixon and forced his impeachment and resignation from office.

In the ensuing decades since the break-in at the Watergate Hotel, it has become a parlor game to figure out why the burglars broke into the office of Chairman O'Brien and who ordered it. Did President Nixon himself order the break-in or did someone else in the White House, acting alone or on orders from others in the Executive Branch? That answer is still not known, but in the intervening time,\ new evidence and old theories co-exist.

Just after the break-in, the top people at the CIA and the FBI went into overdrive to see what actually happened and to deal with any potential fallout from the burglary. As news of the break-in started coming out in bits and pieces, it became evident that a number of the men who were arrested had ties to both the FBI and the CIA.

G. Gordon Liddy had been an FBI agent in the past and was known for his reckless actions over a period of time. On the CIA side, Howard Hunt, Eugenio Martinez, and James McCord had at one time or another worked for the Agency. At the time of his arrest, Eugenio Martinez was still on the payroll of the CIA and that news could not have gone over well at Langley headquarters. There were even rumblings that the CIA had masterminded of the break-in in order to derail the Nixon presidency (or for various other reasons).

There was some talk that the CIA was being blamed, right or wrong, for the break-in itself.

The Nixon administration, too, had gone into overdrive to see what was going on at the Watergate after the men were arrested and see if it would affect them at any level.

On June 23, Nixon received more information on the break-in from his chief of staff, H.R. "Bob" Haldeman in an oval office meeting. Haldeman said, "The FBI agents who are working the case, at this point, feel that's what it is. This is CIA."

Nixon, who was no fan of the CIA (and vice versa), had a good idea what Haldeman was talking about. Nixon was the case officer for the abortive Bay of Pigs invasion of Cuba in April 1961 and had been one of its chief proponents. He knew where Haldeman was going and said in reply:

> Of course, this is a, this is a Howard Hunt operation and exposure of it will uncover a lot of things. You open that scab there's a hell of a lot of things we just feel it would be detrimental to have this thing go any further. This involves the Cubans, Hunt, and a lot of hanky-panky that we have nothing to do with ourselves. This will open the whole Bay of Pigs thing.

But was the Watergate break-in a CIA run operation from the start? In a recorded June 23 meeting between Haldeman and Nixon (which would later become known as the "smoking gun" tape), Haldeman told the president, "the way to handle this now is to have [CIA] deputy director Walters call [FBI] interim director Pat Gray and just say, stay the hell out of this. This is, ah, business here we don't want to go any further on it." Nixon agreed. In that same conversation, Haldeman told Nixon that Pat Gray, the acting FBI director, had spoken to Richard Helms and said, "I think we've run right into the middle of a CIA operation."

At the time of their arrests, James McCord and Eugenio Martinez had the closest ties to the CIA. McCord was a veteran of the CIA's Bay of Pigs invasion in 1961, and served as the security chief at Langley. After leaving the CIA, he opened up his own private security firm in Maryland. During the hearing process, McCord

E. Howard Hunt testifying before Congress in 1973.

blew the lid on the rest of the team, saying that the White House was perpetrating a cover-up of the Watergate affair, after some of the burglars demanded hush money be paid to them in order to ensure their silence.

Eugenio Martinez was a contract employee at the CIA and at the time of his arrest, was still on the Agency payroll. After the burglary, the CIA lied when it said that Martinez had no relationship with the Agency.

Nixon was leary of Howard Hunt right from the moment he heard his name mentioned as one of the burglars. Hunt was a longstanding veteran of the CIA dating back to the 1950s and early 1960s, and was involved in many covert operations including missions in Cuba and other Central American nations. As far as Nixon was concerned, the fact that three men with CIA ties were arrested in the Watergate must have sent him into a panic. What were these CIA men doing, were they ordered to do it and why?

It was obvious that Nixon was paranoid about getting the CIA off the case and he ordered Haldeman and John Ehrlichman to meet with both Helms and General Walters—the CIA Deputy Director. Helms told Nixon's men that the CIA was not connected to the break-in in any way, and that none of the suspects had worked for the CIA in the last two years. That statement was a lie, as Martinez was a current CIA contract officer.

Under huge pressure from the Nixon White House, Richard Helms reluctantly agreed to Nixon's demand that the CIA pressure the FBI into not going ahead with its investigation of the Watergate burglars. Before leaving the meeting an infuriated Helms lashed out

315

at Haldeman saying, "the Bay of Pigs had nothing to do with this. I have no concern about the Bay of Pigs."

Documents released by the National Archives over the past years describe Howard Hunt's connections to the Cubans involved in the Watergate affair. This document had its origins in the records of the Rockefeller Commission. The memo is from David Bellin to William Schwarzer, entitled, "Cuba and the Politicization of Police Power." It reads in part:

> A Cuban explained how the Cubans got into Watergate. They were used to us. When Bay of Pigs operatives like Hunt moved over to Watergate they sent for their old Cubanos. They work like the Mafia. When they want to issue an anti-Communist contract or what looks like an anti-Communist contract, they contact us. We're reliable, intelligent, professional. And we're learning to keep our mouth shut. We're learning to live with this. And we fear the Company [the CIA]. We know the Company. The Company can drop a word and change your life. You don't get a job or a loan for your business, or you're in trouble with police or immigration. To such people the bizarre requirements of Watergate seemed not unusual but SOP.

Nixon used the CIA to his own advantage by ordering Richard Helms to provide him with CIA cables on the Bay of Pigs, information on the assassination of President Diem of South Vietnam, and a file on the Dominican dictator Rafael Trujillo. Nixon wanted these files to find any derogatory information on the Kennedy administration's relationship with these events.

When Richard Helms first learned of the Watergate break-in, he ordered that no one in the agency have anything to do with Hunt or McCord, who obviously had CIA ties. Helms was worried that any leaks of the Agency's past relationship with Hunt or McCord would send the wrong message that the CIA had something to do with the break-in. As far as Helms was concerned, Hunt worked for CREEP (Committee to Reelect the President) at the White House and it was there that any blame would lie. He then tasked William Colby to head the Agency's investigation of the affair.

The FBI had by now traced the money found on the Watergate burglars to a Mexican bank, and also to a man named Kenneth Dahlberg. The total amount of the cash was $114,000, which had originally been in the possession of CREEP. The money directly tied the Nixon administration to the burglars. The $114,000 had originally been deposited in a Miami bank which was controlled by Bernard Barker, one of the men arrested in the Watergate break-in. Unfortunately for the burglars, the money on their persons was sequentially numbered dollar bills which were part of CREEP's operating funds. The Bureau traced the bills back to Barker, and subsequently, to the offices of CREEP.

By now, Helms decided to end any further CIA involvement in what he obviously saw as a White House cover-up. He pressed Gray to investigate those already under arrest, and keep out of any further CIA internal business. Helms asked Walters to write to Gray saying, "We still adhere to the request that they [the FBI] confine themselves to the personalities already or directly under suspicion and that they desist from expanding this investigation into other areas which may well, eventually, run afoul of our operations."

The new documents released by the National Archives on the Watergate-CIA connections are very revealing, and I am going to print here all the relevant material to give the reader the historical context in which it was written and what it all means. First is an "eyes only" report to Teheran for Ambassador Helms from Maury (otherwise unidentified):

At Senate Armed Services Committee party 13 December, I asked Tom Korologos, Deputy Assistant to President for Legislative Affairs, if he could throw light on Baker problem [Senator Howard Baker]. He said in confidence Baker had discussed Agency/ Watergate matter with him and made clear that Baker's central hang-up is thesis advanced by Copeland and St. George that agency staged Watergate in order to entrap Plumbers. Korologos indicated Baker may have been particularly influenced by Copeland allegations.

On 13 December, Lyle Miller, with Baker's permission, received 190 page transcript of Martinez testimony before

Baker. In general, Martinez's account of significant developments consistent with Agency testimony and records available to Baker. Moreover, Martinez said Sturgis denies allegations which St. George attributes to him. However, Martinez did state to Baker that he considered tradecraft of Plumbers unbelievably faulty. From this Baker apparently infers that this faulty tradecraft was deliberate on the part of at least one of the participants who sought thereby to lead other participants into trap. Martinez flatly denied St. George allegation that he was "anyone's double agent.

Understand another advocate of the "entrapment" theory (not necessarily entrapment by CIA, but merely entrapment by a mysterious "third force"). Is Ed Henley, former OGC staffer and more recently senior official with Mobile Oil and known to be on close terms with Baker.

Several days ago in response to a query from Tom Braden we sent Braden a copy of memo given Symington on 7 November and quoted in ref A, Para 4. On 13 December we received from Braden without covering comment, a copy

Richard Helms.

318

of "The Tom Braden Report" of 11 December entitled "Can He Blame It On CIA." Full text not yet appeared in any publication we know of, follows:

Washington—The last turn in the defense of Richard Nixon will be to blame Watergate on the CIA. Such is the view of former CIA Director Richard Helms, and such is the direction in which Sen. Howard Baker (R. Tenn.) and his minority staff on the Ervin Committee are now proceeding. It is not a very salable theory, but it's about all that's left; and if it could be made salable, it might get Richard Nixon off the hook. Consider: If CIA accomplished the break-in, the subsequent White House cover-up might be excused on the grounds that the president had to protect this secret intelligence service. And if the cover-up could be excused on that ground, unrelated crimes such as illegal contributions, forgeries and alleged extortions might be pardoned as mistakes of judgement arising from excessive political zeal. Thus, "some sinister force," General Alexander Haig put it to Judge John Sirica the other day, might eventually be used to explain all three recent magazine articles—two published in the National Review by a former CIA employee named Miles Copeland, the other, published in *Harpers* by Andrew St. George—suggest the President's last stand. Senator Baker has called the attention of all three articles to his colleagues on the Ervin Committee. Copeland alleges that the Watergate operation was CIA's retaliation against the White House for setting up the Plumbers as a rival *apparat*. "McCord took Liddy into a trap," he writes, and "after all, the CIA specialists in operations of the Plumbers kind had a lot to gain by putting the White House clowns out of business." St. George makes a similar allegation and adds detail worthy of 007 and a Fleming novel. "Ah, well," he quotes Helms as telling the young watch officer who telephoned him to report the break-in. "They finally did it. A pity: they really blew it. If the White House tries to ring me, just tell them you reported McCord's arrest already. Said I was very surprised."

Sen. Baker has also asked his colleagues to view a 28-Page memorandum prepared by one of his investigators named George Murphy. Murphy's findings, Baker hints, implicate the CIA. Does the theory that the CIA is at the bottom of the Watergate make sense? Is it a reasonable Presidential Defense? Richard Helms has testified as follows: "I am prepared to swear that no such conversation (with the CIA Watch officer) took place. The quotations attributed to me were never said by me. Of this is am certain." From the time he first learned of the Watergate break-in, Helms had been afraid that it would be blamed on him. Put yourself for a moment in his shoes. You are a career servant. You joined the Office of Strategic Services (OSS) during the war and you stayed on to help a series of Directors build the first US intelligence service. President Lyndon Johnson had made you its Director. You feel the responsibility keenly. Now consider what happens to you in the subsequent administration. First, an old friend of the President, Patrick Gray, is appointed to be chief of your major rival agency. One month later, you are told by H.R. Haldeman that the president has appointed another old friend, General Vernon Walters, to be your deputy. Another month later, and just after the break-in, you and your new deputy are summoned to the White House. You listen while Haldeman tells your deputy that "It has been decided" that he should go to Gray and ask him not to investigate the money found on the burglars because it might expose your operations. For the next few days, the White House calls to discuss the break-in and to suggest that you pay money to the families of those arrested. Eleven days after the break-in and on the eve of your departure for a long-scheduled trip, Gray calls to cancel an appointment you had made with him. With this sequence of events in mind, what would you suppose? That people at the White House might be trying to blame the Watergate on you? That's what Helms supposed and supposes still. [End of the "Tom Braden Report"]

On 14 December Baker met with Robert Bennett of Mullen Company, his father Senator Wallace Bennett and George Murphy to review agency memos covering our relations with Mullen Company [the reader should know that after he left the CIA, Howard Hunt worked for Mullen & Company as a writer, while still having a secret relationship with the Nixon White House]. After meeting, which lasted two hours, Baker emerged and told Lyle Miller that everything Bennett said was consistent with what we had told Baker and it was becoming clearer that Agency not involved Watergate but Baker reserves the option to pursue matter further since he doesn't want to go to his grave without having gotten to the bottom of it. Indicating he is still receiving info apparently implicating Agency. He asked Fred Thompson, Minority Counsel of Ervin Committee, if he should tell Miller "about the money." Thompson advised him not to. Remarking he was not sure of his source. "We have no idea what this refers to." [Fred Thompson would later become a United States Senator and TV actor, starring in such movies and TV shows as *Law & Order*, *The Hunt for Red October*, and *Die Hard 2*.]

The memo ends with these words, "Many thanks for Ref-C which has been discussed with Colby who is commenting thereon to you directly."

This long piece shows just how far some people at the time were willing to go to sacrifice the CIA in the throes of the Watergate break-in, regardless of whether there were any proof. We also have to look into the question of where the authors of the Braden Report got all their information. They must have had good sources inside the intelligence community to report in such detail. We also have to figure out just what Richard Helms knew about the break-in after it happened and whether or not he was being candid in his public remarks regarding the affair. We still don't have the 28-page memorandum that Senator Baker asked his committee friends to review (the one written by George Murphy). The above-mentioned article raises more questions than it answers.

This lengthy article lays out the possible connection between the break-in and the CIA, but we do know that a number of the Plumbers did have ties to the CIA. Eugenio Martinez was still on a $100.00 monthly retainer as an informant on the Cuban exile community in the Miami area. Somewhat later two more men were taken into custody—E. Howard Hunt, White House consultant, and G. Gordon Liddy, who left his White House "plumber" job in late December of 1971 to become an employee of CRP. The past association with the CIA of five of the seven arrested men naturally led to speculation of CIA involvement in the Watergate affair. CIA, confident that it had no involvement in the matter, and unaware of the ramifications that would develop later, proceeded in relatively routine cooperation with the investigating authorities, providing background material on the individuals on whom it had information, and summarizing its more recent known contacts with Hunt (whom the Agency did not initially associate with the Watergate affair).

The following information on Watergate and the CIA comes from a newly released document called "Working Draft—CIA Watergate History" that was obtained by a group called Judicial Watch, and tells the whole story of that relationship. Note: that this wonderful document is available on the web at the Judicial Watch web site:

The role of the Agency in this matter should be considered in two aspects. The first aspect is the actual but limited involvement of the Agency by the White House staff through its requests for Agency support and assistance in presumably legitimate (albeit unusual) activities purporting to be in the national interest. The Agency cooperated, though reluctantly, in producing psychological profiles on Daniel Ellsberg, of Pentagon Papers fame. It also cooperated in giving materials and assistance to Hunt up to the point that it appeared the requested support exceeded the stated purpose. The second aspect is the apparent attempt by members of the White House staff to involve the Agency in suppression of the FBI investigation of an aspect of the Watergate affair, and in what appeared to be an attempt to involve the Agency in a cover-up. The Agency's top officials refused and rebuffed attempts to implicate the CIA.

When the five men were arrested at the DNC

Headquarters on 17 June 1972, the FBI found certain identification documents in possession of two of them which were suspected as having been prepared by the CIA. The ensuing inquires not only established the fact that this was so, but that they had been issued to E. Howard Hunt. This is the first indication that the Agency had of how some of the material issued to Hunt, at the White House request, was being used. Even this took some time since initially the Office of Security, which was handling the matter, was unaware of the issuance to Hunt of the Hamilton alias documents from another Agency component.

The leaking of Hunt's Grand Jury testimony, with the attendant publicity focused on the Agency, resulted in requests from CIA Congressional Committees and subcommittees for an explanation by CIA of exactly what its role had been in the Watergate and Ellsberg affair. To satisfy these Congressional demands and answer their questions, there was an unprecedented parade of past and present top Agency officials to Capitol Hill. In addition to the then Director of Central Intelligence, Mr. James Schlesinger, and Deputy Director, General Vernon Walters, there were appearances by former DCI Helms, former DCI General Robert Cushman, the then Executive Secretary of the CIA Management Committee, Mr. William E. Colby, General Counsel Lawrence Houston, Legislative Counsel John Maury.

The fact that all these important CIA officials were called before the Congressional Committees shows just how vital it was for the Agency to cooperate with the investigation of the Watergate affair, especially since Hunt, Martinez and McCord had previously worked for the CIA.

The material in this chapter, particularly the Tom Braden article called "Can He Blame It on the CIA," and the information coming from Judicial Watch's "Working Draft—CIA Watergate History," sheds new light on the possible role played by the CIA in the Watergate break-in and its subsequent consequences in the aftermath of the Watergate affair.

Chapter 38
Oswald & Kostikov

One of the lingering mysteries of the Kennedy assassination,and the role of the president's alleged assassin, Lee Harvey Oswald, is Oswald's trip to Mexico City. After 55-plus years there is still genuine puzzlement as to why he was there (if he was there at all, as some Kennedy assassination researchers doubt. If was not there, who may have been impersonating him at that critical juncture in the entire Kennedy story?) Over the decades, new information has come to light that the CIA might have been running some sort of intelligence mission in Mexico City at the time of Oswald's arrival, possibly involving the FPCC (Fair Play for Cuba Committee), and a particular KGB assassin/agent who met Oswald when he showed up at the Russian Embassy in that city, Valery Kostikov. Oswald's trip to Mexico City is still a maze within a maze with so many theories and permutations that we still don't really know what was going on.

According to the Warren Commission, Oswald went to Mexico City in order to get a visa from the Soviet Embassy to return to Russia via Cuba. According to the WC, Oswald was eager to get back to Russia, as he was entirely frustrated with what his life in America had become.

What is known is that the CIA was watching Oswald's movements from the time he arrived in Mexico City to the time he left. Why they were so interested in him probably has to do with an ongoing intelligence mission at that time, one that is still not revealed to our satisfaction to this day.

At the time of the Kennedy assassination, the CIA had some comprehensive intelligence gathering activities running in Mexico City. A CIA analyst named John Whitten, a.k.a. John Scelso, who directed an intensive internal report on the Kennedy assassination for the Agency and whose identity had been kept secret for years said of these operations, "They were absolutely enormous. We were trying to follow the Soviets and all the satellites and Cubans. At the same time, the main thrust of the station's efforts was to attempt to recruit Russians, Cubans, and satellite people."

Another twist in the CIA's covert espionage game in Mexico City directly involves Lee Harvey Oswald. Recently discovered documents reveal that a CIA message dated September 16, 1963, informed the FBI that "the agency is giving some consideration to countering the activities of the FPCC, Fair Play for Cuba Committee, in foreign countries." Oswald was the lone member of the FPCC in New Orleans during the summer of 1963 and was arrested in a scuffle with Carlos Bringuer, offering his services in anti-Castro operations while he was handing out pro-Castro leaflets only a short time later. It is interesting to note that the day after this CIA memo dealing with a covert action against the FPCC, which had a direct Oswald connection, Oswald was applying for a Mexican tourist card. Is there any connection?

One of the first things that Oswald did upon his arrival in Mexico City was to make his way to the Cuban Consulate. There, he showed off his "leftist" credentials; his FPCC card, letters from the American Communist Party, a picture of him being arrested in New Orleans after his fight with Carlos Bringuer, and a now disputed membership card for the American Communist Party (it was never proved that Oswald ever belonged to the Communist Party of the US). When he asked for a visa to travel to Russia he was told that he had to go to the Russian Embassy. There, he asked for a visa to travel to Russia and was told he had to wait for months to get his visa. It is at this time that Oswald is supposed to have made a warning that he would "kill Kennedy" in retaliation for his not being allowed back into the Soviet Union.

But here the story becomes mired in mystery. Was it the real Oswald who came to the Soviet Embassy and the Cuban Consulate? The answer to that question seems to be *no*.

The first person to cast doubt on the real Lee Oswald being the man who came to the Cuban Consulate was Sylvia Duran. She was the secretary at the Mexico City Cuban Consulate during the time that Oswald (or someone impersonating him) made his brief sojourn to the Mexican capital. She met with Oswald who was desperately trying to get a visa to get back to Cuba, and then on to the Soviet Union. Sylvia Duran's brief meeting with Oswald caused the CIA a great deal of interest, if not panic, and her testimony regarding Oswald's visit to the consulate would only add to the deepening mystery concerning Oswald's trip south of the border. She told Oswald that she could not issue him a valid Cuban transit visa until he first got clearance from the Soviet Embassy that would approve any travel to the Soviet Union. Oswald left and went to the Soviet Embassy, which was only a short distance away.

A few hours later, he returned to the Cuban Consulate with new passport pictures that he had just taken. Duran accepted Oswald's application and told him to call back in a week. Oswald then said to Duran, "Impossible. I can only stay in Mexico three days." After also speaking with the consul's assistant who explained the same information, Oswald returned later after they assured him that his visa was going to be processed. He urgently requested that the Cubans give him a visa on the spot. Duran called the Soviet Embassy and was told that they had spoken to Oswald and told him that any decision on issuing him a visa would take a few months.

The day after the assassination, the ordeal of Sylvia Duran began. She was arrested by Mexican authorities upon the request of the CIA's Mexico City Station Chief Winston Scott. The arrest of Sylvia Duran was a hot topic at CIA Headquarters as is evident in a cable sent to Scott in Mexico City:

> Arrest of Sylvia Duran is extremely serious matter which could prejudice US freedom of action on entire question of Cuban responsibility. With full regard for Mexican interests, request you ensure that her arrest is kept absolutely secret, that no information from her is published or leaked, that all such info is cabled to US, and that fact of her arrest and her statement are not spread to leftist or disloyal circles in Mexican government.

It is evident from the frantic CIA activity after the president's death that a possible Cuban connection to the events in Dealey Plaza was seriously being considered. It was later revealed that Cuban President Dorticos pointedly asked the Ambassador to Mexico, Armas, in a phone call on November 26, 1963 about a report that Duran had been questioned about money.

Sylvia Duran's story was an important one that could have cleared up any possible Cuban connection to the assassination and her true

Valery Kostikov.

relationship with Oswald. However, the Warren Commission never questioned her on these important matters.

Now, we add the name of a mysterious Russian agent who worked in Mexico City and whom Oswald made contact with while he was there, Valery Kostikov. The documents released in the last two years shed new, valuable light on the activities of Valery Kostikov and we will get to them in this chapter.

Kostikov was a high-level KGB officer who had been serving in the Soviet's Mexican compound since 1960. As described in recently released CIA documents, it is believed that Kostikov was a member of the top secret Soviet Department 13 which was responsible for assassination activity in the Western Hemisphere. Certain members of the CIA tried to paint Oswald as a member of the Communist Party and more importantly, as a Soviet agent in touch with Kostikov. Thus, they tried to falsely to link the Soviet Union somehow with the president's death.

The history of Department 13 dates back to 1936 when the old Soviet Union, under the brutal reign of Joseph Stalin, decided that it needed a terror organization outside the country. During World War II, Department 13 sabotaged German forces in the Ukraine and killed hundreds of Russians who worked with the Germans.

Over the years, the CIA has linked Department 13 to assassination attempts on the late President of Yugoslavia, Marshall Tito, and General Eisenhower during his visit to Korea during the war. Only the top members of the Central Committee could give the approval for any assassination attempt, and in 1963 such action would have had to have the approval of then Premier Nikita Khrushchev. Recent declassified files say that the main job of Department 13 was sabotage against enemy targets. Specially trained KGB agents were tasked with carrying out such assassinations, but sometimes the Russians hired foreigners to do the job.

A CIA document tells the story of a possible Oswald-Department 13 link:

Question—Would KGB have screened Oswald when he was in Russia?

Answer—Yes. They would have close surveillance of him. KGB would have assessed his vulnerability to recruitment. KGB may not have had any interest in him but would know what his vulnerability was. May have gotten compromising photographs.

Question—Would 13th Department have interest?

Answer—Probably not. However, 13th Department dossiers are separate. Nosenko would not have access to any Department 13 dossier on Oswald.

Question—Is it possible that Oswald was recruited after he left Russia?

Answer—It is possible. If KGB had no interest when he returned to the U.S., it could later have interest and could rely on its vulnerability assessment to use the right approach in recruiting him.

Question—Would Oswald be appealing to KGB since he was not stable and was pro-Communist?

Answer—Possibly. It would depend on the job the KGB

wanted done. KGB has often used unstable, unreliable agents. KGB is not very adept to recruiting Americans. KGB is not concerned about an individual who is pro-Communist, but wouldn't like Oswald's getting publicity. However, KGB principally looks for men who need money and who are dissatisfied with their country or life.

Question—There is an unusual conversation between Kostikov and Mirabil, the Cuban Ambassador to Mexico, which takes place only twenty minutes after Kennedy has been shot. Mirabil calls for Yatskov, a KGB counterintelligence officer, but speaks instead to Kostikov. They talk about arrival of a "suitcase." Mirabil asks Kostikov to a picnic but Kostikov declines the invitation.

Answer—The conversation is strange. Perhaps this is some pre-arranged code, otherwise, CIA doesn't understand the conversation.

Question—If Kostikov had been involved, would he have stayed in Mexico City?

Answer—No. He would have been flown out of the country. He stayed there until 1965 and was again assigned there from 1968-71. It is unlikely he was involved in Kennedy's death.

Question—Were any of the employees of the Cuban Embassy who Oswald contacted or might have contacted members of the DGI—such as Duran, Calderon or Azgye?

Answer—The CIA has no evidence that these individuals were DGI.

Question—If Oswald had any contact with a DGI agent, would the government of Cuba be aware of it?

Answer—Yes. However, there have been no reports from Cuba that Oswald contacted DGI. [7]

Now, we get to the heart of what the new documents say regarding Valery Kostikov, and it is interesting reading:

Subject: Valery Kostikov. Kostikov, who was born on 17 March 1935 in Moscow, was assigned to the Soviet Embassy

[7] RIF No. 157-10011-10029: CIA Briefing on (Alleged) Soviet/Cuban Assassinations. Date 1/15/76.

in Mexico City as Vice Consul on 19 September 1961. A fluent Spanish speaker, he had travelled abroad at least three times before this present assignment; moreover, in 1959 Kostikov applied for a visa to accompany Premier Nikita Khrushchev 's party to the United States as an official of the Soviet Ministry of Foreign Affairs, but we have no record of his having come to this country at that time. Kostikov served as an interpreter at international conference at Madrid and Barcelona in 1958 and 1959. In late 1959 early 1960 he attended Soviet exhibitions in Mexico City and Havana; he is known to have been in Cuba from 6 January to 1 March 1960.

The physical descriptions of Kostikov quite accurately fit that of a Soviet case officer who nearly a year ago met in Mexico an FBI-controlled double agent. This double agent's Soviet case officer in the United States has been Oleg Danilevich Brykin of the 13th Department, KGB First Chief Directorate, occupying the overt position of translator-trainee, U.N. Secretariat, New York City. Brykin was stationed in New York from December 1960 to July of this year.

Since arriving in Mexico, Kostikov is known to have traveled three times outside the capital: In March 1963 and again for the first two weeks of September he went to Tijuana, Encenada, and Mexicali, ostensibly for the purpose of purchasing cotton. The US Department of State, however, had reported that during these trips, Kostikov met local representatives of Nocimente Liberation National and Central Compesine Independienta, both large Communist front organizations. In addition, according to FBI sources, Kostikov was accompanied on the September trip by Ivan Alfereyev, and he contacted in Ensenada several persons including Communist sympathizers who previously had been associated with Soviet officials stationed in Mexico City.

Alfereyev, a Pravda correspondent in Mexico, was in close contact with Cuban diplomats and local Communist leaders during a February 1962 visit to Quito.

Kostikov returned to Mexico City for a second tour of duty in July 1968. During this tour he was again assigned to the consular section and was a second secretary. It appeared that he was tasked with following the activities of the Central American communist parties and left-wing groups, and he met often with members of these groups, reportedly providing them with funds and technical guidance. In July/ August 1969, Kostikov made an unusual TDY trip to Moscow lasting three weeks. He made a four-day trip to Havana.

In September/October 1963, Lee Harvey Oswald approached the Soviet Embassy in Mexico City in an attempt to get a visa allowing him to return to the USSR. Kostikov, as a consular officer, handled this visa request. We have no information which indicates any relationship between these individuals other than for the purpose of Oswald's making his visa request.

Kostikov's tour in Mexico ended unexpectedly in September 1971. Our information indicated that he was not due to leave for another three to four months, and at the time of his departure, there was some speculation that the suddenness of his departure was due to the fact that he was known to Lyalin.

While in Mexico he was considered by some to be the most effective and dangerous of intelligence officers in Mexico. He has been described as being without morals, education and manners. Shortly after his arrival in Mexico in 1968, he was arrested in front of a house of prostitution after becoming involved in a fist fight with some locals. It appears this incident did not affect his position in Mexico City, despite the fact that it received a good deal of press coverage.

We are aware only that Kostikov arrived in Beirut in June 1978. We are unable to confirm this. Also, to the best of our knowledge, the KGB has not engaged in such executive action [assassination operations] since 1959.[8]

We now come into further information regarding Kostikov and an operation called Tumbleweed (code named AEBURBLE). This memo is dated 23 November 1963, one day after JFK was killed. It is a memo for the Assistant Deputy Director, Plans from the Acting

8 Letter from David Blee to "Anthony," dated May 21, 1982 marked Secret.

Chief SR Division, subject, Contact of Lee Oswald with a Member of Soviet KGB Assassination Department:

> Kostikov is an identified KGB officer. He was a case officer in an operation which is evidently sponsored by the KGB's 13th Department (responsible for sabotage and assassinations). This operation, which is controlled by the FBI under the cryptonym TUMBLEWEED, involved a German-national resident of Oklahoma who was recruited in Europe and met this year with Kostikov in Mexico City and shortly thereafter with a known 13th Department officer, Oleg Brykin, in New York. The instructions given TUMBLEWEED by the two officers (pinpointing objectives for sabotage) and the circumstances of their involvement in the case, left no doubt that both of them were working for the same KGB component, the 13th.
>
> Of course it is not usual for a KGB agent on a sensitive mission to have such overt contact with a Soviet Embassy. However, we have top-secret Soviet intelligence documents, describing Military Intelligence doctrine, which show that very important agents can be met in official installations using as cover for their presence there some sort of open business.[9]

There is a huge amount of information regarding Oswald's (or someone else's) trip to Mexico City as well as information that is still being kept secret by the government. Right after the assassination, this document was written regarding Oswald and his possible ties to Kostikov.

According to an intercepted phone call in Mexico City, Lee Oswald was at the Soviet Embassy on 28 September 1963 and spoke with the Consul, Valerie Kostikov. This was learned when Oswald called the Soviet Embassy on 1 October, identifying himself by name and speaking broken Russian, stating the above and asking the guard who answered the phone whether there was "anything new concerning the telegram to Washington." The guard checked and told Oswald that a request had been sent, but nothing had as yet been received. The FBI liaison officer, Mr. Pappich, told me on 23 November that the Bureau has reason to believe that Oswald's visit

9 RIF No.—104-10125-10125.

was to get Soviet support for a US passport or visa matter (perhaps the new passport mentioned in the press articles).

Whether or not operation Tumbleweed had anything to do with Kostikov or another undisclosed CIA operation in Mexico is still open for debate. An addendum was written on November 27, 1963 titled "Domestic Intelligence Division" which said, "TUMBLEWEED is a double agent originally recruited by the Soviets in Germany, operated by CIA until his return to the US when he was turned over to the Bureau. He has made trips to Germany and Mexico. CIA has cooperated in handling of matter."

According to the latest material on the case, the double agent in the Tumbleweed case might be a man named Guenter Schulz (we have no other information on Guenter Schulz).

The CIA wrote the following cable regarding the Tumbleweed case as follows:

Bagley stated that he wished to point out that Kostikov, known KGB agent, is the same individual who has been in touch with the Bureau double agent in the case referred to as TUMBLEWEED. (This case relates to a double agent, Guenter Schulz, who is being operated by us against the Soviets. He had contact with the Soviets in Mexico City. [Bagley pointed out that Kostikov has been tentatively identified with the Thirteenth Department of the KGB, which handles sabotage and assassinations].

At the time of the assassination, there were differences of opinion in the US intelligence community regarding whether or not Kostikov was a member of Department 13. In a declassified memo from 1964 from the FBI Director J. Edgar Hoover to the CIA Director, the Tumbleweed case is front and center:

The files of this Bureau do not contain any information to fully support the statement in paragraph five in your proposed draft to the effect that Kostikov is believed to work for Department 13 of the First Chief Directorate of the Committee for State Security (KGB). Our letter dated May 31, 1963, directed to the attention of Mr. James Angleton of your Agency in the Tumbleweed investigation suggested that you consider the possibility that Valery Kostikov may be connected with the 13th Department. Our suggestion was occasioned by our observation of Kostikov's participation in activity observed in the Tumbleweed matter. In response to our May 31, 1963 letter referred to above, Mr. Angleton's letter dated June 25, 1963, captioned "Terrorist" advised that your Agency could locate no information in your files to indicate that Kostikov was a representative of the 13th Department of the First Chief Directorate, KGB.[10]

Hoover also added that he suggested that the CIA avoid "the affirmative expression of the belief in Kostikov's employment by the Thirteenth Department." According to Hoover, "information suggests the possibility, however, no specific information is at hand to definitely support possibility."

The CIA tried to put to bed the question regarding Kostikov and the Tumbleweed case by writing:

1) After examining all of our traces on Kostikov, we are convinced beyond reasonable doubt that he is a staff officer of the KGB. Contributing to this conclusion are his associates, his movements, his Mexican and other contacts and his cover position, as well as his involvement in the TUMBLEWEED operation. 2) Kostikov's involvement in TUMBLEWEED is our only reason to believe that he is connected with the 13th Department. Kostikov was in clandestine contact with TUMBLEWEED (as definitely confirmed by Tumbleweed's photo identification) and arranged Tumbleweed's contact in the US with a KGB colleague of Kostikov's. This colleague was identified by TUMBLEWEED from photos as Oleg Brykin, who has definitely been identified by a reliable FBI source as a member of the 13th Department.[11]

Until we have more information on the Tumbleweed case, Oleg Brykin, and Geunter Schulz, the story of Kostikov cannot be resolved.

10 Best, Emma, "No, CIA's counterintelligence chief didn't mastermind a JFK assassination cover-up weeks in advance," www.muckrock.com.
11 Ibid.

Chapter 39
Carlos Marcello

It is the spring of 1961 and Attorney General Robert Kennedy is seated in his Washington, DC office; the lights are burning bright despite the late hour. The president's younger brother is working the phones on his latest project, the deportation of one of the best known members of the Mafia, New Orleans mob boss Carlos Marcello. Marcello has been a thorn in the side of the Kennedy brothers since the 1950s when Robert sought to curb the power of the American mob from their days as a member of the Senate Subcommittee on Investigations (the McClellan Committee). The committee investigated organized crimes influence in several areas: garbage collection, dry cleaning, frozen foods, pinball games, and jukebox operations. Most important of all, the Committee monitored activities of the Teamsters Union and its powerful president, Jimmy Hoffa. Little known to most Americans at that time, but well known to RFK, was that Carlos Marcello was part of the CIA's secret war to kill Fidel Castro of Cuba. Marcello, like his fellow co-conspirators Johnny Rosselli and Santos Trafficante, had leverage against the Kennedys if he had chosen to use it.

The Teamsters Union was charged with high-level corruption, and during his investigation, Bobby made a trip to the West Coast to look into the charges. He was told of illegal dealings between the Union and various trucking associations. Along the way, he was introduced to many of the men who would later play an important part in John Kennedy's administration and in Robert's later political life.

Bobby called for the establishment of a national crime commission that would be the main intelligence unit for all the various law enforcement agencies of the government. This program never materialized but the Justice Department did set up a Special Group on organized crime. It lasted only two years.

The FBI, under J. Edgar Hoover, established a "top hoodlum program" in which each FBI field office drew up a list of the biggest local underworld figures for constant surveillance. In New Orleans,

335

the biggest fish was Carlos Marcello.

RFK's first problem upon taking office was how to deal with his FBI boss, and Kennedy hater, J. Edgar Hoover. His brother decided not to ruffle too many feathers upon taking office and he re-appointed both Hoover and CIA Director Allen Dulles to new terms at their respective organizations. Those men knew too many secrets and JFK didn't want any more trouble with them than he might otherwise have as he started his new administration. Hoover became Director of the FBI in 1924 and in the years that followed, took the Bureau out of the control of the Justice Department, making it a law unto himself. Bobby planned to change all that, and he ran straight into a blood feud with the irascible Hoover.

J. Edgar Hoover's first and only passion was the fight against international communism that dated back to World War II. Even then, Hoover had to fight to get his own share of the intelligence pie, in competition with Bill Donovan's OSS. In fact, Hoover always felt that there was no organized crime problem in the United States. He once said, "There is no single individual, or coalition of racketeers who dominates crime across the nation."

This high-tension atmosphere in the battle against organized crime prevailed when Robert Kennedy took over the reins of the Justice Department. As the late John Davis wrote in his book *The Kennedys: Dynasty and Disaster,* the battle against organized crime was a mutual arena for the Kennedys. It involved confrontation with real enemies of the people and therefor appealed to their "competitive and moralistic instincts."

Bobby directed the IRS to start income tax investigations of Marcello, Trafficante, and Carmine Lombardozzi, and got an indictment of Louis Gallo for giving false information on a Veterans Administration application. Also indicted were Anthony Accardo—tax evasion, Tony Provenzano—extortion, and Carlos Marcello—conspiracy to defraud. In 1960, the Justice Department obtained 19 indictments of organized crime figures. By 1961, under RFK, that number jumped to 121. In 1961, Justice had 96 convictions of top mob figures. That number rose to 101 in a single year.

As noted, one of Bobby's biggest targets was Carlos Marcello, the crime boss of Louisiana. Marcello lived in the US under a false Guatemalan passport, having entered the country illegally. In

Carlos Marcello.

addition to Louisiana, he controlled organized crime in Texas and much of the Southwest. A story in the *New Orleans States-Item* ofDecember 28, 1960, published before JFK took office, said, "Robert F. Kennedy stated he would expedite the deportation proceedings pending against Marcello after Kennedy takes office in January 1961."

On April 4, 1961, RFK had Marcello deported to Guatemala in handcuffs. Marcello was ultimately able to covertly return to the US by way of the Dominican Republic. The IRS put an $835,000 tax lien on Marcello and in June 1961, a Federal Grand Jury indicted him for having a false Guatemalan passport.

Marcello had a harrowing few days in the jungles of Guatemala, with broken ribs, trying to live off the land until he could get in touch with people who could aid him. It was suspected that Carlos Marcello was flown back to the US by none other than David Ferrie, who played a prominent part in Jim Garrison's New Orleans investigation into the president's death.

At the time of the assassination, Ferrie was in the employ of Marcello's lawyer, G. Wray Gill, working on Marcello's defense against immigration fraud charges. In an ironic twist of fate, Marcello was acquitted of these charges on the same day that JFK was killed.

According to author Michael Benson, "FBI reports regarding Ferrie—which fell into the hands of author David Lifton through WC staffer Wesley Liebeler—indicated that Ferrie flew to Guatemala aboard Delta Airlines twice during the fall of 1963, evidence that Ferrie's detective work for G. Wray Gill was directly related to his defense of Carlos Marcello's immigration fraud charges."[12]

Reporter Victor Riesel wrote, "Federal organized crime investigators had concluded that Carlos Marcello had become one of the two most powerful Mafia leaders in the nation, second only to Carlo Gambino the actual "boss of all bosses."

Marcello sought revenge against Bobby Kennedy and he is reported to have said that the way to accomplish this was to "hit" the president. He told this to Edward Becker in September of 1962: "Don't worry about that little Bobby son-of-a-bitch He's going to be taken care of."

In that conversation with Marcello, Becker began talking about the Kennedys and Marcello got to his feet and in Italian said, "Take that stone out of my shoe." Becker then told Marcello, "You can't go after Bobby Kennedy. You'll get into a hell of a lot of trouble." Marcello answered by saying, "If you want to kill a dog, you don't cut off the tail, you cut off the head" (meaning the president). Marcello finished the conversation by saying that he had a plan to use "a nut" to take the fall for the murder, like they do in Sicily."

Besides Marcello, there were other threats against President Kennedy, one of them coming from Marcello's fellow co-conspirator in the Castro plots, Santos Trafficante Jr. In a meeting with a Cuban exile leader name Jose Aleman Jr., the conversation turned to Aleman's seeking a $1.5 million loan from the Teamsters Union via Trafficante's friend, Jimmy Hoffa. The conversation led to the Kennedys and Trafficante railed against the president as being a dishonest politician who took bribes and was basically no good. Trafficante said, "Have you seen how his brother is hitting Hoffa, a man who is a worker, who is not a millionaire, a friend of the blue-collars? He doesn't know that this kind of encounter is very delicate. Mark my words, this man Kennedy is in trouble, and he will get what is coming to him."

Aleman told Trafficante that Kennedy would be re-elected in

12 Benson, Michael, *Who's Who in the Kennedy Assassination: An A-Z Encyclopedia,* Page 277.

1964. Trafficante then stopped his friend and said with a straight face, "No, Jose, you don't understand me. Kennedy's not going to make it to the election. He is going to be hit."

Upon hearing this, Aleman, alarmed, took his news to the FBI. But once again, nothing was done to prevent any such assassination attempt and then it was too late.

Marcello's threat against the Kennedys was not an isolated theme. In September 1962, Jimmy Hoffa, one of Robert Kennedy's most hated enemies, had a talk with Louisiana Teamsters leader Edward Partin regarding a possible hit on the Attorney General. The plan was to firebomb Robert Kennedy's Virginia home with plastic explosives, and to hire a sniper to kill the president. Partin, who was a government informer, relayed this information to the FBI but nothing was done.

The new documents released by the National Archives in the JFK dump of the past two years shed new light on what the FBI knew about Marcello's deportation from the United States. This information is from an FBI memo dated May 29, 1961 called "CM, Deportation Coop, Guatemala, Return to US Airport, Whereabouts, Paid Off, Assoc, Buss Act, Source. Subject: Carlos Marcello Anti-Racketeering":

> With regards to events which led up to the deportation of Marcello to Guatemala and to activities which occurred thereafter, you may be interested in the following information which was developed by Agent Papich in Guatemala City, on May 12, 1961.
>
> [blank] confided to the Bureau that he had been very much involved in working out arrangements whereby Marcello was accepted by the Guatemalan Government. It was [blank] understanding that Attorney General Kennedy had conferred [blank] and had asked for [blank] assistance in making certain that Guatemala accept Marcello as a citizen of that country. [blank] received instructions from his headquarters to give the matter special handling. [blank] then went to President Miguel Ydigoras of Guatemala to explain to him that the US Government planned to deport him to Guatemala and that in order to effect this deportation

it would be necessary for the Guatemalan government to accept the subject. [blank] appealed to Ydigoras for full cooperation which was granted. At the time this took place the Guatemalan President insisted that matter be handled quietly and that there be no publicity. [blank] informed Ydigoras that as far as he knew there would not be any publicity. The Guatemalan government then officially agreed to accept subject.

[blank] stated that he personally was at the airport on the day when Marcello arrived in Guatemala City on a US Border Patrol plane. He was shocked to observe that there were 15 to 20 reporters gathered at the airport, all waiting for the subject.[13]

[blank] did not know how the information had leaked to the press but he assumed that there must have been some notice given to newspapermen in the US. Because of this sudden appearance of newspapermen, Guatemalan officials found it necessary to process the subject's entry in a clandestine manner and in another building which blocked any contact with newspaper people. This worked successfully and the subject was immediately removed to a hotel in the city.

According to [blank] the newspapermen learned what happened and some of the local writers began criticizing the Guatemalan President for his involvement in the entire episode. Some of the President's political opposition accused him of protecting a hoodlum. Ydigoras became greatly incensed, bearing in mind that his political position is extremely shaky. He accused [blank] of mishandling the entire matter and has refused to deal with [blank] on any other matters since the above-mentioned event.

Because of the pressure being placed upon him by political opposition, Ydigoras realized that it would be necessary to remove the subject. On or about May 10, 1961, Marcello allegedly was to be returned to the US via Pan American Airways, who had agreed to accept him as a passenger even though he would be inadmissible in the US. Pan American reportedly did this because Ydigoras had

13 RIF No. 124-10210-10327.

issued orders cancelling flights of all airlines into and out of the country if they refused to take Marcello as a passenger. Pan American apparently decided to gamble because the threatened cancellation would be seriously damaging to the airlines business.

[blank] stated that Marcello never appeared at the airport and a check at the hotel indicated that he had disappeared. Later, a report was received that Guatemalan officials had forced him into El Salvador, which country had refused to accept subject. [blank] pointed out that as far as he was concerned there was no truth to the story. He was convinced that arrangements were made between Marcello and Guatemalan officials whereby Marcello was able to conveniently move to a finca (farm) in the interior of Guatemala. [blank] has received information from a reliable source indicating that subject is living comfortably and will not leave until a disposition is made of the court action in behalf of the subject, now reportedly pending in Washington, D.C.[14]

In any event, Marcello somehow returned to the United States, landing in Miami where he was allowed to enter the country without being stopped at immigration for questioning. His actions and movements were monitored by the FBI. When asked by reporters what kind of business he was in, Marcello replied by saying he was a "legitimate businessman" who was being harassed by the federal government. By 1975 his net worth was estimated to be around $60 million, (one would have loved to have seen his tax returns).

Upon Marcello's return to the US, Robert Kennedy put more priority on getting two of his main targets: Marcello and Teamsters President Jimmy Hoffa. By a twist of fate, RFK's quest to bag these two prominent mobsters was suddenly ended by the assassination of his brother in Dallas, Texas on November 22, 1963.

But as time went on, the federal government had the final say regarding the illegal activities of Carlos Marcello. In 1981, years after the deaths of John and Robert Kennedy, Marcello went on trial in the so-called Brilab case—short for bribery/labor. He was found guilty in Federal District Court of conspiracy charges stemming

14 Memorandum: L'Allier to Belmont, Re: Carlos Marcello, Anti-Racketeering.

from the trial. Marcello, then 71 years old, was found not guilty of 11 counts listed in the 12-count Federal indictment. His co-defendant at trial, Charles Roemer, a former Louisiana Commissioner of Administration, was also found guilty of one count of conspiracy. The jury subsequently found Mr. Roemer not guilty of three other charges in the indictment. The other defendants in the case—I. Irving Davidson, 59, a Washington lobbyist, and Vincent Marinello, 43, a New Orleans attorney—were found not guilty of conspiracy and all other charges.

The Brilab case stemmed from a yearlong undercover inquiry of public corruption and labor racketeering in Louisiana and the Southwest part of the United States. The lead agency in the Brilab case was the FBI. Another part of the Brilab investigation concerned the activities of the then Speaker of the Texas House of Representatives, Billy Clayton, and two other attorneys who were found not guilty of

Carlos Marcello testifying during his 1981 trial.

the charges brought against them.

The prosecutors in the case said that Marcello was at the center of the conspiracy, and had leverage with many of the leading public figures in the Louisiana area.

During the trial, a tape recording was played in which Mr. Roemer seemed to agree to taking $43,000 a month in return for helping the "pseudo-salesmen gain a state insurance contract. According to the tapes and to testimony, Mr. Roemer in September and October of 1979, accepted two payments amounting to $25,000 described by prosecutors as bribe money." Mr. Roemer admitted at trial that he had, in fact, agreed to take part in the bribery plan proposed by the undercover agents. But he said that he had no plan of doing anything illegal in return for the money. He said he accepted the $25,000 as a campaign contribution to then gubernatorial candidate, State Senator Edgar Mouton.

> Government testimony and tapes disclosed that Mr. Roemer sent Mr. Marcello a document outlining state insurance bid specifications. They showed that Mr. Roemer, after getting word of the undercover operation, sent a message to Mr. Marcello asking him to destroy the papers. But a state insurance consultant testified that the document "could not possibly" have given a prospective bidder an advantage in seeking the insurance contract.[15]

Marcello was sentenced to a term of seven years and was interned at the United States Medical Center for Federal Prisoners at Springfield, Missouri where he was being treated for cancer. On May 21, 1987, Marcello was transferred to another prison at Texarkana.

Carlos Marcello's name will always be connected to the Kennedy assassination and his efforts to aid the CIA in its plots to kill Castro. However many Brilab tapes the FBI recorded of Marcello over the years, they never picked up a "smoking gun" relating to his possible participation in the Kennedy killing. Carlos Marcello died on March 21, 1993 in Louisiana of a stroke: his secrets, too, went with him to the grave.

---

15 No author. "Brilab Jury Convicts Carlos Marcello and Former Louisiana Official," New York Times Archives, 1981.

Chapter 40
Sam Papich

Sam Papich was the FBI's liaison to the CIA during the time of the CIA-Mafia plots to kill Fidel Castro as well as being on the front lines of the spy game against the Russians during the Cold War era. He was privy to some of the most important secrets coming out of the CIA and the FBI, and bucked heads with two of the legendary spy hunters of the time, James Angleton and J. Edgar Hoover. He also worked such high profile spy cases of World War II, including the case of the Yugoslav playboy and double agent Dusko Popov.

Papich played football at Northwestern University at the tackle position. He got his degree in engineering in 1936 and worked for a while at a Chicago insurance company while he went to law school at night. On weekends, he played for a team called the Chicago Gunners, a pro team that was financed by a local lumber company. He joined the FBI in March of 1941, a few months after the United States entered World War II. He first worked under the guidance of FBI agent Bud Foxworth in New York, following Dusko Popov around the city and informing his superiors on what Popov was doing. He was soon sent to Brazil and other parts of Latin America, and after the war ended, served as the legal attaché in Rio de Janeiro. After his stint in Latin America he returned home and was assigned to the Bureau office in San Francisco where he worked against the Mafia in that city. He then came back to DC where he was assigned to bank robbery cases, most of which he didn't like. It was at this time that Hoover ordered him to take on the position of liaison between the CIA and the FBI, a job he'd handle for years to come and therefore have a front-row seat for the unveiling of our nation's covert history. As Papich began reading the intelligence files supplied to him on the relationship between the CIA and the FBI, he was shocked by what he saw. He would later say of this time, "Reading those files gave me a picture of two warring agencies. It was that bad."

On one of his first trips to see the Director of Central Intelligence, Walter Bedell Smith, the two men got into a heated discussion which almost ended badly for both sides. Smith said to him, "You go back down to Ninth Street and tell J. Edgar Hoover to stick it up his ass." Before the meeting ended, Smith told Papich, "Lets calm down."[16]

Lawrence Houston, who was a leading member of the CIA for decades, had this to say about Papich: "Most people at CIA liked Sam very much. Difference in background was not a problem with Sam—I didn't even know what Sam's background was—but he was able to talk to anyone on a nice, easy basis. Sometimes he'd just sit around and talk. I liked him. He had a rough life, but he had the confidence of both sides, which was remarkable in that job. He was one of the major influences keeping relations as good as they were."

FBI agent Robert Lamphere, one of the Bureau's most respected agents, said of Papich, "Things improved when Sam took over liaison. My view, shared I think by Sam, was that we should think first on what was good for the United States and that problems between the two agencies, which were inevitable, should be worked out without having them grow like a cancer. In many instances I thought the FBI was being unreasonable in making big problems out of fairly small ones."

As it relates to the Cuba plots under Kennedy and Eisenhower, by 1961, J. Edgar Hoover had discovered to his surprise the secret dealings between the CIA—in the person of Sheffield Edwards—and Johnny Rosselli and Sam Giancana. Hoover discovered the plots in an indirect way—the bugging of singer/comedian Dan Rowan's hotel room in Las Vegas by Robert Maheu and Arthur Bellitti. Hoover had been going after the mob in Las Vegas for some time and when the CIA and his own organization learned of the botched job against Rowan, the secret of the CIA vs. Castro came spilling out.

Hoover was angry that his investigation of the mob was being compromised by the CIA and he immediately sought an answer from Sheffield Edwards. A meeting between Hoover and Edwards took place on May 3, 1961 at which time the CIA head of Security (Edwards) told Hoover about the Agency's relationship with Rosselli and Giancana, and "Phase One" of the Castro plots. On May 21, 1961, Hoover sent a memo to Robert Kennedy telling him of his meeting with Edwards and the information gleaned from that sitting.

It was at this time that Sam Papich was informed by Hoover of

16 Riebling, Mark, *Wedge: The Secret War Between The FBI and the CIA,* Alfred Knopf, New York, 1994, Page 114.

his meeting with Edwards, and Papich, who was dealing with both intelligence agencies at the same time, told William Harvey, who ran the Executive Action arm of the CIA, of the news. Harvey asked Papich to tell him if Hoover was going to tell John McCone, the new head of the CIA. It is now almost certain that McCone did not know about his own agency's involvement with the mob.

According to author Gus Russo, in his book *Live By the Sword*, in later years, Papich told the HSCA that the FBI kept Robert Kennedy informed of its information on the plots to kill Castro. According to Papich, Robert Kennedy did not disapprove of the plots but was concerned that the news not get out.

The newly released documents regarding Sam Papich shed new light on his relationship with James Angleton and the relationship between the CIA and the FBI during the Cold War years. The following records come from the files of the Rockefeller Commission from James Roethe, "Subject: Summary of Interview with Papich, Sam, J.," dated March 5, 1975:

> Secret—During this period Papich developed a good relationship with Jim Angleton of Counterintelligence and found he could work effectively with Angleton. In the early 1960s, the relationship between the two agencies was probably the best that it ever got. While some flaps continued to occur, both agencies seemed to be making an effort to learn the responsibilities and jurisdiction of the other.
>
> Relationships Between 1965 and 1970—During the Johnson administration, there was a deterioration or a cut in the number of projects directed towards the Soviet's. Hoover's desire to become engaged in extensive counterintelligence work lessened. Many of the FBI's programs to identify illegal aliens attempting to penetrate the US Government broke down. Hoover became extremely cautious and conservative in the area of counterintelligence, which greatly disturbed Papich, who felt strongly about the Soviet threat and who was convinced that strong counter-measures were necessary.
>
> During 1967 and early 1968, Papich saw no signs from Hoover that the programs and projects that Papich felt so necessary would be reinstated. Papich was receiving the

FBI agent Sam Papich.

message that his relationship with Hoover was coming to an end. Papich was physically and mentally worn out trying to keep the two agencies working together. In 1968, Papich wrote a polite letter to Hoover expressing his concern with what was happening in the area of counterintelligence. He appealed to Hoover to reinstate some of the effective programs aimed at Soviet penetration of the United States. While Hoover was extremely angry at Papich for writing such a letter, he did not fire him to the surprise of many. Further appeals by Papich to Hoover to reinstate programs were of no avail. From that point on, the relationship between Papich and Hoover chilled and any idea that Papich brought Hoover from the CIA concerning joint counterintelligence efforts was generally rejected and accompanied by a critical remark.

While Papich's 1968 letter had brought no change in Hoover's attitude, Hoover did keep Papich on as liaison. In the fall of 1969, Papich confided to his wife that he was seriously considering retiring in the spring of 1970. By the first of the year he realized that his career was effectively at an end and that he could no longer effectively accomplish his responsibilities as liaison between FBI and CIA. He decided to submit his letter of resignation, to be effective in early April of 1970.

Under Hoover there was little exchange of ideas at the highest levels of the CIA and FBI. This was merely Hoover's style. Papich was able to get people exchanging ideas at the working level and this was done with Hoover's approval. Papich supported CIA innovative approaches to targets of mutual interest to both agencies and frequently became involved in conflicts with Hoover for such interest and action. When any CIA promoted projects were approved, the responsibility was placed on Papich to assure there would not be any invasion of FBI jurisdiction or violation of agreements.

Papich also advocated the exchange of lectures between the CIA and FBI to give the two agencies some understanding of what the other agency was doing. Such an exchange of lectures and training facilities did not come about until about the time that Papich retired. Papich also suggested an actual trade of personnel for short periods of time so that personnel from one agency could become familiar with the various problems that faced personnel from the other agency on the working level. This suggestion was never approved while Papich worked for the FBI. Papich reiterated the fact that he had a very good working relationship with Jim Angleton. He feels that this relationship was probably responsible for the FBI's arrest of the Russian spy Rudolf Abel. Papich cooperated with Angleton, and the information obtained led to Abel's arrest and conviction.

Criminal Cases—Papich is not aware of any instances when the CIA has undertaken law enforcement tasks in the United States. This does not mean that there was not some cooperation between the FBI and CIA in criminal cases. For instance, Angleton's overseas agents would frequently obtain information connecting Americans with criminal activities in the US. Angleton would contact the FBI and together Papich and Angleton would develop the CIA's source of information to assist the FBI. A good example of this led to the arrest and conviction of a New York City official during the Lindsay Administration.

Papich's Philosophy and Miscellaneous Items—It is

Papich's belief that while the intelligence services of the United States presently obtain great amounts of information through new technological developments, they are still unable to read the minds of leaders of foreign countries. Consequently, they must attempt to penetrate through clandestine efforts. The only way to successfully penetrate is to permit those conducting the operation to go about their business unburdened by numerous reporting requirements. Papich's philosophy is "If you want the job done right, give me X number of men and leave me alone." He questions whether this philosophy can be adopted in the United States in 1975, as faith in the leadership is an essential factor. He believes that such operations can be controlled and overseen by the Director of the CIA, the Director of the FBI, and the President. Papich indicated that the differences between Hoover and Sullivan have nothing to do with CIA. Hoover was convinced that all dissident groups were directed by the Communist Party, whereas Sullivan disagreed. These differences affected the Hoover-Sullivan relationship only after Papich retired.[17]

Among the released documents is a write-up of a long interview with Papich concerning the CIA-Mafia plots to kill Castro and the Agency people he came in contact with regarding this operation:

Papich stated that he was aware, in general, of the CIA's anti-Castro activities in Miami, but not of specific operations. He knew the chiefs of the Miami operations, but was only interested in the domestic aspects of that operation.

Papich heard that Attorney General Kennedy had direct communication with the CIA. He described the Attorney General's involvement in the intelligence community as beginning almost immediately upon the commencement of the Kennedy administration. He stated that Attorney General Kennedy was involved in, and aware of, the whole range of intelligence activities. He stated that the Attorney General would put pressure on the intelligence community for results. He stated that while the Attorney General's involvement with

17 RIF No. 157-10011-10093:. Summary of Interview with Sam Papich.

the intelligence community began prior to the Bay of Pigs, his involvement increased after this operation.

Papich stated that when the wiretap was discovered [on Rowan's phone in Vegas] it really hit the fan. He stated that when the tap was found, the intelligence of the Bureau would have been on top of the situation. He stated that he would have talked to a Mr. Andrews of the organized crime section after discovering the involvement of the underworld in this operation. He stated that Courtney Evans' interest in this operation would have been Giancana's relationship to the wiretap, and not to the CIA's involvement. He stated that Courtney Evans's reports would have reflected this involvement as a potential impediment to prosecution. He did state that when the Bureau learned of the wiretap and its relation to the CIA, everyone at the Bureau was really upset. He also stated that the Attorney General didn't want this connection surfaced.

Papich stated that with respect to the CIA underworld connection, he would monitor agency contact with these people. He would report these contacts to the domestic intelligence section of the Bureau and they in turn would relate this information to Courtney Evans. He stated that he would file a memo of every contact to him by personnel at the CIA. He stated that he was briefed on every meeting with Rosselli and the other underworld figures. He stated he was told the nature of the talks. While the Office of Security handled this operation, Edwards was the individual at the CIA who kept Papich briefed. He stated that at this time he believed there were two or three meetings with the Attorney General about this operation, but doesn't know the specifics, nor was he present at any of these meetings. He stated that his reports would go to the intelligence division, the organized crime section and the Director of the FBI.

Papich stated that the Attorney General would not have gone to the Bureau in order to find the object of this operation. The Attorney General would have found out the nature of the operation by contacting the DCI directly, He found it difficult to believe that McCone would not have known of this operation. However, he never discussed this operation with McCone. He did state that he had ready access to Mr. McCone and that they discussed many subjects. He stated that the Bureau's arrangement with the CIA was worked out prior to the McCone administration. He also stated that the Bureau had no pre-wiretap information on this operation. After the wiretap was discovered, the Bureau was aware of the CIA's involvement, and the Attorney General was kept informed.

Papich was quite certain that he would have filed a memorandum of every contact with underworld figures as related to him by William Harvey. He also was certain he would have done the same with information given him by Edwards. Papich stated that he told Harvey from the beginning of the stupidity of using underworld figures. He stated that he believed when Harvey took over the contact with the underworld figures, he was only doing so because they were strapped with these people. As far as the FBI was concerned, the damage had already been done with respect to the problems of prosecuting these underworld figures. He stated that the FBI would not have been privy to much of what the Attorney General would have known about this and other foreign intelligence matters.

The agreement between the CIA and the FBI was an understanding that the FBI would be informed by the CIA of any contacts with underworld people, of their movements, and any intelligence which directly or indirectly related to organized crime in the United States. This information would include the movement of these figures, their activities, their travel, and any meetings.

He again stated that everyone in the Bureau was madder than hell about the Agency's involvement with these underworld figures. To the best of his knowledge, he never heard that the Attorney General was mad about this contact. It was his understanding, that the underworld figures were not being used operationally. When shown the references in the May 22, 1961 memorandum to this operation involving anti-Castro activities and dirty business, Papich stated he

351

didn't ask what the operational use of these figures was, or get clearance from above for staying out of this operation. He did state that the Bureau kept the Attorney General advised on what it learned of this operation. He stated that the Attorney General was concerned that this operation would become known, and didn't want it to get out. Finally, Mr. Papich was most concerned that people at the Committee understand what the nature of these times were. He stated that everyone's primary concern were with actions directed against the Soviet Union. That actions directed against Castro's Cuba were an extension of this policy. His primary concern, as a member of the Bureau's domestic intelligence section, was with Soviet operations in this country. He feels it is very important to have an intelligence community in this country, and feels that the Committee's work perhaps is jeopardizing this important resource.[18]

These documents relating to the activities of Sam Papich open up a new area of understanding regarding how the Bureau and the CIA operated (or didn't) during the Cold War years, and especially, the inner workings of both agencies regarding the CIA-Mafia plots to kill Castro and destabilize his regime.

---

18 RIF No. 157-10002-10151: Interview With Sam Papich, 8/22/1975.

Chapter 41
Jorge Volsky/Tad Szulc

Besides the AMLASH (Rolando Cubela) project, the CIA, by late 1963 and beyond, turned its attention to ousting Castro from power by making alliances with various Cuban exile groups based in Miami and elsewhere, along with a secret network of dissident Cuban military officers who were willing to do the Agency's work. The code name for this operation was AMTRUNK, and its primary purpose was to instigate a revolt inside the Cuban military. But this plan was not entirely run by the CIA; the State Department also had a hand in its inception.

Called "Operation Leonardo," some of its original parties were George Volsky (AMTRUNK-1), Cuban exile leader Nestor Moreno, and *New York Times* reporter Tad Szulc, who had a good working relationship with both John and Robert Kennedy. In early 1963, this plan was presented to the Kennedy White House at a meeting with the State Department Cuban Coordinator, Robert Hurwitch. The administration then went to the CIA asking to develop a program to divide the Castro regime from within. But unexpectedly, some members of the CIA, including the powerful chief of the JM/WAVE Station, Ted Shackley, did not like the idea at all. Shackley believed that the "AMTRUNKERS," as he called them, were not entirely loyal to the CIA and were using their relationship to further their own ends, and asked that the plan be dropped as soon as possible.

It now seems that the three principal agents in the AMTRUNK affair named above were not on the CIA's list of good friends. All three men were anti-CIA, and US government, and would accept assistance from anyone who would aid their cause. But the most striking objection was that the trio were not under any CIA control. Szulc got the most heat from the CIA, saying that while he was not directly involved in the operation, he was fully briefed by Moreno. Another strike against him was his close contact with the Kennedy White House, and the CIA's fears that he might pass along secret information to the opposition (whoever that might be).

During the Kennedy administration, Tad Szulc was a veteran reporter for the *New York Times* who was on good terms with many of the men who worked for the New Frontier. On November 8, 1961, Attorney General Robert Kennedy met with Tad Szulc to discuss the situation in Cuba. It was now seven months after the Bay of Pigs invasion, and Operation Mongoose was in full swing. The meeting was off the record, just a chat between two friends. RFK wanted to feel out Szulc to find out what the reporter thought of the administration's current policy toward Cuba.

At no time during their meeting did the word assassination come up. Before the meeting broke up, RFK asked Szulc if he would like to meet the president the next day. The reporter agreed and a meeting was set up. The next day, Szulc was taken into the Oval Office by the president's Special Assistant, Richard Goodwin. Just before the meeting ended, the president asked Szulc the following question, "What would you think if I ordered Castro to be assassinated?" The reporter told the president that if Castro was killed it would not necessarily change the political situation in Cuba, as someone else would take his place. He also said the US should have no role in political assassinations. Szulc testified to Congress that President Kennedy then said, "I agree with you completely."

Szulc remarked further, concerning his conference with JFK:

> He [President Kennedy] then went on for a few minutes to make the point how strongly he and his brother felt that the United States for moral reasons should never be in a situation of having recourse to assassination. JFK then said he was testing me, that he had felt the same way—he added, I'm glad you feel the same way because indeed US morally must not be part of assassinations. JFK said he raised the question because he was under terrific pressure from advisors (think he said intelligence people, but not positive) to okay a Castro murder, and he was resisting pressure.

When Kennedy aide Richard Goodwin testified before the HSCA he said that Szulc said that JFK told him in reference to a Castro assassination order, "We can't get into that kind of thing, or we will all be targets."

The encounter between JFK and Tad Szulc is important for two reasons. First, we have the president actually talking about assassinating Castro (he had to have gotten the idea from someone) and second, the fact that Kennedy suggested that some people in the intelligence community were putting pressure on him to act against Castro.

Jorge Volsky (AMTRUNK-1), a.k.a. "Chico," was a Cuban citizen of Polish origin. He lived in Poland from 1921 until 1939. During World War II, he served in the Royal Air Force Polish Group, spent some time in a Russian prison in the 1940s, and then enlisted in the Polish Air Force under the British Command. After the war ended, Volsky established a penpal relationship with a Cuban girl. He was able to get into Cuba without a valid passport and married the woman. In Cuba, he was the owner of a publicity company from 1947 until 1961, when he came to the US. He was a Castro supporter and was allegedly arrested shortly after the Bay of Pigs invasion and then released.

Once in Miami, Volsky met Paul Bethel who was in charge of the Miami office of the USIA and immediately went to work for them. Bethel, it seems, was also working for the JM/WAVE Station from

Tad Szulc at the *New York Times*, 1961.

October through December 1961.

Volsky also met Tad Szulc, spoke Polish with him, and a strong friendship began. Szulc arranged a meeting for Volsky with Richard Goodwin in August, 1962. During the Cuban Missile Crisis, Volsky made covert contact with Major Manuel Pineior Losada, Chief of the DGI, the Cuban external service.

In late 1962, Volsky devised a plan to split the Castro regime. He immediately told Szulc who got in touch with his friends at the State Department and at the White House.

One of Volsky's contacts in Miami was Raul Rivas, a member of the anti-Castro exile group JURE. In March 1963, JURE created an intelligence group to infiltrate agencies of the US Government. A JURE official, named Jose Aguiar, was making a list of CIA agents and their assigned tasks for JURE, and Volsky assisted him.

On June 6, 1963, the head of JURE, Monolo Ray, arrived in Miami from Puerto Rico and ordered that no more attacks be made on the US government, as he was going to have a talk with Robert Kennedy in Washington regarding the Cuban situation:

> On June 27, 1963, Ray returned to Miami from Washington, went directly to JURE offices, held a meeting, and said he had gained more information from his Washington contacts in the last month than he had in the two previous years. Ray said that the CIA agents are more dangerous than the Kennedy administration as the administration will end but the CIA always stayed and their memory is longer than that of elephants, the never forget or forgive.

It was also reported by sources that Volsky told refugees with knowledge of Cuban affairs not to talk to the CIA as they were the enemies of the Cubans who wanted to fight Castro.

The following short excerpt comes from a document prepared by the HSCA in its investigation of the JFK case regarding Volsky, "The analyst speculated that Volsky's knowledge of clandestine methods of operations, together with his Russian prison background, and his ingenuity as a middleman in US Government/CIA activities, made him an excellent candidate for a Communist penetration agent." Like those of Cubela-AMLASH, George Volsky's bona fides were deeply questioned by the CIA.

The stories of Jorge Volsky and Tad Szulc are so intertwined that the writer feels it necessary to present their stories in one chapter in order to give the proper historical perspective. The documents have a lot to say about each man and I'll endeavor to provide that insight. Said the document:

> As the result of Volsky's cultivation in Cuba of American journalists, in particular Tad Szulc, Volsky had influence with certain elements of the American press, especially the *New York Times* and the *Washington Post*. Volsky and Szulc had a close relationship in Washington and Miami, were in touch periodically by phone and personally, and conversed in Polish. Volsky was a source of information for Szulc and evidently influenced his thinking, manifested in a book written by Szulc entitled *The Cuban Invasion—The Chronicle of a Disaster,* which was particularly critical of the CIA, not only concerning its failure at Bay of Pigs, but details of many other aspects of CIA.
>
> In January 1964, JURE completed plans to send youths to all Latin American universities to lecture concerning CIA betrayal of US policy. In 1964, Volsky was a stringer for the Washington Bureau of the *Times* which is believed to have been a special Szulc-engineered deal.

Other Government Agencies' Knowledge of Volsky:

> USIA—Volsky was cleared in December 1961 for unlimited purchase order as a writer. He apparently had no access to classified information.
>
> INS—In 1965, INS requested name checks on Volsky and his son. A Special Private Bill had been submitted to grant Volsky US citizenship. Unfortunately the CIA response on Volsky senior was "N.D." [no derogatory] which obviously was not a true statement. Volsky became a naturalized US citizen on 10 April 1969.
>
> FBI—An FBI report of January 1974 re Orlando Bosch Avila, indicates that Volsky, of the *New York Times,* was

collecting money from Cuban doctors on behalf of Bosch. On 14 August 1974, the Miami Station provided the Miami FBI Office comprehensive traces on Volsky in response to a July 1974 FBI request for any action the Bureau deemed necessary. Miami Station advised the FBI that the Agency had not conducted any investigation, and that the information included in the trace was in Agency files because at the time of collection it was considered foreign intelligence.

The CIA was so alarmed by Volsky's bona fides they wrote that the possibility existed that he "might be a singleton, sleeper, or stringer for the RIS. Further, that if that theory proved false, Volsky violated his USIA position by reporting to JURE and damaging the US and CIA by his propaganda programs."[19]

If the CIA had reservations regarding the activities of Jorge Volsky, they certainly had reason not to trust Tad Szulc, as the government documents disclose. Here are the salient points regarding the *Times* correspondent:

Szulc has been under suspicion as a hostile foreign agent since 1948 when the FBI reported (apparently from a [blank] source) that he was a Communist. He brought himself to the attention of the CIA in August 1959 in Santiago, Chile by claiming (falsely) to be "cleared" and requesting contact with an Agency representative. This was the first of many such incidents in Latin America, and resulted in a warning to all Latin American Stations to beware of Szulc and his efforts to interview Agency personnel. It also resulted in continuing watch of his movements and activities because they represented a threat to the cover of Agency personnel. By 1960 his reputation was so widespread that several different CIA officers called for an investigation that would clear up "once and for all" his suspected connections with a hostile intelligence service. He was in frequent contact with Communist Party leaders and functionaries throughout Latin America, constantly sought out and elicited information from US Embassy officers, frequently mentioning the names of other CIA officers with whom he was acquainted.

19 RIF No. 104-10103-10109: Memo Re Jorge Volsky, 2/14/1977.

Although the suspicions have increased, and Szulc's anti-Agency activities have become much more serious and blatant in the 1970s, it has not been possible to clear up any of the suspicions about his motive or his possible connections with a foreign intelligence service. There have been numerous reviews of his files and the interest in his activities has extended from the case officer level, to the DCI. In fact, it is not possible to come to any clear conclusion about this man, and the notes below are simply illustrative of the kinds of things that keep the suspicions alive. It is important to note that Szulc's activities can be explained by the combination of his personality, ambition, and the demands of an investigative reporter for the NYT. He is an aggressive, insensitive, and persistent journalist with the family connections (Ambassador Wiley) and ability to develop the kinds of contacts appropriate to a successful correspondent for a paper like the NYT.

Nevertheless, there are elements throughout his entire career that are almost designed to arouse suspicion. For example, a [blank] source in Rio de Janeiro reported that Szulc was "directed" by the Polish regime in Warsaw to seek employment in US journalistic circles. This report runs like a thread throughout his file and is repeated and garbled in several versions over the years. The report has never been adequately explained and was apparently never reported in full to [blank] by the [blank] representative in Rio. This report and other questions that arose early in his career were, however, just the earliest elements that aroused suspicion.

Because he became so well-known to so many Agency officers, his name and reputation have become the subject of discussion on many occasions. One senior operations officer stated in 1975 that a Soviet agent could not be more beneficial to the Soviets and the Communists cause than Szulc has been. Although he presented a generally anti-Communist view prior to quitting the NYT in 1972, it is noteworthy that he arranged extensive, favorable TV coverage of the Communist-dominated Ligas Campesinas in Northeast Brazil and that one of the most important anti-

Castro operations, AMTRUNK, in which he was involved from the beginning, was disastrous for all participants. More indicative of his true beliefs, however, are the articles he had written since Watergate. They have become increasingly critical of the CIA and of the USG generally and have damaged US image and prestige.

The notes below are somewhat random examples of elements in Szulc's file that bring him under suspicion. As mentioned above, they in no way point to a firm conclusion. For further information on Szulc during the period 1963-1964, see the CI review prepared at Miami Station on Jorge Volsky in 1964. Fitzgerald assured the DCI that the highest priority had been assigned to the above program with SAS.

Comment: See the AMTRNK Operation paper attached biographic sketch on Tad Szulc, a possible foreign agent. Szulc claimed to have had direct access to President Kennedy, Attorney General Kennedy, and McGeorge Bundy since early 1961. If true, that would have placed him in a position to be used as a possible channel by which policy information on CIA operations and activities conceivably could have gotten to the Cuban Government or the Soviets.[20]

This damning memorandum offers up the following questions regarding Tad Szulc. Did the Kennedy brothers know of his possible role as a foreign operative when the President and his brother were having high-level, secret discussions with him in the Oval Office? Did the Director of the CIA or any other Agency officer tell them of their suspicions regarding Tad Szulc?

The connections between Jorge Volsky and his friend Tad Szulc should have been a warning sign to those in the Kennedy administration who were conducting a covert war against Fidel Castro. Maybe they did not know about either man's past. If they did, then the story of the Castro plots might have been different.

---

20 Memorandum Subject: Tadeusz (Tad) Szulc AMCAPE-01, 14 February 1977.

Chapter 42
ZR/RIFLE and QJ/WIN

Among the thousands of files released over the years via the JFK Records Act, are significant new developments on one of the most secret projects of the Kennedy administration, code named ZR/RIFLE. Along with this material are important files concerning the identities of two agents associated with the program and the so called "Executive Action" organization, code named QJ/WIN and WI/ROGUE.

Project ZR/RIFLE first came to light during the Church Committee hearings in 1975 that dealt with both illegal CIA domestic activities and the Kennedy assassination. This program, established in the early days of the Kennedy administration, was originally set up to get rid of Fidel Castro. It turned into a nightmare, finally involving plots to kill Patrice Lumumba of the Congo, as well as other foreign leaders whose policies did not jibe with US interests. Project ZR/RIFLE also had domestic ramifications as well, involving militant anti-Castro Cubans whose goal was to establish their old business interests in Cuba.

Besides the Cubans, this top-secret project may have tenuous links to the JFK assassination on November 22, 1963. The Executive Action capability included "the development of a general, standby assassination capability." This program included research into the long-term possibilities and capabilities of killing foreign leaders. Despite all the intensive planning for Executive Action, in reality, the program was never carried out.

The man put in charge of Executive Action (whose name has appeared previously in this book) was a tough, action-oriented CIA officer named William Harvey. Harvey was well equipped to deal with this new type of operation, having been one of the key players in the CIA's secret war against Castro, Harvey called ZR/RIFLE "the magic button," and "beyond the last resort and a confession of weakness." In the notes he left behind, Harvey never used the word "assassination," instead, when dealing with ZR/RIFLE, his favorite expressions were "maximum security," and "non-attributability."

The files show that the Kennedy administration was well aware of Project ZR/RIFLE as early as February 1961. According to the released CIA Inspector General's Report on the plots to kill Castro, "Project ZR/RIFLE was covered as an operation (ostensibly to develop a capability for entering safes and for kidnapping couriers"). Harvey has a note that on November 15, 1961, he discussed with Richard Bissell, a top CIA officer, the application of the ZR/RIFLE program to Cuba.

The ZR/RIFLE project was one of the most secretive ever undertaken, with meetings taking place behind locked doors and thing committed to paper. The agencies hired two mercenaries to become part of a team who are forever known by their code names, WI/ROGUE and QJ/WIN.

It now seems clear that President Kennedy, and probably his brother Robert were aware of the ZR/RIFLE/Executive Action programs (that issue is still being debated by researchers). Whether JFK ordered that Fidel Castro be "terminated," or knew of the CIA-Mafia plots (the Maheu-Rosselli-Giancana-Trafficante connection) is still in dispute. It is very possible that the forces unleased via Executive Action, vis a vis the Cubans, QJ/WIN-WIROGUE, and the various plots to tie in Lee Harvey Oswald as a follower of the Castro regime, thus making him a Castro dupe in the assassination of the president, may have led to the tragedy in Dallas.

Harvey stated that when he took over the Cuba plots, he was taking over an on-going operation. Harvey was given the job as Cuba chief in a briefin by Richard Bissell in late 1961 or early 1962. He met with Sheffield Edwards in February 1962, and was briefed on the full aspects of the Castro operation. The Assassinations Report has this to say concerning Harvey's taking over the Castro function:

> After Harvey took over the Castro operation, he ran it as one aspect of ZR/RIFLE, however, he personally handled the Castro operation and did not use any of the assets being developed in ZR/RIFLE as being synonymous. The overall Executive Action program came to be treated in his mind as being synonymous with QJ/WIN, the agent working on the overall program. He says that when he wrote of ZR/RIFLE, QJ/WIN, the reference was to Executive Action capability; when he used the cryptonym ZR/RIFLE alone,

referring to Castro.

On November 22, 1963, while the United States and the world were still reeling in shock from the assassination of President John Kennedy, a seemingly unrelated incident took place in Dallas. United States officials expelled a known deserter from the French army who also had connections to the outlawed OAS that had been battling France over the status of Algeria. This mysterious figure was later identified as Jean Souetre who also went by the names of Michael Roux and Michael Mertz (this author has written extensively on the French connection to the JFK assassination in the book *JFK: The French Connection*).

Souetre was seen in Fort Worth on the morning of the assassination and was placed in Dallas that afternoon. What this French soldier of fortune, ex-heroin smuggler, and gifted assassin was doing in Dallas at the same time that President Kennedy was being struck down is open to speculation.

It has been suggested by Kennedy assassination researchers that Souetre was QJ/WIN. Souetre's background and that of the mysterious QJ/WIN are tantalizingly similar.

Souetre served as a paratrooper in the French Air Force as a captain. He served in Algiers from 1955 to 1959. It was in Algiers that he took up the anti-de Gaulle position on the freedom of Algeria and deserted from the service. He and his like-minded compatriots formed an underground group of officers in the Oran Province of France. It was at this time that he joined the OAS. He was arrested in 1961, charged with sedition, and served one year of a three-year sentence. It is believed that Souetre had a hand in the various plots to kill French President Charles de Gaulle.

A released CIA document says that QJ/WIN was under written contract as a principal agent with the primary task of spotting agent candidates. It goes on to say that he was contacted by someone in the government "in connection with an illegal narcotics operation in the US." Ex-CIA director Richard Helms said of QJ/WIN that he was the man to see if a murder sanction was ordered.

Souetre hotly denied any involvement in the president's murder and said that the only time he was in the United States was in 1974 or 1975. He said that he was in Spain at the time of the president's assassination and that Michael Mertz might have been in Dallas using his name. But that does not hold up as Souetre used the alias of Michael Victor Mertz.

Souetre said that he was never contacted by any American authorities until almost 20 years after November 22, 1963. Then living in France, he said that he was contacted by a friend who lived in the US who told him he was under investigation in connection to the president's death. The "friend" further stated that he had a note that would "surely interest him." Souetre never said who his "friend" was, but shortly after getting the note he was visited by two reporters. He stated that they asked him the same questions sent to him by his friend.

How did Souetre's "friend" know what queries the two visitors had in mind?

In talking about the Kennedy assassination, Souetre said, "but I believe that certainly there is a French connection to the assassination and that Mertz may well have been involved. Though if he was, I am sure he was not acting alone."[21]

Michael Mertz served in the German army in 1941, deserted in 1943, and joined the underground fighting the Germans. He adopted the name Major Baptiste and enlisted in the French army with the rank of captain. He was decorated by President de Gaulle for bravery and sometime in the 1950s joined the SDECE—French intelligence.

Mertz married in 1947 and his father-in-law was linked to illegal activities including whorehouses in Montreal. Whether his father-in-law provided the push or he did it on his own, Mertz infiltrated the illegal OAS and became the eyes and ears of French intelligence. In 1961, he was arrested along with other OAS members for carrying out an attack against De Gaulle. All of those who participated in the attempted assassination plot against de Gaulle were prosecuted except Mertz.

It was during this period of time that Mertz entered the gunrunning and drug smuggling market and fled to Canada to pursue his lucrative activities. American authorities suspected him of drug dealing and asked the French to curtail his activities. They refused.

In 1969, Mertz was turned in to US authorities but posted bond one year later. He was found guilty of drug running, served a five-

21 Kross, Peter, "JFK and the French Connection," *Back Channels*, Vol. 1, No. 1, October 1991.

year prison term, and returned to France where he became a wealthy man.

The similarities between Mertz and Souetre are very close. Could they be the same person? An intriguing sideline to the Mertz story concerns an FBI document that states that three people—John Mertz, Irma Mertz, and Sara Mertz—left Texas on November 23, 1963, one day after the president's assassination, flying on Pan Am to Mexico.

The document dump that was made in the past two years reveals a 13-page report on events called "Project ZR/RIFLE and QJ/WIN Assassinations." The report, which is dated April 30, 1975 and marked "Top Secret-Sensitive," was sent to the file from a Mason Cargill:

> On April 25, 1975, I was given three file folders containing material on the above subjects by Mr. Joseph Selzer of the Inspector General's staff. According to Mr. Selzer, his review of these files indicates that the basic purpose of ZR/RIFLE and its asset QJ/WIN was the [blank]. He assures me that there is nothing in these files which refer explicitly or implicitly to assassination or "executive action" in any form. His opinion is that clandestine operatives of the type who wrote the documents contained in these files would never commit to writing anything having to do with the subject of assassination.
>
> Dispatch, dated 1 November 1960, to Chief of Station [blank] and Chief of Station, Luxembourg, from Chief KUTUBE/D at headquarters. This three-page dispatch apparently deals with a mission on which a recruited agent, Jose Marie Andre Mankel, will be sent from Luxembourg, where he was recruited, to Dakar for the purpose of recruiting certain other agents from among criminal elements there, specifically Corsicans. The purpose for which these agents would ultimately be used is not clear from this dispatch. However, paragraph 2a reads as follows: In view of the extreme sensitivity of the objective for which we want him to perform his task, he was not told precisely what we want him to do. Instead, he was told that we have evidence of Soviet

operations among nationality groups in Africa, specifically, Corsicans, and that we would like to have him spot, assess, and recommend some dependable, quick-witted persons for our use. Comment: It was thought best to withhold our true, specific requirements pending the final decision to use Mankel. He agreed to go on the trip for us.

Cable, dated November 3, 1960 from Director to stations at Luxembourg and [blank]. This cable contains the first identification of Mankel with the code name of QJ/WIN. The cable reads as follows: [blank] 147 on QJ/WIN trip [blank] pouched both stations 3 November. Confirm receipt by cable.

So, now we know that the elusive agent named QJ/WIN was Jose Marie Andre Mankel.

The long report on QJ/WIN contains more detailed information and I will tell the most important developments throughout the rest of this chapter:

Please inform Mankel he should proceed to Leopoldville as soon as shots completed. Not necessary have Congo visa. Should go Paris and take Air France flight to Brazzaville and can obtain visa for Brazzaville in Paris.

Unless you advised to contrary by Altman, brief QJ/WIN on Dakar mission, using notes left during Rabney visit. Please insure he thoroughly rehearsed all details since we anticipate he will go from Leopoldville to Dakar with no opportunity reviewing briefing.

The file contains several documents apparently describing various Italians in the area of Trieste who have the capability to break and enter and crack safes. They appeared to be of questionable morality. Reports on the safecrackers were transmitted in a dispatch from the Chief of Station in [redacted] to the Chief, KUDOVE/D. The names of the safecrackers in question are Sabatti, Cuccangna, and Bernardini. [We now have the names of the safecrackers to add to the story of QJ/WIN and his activities.]

It indicates that one purpose of QJ/WIN's presence in Leopoldville is to recruit a major in the Yugoslavian air force, through framing him up in an illegal smuggling transaction. This recruitment is apparently for Yugoslavian government.

Cable, dated December 14, 1960, from HQ to Leopoldville. The cable criticizes Leopoldville for using QJ/WIN for the purpose of recruiting the Yugoslav major, since this was not his primary purpose in Leopoldville. Cable contains the following statement: "Would like restrict QJ/WIN to activity directly pertinent his mission Leopoldville or forth-coming mission Dakar and possibly elsewhere (e.g., Milan) for KUTUBE/D purposes. He our only asset of this type and we wish keep him clean of any operational involvement other than that originally planned for him." This is the first cable from HQ on which the name of William Harvey appears.

Cable, dated December 17, 1960, from Leopoldville to Director. This cable concerned a new asset entering the picture for the first time, who arrived in Leopoldville on December 2. The cable states that WIROGUE was the asset with whom initial contact has been made in Leopoldville. WIROGUE is living in the same hotel as QJ/WIN with whom he conversed. QJ/WIN has reported: WIROGUE had offered him $300 per month to participate in intel net and be member execution squad. When QJ/WIN said he not interested, WIROGUE added there would be bonuses for special jobs. Under QJ/WIN questioning, WIROGUE later said he working for PBPRIME service.

QJ/WIN then proceeded on CIA orders to Italy in order to recruit more agents for his work, but the cables say that no mention of the CIA or US Government was to be made to these people:

Cables which follow seem to indicate that the people QJ/WIN was to recruit were intended to be professional burglars. There is no indication that they are intended to be assassins. There are many other indications that these recruits were intended for safecracking and breaking and entering. QJ/WIN told them he could offer a job for a large firm which wanted certain commercial documents stolen.

Subsequent cables and dispatches indicate other efforts on the part of QJ/WIN to recruit safecrackers in France and Italy. Correspondence and cables indicate that one James Rabney from CIA headquarters visited Europe in April and March of 1961 for the purpose of meeting with Mankel to discuss possible recruits for safecracking operations.

Dispatch dated December 15, 1961, from Chief of Station in Luxembourg to HQ, Chief, KUTUBE/D. It discussed the efforts of QJ/WIN to recruit two safecrackers in Switzerland. It indicates that two French citizens, named Santelli and Garioni were asked to come to Switzerland under false pretenses by QJ/WIN for the purpose of being interviewed. The following passage in the dispatch indicates clearly these men were to be recruited for the purpose of the safecracking and surreptitious entry. "During the interview with Santelli, Garioni observed that for a night job he would need an assistant to help him with carrying the equipment and to act as lookout. He said he would prefer to do the job during working hours; for this he would get three or four others to help him and force someone in the office to open the safe.

Dispatch dated February 2, 1962, from Chief of Station Luxembourg to HQ, Chief, KUTUBE/D. It discussed the efforts of the Luxembourg station to provide acceptable cover for Mankel in Germany, where the Agency has decided to locate him. The plan seems to be for Mankel to develop a business as an art dealer in some German town selling French paintings. It is contemplated that the Agency will supply the initial capital for the formation of his business. The final sentence in this dispatch asked HQ for projected operational plans for QJ/WIN.[22]

At this time there was some discussion at Langley headquarters about whether to send QJ/WIN to the Congo or have him remain in Europe. It was then decided by the top brass to keep him in Europe, at least for a while. The cable, dated May 24, 1962 said, "Decision made to keep QJ/WIN Europe. Leopoldville assignment canceled. Cable also indicates that HQ approves of Mankel's proposed move

22 All of the above material comes from RIF No. 157-10003-10490: Project ZRRIFLE and QJ/WIN.

to Germany, probably Baden-Baden."

The CIA also had discussions regarding some of the safecrackers they were going to use in future endeavors. In a dispatch dated July 3, 1962, they talked about two references "which may be somewhat disturbing: One candidate is stated to be willing to use gun; the second wanted to know if he should be armed for job—ready to go to the end."

A dispatch dated February 14, 1963 said that QJ/WIN's services were ended. A person named Rozeney told him that the operation he was scheduled to go on was shelved and therefore his contract, which ran out on 29 February, was not renewed. "He was reassured that this action did not result from anything had done and his past cooperation was appreciated."

But if QJ/WIN thought his employment with the CIA had ended, he was mistaken. The remaining pages in this document talk about his trip to the Congo and what he was supposed to be doing in the heart of Africa.

A memorandum dated January 31, 1961, for Chief, Accounts Branch, Finance Division from Justin O'Donnell, reads as follows:

QJ/WIN was recruited in Frankfurt 1 November 1960 to undertake a one-shot mission to the Belgian Congo. Because the mission potentially involved great personal risk to him and he was obliged to separate himself from his business affairs, it was agreed orally by this writer with QJ/WIN that his compensation would be at the rate of $1,000 per month, plus his expenses, for a period of not less than one month and not more than two months. These two financial memorandum, numbers 1 and 2, here, seem to indicate a one-shot purpose for QJ/WIN in connection with a Congo operation, which seems inconsistent with many of the papers in the operational file reviewed above, which indicated an ongoing relationship with QJ/WIN for the purposes of recruiting safecrackers and burglars. These financial memorandums are certainly quite consistent with a plan to use QJ/WIN for a one-shot assassination attempt in the Belgian Congo. It is unclear that merely recruiting safecrackers and burglars or even performing safecracking and burglary missions, would have involved potential great "personal risk" to QJ/WIN.

This memo now begins to refer to the Executive Action/ZR/RIFLE program headed by William Harvey:

> The first two pages portray the objective of ZR/RIFLE to be that of procurement of code and cipher materials by burglary and safecracking. However, subsequent pages, particularly the last four legal size pages in this file, contain what appears to be the outline of something which could be the establishment of an "executive action capability" although these words are not mentioned nor is the word "assassination."

A memorandum, dated February 19, 1962, from Richard Helms, Deputy Director (Plans), to William Harvey, has the subject: "Authorization of ZRRIFLE Agent Activities." This memo authorizes Harvey to retain the services of QJ/WIN "and other such principal agents and subagents as may be required. Memorandum does not state the purpose of the ZRRIFLE project.

Filed immediately after a memorandum dated March 6, 1969, from Richard Helms to William K. Harvey, is a normal business size white envelope containing the following notation on the front in penciled handwriting: "Lloyd very personal from Bill H." Within

Richard Helms being sworn in as director of the CIA.

this envelope in penciled handwriting, "John Rosselli, alias John Ralston-Wm. Walker."

The last paragraph closes down the entire project. "This memo states that QJ/WIN is currently not being used for any operational purposes. It discussed whether or not he should be retained as an agent. Paragraph two seems to indicate that the executive action portion of QJ/WIN's project, if any, has been terminated. This paragraph reads:

> As far as the ZR/RIFLE aspects of this operation which has been covered under the QJ/WIN authorization for security reasons and which Fletcher M. Knight is fully familiar as I orally advised you on June 26, 1963, except for one precautionary "lifeline," aspects of this case have been terminated and need on longer except perhaps for minor accountings, be considered as a part of this project.

Let's now consider what we've learned from this very long, and well-written document regarding QJ/WIN and the Executive Action program.

A French assassin named Jean Souetre, aliases Michael Roux and Michael Mertz, was in Dallas on November 22, 1963 and was then taken out of the country. Why he was there on the day the president was killed is still an open question. Jose Mankel went by the code name QJ/WIN. The names of the safecrackers whom Mankel was to recruit were Sabatti, Bernardi, and Cuccangna. QJ/WIN tried to enlist two Frenchmen in Switzerland named Santelli and Garioni. The Executive Action program was headed by William Harvey and ultimately controlled by Richard Helms, who would later become DCI. QJ/WIN and his fellow agent, WIROGUE, were sent to the Congo on a secret mission where a plan to assassinate Congolese President Patrice Lumumba was being hatched by outside forces.

While a lot of material on this topic has been released in previous years, the information presented in this long document adds to the historical record concerning the activities of these two assassins, as well as the entire ZR/RIFLE-Executive Action program. Hopefully, in years to come, we'll get more information regarding this most important topic.

Chapter 43
The Defection of Joseph Dutkanicz

The story of the defection of Lee Harvey Oswald to Moscow was one of the most notorious cases during the Cold War era. Whether Oswald was really a "defector" or just a plant sent by the United States government is still a mystery. The Oswald defection surely got the attention of the CIA and other interested agencies of the US intelligence community, and they did everything they could to figure out what the former Marine was doing in Russia during his stay. But Oswald was not the only member of the United States armed forces to defect to the Soviet Union as the 1960s began. One of the others was Army Sgt. Joseph Dutkanicz whose story began in 1958 when he was recruited by a representative of Soviet intelligence in West Germany. The files on the Dutkanicz case say the following regarding the circumstances of his defection:

A combination of threats and inducements were used to gain his cooperation. He admits having had four meetings with his Soviet handlers during a two-year period, but claims he supplied only limited information to the KGB. There are, however, substantial indications that the compromise was greater. His espionage activity was terminated by his defection to the USSR in June 1960. He was subsequently exploited for propaganda purposes by the Soviets. Details of his complicity were obtained from statements made by Dutkanicz to US officials in Moscow.

The documents reveal what Sgt. Dutkanicz' job was prior to his defection. "Dutkanicz's principal mission was to report changes in the status and disposition of USAREUR forces indicating possible preparation for hostilities. He also admits receiving detailed instructions from the SIS which probably included additional collection of EEI, but he did not elaborate on these missions."

Here is the background of Dutkanicz as reported in memo under the heading "Hostile Service: Soviet Intelligence, Service (SIS), probably State Security Service (KGB)."

Dutkanicz was a naturalized US citizen who was born in Poland, and was shipped to Germany in 1943 as a slave laborer and who immigrated to the United States after World War II. He was drafted into the US Army in 1951 and was a sergeant in the 32nd Signal Battalion, Darmstadt, at the time of his defection. He is a convinced liberal and has espoused leftist causes which led to a review and revocation of his Secret clearance in January.

Dutkanicz claims he was approached by KGB personnel in 1958 while drinking in a bar at Crumstadt, near Darmstadt. In the initial conversation, a combination of threats and inducements were used to obtain his promise of cooperation. The threats were mostly implied and directed against relatives in Poland, his immediate family in West Germany and him personally. Inducements consisted of promises to assist relatives residing behind the Iron Curtain. He also admits having been offered money on several occasions, but allegedly refused to accept payment for his espionage activities. Dutkanicz claims that the controlling agency was the KGB. He admits having four meetings with the KGB representatives, who were allegedly from Vienna, Austria, during the period 1958 to 1960. He was furnished an accommodation address which he no longer remembers and was given secret writing materials. He claims to have sent only four letters to the accommodations address and he alleges to have furnished only negative imminence reports.

In May 1960, Dutkanicz began his preparations for his defection to the Soviet Union. He told his handlers that he was being investigated for security reasons and said that he wanted to defect with his wife and family to the USSR via Austria and Czechoslovakia. He was contacted by KGB officers on June 26, 1960 in Bratislava, Czechoslovakia, not far from Vienna. He and his family then drove to Lvov, USSR, with a Soviet escort. In an unusual move, the Soviets allowed his wife to return to the United States in March 1962, but his children stayed in Moscow. He was allowed to accompany his wife to the US Embassy in Moscow for making the necessary preparations for her return. During this period Dutkanicz made a statement concerning his espionage activities in behalf on the KGB.

The memo regarding Sgt. Dutkanicz then goes into great detail regarding his arrest and the reasons for the activities he undertook leading up to his defection:

> Although Dutkanicz's confession was obtained under unusual circumstances, his statements appear substantially true although obviously incomplete. A strong possibility exists that he worked for the KGB for a longer period than he admits, and it is probable that Dutkanicz provided the KGB with considerably more information than negative imminence reports. His statements that his SIS recruiters were from Vienna is possibly correct and is supported by his alleged defection route. His statement that he refused payment from the SIS seems unlikely, since he reportedly was spending considerable amounts of money before his defection. The case is of unusual significance since it constitutes one of the most serious known penetrations of USAREUR forces by hostile intelligence. Also important is the fact that Dutkanicz's defection was apparently instigated by the Soviets for propaganda purposes after he lost access to sensitive information.[23]

This short summary of Sgt. Dutkanicz, is of more significance when seen against the defection of Oswald. While both men were in the USSR at approximately the same time, their cases could not have been more different in scope and intensity. Dutkanicz was recruited by the SIS and was aided and abetted in his efforts to reach the Soviet Union. He was a real spy in that he gave some information to the KGB while Oswald never revealed anything of value to them. He admitted to having four meetings with his handlers during a two-year period. There is nothing in the historical record that Oswald had any relationship with any Soviet "handlers" while he was in the Soviet

23 RIF No. 104-10005-10316: Case Summary of Soviet Army Defector Stg. Joseph Dutkanicz.

Union. There were reports from the KGB who tailed Oswald and knew a lot of his activities in the Soviet Union, that Oswald was not stable and that they could not gain any reliable information from him.

Dutkanicz was recruited by the Soviets in Germany, while Oswald was never "pitched" by the KGB (as far as we are aware). The United States government, i.e., the CIA, took great exception to his defection and what information he could give the Soviets. While Oswald said he was going to spill the beans to the Russians about his time as a radar operator in Japan (i.e., his knowledge of the U-2 spy plane), there is no evidence that he did anything of the sort.

As concerns the Warren Commission Report, there was no mention of the defection of Sgt. Joseph Dutkanicz. Even if he had been mentioned in the report, it would have made little difference in its final conclusions, just another footnote about a US defector to the Soviet Union during the Cold War era.

However, if the Warren Commission had no interest in the Dutkanicz defection, that was not the case at Langley headquarters. A memo was written on October 2, 1964, by Lee Wigren, Chief of "R" (research and analysis) in the Counterintelligence branch of the Soviet Russia Division entitled "Questions Concerning Defectors Joseph Dutkanicz and Vladimir Sloboda," mentions that his wife "indicated that he had CIC [Counterintelligence Corps] connections," a rather interesting quote from the wife of a new defector to the Soviet Union.

Another source says Mrs. Dutkanicz told State Department officials that her husband: "In an interview at the American Embassy Moscow on 5 December 1961, she indicated that their trip behind the Iron Curtain "had been made possible because her husband worked for the CIC and as allowed to do things an ordinary GI could not do."[24]

In the file that the CIA had on Sgt. Dutkanicz there is a written notation by Mr. Wigren who suggested that, "his Army assignment may have included intelligence functions of some kind." That reference is interesting because many researchers into Oswald's life in the military suggest that he was sent on some sort of intelligence mission either on behalf of the CIA or the Office of Naval Intelligence.

The Counterintelligence report on the case for the Department of State dated November 1960 and marked "Secret" says the following:

We are informed that Dutkanicz has had difficulties with

24 Newman, John, *Oswald and the CIA*, Page 188.

his wife and that she reported that he had relatives in the USSR and that he admitted that he was a Communist and that he had associated with German Nationals who were Communists.

No sooner than he had defected, however, Dutkanicz was talking with a CIA informant inside the Soviet Union. From the JFK files released by the CIA in 1994 comes the startling news that on July 10, 1960, Dutkanicz met a "clergyman" in the lobby of the Intourist Hotel Lvov. The "clergyman" submitted this account of his encounter with Dutkanicz to the CIA that same July.

> On the morning of Monday, 10 July 1960, at about 0930-1000 hours, I chanced to meet one Joseph Dutkanicz allegedly a defected US citizen in the lobby of the Intourist Hotel in the city of Lvov, USSR. I was recognized and approached by Mr. Dutkanicz while making my way up the hotel stairway toward my hotel room. After the customary greetings, I suggested he accompany me to my room where we remained for not more than ten minutes. Since I had arranged that morning for a private conducted tour of Lvov our conversation dealt primarily with the points of interest I was scheduled to see.[25]

The men were supposed to meet later that day for supper but the "clergyman" said, "I never saw him again as he failed to keep his appointment." This raises more questions than answers. Who was the "clergyman" that Dutkanicz met and why was he in Lvov in the first place? Was he some sort of Agency spy, as is hinted at by John Newman in *Oswald and the CIA*? Was he sent to Lvov to meet clandestinely with Dutkanicz for some ulterior purpose? Was he supposed to have met with him so could report back to the CIA what the defector was saying or doing in the USSR? We also don't know for sure whether Oswald met with Dutkanicz while the two men were in Russia, nor are we aware whether either of them knew the other (two defectors being in Russia at the same time is quite a coincidence).

The defection of Sgt. Joseph Dutkanicz is just one more story without a plausible ending that still needs to be explored.

25 Ibid,. Page 189.

Chapter 44
The Secrets of Robert Maheu

The name of Robert Maheu has been featured in a number of chapters of this work. He was the intermediary between the CIA and the Mafia in the US government's secret war to kill Fidel Castro of Cuba, as well as the man to see in the secret world of Washington DC politics and espionage. In his prime, Robert Maheu was the owner of a private detective agency in Washington and had high-priced clients in both the political and social world. One of his most valued clients was none other than Howard Hughes, the reclusive billionaire. It was Maheu's job to look after Hughes' political and business affairs. In his early days, Maheu worked for the FBI and the CIA, from 1954 to 1960. Maheu came in contact with both sides of the law, having buddies at the CIA and FBI, as well as socializing with certain members of organized crime, most notably, Johnny Rosselli. From the early 1950s, the CIA paid Maheu $500.00 per month to carry out covert jobs that the Agency could or would not do.

In 1960, CIA officer James O'Connell (Maheu's project officer at the Agency) met with Maheu and asked him to recruit his Mafia pal, Johnny Rosselli in a clandestine plot to kill Castro.

Maheu told Rosselli that at the same time that Castro would be killed, an American-sponsored invasion of Cuba was to be initiated. That must have been great news to Johnny Rosselli, whose Mafia colleagues had lost millions of dollars when the former Cuban dictator Batista was overthrown by the young, brash Fidel Castro and his followers. Castro closed down the lucrative casinos that brought millions of dollars into Mafia coffers and also lined the pockets of Batista. Thus, the first American-sponsored attempt to kill Castro took place fully one year before John Kennedy was elected President of the United States.

Robert Maheu was to be the "cut-out" between the mob leaders selected by the CIA—Sam Giancana, Santos Trafficante, and Jonny Rosselli—the man who would initially bring them all together. Maheu was brought out of "retirement" for this most sensitive assignment, one that was right up his highly politically savvy ally.

The records on Robert Maheu that were released are a treasure trove of information regarding his most interesting career that spanned over two decades on the firing line of American politics:

> Mr. Maheu was recruited by the Office of Security in March 1954. He was previously known to Mr. Robert Cunningham (deceased), who was, at that time, Chief, Special Security Division, through their mutual employment by the FBI. Cunningham saw in Maheu a covert asset who could be utilized by the Office in extremely sensitive cases. With the approval of the Director of Security, Subject was offered a proposition wherein he was to receive $500.00 per month, with the stipulation that he move into his own office and that he be on call for any assignments by the Office of Security. He agreed to this and immediately took steps to move out of his area, where he rented desk space in a suite occupied by Carmine Bellino, a former FBI agent and CPA.
>
> In July of 1954, Maheu was engaged by "British shipping interests" to check on Aristotle Onassis's activities while in the United States. This included technical coverage of Onassis' New York office. It was later learned that the principal "British interest" was Stavros Niarchos and that the ultimate goal of this task was to scrap the Onassis/Saudi oil deal. Maheu took the job but conditioned his acceptance with the fact that he would do nothing inimical to the US Government. Any information developed of interest to the US was to be passed by Maheu to the appropriate Government agency.

During his time working on the Onassis/Saudi deal, Maheu informed his bosses at the various US intelligence agencies on what he had learned. Some of the people he talked to were John Foster Dulles who was Secretary of State under President Eisenhower, FBI Director J. Edgar Hoover, and Vice President Nixon.

In August 1954, Maheu told his superiors of his relationship with Niarchos and was given secret communication materials with which he could contact his bosses. International litigation erupted as a result of the Niarchos/Onassis matter; as a result of Niarchos claiming government privilege in the case, the CIA was subsequently identified as being the government agency involved. Files reflect extensive correspondence furnished by the Office of General Counsel regarding the Onassis matter:

On 16 August 1954, Subject was granted a covert security clearance for utilization as an agent under Project [blank] in the Near East. On 30 August 1954 he was granted a similar clearance to permit his use in the United States as a covert associate under Project LPHIDDEN. In November of 1957, a cable from [blank] indicated that Mr. Maheu had allegedly been involved in a violation of the Mann Act in procuring and transporting prostitutes for [blank] visit to the United States in 1956. Mr. Maheu contacted this office to advise that the allegations were without foundation and stated that he would take steps immediately to have his attorney see that appropriate [blank] officials would retract the charges. This was subsequently done. Edward Bennett Williams acted as Maheu's lawyer in this matter.

In June of 1959, a covert security approval was issued for the use of Maheu by IO Division in order for him to be approached and advised of agency interest in International Labor. Files of this office do not reflect whether or not this was done. On 7 October 1959, a covert security approval was granted for Mr. Maheu's use in the United States. The request for approval indicated that subject might be employed by the [blank] to handle [blank] public relations in the United States.

In August of 1960, Richard Bissell, the then DD/P contacted the Director of Security regarding the Rosselli matter. In 1966, information was received by the Agency indicating that the Senate Administrative Practices Subcommittee, under the chairmanship of Senator Edward Long, had advised Maheu that his testimony wad desired concerning his relationship with Onassis and Stavros Niarchos, Sam Giancana and (blank). The subcommittee interest was invasion of privacy and particularly the use of audio devices by private investigators. In July of 1966,

Senator Long was alerted to the fact that the Agency had had sensitive operational contacts with Maheu. Sen. Long was told that the Agency had used Maheu over the years on a number of occasions but that he had never been asked to engage in any wiretapping and had never engaged in any such activities on our behalf. Office of Security files do not indicate whether or not Maheu did appear before this Subcommittee, although it appears that he did not.

In January of 1971, in light of the involvement of Maheu in a suit between executives of the Hughes Company and Maheu, the Director of Security recommended to the DCI that all existing clearances with Maheu and Associates be terminated. The DCI concurred in this recommendation.

Files of this Office reflect that Subject's company, Maheu and Associates, cooperated with the Agency in supporting the activities of an [blank] GLOBE agent [blank] in Ecuador. [Note—There is no information on what the GLOBE operation was about].

A memo from the Chief, Central Cover Staff to the Inspector General dated 10 October 1973, delineates the relationship between CCS and Robert Maheu and Associates.

Subject's son Peter Maheu was a staff employee of the Agency and of this Office from 1963 to 1964. He was a clerical employee. In February of 1969, Peter Maheu was granted a covert security approval as an employee of Maheu and Associates for use on Project QKENCHANT.

So, the new information from the Maheu file says that his son Peter Maheu was an employee of the CIA and worked for a project called QKENCHANT.

The file on Maheu now turns to the CIA-Mafia plots to kill Castro is under the heading "The Johnny Rosselli Matter."

Robert Maheu was contacted, briefed generally on the project, and requested to ascertain if he could develop an entrée into gangster elements. Mr. Maheu advised that he had met one Johnny Rosselli on several occasions while visiting Las Vegas. Maheu knew Rosselli only casually through clients but had been given to understand that Rosselli was a high-ranking member of the "Syndicate" and controlled all of the ice making machines on the Strip. Maheu was asked to approach Rosselli, who knew Maheu as a personal relations executive handling domestic and foreign accounts. Maheu was to tell Rosselli that he had recently been retained by a client who represented several international business firms which were suffering heavy financial losses in Cuba as a result of Castro's actions. These firms were convinced that Castro's removal was the answer to the problem and were willing to pay a price of $150,000 for its successful accomplishment. It was to be made clear to Rosselli that the United States Government was not and should not become aware of this operation.

Maheu met with James O'Connell of the CIA on 14 September 1960 at the Hilton Plaza Hotel in New York where the entire operation was explained. O' Connell was to be Rosselli's point of contact in the operation until May 1962, when he was assigned to an overseas posting. At first, Rosselli didn't want any part of the operation but "through Maheu's persuasion he agreed to introduce him to a friend, Sam Gold. Rosselli made it clear that he would not want any money for his part, and he believed that Gold would feel the same way. Neither of these individuals were ever paid out of Agency funds." It later turned out that "Sam Gold" was in fact, Sam Giancana, and the person named "Joe" who was also introduced to Maheu was really Santos Trafficante. Both men were on the list of the most notorious mobsters Robert Kennedy wanted for prosecution for various crimes committed in the United States. Giancana was described as the Chicago Chieftan of the Cosa Nostra and successor to Al Capone. Trafficante was identified as the Cosa Nostra boss of Cuban operations.

When discussing the Castro hits, Giancana suggested that poison be used in the attempt, as it would be much easier than using a sniper for the operation. Giancana said he could use a man named Juan Orta to poison Castro's food at the proper time and place. Orta, a one-time Cuban official who had been receiving kickback payments for a gambling interest and who still had access to Castro was the man for the job.

Orta was supposed to have received six pills of high lethal content from "Joe" but he got cold feet and asked out of the assignment. He suggested that another person be given the assignment, but that did not take place. Another high-placed anti-Castro leader named Dr. Antonio Varona said he'd do the Castro hit using his own resources. He asked for $10,000 for the job, as well as $1,000 for communication equipment. The document says, "Dr. Varona's potential was never fully exploited" as the mission was canceled shortly after the Bay of Pigs episode. Varona was advised the offer was withdrawn, and the pills were retrieved.[26]

In May 1962, William Harvey took over as Rosselli's case officer and it is not known if he was used officially from that point on. It was subsequently learned from the FBI that Rosselli had been convicted on six counts involving illegal entry into the United States some time during November 1967.

On December 2, 1968, Rosselli and four other individuals were convicted of conspiracy to cheat members of the Friars Club out of $400,000 in a rigged gin rummy game. Mr. Harvey reported his contacts with Rosselli during November and December of 1967 and January of 1968. Rosselli was facing deportation at that time but felt that he would win an appeal. Says the file on Maheu and Rosselli:

> On November 17 1970, Mr. Maheu called James O'Connell, Rosselli's first case officer, to advise that Maheu's attorney, Ed Morgan, had received a call from Thomas Waddin, Rosselli's attorney, who stated that all avenues of appeal had been exhausted and Rosselli faced deportation. Waddin indicated that if someone did not intercede on Rosselli's behalf, he would make a complete expose of his activity with the Agency. On 13 November 1970, Mr. Helms was briefed on this latest development and it was decided that the Agency would not in any way assist Rosselli. Maheu was advised of the Agency's position and was in complete agreement. He stated that he was not concerned about any publicity as it affected him personally should Rosselli decide to tell all. Subsequently Rosselli or someone on his behalf furnished Jack Anderson details of the operation. Anderson

26 RIF No. 104-10122-10141: Robert Maheu.

wrote two columns regarding this operation on 13 January 1971 and 23 February 1971. Rosselli was last known to be in the Federal Penitentiary in Seattle, Washington.

The CIA went to extradionary lengths to find out as much as they could regarding the actions of Robert Maheu and his participation in the Cuba plots as can be seen in a memo for the Director of the CIA. The subject was "Pros and Cons of the Robert Maheu Case" and it was written by Howard Osborn, Director of Security. The "Pros and Cons" memo starts by saying:

> Senator Long has been told by Morris Shenker, his personal attorney, that Robert Maheu was involved in certain assignments for this Agency. He is specifically aware of our interest in the Onassis/Niarchos Case, as well as our use of Giancana (not the mission). Senator Long allegedly agreed to withhold the subpoena of Maheu if the Agency confirms Maheu's statement that he has been utilized in the past on sensitive assignments for CIA. Senator Long reportedly does not desire to know any of the particulars and reportedly agrees not to get the Agency involved through other witnesses that may be called.

Below are the highlights of the "Pros and Cons" that the CIA wrote about in the Maheu case.

> Pros: The Agency will not become involved and no publicity will ensue. This undoubtedly would also have a number of advantages for Maheu personally, since he would not be involved. The Agency would be in a position of having attempted to cooperate with the Senate Committee by informing them of our interest in the matter. We would be more sure of having the fullest support of Maheu, Morgan and Shenker since we have attempted to solve the problem and our attempts have failed through no fault of our own. We have made no admissions and have furnished no validation to the Committee concerning our association with Maheu. We have not admitted to the Committee our involvement

in the Onassis or Giancana affairs. We are in a position to simply deny any involvement in wire-tapping in the Maheu case, which after all, is the purpose of the hearings of the Long Committee.

Now, to the Cons: The Senator could withhold the use of this information at this time, but could utilize the information later if he desired to do so. He could withhold use of the information at this time, but have his Committee Staff dig into the matter more deeply to develop the full story in the case at a later date. He could advise other individuals on the Hill that he had withheld the subpoena of Maheu due to the Agency's involvement in the two cases. Maheu will be subpoenaed and upon inquiry into the Onassis and Giancana affairs, will refer the Committee to the Agency. This will publically surface our connection. Even though Maheu refers the Committee to the Agency in this matter, the Giancana situation could be most embarrassing. First of all, even though Maheu would not be involved in the questioning, the Committee might call Giancana to testify. The attendant publicity would possibly identify Maheu as an Agency intermediary to other members of the Giancana family. If Maheu's association with the Agency is publically identified, this may cause [blank] to volunteer information on the Djakarta incident. The Senator could also leak it to the Press.

We risk arousing the ire of Maheu, Morgan, and Shenker because of our lack of cooperation. Since the Senator has reportedly been informed of our involvement with Maheu and we have not acknowledged it, he may then feel free to dig into the matter completely since we have not furnished him with the information. Giancana may be called to testify and we could not control Giancana. [blank] could come into the picture as a result of the television publicity involving Maheu. Our involvement in the Giancana situation would become known to other members of the Giancana family.[27]

The CIA's use of Robert Maheu as a cut-out between the mob and the Agency in the beginning was a dangerous game that really had no good ending. Maheu could have gone "rogue" at any time

27 RIF No. 104-10122-10311: Pros and Cons of the Robert Maheu Case.

but felt an obligation to the intelligence establishment that got him started after the war. He knew about all the loose ends surrounding the CIA-mob plots, including the relationship between the McGuire sisters act in Las Vegas, the wiretapping of the phone of singer Dan Rowan, and the fact that Sam Giancana was having an affair with the aforementioned Phyllis McGuire. How much could he have gotten if he blackmailed the Agency, and what ramifications would that have had at the time? The fact that the CIA made up a Pros and Cons list regarding Maheu shows how threatening they thought he might be under different circumstances.

But the story of Robert Maheu does not end there. Information gleaned over the years describes the testimony of Joseph Shimon, a man well connected to the mob and the intelligence services in the late 1960s, who gave his own account of the Las Vegas wiretapping case mentioned above.

According to the documents:

> Shimon stated that the wiretap in Phyllis McGuire's hotel room in Las Vegas, Nevada, did not involve the CIA. He stated that Maheu had the wiretap installed per arrangement with Sam Giancana. Maheu was paid $5,000 by Giancana to have a bug placed in the hotel room because he was concerned that his girlfriend was having an affair. Giancana could not have done it himself because he was persona grata in Nevada. When the wiretap was discovered, Shimon stated that Bob Maheu went absolutely nuts. The FBI was on to Maheu soon after the wiretap was discovered and it was Maheu that put the FBI onto Johnny... Shimon stated that when the FBI came to Rosselli that they decided to go to the CIA in order to work something out. Shimon said that when the CIA involvement with the wiretap on Phyllis McGuire was revealed, Sam Giancana went nuts. Sam, it seems, was most irate at the idea that someone else had engineered that wiretap.

One can only wonder whether, if Robert Maheu knew all the facts regarding what was to happen in the coming years, he would have signed up to begin with.

385

Chapter 45
Schweiker and Hart

By the late 1960s and early 1970s, the criticism of the Warren Commission Report began to grow more loud in the United States and across the world. The Warren Commission's 700-plus pages was a rush to judgment that left a lot of people wondering if the government had lied to them regarding the circumstances surrounding the assassination of the 35th president of the United States. In the late 60s, the people of the United States had not seen the grizzly pictures taken by Abraham Zapruder, who was standing near the grassy knoll and filmed the assassination as it took place. For years, the Zapruder film, as it was called, was locked away in a safe in New York City in the offices of Time-Life which had bought the rights to the film. When it was finally aired years later, the American people saw just what happened to President Kennedy as he rode through Dealey Plaza, and the angle of the shots that struck him. Whoever planned the assassination did not take into account that a person would capture the assassination as it happened on film. The Zapruder film changed everything as far as the assassination was concerned among the American people. Calls for another investigation began sweeping through the halls of Congress and the national legislators finally buckled to the pressure. The belief that there was a conspiracy in the Kennedy assassination took new life and a new era of investigations began to take shape.

It wasn't until 1976 that the Congress of the United States approved a bill that would look into the assassination of JFK and Martin Luther King. The House and Senate created their own investigative panels and an eager nation looked toward them to answer the questions that the biased Warren Commission failed to pursue. The Senate created a panel chaired by Idaho Senator Frank Church (The Church Committee) to investigate domestic assassinations and illegal CIA abuses. The House of Representatives established the HSCA, House Select Committee on Assassinations. For all their imperfections, these investigative panels, especially the Church Committee, were a blessing as far as finding out the darker side of the CIA in the 1960s. The committee revealed the CIA-Mafia plots to kill Fidel Castro, massive illegal CIA abuses at home, and the so-called "Family Jewels," a number of illegal CIA actions that hit the nation's front pages.

When the committee finished its report, it was published under the title "Book V: The Investigation of the Assassination of President J.F.K.: Performance of the Intelligence Agencies. "This report, also called the Schweiker-Hart Report after its authors, Senators Gary Hart and Richard Schweiker, discussed the performance of the CIA and the FBI in the investigation of the assassination of President Kennedy. The report analyzed the outstanding question of whether and by what degree the CIA and the FBI withheld relevant information from the Warren Commission, which was assigned to find out who killed the president and why. Among the news that came out of the report was the fact that the CIA was working with the Mafia to kill Castro, and that one of its members, former CIA Director Allen Dulles, never informed his fellow commissioners of that important fact. The committee found that the evidence "indicates that the investigation of the assassination was deficient" and "impeaches the process whereby the intelligence agencies arrived at their own conclusions."

Who were the two leading Senators who played such a large part in Congress's investigation into the Kennedy assassination?

Richard Schweiker was born on June 1, 1926 in Norristown, Pa. He served in the Navy during World War II and later graduated from Pennsylvania State University in 1950. He worked for a time as a manufacturing and sales executive. He was a member of the Republican Party and was elected to Congress in November 1960.

In September, 1976, Richard Schweiker was chosen to become a member of the House Select Committee on Assassinations. As Schweiker began his investigation he quickly found out about the abuses of the intelligence agencies including the fact that the FBI was harassing dissident political groups inside the US, and how the CIA, Army Intelligence and the National Security Agency were involved in domestic snooping. Also how the intelligence agencies had planned assassinations of foreign leaders. Schweiker said upon learning of these events, "I've learned more about the inner workings of government in the past nine months than in my fifteen previous years in Congress." Schweiker never in his mind believed that the US intelligence agencies would become a rougue sector of government and he said upon learning about these abuses, "That was so repugnant and shocking to me, that I did a backflip on any number of things."

For example, when he learned that Castro had made incendiary comments regarding the attempted assassination plots on his life by the mob, and said that American political leaders better watch what they said and did (some people believed this was a threat against JFK himself), Schweiker made the following comments, "But that statement had to have meaning, particularly to Allen Dulles." Schweiker thought Dulles' failure to tell the Warren Commission of the Castro plots was "a cover-up of sensational proportions."

As he read and re-read all the materials coming out of the National Archives pertaining to the Kennedy assassination, he became more convinced that a new investigation was needed.

He then issued the following statement regarding what he'd learned. "Recent disclosures have devastated the credibility of the WC Report. I call for a new, vigorous and meticulous inquiry (mentioning the attempts on Castro's life)." He also cited testimony that the FBI had destroyed and suppressed evidence about its association with Oswald, adding that a transcript of a previously "Top Secret" Warren Commission session revealed that Allen Dulles bluntly told his fellow members that J. Edgar Hoover would probably lie if called to testify.[28]

As the Schweiker-Hart subcommittee members began their work, they were immediately thrown into a puzzle surrounding Antonio Veciana, the leader of the militant anti-Castro group Alpha 66. Veciana told the committee about his meeting with a CIA officer named Maurice Bishop. He said that in August 1963, he saw Bishop meet with Lee Harvey Oswald in Dallas, Texas. Veciana told the committee that Bishop had organized and funded the Alpha 66 raids on Soviet ships that were docked in Cuba in 1963. Veciana said regarding this incident:

> It was my case officer, Maurice Bishop, who had the idea to attack the Soviet ships. The intention was to cause trouble between Kennedy and Russia. Bishop believed that Kennedy

28 Fonzi, Gaeton, *The Last Investigation,* Thunder's Mouth Press, New York, 1993, Page 31.

and Khrushchev had made a secret agreement that the USA would do nothing more to help in the fight against Castro. Bishop felt-he told me many times-that President Kennedy was a man without experience surrounded by a group of young men who were also inexperienced with mistaken ideas on how to manage this country. He said you had to put Kennedy against the wall in order to force him to make decisions that would remove Castro's regime.

Schweiker was convinced that Bishop was really CIA agent David Atlee Phillips. Senator Schweiker arranged for a meeting between Veciana and Phillips at a meeting of the Association of Retired Intelligence Officers in Reston, Virginia. At that meeting, Phillips denied knowing Veciana, despite having met someone named "Bishop" in Dallas with Oswald. Following the meeting, Veciana told Schweiker that Phillips was not the man known to him as Bishop:

> Schweiker was unconvinced by this evidence. He found it difficult to believe Phillips would not have known the leader of Alpha 66. Especially as Phillips had been in charge of covert action in Cuba when Alpha 66 was established. Another CIA agent who worked in Cuba during this period, claimed that Phillips used the code name, Maurice Bishop.[29]

Sen. Schweiker had his doubts about what Oswald was really doing in Russia and his possible links to US intelligence. He told author Anthony Summers a lot of information for Summers' book *Conspiracy*. He said of Oswald, "Either, we trained and sent him to Russia, and they went along and pretended they sent him back to fake us out, or in fact, they inculcated him and sent him back here and were trying to fake us out that way."

Schweiker also had very interesting information to give Anthony Summers regarding the workings of the Warren Commission. In 1978 he told Summers that, "the Warren Commission has collapsed like a house of cards. I believe that the Warren Commission was set up at the time to feed pablum to the American people for reasons not yet known, and that one of the biggest cover-ups in the history of our

29 Richard Schweiker-spartacus-educational.com.

country, occurred at that time. He said this regarding Oswald's time in New Orleans in the summer of 1963:

> I think that by playing a pro-Castro role on the one hand and associating with anti-Castro Cubans on the other, Oswald was playing out an intelligence role. This gets back to him being an agent or double agent. I personally believe that he had a special relationship with one of the intelligence agencies, which one I'm not certain. But all the fingerprints I found during my eighteen months on the Senate Select Committee on Intelligence point to Oswald as being a product of, and interacting with, the intelligence community.

In previous chapters in this book, I have made reference to Oswald's time in New Orleans prior to the assassination and his associations with Guy Banister and David Ferrie. Schweiker told Summers that, in regard to the New Orleans chapter of the assassination story, "We have evidence which places at 544 Camp Street (Banister's office) intelligence agents, Lee Oswald, the mob, and anti-Castro Cuban exiles. It puts all these elements together in a way than has never been done before."

Schweiker also had a lot if misgivings regarding Oswald's visit to Mexico City and the absence of tapes of people coming and going at the Cuban Consulate and the Russian Embassy. "He charges that the CIA deliberately concealed the existence of Mexico pictures from hi sstaff, and has expressed belief that a CIA cover-up is still going on."

After Richard Schweiker left the Senate, President Ronald Reagan appointed him as the Secretary of Health and Human Services. He later served as president of the American Council of Life Insurance.

Gary Hart, Schweikers's Senate colleague, was born in Ottawa, Kansas on November 28, 1936. He graduated from Nazarene College in 1958, Yale Divinity School in 1961, and then attended Yale University Law School. He soon found a job with the US Department of Justice, working there from 1964 to 1965. He then became special assistant to the solicitor of the Department of the Interior from 1965-1967. After leaving that post, he began his own law firm in Denver, Colorado.

In 1972 he turned to national politics and ran Senator George

McGovern's presidential campaign, only to have McGovern lose to Richard Nixon in a blowout election. In 1972, after the scandal of Watergate, Hart was elected to the Senate. In 1975, Hart was appointed to the Church Committee, whose other members were Walter Mondale, Richard Schweiker, Philip Hart, Howard Baker, and Barry Goldwater. The Committee investigated misuses on the part of the FBI and the CIA which, in later years, put restraints on their internal domestic activities. In September 1975, a he was appointed as a member of a sub-committee made up of Hart and Schweiker to review the performance of the intelligence agencies and their misdeeds. On May 1, 1975, Hart said, "I don't think you can see the things I have seen and sit on it."

In an interview he gave to the *Denver Post,* Hart said discussed the activities of Lee Oswald:

> ...he said the questions that needed answering included: "Who Oswald really was—who did he know? What affiliation did he have in the Cuban network? Was his public identification with the left-wing a cover for a connection with the anti-Castro right wing?" In the interview Hart went on to say that he believed Oswald was probably operating as a double agent. He thought this was one of the reasons why the FBI and the CIA had made a conscious decision to withhold evidence from the Warren Commission.[30]

In 1983, Hart announced a presidential run on the Democratic ticket in 1984. He won a number of primaries, but lost the nomination fight to Walter Mondale.

In 1985, Hart and his fellow Senator William Cohen wrote a political thriller called *Double Man.* Bob Woodward wrote a review of the book saying, "This is an expertly crafted thriller that is full of many uncomfortable plausibilities. Though it is labeled fiction, it dances knowledgeably with many old and new ghosts, including the CIA, the KGB, the Kennedy assassination, terrorism, and a range of state secrets. The *Double Man* has to be taken, minimally as a grim warning about the intelligence services in our own country and elsewhere."

In 1987, he became embroiled in a sexual scandal involving a young woman named Donna Rice which made national headlines and

30 Gary Hart-Spartacuts-educational.com.

ruined his potential nomination for president forever. In 2018, a movie on Senator Hart called *The Front Runner* was released in theaters.

On June 24, 1976, Senators Frank Church and Richard Schweiker held a press conference concerning the release of the Senate Select Committee Warren Commission Report that they had been working on for some time. Senator Church gave praise to Senators Schweiker and Hart for their dedication and hard work for the committee. Senator Church stated that "the report's central conclusion is that senior officials of both the CIA and the FBI failed to turn over relevant information to the Warren Commission. "Senator Church indicated that the reasons for the failure to turn over this relevant information are unclear and then quoted from the report to the effect that the possibility exists that this nondisclosure was intentional. Senator Church closed his statement by recommending "that the matter be referred to the newly created oversight committee with the recommendation that the committee continue this investigation to resolve unanswered questions." Senator Church then passed the microphone to Senator Schweiker who continued the press conference by taking reporters' questions. Here are some of them:

Question: The report states there is no hard evidence of a conspiracy. Is there circumstantial evidence?

Answer: Sen. Schweiker answered that the report leaves unanswered many questions that need to be resolved and there is sufficient evidence to warrant additional investigation.

Question: What are the names of the senior intelligence officers who withheld information from the Warren Commission?

Answer: Sen. Schweiker replied that Hoover and Helms failed to provide the Warren Commission with all relevant information but beyond those two individuals the investigation has not been completed.

Question: Allen Dulles who was a member of the WC knew about assassination plots against Castro. Why didn't he provide the Warren Commission with this data?

Answer: Schweiker replied that there is no indication any other member besides Allen Dulles knew of the assassination plots.

Question: What is left to be done in the way of investigation?

Answer: Senator Schweiker replied that the question of how high up and the purpose of the "cover-up" needs to be pursued, as well as several other leads not identified within the report.

Question: Was AMLASH a double agent?

Answer: Sen. Schweiker replied that the Cuban government had an excellent intelligence network in the US and the question of whether AMLASH was a double agent and whether Castro knew of AMLASH's activities with the CIA is a very important issue.

Question: You have indicated that you do not have faith in the Warren Commission investigation, therefore, do you then not believe that Oswald was the lone assassin?

Answer: Senator Schweiker replied that the Warren Commission was missing several ingredients when they made their investigation and therefor he (Schweiker) could make no decision on the matter.

Question: Is there enough evidence to reopen a full-scale investigation of the Kennedy assassination?

Answer: Sen. Schweiker replied that if Oswald had been convicted the trial would later have been declared a mistrial solely on the basis of the FBI's destruction of Oswald's note in the Dallas office. He added that yes there is enough evidence to open a full-scale investigation, but the next step would be for the oversight committee to pursue the leads.

Question addressed to Sen. Church: Was there a reason for the cover-up?

Answer: Sen. Church replied he had no judgment on that. There could be many reasons "we just don't know."

Question: How far did the cover-up go?

Answer: Sen. Schweiker replied that he doesn't know, his committee ran out of time to pursue this and this is the next logical lead to pursue. He added that Mr. McCone has testified that he did not know of CIA attempts to assassinate Castro. Sen. Church interjected that the state of the investigation does not show whether there was a conscious effort to cover up. Sen. Church said there could be several other reasons such as one frequently pointed out that since Allen Dulles was on the Warren Commission there was no need to tell the Commission.

Question: Are any of the participants in the cover-up still employed by the CIA or FBI?

Answer: Sen. Schweiker replied it would be unfair to answer

this question and that there could or could not be current employees involved.

Question: What about the interest of President Johnson in 1967?

Answer: Sen. Schweiker replied again this was an example where they did not fully reopen the investigation and conducted only a pro forma inquiry where several important leads "fell through the cracks."

Question: Is there any new information in the report?

Answer: Sen. Schweiker replied a couple of leads such as Cuban intelligence agents moving in flights in cockpits within Mexico and the US and then on to Cuba.

Question: Do you know that the man riding in the cockpit of the aircraft was a Cuban intelligence agent?

Answer: Sen. Schweiker replied that there is strong evidence that one of the Cubans mentioned in one of these two leads in the report was a Cuban intelligence agent.

Question: What are other motives in President Kennedy's assassination?

Answer: Sen. Schweiker replied that he hated to speculate on this matter and that it could have been Castro retaliation, retaliation by anti-Castro groups or it could even involve the Mafia.

Question: Since you say Mr. Helms did not fulfill his responsibility in this regard, what are you doing to terminate his ambassadorship?

Answer: Sen. Schweiker replied he had made no judgment on this matter and will wait for the oversight committee continuance of the investigation.[31]

The Church Committee and the two-man Kennedy investigation that was run by Senators Hart and Schweiker answered a lot of questions regarding the Kennedy assassination but were stalled at almost every way station by the FBI and the CIA. Those two agencies had a lot to lose from revealing their most vital Oswald-related information and they certainly were not going to give it to the Congress which they did not trust. And so, the matter rested without any conclusive answer one way or another. Had Gary Hart become president, he might have had the power to re-open the Kennedy assassination probe but that, of course, did not take place.

31 RIF No. 104-10096-10193: Senators Church and Schweiker News Conference Concerning Release of Senate Select Committee Warren Commission Report, 24 June, 1976.

There is one more interesting fact regarding Gary Hart and his JFK assassination investigation that has to be told, and it involves the CIA's most elusive assassin at that time, QJ/WIN.

In July 1975, while Senator Hart was returning from a trip to Moscow, he received an unsigned note that was left for him. The note said he would be contacted in Holland while on a stopover and that he'd be told what to do next. After hours, Hart slipped out of his hotel and went to a bar near his hotel to meet someone he'd never met. The man he was supposed to meet that dark night was the elusive CIA assassin known as QJ/WIN who was front and center in the plots to kill Patrice Lumumba of the Congo.

Before leaving for his European trip, Hart had met with CIA Director William Colby to arrange a meeting with QJ/WIN while he was overseas. When Hart's contact arrived at the bar, it was not QJ/WIN, but his representative:

> He told Hart that WIN had come that evening from a neighboring country. WIN had asked who Hart was, and why he wanted to meet him. When the CIA man admitted that Hart was involved in an investigation of Kennedy's death, WIN angrily declared that he would not meet with Hart, and abruptly left the room.
>
> Clearly Hart was intrigued by this mysterious man whom he had failed to meet. And clearly he felt there was much to be gained in questioning him about his legendary career. Conversely, the CIA ought to have much to lose by allowing WIN to be questioned. And given the lengths to which they had gone to conceal his identity, it seems strange that they would so willingly have agreed to bring him to Hart. It is a curious event in the history of the investigation and intelligence, or perhaps we should call it a non-event, since the meeting never took place. We must ask, therefore, what this non-event might mean; what purpose it might have served.[32]

Who knows how history would have changed if Hart had met QJ/WIN that night?

---

[32] Rivele, Stephen, *Death of a Double Man.*

Chapter 46:
Dorothy Hunt and Watergate

It seems that there is always a connection between the Watergate affair and the assassination of President Kennedy. We can name the "usual suspects" who were linked to both events: Howard Hunt, Frank Sturgis, and their other hangers-on. Howard Hunt's wife, Dorothy Hunt, is the subject of this chapter based on information gleaned from various sources including the on-line investigative company called Muckrock which has been an invaluable source in revealing new information on the underside of American political history. The Dorothy Hunt story reveals information about her links to some of the other participants in the Watergate burglary, her personal relationship with her husband, the contents of Howard Hunt's safe, and the circumstances surrounding her tragic death in a plane crash while she was carrying $10,000 bound for the Watergate burglars.

On July 5, 1972, two agents of the FBI, Special Agents Daniel Mahan and Donald Stukey, had an interview with Mrs. Hunt. The interview was conducted at Mrs. Hunt's residence at 11120 River Road, Potomac, Maryland. The two FBI agents worked out of FBI offices located at 12th and Pennsylvania Ave. N.W. in Washington, DC. At the interview, Mrs. Hunt identified herself as the wife of Howard Hunt who lived at the same residence.

"SA Mahan advised Mrs. Hunt that she was being contacted concerning information she may possess concerning a burglary at the offices of the Democratic National Committee (the Watergate complex), 2650 Virginia Ave, N.W. Washington, DC, which occurred on June 17, 1972." She told the agents that she didn't know anything regarding the break-in, but that she doubted that Howard had been associated with any of the men who were subsequently arrested.

> Mrs. Hunt stated that she does not feel that she possesses
> any information which is directly related to the burglary at
> the Democratic National Headquarters and that the only
> information she possesses concerning this burglary is what

she has read in the local newspapers. Mrs. Hunt noted that she has read considerable information to the effect that her husband, E. Howard Hunt, Jr., may have been associated with the individuals who were arrested for the burglary of the Democratic National Committee Headquarters (DNCH) but stated that she doesn't feel that her husband is involved with these men.

The agents then proceeded to show Mrs. Hunt a number of photographs and letters, some of which she was able to identify. Five of the photographs were of the Watergate burglars, who were connected to her husband:

> Significantly, her statement of meeting one of the burglars through her husband at the 1971 Bay of Pigs reunion lends credence to later statements that this was when and where Howard Hunt reconnected with Bernard Barker in the lead-up to the Watergate affair.
>
> Mrs. Hunt stated that she is familiar with the photograph of [blank] as he is an individual who is known to her as [blank] whom she has known for more than ten years. Mrs. Hunt stated that she met [blank] more than ten years ago as her husband was instrumental in organizing the "Bay of Pigs" invasion and [blank] was also active in that operation.
>
> Mrs. Hunt selected a photograph of [blank] and stated that he is an individual she met during April 1971, at the ten year commemoration of the Bay of Pigs invasion which was held in Miami, Florida. Mrs. Hunt stated that she knew this individual only as [blank].
>
> SA [blank] asked Mrs. Hunt if the name [blank] is known to her. Mrs. Hunt stated that she is familiar with the name [blank] as an individual who worked for the CIA and retired to the State of Florida following a heart attack.
>
> SA [blank] displayed a series of two black and white photographs of unknown white males and a series of letters which were signed [blank]. Mrs. Hunt identified the photographs as photographs of [blank] (also known as [blank]) a citizen of Argentina whom she met in Tokyo, Japan.

This document obtained by Muckrock reveals the names of the two people mentioned above by Dorothy Hunt as "Bob" and Juan Carlos Quagliotti, a Uruguayan national. Mrs. Hunt identified the photographs as pictures of Ernesto Herrera, also known as "Chango."

The Muckrock documents then tells the story of the challenges the Hunts faced in their marriage, one that almost ended in divorce, as well as certain letters in her care.

Mrs. Hunt stated that she also recognizes the letters as letters that she had exchanged with [blank—possibly Juan Carlos Quagliotti]. Mrs. Hunt explained that during the late 1950s and early 1960s, she and her husband were having considerable difficulties in their marital relations. She stated that her husband spent a considerable amount of time [in his job as a member of the Central Intelligence Agency] and that she learned he was carrying on extramarital affairs with other women. Mrs. Hunt stated she sought solace for her marital difficulties by carrying on extramarital affairs with the aforementioned individuals.

However, no matter how hard their marriage was as that time, they decided not to split up due to the fact that they had children and for other personal reasons. Dorothy told the FBI that she "gave [her husband] the letters, photographs and other materials she had received from these individuals. She assumed that he had destroyed them, at her request. Mrs. Hunt stated that she is shocked to find these letters and other materials in the hands of the FBI as she had believed that they had been destroyed more than ten years ago."

Information relating to the Hunt letters/pictures is given by renegade CIA officer Philip Agee who wrote a blockbuster book called *Inside the Company: CIA Diary.* According to Agee, Quagliotti was a Uruguayan lawyer and rancher and a "political contact of the Montevideo station." He was supposed to have been given the code name AVIATOR. Agee said that Quagliotti was "concerned with the decline in government effectiveness" and "was active in trying to persuade military leaders to intervene in political affairs." Agee said that while the CIA had contact with him, it did not "finance or encourage him." Agee's most interesting claim about

Quagliotti relates to a flurry of security moves that he caused at the end of May 1965."

Quagliotti was supposed to have been arrested for "the printing and distribution of a distorted version of an article written in 1919 by President Beltran's father, on justification of military intervention in politics."[33]

The files released by Muckrock hint that Dorothy Hunt may have had an affair with Quagliotti who was a known political agitator in his home country "especially given that she had, like her husband, worked for the US government and that, according to a book co-written by Howard Hunt, she had also acted as a source and asset for the CIA. Did she eventually pass that information on to Howard? Did she provide Howard—and the Agency—information about Quagliotti when she confessed the affair, like she had previously done with information whisked from the Argentinian embassy?"

These documents now go on to another topic, that of a pistol that was in the possession of Mrs. Hunt. The FBI agents who interviewed her showed her an automatic Colt revolver with a pearl inlaid handle, serial number 321803. Mrs. Hunt recognized the gun and told the agents that it was her "personal weapon" and that she had thought it was in a closet at home. If that was true, how did the FBI agent get hold of it? She told the agents that she had been given the pistol "prior to 1945 when she traveled to China to work on behalf of the US Treasury Department." Her son, St. John Hunt, said she told him that she obtained the small semi-automatic pistol while "she was in Bern and told me she kept it within reach during these midnight trysts." Mrs. Hunt moved from Bern to China in 1946.

> Mrs. Hunt stated that she had nearly forgotten about the gun but stated that she does not know how or when this gun was removed from her residence. She stated that her husband possesses a German Luger pistol and that she is certain that it is still at her residence as she observed it the evening hours of June 24, 1972.

It turns out that Mrs. Hunt's gun was part of a large number of articles taken from Howard Hunt's White House safe that was

33 "FBI file reveals some of the secrets of Howard Hunt's White House safe," www.muckrock.com.

opened in the wake of the Watergate scandal on orders from John Dean. The Bureau got custody of the gun the day before interviewing Dorothy. Coincidentally, one of the two agents who recieved the boxes containing most of the materials retrieved from Hunt's safe was one of the two agents interviewing Dorothy Hunt.

Now to the contents of Howard Hunt's safe that was opened on June 17, 1972. White House officials, including John Dean, spent a few days going over the contents of the safe before turning them over to the FBI. The materials in the safe were given to acting FBI Director L. Patrick Gray who kept them for six months before burning them in late December 1972. Gray would later admit burning these items to the Senate Watergate Committee. What Dean found in the safe was a treasure trove of material that was later made public.

Among the items found in the safe were the following: a loaded .25 caliber pistol (the one owned by Mrs. Hunt), the attaché case of burglar James McCord loaded with electronic surveillance equipment and a tear gas canister, CIA psychological profiles of Pentagon Papers leaker Daniel Ellsberg, papers from the Pentagon Papers, memos to and from Nixon aide Charles Colson, two falsified diplomatic cables implicating President Kennedy in the 1963 assassination of South Vietnamese President Ngo Diem, and a dossier on the personal life of Senator Edward Kennedy. It was later reported that Nixon aide John Ehrlichman advised Dean to throw the contents of the safe into the Potomac River.[34]

In a later development to this story, *Washington Post* reporter Carl Bernstein, talked with an assistant who worked for Charles Colson in the White House, and learned that Hunt had been investigating Kennedy's checkered past. Of particular interest was the Chappaquiddick incident in which a woman named Mary Jo Kopechine, who was riding in Ted Kennedy's car died when the vehicle plunged into a canal. Ted Kennedy went for help, not trying to save her. Hunt was looking for any dirt he could find in anticipation of Kennedy's possible run for president in later years. Charles Colson, a close intimate of Nixon's, and his friend H.R. Haldeman were "absolutely paranoid" about a Kennedy campaign.

We now turn to the last tale in the saga of Dorothy Hunt, that of her sudden and tragic death in a plane crash which took the lives of

---

34 History Commons: The Nixon Administration and Watergate. June 19, 1972: Dean Orders Falsified Documents Removed from Watergate Burglar's Safe.

44 other people on December 8, 1972 when United Airlines Flight 533 crashed upon landing at Chicago's Midway Airport.

The crash, as with most areas of the Watergate affair, goes back to the roles of the burglars and their secret funds. Hunt and his fellow Plumbers were regularly receiving hush money payments from the Nixon presidential campaign to remain quiet about their illicit activities. Hunt was under immense pressure to save himself as his sentencing was due, and he refused to go along with the cover-up anymore. He threatened to reveal what he knew regarding the break-in at DNC Headquarters.

His wife, Dorothy, helped bring off a payoff deal with Nixon aide Charles Colson, and James McCord, who would later claim that Dorothy said that her husband had information that would "blow the White House out of the water." She was upset, according to Colson "at the interruption of payments from Nixon's associates to Watergate defendants." Former Attorney General John Mitchell, the head of Nixon's re-election committee, arranged to have Nixon aide Fred LaRue pay the Hunts $250,000 to keep their mouths shut.

On the day of the crash, Mrs. Hunt had arranged to meet with CBS journalist Michelle Clark for some unknown reason, but one can speculate that it had to do with the Watergate scandal. Also in the ill-fated plane was Illinois Congressman George Collins. Mrs. Hunt was reportedly carrying on her person $10,000 in cash as a partial payoff for the burglars.

A few days after the crash of United Air 533, President Nixon was informed of the event by H.R. Haldeman and John Ehrlichman who told the president that Mrs. Hunt had paid out $250,000 in cash to her husband and the other Watergate burglars. The cash was delivered to Mrs. Hunt from White House courier Tony Ulasewicz, who took cash from the White House and stored it in a rental locker at Washington's National Airport. In October 1974, Watergate burglar Bernard Barker confirmed that Dorothy Hunt was the burglars' connection to the Nixon White House. Barker later said that months after the burglary he met with Dorothy Hunt in Miami, where she told him, "From now on, I will be your contact."

Within hours of the crash of United 533, law enforcement officers rushed to the scene. A reporter named Lalo Gastriani later said that the crash site was swarmed by "a battalion of plainclothes operatives in unmarked cars parked on side streets. Some of the neighbors said the operatives looked like "FBI types," and one witness said she recognized a "rescue worker" as a CIA agent (how this person came to that conclusion is unknown). In later years the future FBI Director, William Ruckelshaus, admitted that his agency had 50 agents at the crash site. In a side note, one of Charles Colson's aides, Egil Krogh, who was involved with the White House "Plumbers," was named as undersecretary of transportation one day after the crash. The position gave Krogh direct control over the two agencies responsible for investigating the crash. Also, another Nixon aide, Dwight Chapin, would become a top executive at United Airlines.[35]

While the Nixon White House was trying to figure out what to do in wake of the death of Mrs. Hunt, her husband, Howard, had much up his sleeve regarding his legal troubles. While on trial, Hunt told his fellow burglars, Frank Sturgis, Virgilio Gonzalez, Eugenio Martinez, and Bernard Barker that if they plead guilty and kept their mouth shut, the White House would help them financially to take care of their families if they went to jail. Hunt then plead guilty, leaving his fellow conspirators to their own ends. Barker would later explain why Hunt plead guilty. He said that Hunt was overcome with emotion after the death of his wife and said to Barker, "Well, you do what you want, but I am going to plead guilty."

When Barker asked Hunt why he made that decision, Hunt said, "We have no defense. The evidence against us is overwhelming." When Barker asked Hunt about Liddy and McCord he replied, "Liddy and McCord are in a different sector. We are in one sector and they are in another. They have their own plan." Over the next several days, Barker, Gonzalez, and Martinez also plead guilty, following in Hunt's footsteps.

We now come to the conversations regarding the death of Mrs. Hunt between the president and John Dean. Dean had several conversations with President Nixon regarding the Chicago plane crash, but what he did not know as he talked, was that their conversations were being taped. Dean told the president that Dorothy Hunt was carrying $10,000 in her person that was to be distributed to the Cubans who were involved in the break-in. Dean told Nixon, "You've got them, an awful lot of the principals involved who know.

35 History Commons: December 8, 1972: Wife of Watergate Plumber Dies in Suspicious Plane Crash.

Some people's wives know. Mrs. Hunt was the savviest woman in the world. She had put the whole picture together." This reference possibly referred to the fact that Mrs. Hunt knew all the facets of the cover-up, including what part each of the burglars played when they broke into the DNC Headquarters.

Nixon had this to say regarding the death of Mrs. Hunt according to John Dean:

> "Great sadness. As a matter of fact there was discussion with somebody about Hunt's problem on account of his wife and I said, of course communication could be considered on the basis of his wife's death, and that is the only conversation I ever had in that light."
>
> Dean agreed with the president, "Right. So that is it. That is the extent of the knowledge."

John Dean was not the only one of the president's close advisors to have conversations with him regarding the death of Mrs. Hunt. The president spoke with H.R. Haldeman regarding the incident and told him the basics of what happened. But then the conversation turned to the ten grand that she was carrying. At this point the president grew angrier by the minute. Haldeman told the president that investigators were probably going to trace the serial numbers of the money. Nixon then said, "Who gave 'em to him? We didn't." Haldeman then continued by telling the president, "You know, whether its theirs, or there's payoff money involved in it, it could be some of it, a lot of bills."

The president then asked Haldeman if Hunt had some explanation for the money and Haldeman replied, "They might not be able to track it, he may have been smart enough to wash it." Nixon then asked Haldeman, "Suppose, incidentally, this money is tracked back, who is it tracked to? They put together some cash to take care of these people. I don't know where it came from. I assume they were smart enough to do it so that it was not traceable cash, as the other stuff."[36]

As the days went on, Nixon was still fixated on the money carried by Dorothy Hunt. He continued to pester Haldeman about

36 Dean, John, *The Nixon Defense: What He Knew and When He Knew It,* Viking, New York, 2014, Page 186.

the money. Haldeman told Nixon that John Dean was looking into the matter and found out that Mrs. Hunt was carrying the money to Chicago to make an investment in a Howard Johnson restaurant with some other people who dealt in other such investments in cash. Dean said the money was in the possession of the Chicago Police who would turn it over to Howard Hunt at a later date. Haldeman said, "John [Dean] doesn't know whether it's traceable or not. He's not particularly concerned, but he doesn't think it is." Another interesting piece of information is that Mrs. Hunt purchased a large amount of flight insurance, paying either $200,000 or $250,000, prior to boarding the ill-fated plane.

The destruction of United Flight 533 at Chicago's Midway Airport is the last piece of the Watergate story to be revealed. Was there a conspiracy in the downing of the jet carrying Dorothy Hunt and her $10,000 in hush money, or was it just a tragic happenstance? Was her role as a conduit for the other Watergate burglars her only involvement in the Watergate affair, or is there some other story regarding Mrs. Hunt that we still don't know?

The detail in the materials that came via Muckrock are interesting in themselves. We have information about Mrs. Hunt's personal gun that was found in her husband's White House safe that she believed was still in her possession. She was possibly involved in an extramarital affair with a known foreign agent named Juan Carlos Quagliotti—did Howard Hunt know about it? The historical record is still wanting a clear-cut answer to just what Mrs. Hunt knew regarding the events of the Watergate break-in itself and the role played by her husband. We know for a fact that the Nixon White House was extremely paranoid about what what would happen after the plane crash, vis a vis the money she was carrying, and what it was going to be used for. Haldeman and the president were talking about how the aftermath of the crash would affect the cover-up of the Watergate incident and how best to contain it, lest it come directly to the door of the Oval Office. They talked briefly of a commutation of Howard Hunt's sentence, but dropped the idea without any further discussion. All of these details leave as many questions outstanding as they answer. But in the long run, Watergate is still something to be talked and written about even, after the passage of all this time.

Chapter 47
The Case of Peter Karlow

One of the interesting finds in the JFK documents is a memorandum written by the FBI regarding the case of a suspected mole in the bowels of CIA headquarters in Langley, Virginia, named Peter Karlow. The person who told the Agency of the suspected mole was none other than Major Anatoly Golitsyn of the KGB who defected to the United States from Helsinki, Finland in December 1961. Golitsyn is forever linked with the defection of another Russian spy named Yuri Nosenko whose exploits have been recorded in this book and many other books and magazine articles over the decades.

When Golitsyn defected he began to regale his listeners with the most fantastic stories imaginable. One item of particular interest caught their full attention. He said that the Russians had infiltrated a mole inside CIA headquarters, someone who had been there for a long time. All CIA counterintelligence plans were known in Moscow Center as fast as they were put in motion. When asked who this mysterious mole was, Golitsyn said he did not know his real name, but he gave some tantalizing clues. The person had previously served in Germany, the man was of Slavic background, and went by the code name SASHA. Golitsyn added that the man's name probably began with the letter K. He also added that the man's last name probably ended with the letters "sky." With these alluring clues, the CIA began a yearlong mole hunt looking for the sleeper agent who had penetrated the inner sanctum of the CIA. By the time the search for the mole ended, the CIA's Counterespionage section would be torn apart and many innocent men's lives would be in ruin.

As soon as Golitsyn was safely ensconced in a CIA safe house, the hunt for the mole began in earnest. Anyone connected with foreign counterintelligence was gone over with a fine-tooth comb and the field was soon narrowed down to a few suspects. One person who seemed to fit all the categories laid out by Golitsyn was Peter Karlow, whose real name was Klibansky, which ends in "sky," as mentioned by Golitsyn. Was Karlow/Klibansky the mole?

The Klibansky family came to the United States from Germany

in 1910. The elder Klibansky got a job as a singing teacher. Both mother and father became naturalized American citizens in 1921, and their son, Serge Peter, was born that same year.

In 1937, Peter officially changed his name to Karlow, and graduated from the McBurney Prep School. He was awarded a scholarship to Swarthmore College, and joined the Navy when the United States entered World War II. He soon found himself in the OSS and remained in that capacity until the conflict ended. His most important duty while posted to the OSS was carried out on the island of Corsica, where he was assigned to a PT boat base. Karlow was part of a 15 man intercept platoon located near the island of Elba. One of his duties was to locate German planes that made attack runs against the US military in Corsica. In February 1944, while on a mission aboard a boat, an explosion from a German mine tossed him over the side and killed most of his crew. In the ensuing hell, Karlow lost his left leg above the knee. At age 22, he now had to wear an artificial limb for the rest of his life. After the war, he and many other veterans of the OSS joined the CIA (he was accepted in 1947).

In 1946, on year before his entry into the CIA, Karlow was asked to write a history of the OSS. He worked on the narrative with legendary OSS officer Kermit Roosevelt, a grandson of former President Theodore Roosevelt. The classified study was an in-house publication that was read by only those invited to view its secrets. Many years later, the manuscript was finally released to an eager public under the title *War Report of the OSS*.

In the 1950s, under orders from Richard Helms, he was sent to Frankfurt, Germany to set up a technical lab where he could refine his espionage/technical skills. He worked out of the CIA station in Karlsruhe, and within six months, had a prosperous business up and running.

One of his duties was to supply clandestine espionage tools for the secret agents whose job it was to parachute into Soviet-held parts of Eastern Europe. His team made lock picks and specialized guns, forged papers, all the necessary items needed for clandestine warfare. Karlow's specialty was to create perfectly forged identity papers that he and his team called the "7922nd Technical Aids Detachment (TAD) of the United States Army."

During his stay in Germany, Karlow married a woman named

406

Elizabeth Rausch, who later joined the CIA. She worked with her husband in the technical gadgets department in Germany. She also worked in the counterintelligence division, leaving in 1953 when their first child was born.

Peter Karlow left Germany and by 1956 was back in the United States. He now had a job in the Eastern European Division as the Deputy Chief of the Economic Action Department. By 1959, he was Secretary of the Technical Requirements Board.

For the next two years, Karlow performed his duties unencumbered by the secret events that were going on around him. As 1962 arrived, he did not know that Anatoly Golitsyn would collide with his peaceful life.

As the CIA began to piece Golitsyn's information together, they came to the conclusion that their main suspect was Serge Peter Karlow. Not wanting to tip him off, they decided he was to be transferred to a new job, one that did not allow him access to really sensitive information. He was called into the office of Richard Helms who told him that the Kennedy administration was starting up an office that would handle foreign policy crisies, and that Karlow had been picked to represent the CIA. As Karlow began his new assignment, he had no idea that he was under investigation as a Russian mole.

As time went on, Karlow received a sudden and unexpected visit from two FBI agents. They came to see him on an unrelated case concerning a German forger he had known. They said that this person wanted to defect to the Russians, and could he tell them anything about him. Karlow was very helpful and he was mystified why the Bureau had bothered to see him in the first place. Later, other agents came to his home and told him they believed a person on his block might be a German spy. They asked if it would be OK for the Bureau to set up a listening device in Karlow's garage. Karlow agreed to their request. Soon, he realized that his own phone was tapped and knew something untoward was going on.

When Karlow traveled to Philadelphia to get a new artificial limb (the CIA believed he was going to meet a Russian contact) he was followed by FBI agents, who were dumfounded when they realized what he was doing in the City of Brotherly Love.

For Karlow, the signs were all beginning to make sense. He was being followed for some reason of which he was not aware. Another blow to his psyche came when he was turned down for a job in the Technical Services Division.

On February 11, 1962, he was told to report to the Washington Field Office of the FBI where he would assist agents on a sensitive yet unnamed case. When Karlow showed up he was greeted by two FBI agents, Aubrey Brent and Maurice Taylor. He was told up front that he had "the right to remain silent," a sure indication that he was being accused of some crime. He was dumfounded when the agents told him he was accused of being a Russian mole. His flawless 22-year career in the CIA was now at an end.

He was interrogated by government agents who wanted to know all about his family ties to Germany and tried to cajole him into admitting he was SASHA, all to no avail. Shortly before he left the Agency, Karlow confronted Richard Helms and his boss, James Angleton. Angleton told him, "There is more that goes on around here than I can possibly explain to you. It has to do with a Russian defector." Karlow now recognized where the accusations had come from. As he left the CIA for the last time, he vowed to clear his name.

After leaving the CIA, Peter Karlow worked in the private sector, doing everything to clear his reputation. By the 1980s, 20 years after he was forced out of the CIA, the nation's mood as far as the intelligence community was concerned, had changed. In the 1970s Congress held open hearings on the CIA's abuses, both at home and abroad. With new access to previously classified CIA files, Karlow got help from then CIA Director William Webster. Webster, after reviewing the evidence against Karlow, decided that he had been unfairly relieved of his duties. He was awarded $700,000 in back pay and reparations for his loyal service to the country, and now had his good reputation back. Congress passed a special bill on Karlow's behalf called "The Mole Relief Act."

In a secret ceremony, Karlow was awarded the intelligence Commendation Medal and an award that was signed by DCI Webster.

In an ironic twist to the Karlow case, James Angleton, the CIA's chief spycatcher, was himself believed by some of his CIA colleagues to be the elusive SASHA.

The above has been the historical record relating to the background of Peter Karlow and the suspected mole called SASHA. Now, we have the records on the Karlow case that were released by the National Archives over the past several years:

Vienna: [blank] estimated that Karlow probably made 12-15 trips to Vienna during this period (1950-53) for Agency purposes. He recalled that the Agency was servicing a number of requests from Vienna; that at one time, "We had a riotous operation going there and [blank] needed some help. [blank] believed that [blank] could furnish substantial information regarding Karlow's activities in Vienna.

[blank] recalled that during this particular period there were no travel restrictions on American personnel in and around Soviet zone [blank] could not recall how long Karlow remained in Vienna on his trips there.

Karlow stated that he had stayed with Agency associates on some visits to Berlin and on one or more occasions he stayed at the Harnach House, an Army guest house for the Berlin command. Karlow also stated that after his marriage he and his wife had gone to Corsica on two occasions, and to Rome, and had spent New Year's Eve 1952-53 at a small town in Austria. These were purely personal trips. He said he did not recall having taken a trip to Berlin for purely personal purposes. Karlow stated that before their marriage, "Libby" Rausch had gone to Berlin and stayed at the residence of William Harvey. Karlow said he had not visited Berlin with "Libby" before marriage but recalled he had done so on one occasion after marriage and he recollected he had become ill on the train from some oysters he had eaten.

Karlow explained in early February 1950, he proceeded to [blank] and took over as Chief of TAD which was located in the [blank] suburb of [blank] and had mail address APO 709. Karlow resided in an apartment located in an adjoining building. Karlow advised when he assumed charge of [blank] the unit consisted of only about nine persons. From recollection Karlow identified TAD personnel as follows: Major Robert Harris, the previous Chief of TAD, and a former officer of National Security Agency (NSA), Captain Guy Drennan, also formerly with NSA, and currently night Duty Officer with the Intelligence Branch of the Department of State; and [blank[, a civilian scientist-chemist, who became deputy of Karlow and had a small laboratory with several technicians and operated what Karlow described as a postal censorship.

[blank] advised that because of the wide area that TAD was servicing on behalf of the CIA, it was necessary that number of TAD personnel be constantly travelling. [blank] remarked that he was travelling steadily and that Karlow was a frequent traveler in behalf of TAD. [blank] could recall no specific dates of trips by Karlow during the period 1950-1953, but furnished the following information. [blank] recalled that during this particular period there were no travel restrictions on American personnel in and around Vienna; that frequently one was not aware he was even in a Soviet zone. [blank] could not recall how long Karlow remained in Vienna on his trips there.

The documents then refer to an interview that Karlow gave to an unidentified person (most likely from the CIA) in which he touched on some matters relating to Agency work in Berlin and other people in the CIA that he worked with:

[blank] said he is acquainted with Harry Rositzke, who is also employed with CIA. [blank] said his association with Rositzke is not new and has never been close. He said he is unable to recall exactly when he became acquainted with Rositzke but he associates their meeting with a period shortly following World War II. He is unable to state how they became acquainted because they have never been assigned to the same work.

The interview turns to a man named Houck who was employed by the Agency in Berlin:

He mentioned Houck was still Chief of Base at Berlin and said he saw Houck. Karlow explained that military orders were necessary for any travel into Berlin, including flights by Pan American Airways, which also operated under military control. He stated the orders for travel was involved.

Karlow related one of his men from TAD, [blank] was stationed in Berlin under the name Daniel O'Neill. He thought this was in 1951 or after 1951. He also stated that other men from TAD had temporary duty in Berlin and recalled vaguely the photography men had set up some new equipment and dark room there. [blank] had visited Berlin in connection with some Polish matter. Wesley Parcells on some German "things" and [blank] the chemist, in connection with some case.

Karlow said he could not say whether he was in Berlin in August 1951, but recalled he was there on at least one occasion in the summer because he clearly remembered how early the sun rose in the morning.

Karlow stated that he rarely became involved in operations and was usually occupied in making arrangements and setting things up for use of the facilities of TAD. He recalled, however, he was involved in an operation with [blank], and Harry Rositzke of the SR [Soviet Russia] Division and flew to Berlin in 1952 in this connection. Karlow explained the operation involved a planned attempt to steal the latest made model MIG fighter plane and great preparation had been made but at the last minute the adventure was called off because of possible political and diplomatic repercussions.

Karlow first said he was unable to recall visiting Berlin in 1953 but later said he recalled seeing William Harvey, Chief of Station (December, 1952 to August 1959) on more than one occasion so he supposes he did make such visits. When informed that it was understood that Karlow had been to Berlin ten to fifteen times in the period 1950-1953, Karlow offered no objection and said it was possible that this was true. With reference to his later assignment in Munich from November 1953 to the end of 1955, Karlow stated he was fairly certain he had not visited Berlin during this period.[37]

The above-mentioned CIA officer named Harry Rositzke was a major player in the CIA's early operations against the Russians in

---

37 RIF No. 124-90092-10016: William Harvey, 3/5/1963.

Berlin just after the end of World War II and into the Cold War era. He ran all paramilitary operations against the Soviets from his base in Munich, and was ready to end all behind-the lines operations in 1955. One veteran of these missions, a CIA officer named Donald Morris, said of this time, "they kept the KGB occupied, confused." Harry Rositzke also worked as the CIA Station Chief in India during the Kennedy administration and ran head on with Ambassador John Kenneth Galbraith as to how the CIA station was to be run.

Peter Karlow's career in the CIA can be viewed in two different phases. First, his long-standing work for the infant CIA in Berlin and other Cold War hot spots such as Vienna, where he plied his trade in the secret war against the Soviet Union, working with such people as William Harvey and Harry Rositzke, and others. The other part of his career was the hardest, the time when he was accused of being a traitor inside the CIA which almost ruined his life and career. If it weren't for the leadership of the CIA in the 1970s, and the mole relief bill that was passed by Congress, who knows what the ultimate outcome of his life would have been.

What we've learned from the files released on Karlow is the fact that Pan American Airways was a conduit for the CIA during the Cold War era, like others would be used in Vietnam and Korea, as well as the fact that he was involved in a dangerous operation to steal a Soviet MIG fighter that never took place.

Chapter 48
The Riddle of AMLASH

Besides the CIA's external efforts to oust Fidel Castro, the Agency used a number of internal assets inside Cuba for its own purposes. One of the most important agents, and one that would prove to be the most controversial in the efforts to remove Castro from power, was one of the Prime Minister's most trusted advisors, Rolando Cubela, a.k.a. AMLASH.

Cubela was just a part of the two-track effort to remove Castro, the CIA-Mafia plots and the Kennedy administration's not-so-secret war called Operation Mongoose. It is safe to assume that by the end of 1962, even Fidel Castro knew of the underworld efforts to kill him, but he probably did not link them to the CIA. But this was not the case with the CIA's association with Rolando Cubela.

The first meeting between the CIA and Rolando Cubela took place in Mexico City on March 9, 1961. He was interviewed in order to find out his views on the Cuban revolution. Cubela did not give the questioner any favor and the meeting ended.

In 1961, Cubela was the second ranking member of the Directorio Revolucionario (DR), a revolutionary group of students who had worked for the overthrow of the Batista regime. It is believed that Cubela was part of the team that killed Lt. Col. Antonio Blanco, the head of Batista's military intelligence unit in 1956. Cubela's DR group, while working for the same goals as that of Fidel Castro's 26th of July Movement, did not see eye to eye with that movement, and the two groups kept each other at a distance. In the final days of the Cuban Revolution, Cubela's group took over the presidential palace, refusing to turn it over to Che Guevara, but finally, and reluctantly, it deferred to Castro. When Castro finally took power, Cubela held the rank of Major in the Cuban armed forces.

The CIA's Inspector General's Report on the early days of Cubela and his relationship to Castro says that prior to his appointment to the post of Cuban Military Attaché to Spain and his subsequent departure for Madrid on 27 March 1959, Ronaldo Cubela frankly expressed to Prime Minister Castro his dissatisfaction over the present situation in Cuba. Cubela privately told intimates that he was so disgusted with Castro that if he, Cubela, did not get out of the country soon, he would "kill Castro himself."

After the Agency heard of Cubela's anti-Castro remark, new covert dispatches were sent to him and further meetings were arranged. Thus, the AMLASH operation was born.

Now that the CIA had established a relationship with Cubela, he informed his new handlers that he wanted to defect to the US. This news was given to the JM/WAVE Station in March 1961. Along with Cubela, another man deeply involved in the CIA-Mafia plots to kill Castro, Juan Orta, also wanted to defect. But the CIA nixed the idea because of possible awareness of Castro's security forces concerning Cubela's and Orta's ties to the United States.

By June of 1962 Cubela had contacted the CIA once again and told them that he would be attending the World Youth Festival in Helsinki, Finland and that he still wanted to defect. At this point, the FBI, through one of its sources, was advised of the Cubela defection plan and they in turn asked the CIA for confirmation. That information was indeed given, and the two top US intelligence agencies were now monitoring Cubela's activities. The IG Report goes on to say that the CIA was in touch with an unidentified asset who would be willing to aid in the defection of Cubela. This unnamed informant and a CIA agent met in New York City on July 13 and 14, 1962 at which time an unofficial relationship was cemented.

From July 30 to August 6, 1962, this unidentified asset arrived in Helsinki to meet with Cubela. After hours of intense discussions, Cubela changed his mind and decided to be an agent in place for the CIA, rather than defect to the US.

In the middle of August, Cubela and his Agency contacts met once again, this time in Copenhagen and Stockholm, but nothing of importance came out of these meetings. However, minutes from one meeting show Cubela's state of mind regarding future action against Castro. This is what the CIA had to say:

> At one time when we were discussing the various aspects of Cubela's further role in Cuba, we used the term "assassinate." The use of this term, we later learned from [deleted] and from Cubela himself, was most objectionable

to the latter, and he was visibly upset. It was not the act he objected to, but rather merely the choice of the word used to describe it. Eliminate was acceptable.

In the middle of August, representatives of the CIA and Cubela met in Paris for an intensive, two-week series of meetings and training sessions. A Spanish speaking case officer came to France and Cubela was given S/W training, and was taken to the south of France where he was given demolition training and taught other clandestine warfare methods. He was also asked to take a polygraph test but he refused. The CIA wrote its final comment after Cubela's Paris training session, "Have no intention give Cubela physical elimination mission as requirement but recognize this something he could try to carry out on his own initiative."

So now it seemed that the one man the CIA wanted to use in a plot to either kill Castro, or to use in some way to bring about the demise of his government, was not trusted by the Agency to carry out his highly sensitive mission. But for lack of any other agent in place, the Agency pinned their hopes on Cubela, despite the many warning signs that trouble might be ahead.

In the early part of September 1963, AMLASH went to Porto Alegre, Brazil to attend the Collegiate Games as a representative of the Cuban government. He was met there by a number of CIA officers and by his friend from revolutionary days, now also working for the CIA, code named AMWHIP. He told his CIA colleagues that he wanted to approach a number of Cuban army officers who were anti-Communist but were pro-Fidel about his secret ties with the US, but was reluctant to do so.

In documents released by the JFK Records Act, this meeting had some importance. According to the documents, AMLASH told AMWHIP he felt there were only two ways of getting rid of Castro. The first was an invasion by US forces that AMLASH knew was out of the question, and the second was an "inside job." AMLASH indicated he was awaiting a US plan of action. He referred to the explosives demonstration that the CIA gave him earlier as "too cumbersome" for his purposes.

Not only did the CIA know of Cubela's relationship with some of the anti-Castro elements on the island, but so did Fidel Castro himself. In a September 19, 1963 cable from the CIA's JM/WAVE station in Miami to headquarters, states that AMLASH was part of an anti-Communist group whose members were well known to the Castro government, and that "Fidel is allegedly aware of the two groups and acts as moderator between them in order to maintain cohesion in the government of Cuba."

In the fall of 1963 Cubela traveled to Europe winding up in Paris in early October. There he met a case officer named "O" who sat down and heard Cubela spill his guts. Cubela said that he was mad that he was given "low level" tasks to perform, saying that he believed that he had a more important role to perform. Case officer "O" assured him that that was not the case and said that his possible role was being given consideration at the "highest levels" within the Agency. With this problem, which had undoubtedly been bothering him considerably, off his chest, a much more relaxed AMLASH departed, restating his desire to return to Cuba to undertake "the big job."

A CIA memo on Cubela confirms his disaffection with Castro.:

> He was politically ambitious but in the post-Batista days was outmaneuvered by Fidel Castro so that, as Fidel's star ascended, Cubela's declined. It would appear probable that Cubela's interest in eliminating Castro stems in part from a personal grudge and in part from political ambition but not from ideological principle. He does not appear to have been a communist at any time but he defended communists and participated in communist sponsored conferences. He participated in anti-US activities.

The IG's report says this about the Orta-Cubela connection:

> This is one of the three name links we found in the AMLASH file between Rolando Cubela and persons involved in the gambling syndicate episodes. The other two links are even more nebulous than this. If Cubela was in fact one of the gangsters' assets inside Cuba, that fact was unknown to either the CIA officers running the gangster episodes or those handling Cubela.

On August 22, 1962, Cubela left Prague, Czechoslovakia for Havana. This was the last time he was met by the CIA until he next left Cuba in September 1963, a long time in which he was out of the CIA's hands. In relation to this time period in which Cubela was back in Cuba, the CIA reported, "It is noted at this point that AMLASH was not a recruited agent at that time—nor was he ever for that matter. By the end of August 1962, the CIA relationship with AMLASH/1 had made no real progress."

There had been longstanding concern among certain CIA officers about Cubela's bona fides during their meetings with him. If Cubela was acting as a double agent for Castro at this early date (and there is no concrete proof one way or another), his one year absence from his CIA controllers must have allowed time for much mischief to take place. Without constant CIA supervision, Cubela, if he was indeed working as a double for Castro, could have given him up-to-the-minute information on his meetings with the CIA in the various locations where they met, and divulged the plans they had discussed. On the other side of the coin, if Castro had somehow penetrated the Cubela-CIA connection, he could have allowed his one-time friend to continue his clandestine relationship with the CIA and watch what happened on the sidelines without revealing to Cubela the CIA's misgivings about him.

Whether or not these misgivings on the part of the CIA were correct, they did have future contact with him. The Senate Select Committee on Assassinations took a close look at the entire AMLASH case and was very precise in its narrative of the situation. Regarding the CIA's renewal of its contact with Cubela the committee wrote,

> If it is narrowly correct to state that the exact purpose for renewing contact was not known to the authors of the SSC Report, it nevertheless is quite clear why he was met. He was an important potential asset whose usefulness remained to explored. At this point, not only was there "no evidence" that an assassination operation was intended, it is quite clear that it was not under consideration. The problem at that time was how to deal with the man.

In their evaluation of Cubela at the end of September 1963, the

CIA had little good to say about their agent in place. If they had anyone else that was as close to Castro as Cubela was, the CIA would no doubt have completely severed their relationship with him. But that was not the case:

> At the conclusion of the meeting with AMLASH, headquarters cabled on 9 September that based on what little feel headquarters had, AMLASH appeared hopeless as an intelligence performer and should be approached as a chief conspirator allowed to recruit his own cohorts. He should be urged to recruit a few trusted friends to assist him, initially in FI and Ops reporting and then progress to sabotage and more serious matters on an orderly basis.

Cubela was now getting nervous about his situation and asked the Agency for a meeting with a high-level US government official. He told the CIA that he was "convinced that if such meeting does not take place at this time it will be almost impossible come out again and we will be in same situation as last year with no definite decision." The high official AMLASH wanted to see was Attorney General Robert Kennedy.

Instead, Cubela met with Desmond Fitzgerald, a senior CIA officer who ran the Special Affairs Staff, which was the CIA branch that ran all Cuban affairs, including the Cubela operation. In 1964, Fitzgerald was named Chief of the Western Hemisphere Division, and in June 1966, he succeeded Richard Helms as deputy director for plans at Langley headquarters.

Fitzgerald met with Cubela in Paris on October 29, 1963, and told him that he was a personal representative of Robert Kennedy. He told Cubela that the US was prepared to give him all necessary assistance and support any anti-Communist group of his choosing in Cuba that could succeed in toppling Castro from power. He remarked that American support would only come after a successful coup.

During their meeting, Cubela told Fitzgerald that he was getting tired of being put off by the CIA because "he did not receive technical assistance from a US government technician. Fitzgerald then authorized Cubela's being told that he would be given a cache which could, if he requested it, include high powered rifles/w. scopes."

418

During this meeting, Fitzgerald, in order to gain Cubela's trust, told him that Robert Kennedy was aware of their meeting and that he personally approved of Cubela's plan (this was not true):

> Nothing of an operational nature was discussed at the Fitzgerald meeting. After the meeting, AMLASH stated that he was satisfied with the policy discussions but now desired to know what technical support we could provide him.

Cubela's reaction to his meeting with Fitzgerald was spelled out by his associate, code named AMWHIP, a few weeks later. AMWHIP said that Cubela was not pleased with the support he was receiving from the US.:

> While AMLASH was satisfied on policy grounds, he was not at all happy with the fact that he still was not given the technical assistance for the operation plan as he saw it. AMLASH could not understand why he was denied certain small pieces of equipment which promised a final solution to the problem, while, on the other hand, the US gave much equipment and money to exile groups for their ineffective excursions against Cuban coastal targets. AMLASH accepted the fact that he had to work with the CIA, but CIA might lose him if it continued to procrastinate. AMLASH talked about going to the French terrorist group, the OAS, but realized that was not feasible.

Desmond Fitzgerald was a busy man during the week of November 13-22, 1963. He met with Cubela a number of times in Paris, going over every detail of their relationship. On November 13, the CIA wrote a note regarding a meeting of that day which said:

> In summary of meeting it was emphasized that the above support will be forthcoming only after a real coup had been effected and the group involved is in a position to request US (probably under OAS auspices) recognition and support. It was made clear that the US was not prepared to commit itself to support an isolated uprising, as such an uprising can be

extinguished in a matter of hours if the present government is still in Havana.

Despite the misgivings on both sides, Fitzgerald's talks with Cubela in Paris were sufficiently positive for him to recommend to his superiors at CIA HQ to trust him. In a CIA memorandum of November 18, 1963, the Agency approved of Cubela's coup attempt. Headquarters also gave the go-ahead to provide him with the rifles and scopes which he previously requested. On November 20, 1963, the CIA sent a message to Cubela asking him to postpone his trip back to Cuba for further talks. Cubela said that he would remain in Paris "If it is something interesting." The purpose of the discussion was to inform him of the "technical support," i.e., guns, scopes, etc. that he had requested were approved. The next meeting would take place in Paris on November 22, 1963.

Cubela met with his CIA case officer in Paris to discuss their next step in the Castro plots. Cubela stated that while he wanted to do away with Castro, he was not willing to lay his life on the line. He told his case officer this astounding news, and the case officer rather reluctantly passed the word back to Langley. During the meeting, the case officer gave Cubela a ballpoint pen that was rigged with a hypodermic needle, and suggested that a substance called Black Leaf 40, which was a poison, be put inside the pen to be used as an assassination weapon. Cubela was told that the needle was so precise that the person who was injected would never feel it. Years later, a CIA officer who was deeply involved in the passing of the poison pen to Cubela remarked that Cubela asked the CIA to "devise some technical means of doing the job that would not automatically cause him to lose his own life in the try."

Cubela then said that he was returning to Cuba and was determined to initiate a coup against Castro, with or without US help. He asked that certain other military equipment be sent to him inside Cuba, including 20 hand grenades, two high-powered rifles with telescopic sights, and about 20 pounds of C-4 explosive and other related equipment. This material would be left on a friend's farm in Cuba:

As they were coming out of the meeting, [blank] and

Cubela were informed that President Kennedy had been assassinated. Cubela was visibly moved over the news. He asked, "Why do such things happen to good people?" We do not know exactly how long this meeting took place, but it is likely that at the very moment President Kennedy was shot, a CIA officer was meeting with a Cuban agent in Paris and giving him an assassination device for use against Castro.

Immediately after the president's assassination, Fitzgerald gave orders that all use of AMLASH was to be temporarily put on hold. With nothing more to do, the case officer who was with Cubela in the November 22, 1963 meeting returned to Washington the next day.

Cubela left Paris on November 27, 1963, and arrived in Cuba on December 1. He must have been quite concerned about just what role he would play in the Castro plots now that JFK was dead and there was a new American president in the White House. He also must have been distrustful of the CIA, and know that they did not trust him completely. But he also knew that in order to keep up his façade as long as possible he had to keep his secret life from reaching the ears of Castro (if he wasn't already working as a double agent for the Cuban government).

The new president, Lyndon Johnson, heard about suspicions that the Cubans might have had a role in Kennedy's death, and decided to put a hold on any more US efforts to topple Castro until a full review of the situation could be worked out.

According to the declassified history of the AMLASH case, the last file on Cubela's activities came in December 1963. It reads in part:

> 22 November, Mr. Fitzgerald assured subject that this agency would give him everything he needed (telescopic rifle, silencer, all the money he wanted). The situation changed when [blank]. Mr. Fitzgerald left the meeting to discover that President Kennedy had been assassinated. Because of this fact, plans with subject changed and it was decided that this agency could have no part in the assassination of a government leader (including Castro) and it would not aid subject in his attempt. This included the following. We would

421

not furnish the silencer, nor scope nor any money for direct assassination; furthermore, we would not lift a finger to help subject escape from Cuba should he assassinate Castro.

So much for sticking up for the good guy!

There have been a good number of documents relating to the AMLASH case released in the past two years, and the rest of this chapter will deal with them as it relates to Cubela and his plots to kill Castro.

The first of these is a contact report dated November 25, 1963. Persons Present: AMLASH/1, Matthew Ontpich (alias Nicholas Sanson): Time and Place: 22 November 1963, Charlie Gray's Apt, Paris, France:

> AMLASH/1 stated that he was returning to Cuba fully determined to pursue his plans to initiate a coup against AMTHUG [Fidel Castro]. Subject was pleased to read a copy of President Kennedy's 18 November speech in Miami and was even more pleased to hear that Mr. Clark (DAINOLD) had helped prepare the President's speech. ONTRICH reiterated the assurances given by DAINOLD of full US support if a real coup against AMTHUG regime is successful. AMLASH continued to insist that as long as AMTHUG is around the number of individuals knowledgeable of a coup against the regime must be kept to an absolute minimum. The individuals in whom AMLASH/1 has the most confidence and whom he believes can be trusted in the initial stages of the operation if it is necessary to cut other individuals are: Cmdte Efigenio Delagdo, AMTRUNK/10, Jose Naranjo Morales, Mayor of Havana, Jose Assef, former sub-Sec, Ministry of Interior and presently Assistant to Naranjo, Municipality of Havana. AMLASH/1 feels that once AMTHUG is removed, the following officers can be counted on to support the coup: Cmdte. Raul Diaz-Arguelles Garcia, Nieves brothers, Capt. Fausto Lopez Miranda, Capt. Juan Nuiry Sanchez who is a close friend and can influence stand of Capt. Felipe Guerra Matos.
>
> Since he was returning via Prague, AMLASH/1 did not

desire to carry any incriminating materials with him. In order to provide him time to establish his normal pattern once he returned to Havana, it was agreed his S/W material would not be sent to him until sometime between 5-15 January 1964. AMLASH/1 suggested and C/O agreed he should not engage in any activity which may draw suspicion to him for at least a month. During December he planned attending the various anniversary functions coming due during this month and again speaking in Santa Clara as he had done each year in the past on the anniversary date of the battle of Santa Clara. He also felt this would give him an opportunity to check the pulse of his friends in that city.

The files then go into the question of whether Cubela was working for Castro all along:

The record: The file shows that since April 1959 and repeatedly since then, AMLASH/1 has threatened to eliminate AMTHUG-1, but has not done so. He also was reportedly on the verge several times of defecting but never did. There are numerous reports of varying credibility that he has been and is a Castro agent. His character is such that he has been described in a report as a "probable thief," a possible user of narcotics, a homosexual or a friend of homosexuals but also an exceedingly brave man. Various reports indicate that he is a heavy drinker and a party lover. Thus a person with such traits could reasonably be believed to be involved in irregular financial transactions.

Conclusions: While it cannot be discounted that AMLASH/1 may be a Castro agent, it may be that he has been sincere in his dealings with KUBARK [CIA]. Resolution of doubts through LCFLUTTER interview has been impossible since AMLASH/1 hit the ceiling when the matter was first mentioned.

Presumably, KUBARK's interest in AMLASH/1 is to see him carry out his mission to eliminate AMTHUG/1. The above proposal may actually stimulate the desired action. If AMLASH/1 is questioned by the regime in connection with this charge, and should the investigation involve a certain amount of harassment and unpleasantness, he might well reach the conclusion that the time to take matters into his own hands (which he has threatened to do for several years) has at last arrived.

If AMLASH/1 is a Castro agent and Castro should be aware of AMLASH/1's relationship with KUBARK, Castro might conclude that AMLASH/1 received the money from KUBARK, banked it without reporting it, and was in fact working with KUBARK against Castro. (At the recent meetings in Paris, AMLASH/1 asked us for $10,000. We did not give him this sum, though AMWHIP/1 gave him $7,000).

If for any reason the regime should do away with AMLASH/1, his alleged sympathizers in the Armed Forces might feel they must react at once to save their own skins. Given the tense political situation in Cuba today, this is not out of the question and certainly this proposal could split the regime more.

The documents then mention someone named Jose Rebellon:

[He] is a non-controversial good target for inclusion in this AMSNEAK play for the following reasons: He is close to Castro, as well as to AMLASH/1, and has a Communist background. He is familiar with the $80,000 account opened in a Swiss bank by Ambassador Carrillo in the fall of 1964. Rebellon has been authorized by Castro to draw on that fund for purchases related to Castro's pet projects. Castro might think Rebellon had raided Castro's own official fund. As with AMLASH/1, any action by the regime against Rebellon might widen splits in Cuba and bring about further political uneasiness and tensions in interpersonal relationships that we desire.[38]

With Cubela now back in Cuba, things began to unravel fast for him. Upon arriving home, he had an unexpected meeting with Fidel Castro. During their conversation, Castro never let on that he

38 RIF No. 104-10215-10227: AMLASH/1, Matthew Ontpich, (alias Nicholas Sanson).

knew of Cubela's secret affairs and chided him for not paying close enough attention to the Cuban revolution. "Fidel also told Cubela that because of Cubela's unstable character, his fondness for an easy life, and his lack of concern for the problems of the people, Cubela alone was responsible for his increasing isolation outside the revolutionary process. But, Fidel told him, if he really would correct this and was ready to devote himself seriously to any activity in the many fields in which the revolution pursues its work, we would all be ready to help him."

Cubela told Castro that he was not out to do harm to the revolution and had no connection with any dissident elements. Castro did not believe his old friend and ordered the state security apparatus to double their surveillance of Cubela.

Between February 26, 28, 1965, Rolando Cubela, Alberto Blanco, Ramon Guin Diaz, and a few other conspirators were arrested by Cuban security forces. Cuban police found the telescopic sight that was given to him by the US in his apartment, along with the FAL rifle and the other military equipment that he brought back from Spain. For the CIA, the AMLASH plot, which had been flawed from the start, had come crashing down.

On March 7, 1966, a sweltering day in Havana, Rolando Cubela, a.k.a. AMLASH, the CIA's reluctant spy, was put on trial for plotting to kill Fidel Castro, along with another top-level Cuban exile named Manuel Artime. The trial was covered by the Cuban press as well as the news outlets in the United States. The CIA in particular kept an active watch on the goings-on in the Cuban courtroom and watched Cuban justice (such as it was) with deep suspicion.

Like all aspects of the Cubela case, his circumstances while in jail were open to debate. Cubela told the court about his so-called personal "weakness," his playboy attitude in plotting the Castro assassination with Manuel Artime. The CIA learned from its sources that Cubela did not reveal the names of the real military leaders with whom he was in contact during his schemes to overthrow the Castro regime. According to the CIA, when Cubela learned of the charges brought against him he used as his defense his own personal failings, such as his mental disability (if there was one), his fancy for gay parties, and the "dolce vita," or good life, in Havana. He alluded that it was these traits that led him to plot Castro's assassination, a false premise but one he decided to use in order to save him from execution.

Cuban justice was swift and the rule of law was nowhere to be found. He was found guilty of the charges brought against him and sentenced to a prison term of 25 years. Cubela's father was the only relative allowed to be in court and watch his son on trial. His mother, Virginia Secades Zelanda, was not allowed to witness the proceedings and was taken from the court in order to spare her any more anguish.

For whatever reason, "the statements which the prosecutor made against Cubela at the trial were not as harsh as those which the defense attorney allegedly made in his favor. Cubela's defense was twisted and slanted towards the charges that had been pressed against him and the motivation of his guilt."

Cubela plead guilty to the charges brought against him and signed a statement saying he was sorry for his deeds. A source that reported on the trial to the CIA said that Cubela's guilty statement "was the only way in which he could avoid receiving the death penalty."

This source told the Agency a very interesting bit of information that might have played a role in Cubela's proceedings in court. He revealed that two or three days before the trial began, Cubela met with Raul Castro, Fidel's brother, at which point it was decided what Cubela should say at the trial in order to avoid the death penalty. "Cubela was to accept his guilt, but insinuating that "deviationism," not treason, had motivated his actions."

If Cubela did have this conversation with Raul Castro, it leads to

Rolando Cubela with Fidel Castro, circa 1963.

some very interesting possibilities regarding his actual relationship with the Castro brothers. Was his agreement to plead guilty a foregone conclusion, mutually agreed upon by Cubela and Fidel and Raul, well in advance of the trial? Was Cubela's promise to plead guilty part of a pact between him and the Castro brothers, and they were all just going through the motions of a sham trial?

The documents in the Cubela trial reveal much useful information about what was going on during that hectic time:

> During the reported conversation of the trial, there is no indication whatsoever that Cubela revealed anything more than his "weakness, playboy attitude, etc.," in plotting with a man like Artime to assassinate Castro. Under private interrogation to date there is no known possibility that Cubela has revealed the names of the real military leaders with whom he really was in contact with and with whom he discussed the overthrow of Castro, because none of these major individuals, whose names are known to us, have been arrested or detained.
>
> Cubela has been reported by several sources to have been drugged. The clear, precise, careful, educated statements he made throughout the trial do not bear this out comment to any degree. A handwriting analysis done by Mrs. Hall of TSD in April 1965 bears out many of the underlying subtleties he showed in the trial. To quote a few, "He is a cool and calculating observer who relates the smallest details to their larger aspects. He possesses great facility in expressing himself in word and script. He has some skill in adjusting his style to that of the people he is talking to. While he can be rather eloquent, he is not likely to divulge anything which should be kept secret. He has his feelings and impulses under the strictest control. He is a role player who may appear more natural and spontaneous than he actually is. He can exercise various deceptive mechanism in the most adroit fashion, and while demonstrating a smooth behavior."[39]

In one of the many documents on the AMLASH case there is a notation regarding the possible knowledge of the Castro regime of

39 Memorandum for the Record: The Cubela Trial, 14 April 1966.

Cubela and his plots that the writer is now turning his attention to. The important paragraph reads as follows:

> Later documents on AMLASH are also relevant to the September-November 1963 AMLASH operation. Several such documents report information received to the effect that Fidel Castro had long been aware of AMLASH's plots against him. For example, AMLASH's one time Cuban mistress was believed to be working for Cuban intelligence and her brother was known to be working for Cuban intelligence. [blank] to DIR in December 1964 warns that AMLASH's objective may be known to too many Cubans. And, one CIA informant reported in 1966 on one known double agent of Cuban intelligence working for CIA and said the CIA's Cuban operations had been penetrated at a high level by Cuban intelligence. He identified this latter person only as one of the Cuban exiles who was knowledgeable of a number of the most important operations. Nevertheless, AMLASH's file contains nothing to indicate any detailed analysis of these possible penetrations of the CIA's AMLASH operation, although a cryptic handwritten note on at least one report rejects the suggestion that AMLASH was himself reporting to Castro.[40]

Rolando Cubela was a very lucky man, even as he languished in a Cuban jail. It was decided by Fidel Castro that Cubela, despite the seriousness of the charges brought against him, was to be given a reprieve. Although the exact circumstances are not known, it was decided to commute his jail term and eventually make him a free man. Was Cubela's acknowledgement of his past misdeeds a quid pro quo for his release from jail? Was this the plan all along? In time, Cubela was finally released from prison and resumed his work as a cardiologist in Havana.

The entire AMLASH operation would in later years, bring more controversy among those who participated in it. For example, CIA Director Richard Helms told the Rockefeller Commission that he did not believe the AMLASH operation was relevant to the investigation

40 RIF No. 157-10005-10421: Connection Between Amlash Operation and JFK Assassination, .

of the assassination of JFK. He also testified that he believed that the AMLASH project was not intended to be an assassination plot against Castro. All this flies in the face of the CIA's actions in giving Cubela a poison pen on November 22, 1963 for use against Castro, and for the years of encouragement in aiding him in the Agency's plans to kill Castro.

A contrasting view of the AMLASH project comes from Joseph Langosch (an alias), who, in 1963, was the Chief of Counterintelligence for the CIA's Special Affairs Staff (headed by Desmond Fitzgerald) that ran all Cuban matters. Langosch's job was to safeguard the SAS against penetration by foreign intelligence services (KGB, DRE), particularly the Cuban intelligence service. According to Langosch's testimony:

> The AMLASH operation prior to the assassination of President Kennedy was characterized by the SAS, Desmond Fitzgerald and other senior CIA officers as an assassination operation initiated and supported by the CIA.
>
> Langosch further recollected that as of 1962 it was highly possible that the Cuban Intelligence Services were aware of AMLASH and his association with the CIA and that the information upon which he based his conclusion that the AMLASH operation was insecure was available to senior level CIA officials, including Desmond Fitzgerald.

But, muddying the waters just a little, comes the testimony of another top Agency officer who contradicts Langosch's findings.

The Senate Intelligence Committee received an affidavit from a man named Ken Pollack (a pseudonym) who served as Executive Officer for Desmond Fitzgerald during the time he was SAS chief. Pollack knew about the AMLASH operation and said it was not characterized as an assassination operation:

> To the best of my knowledge, Mr. Fitzgerald considered the AMLASH operation to be a political action activity with the objective of organizing a group within Cuba to overthrow Castro and the Castro regime by means of a coup d'état. I heard Mr. Fitzgerald discuss the AMLASH

operation frequently, and never heard him characterize it as an "assassination operation." Mr. Fitzgerald stated within my hearing on several occasions his awareness that a coup d'etat often involves loss of life.

He further stated, "Desmond Fitzgerald did not characterize the AMLASH operation as an assassination operation, the case officer did not. I, as Executive Officer, never discussed any aspect of the AMLASH operation with Joseph Langosch."

While the accounts of Fitzgerald, Langosch and Pollock, may differ, when the Church Committee studied the ramifications of the AMLASH project, they came to one important conclusion:

Based upon the presently available evidence it is the Committee's position that such information, if made available to the Warren Commission, might have stimulated the Commission's investigative concern for possible Cuban involvement or complicity in the assassination.

As J. Lee Rankin commented regarding the Committee:

When I read the Church Committee's report—it was an ideal situation for them to just pick out any way they wanted to tell the story and fit it in with the facts that had to be met and then either blame the rest of it on somebody else or not tell any more and polish it off. I don't think that could have happened in 1964. I think there would have been a much better chance of getting to the heart of it. It might have only revealed that we are involved in it and who approved it and all that. But I think that would have at least come out.

The Cubela story is still one of the most discussed enigmas in the Kennedy assassination story, one that will probably not be resolved until all the documents that are still locked up in the National Archives are finally revealed.

Chapter 49
Yuri Nosenko: The Second Defector

Three months after the assassination of President Kennedy, the CIA was rocked with the beginning of one of its most formidable cases in its history, one whose ramifications are still being hotly debated by historians and by the CIA itself. On January 20, 1964, a KGB officer named Yuri Nosenko decided to defect to the US. At the time of his "defection," Nosenko was one of the highest-ranking Russian intelligence officers to come westward. Nosenko worked for the second directorate of the KGB's Seventh Department-the section that oversaw all visiting American tourists to the Soviet Union. At the time that Nosenko was monitoring the few Americans to set foot on Russian soil, his branch was keeping tabs on a recent American defector, a former Marine named Lee Harvey Oswald.

The Oswald case would come to haunt the CIA when Nosenko arrived in the United States for good in January of 1964. The Warren Commission which was investigating the Kennedy assassination knew of Nosenko and his revelations concerning Oswald but they did not pursue the matter. His other bombshell was the fact that the CIA was infested with "moles" which were feeding the KGB all sorts of top-secret information coming from Langley headquarters. For the members of James Angleton's Counterintelligence Staff, Nosenko was the devil incarnate, a man who came to destroy the CIA. Furthermore, he was the man Anatoly Golitsyn said would follow him in a massive disinformation program.

Nosenko first made contact with the CIA in 1962 while he was in Geneva, Switzerland in his capacity as chief of security for the Soviet delegation to the disarmament talks. In a bit of bad luck, Nosenko lost all of the money he was given by the KGB on his first foray to the West. He had to get the money back before his KGB pals could discover his indiscretions. In a hasty decision, he decided to approach the Agency and offer to sell information to the US for 900 Swiss Francs.

The CIA was very much interested in what Nosenko had to offer and he was soon debriefed by two top notch officials, Pete Bagley, a

CIA case officer who was stationed in Bern, and George Kisvalter, who arrived from Washington to act as an interpreter.

Nosenko arrived at the CIA safe house a bit tipsy from all the liquor he had been consuming. Still, he had quite a tale to tell. He said that the walls of the American embassy in Moscow were bugged by the KGB. After intensive interrogations, Bagley sent a cable to Washington saying, "Subject has conclusively proved his bona fides. He has provided info of importance and sensitivity. Willing to meet when abroad and will meet as often and as long as possible (until) his departure from Geneva on 15 June." Nosenko told Bagley and Kisvalter that they should not try to contact him once he returned to the Soviet Union—it would be too dangerous. Instead, the CIA men gave Nosenko a secure telephone number, as well as the code name AE/FOXTROT.

Recent documents from the CIA regarding the bona fides of Nosenko make interesting reading, to say the least:

Subject: The Bona Fides of Yuri Nosenko: KGB officer Yuri Nosenko first contacted CIA in Geneva in June 1962. Over the course of five meetings he provided sufficient information to enable the two officers from the CIA's Soviet-Russia Division who met him to establish that he was a bona fide source. The major information furnished by him at that time was the identification of a US code technician who had been recruited by the KGB, and the identification of the location of KGB microphones in the US Embassy in Moscow, 52 of which were later found.

When CIA's Counterintelligence Staff was informed of Nosenko's 1962 approach, its management regarded this news within the context of what they had been hearing from a KGB defector whom they had been debriefing, Anatoly Golitsyn. Golitsyn, who had defected in December 1961, was a counterintelligence officer who was obsessed with the subject of KGB deception operations. Even though Golitsyn was diagnosed in early 1962 as a "paranoid personality," the CI Staff had complete faith in the validity of his theories and analyses. A sanitized version of Nosenko's information was therefore show to Golitsyn, who flatly concluded that

Nosenko was acting under KGB control. The CI Staff accepted Golitsyn's analysis and persuaded the management of SR Division also to accept it.

By the time Nosenko was again heard from, in January 1964, again in Geneva, the management of SR Division and CI Staff was firmly committed to the position that Nosenko was part of a KGB deception operation. Nosenko actually defected on 4 February 1964.

In October 1964, the DCI turned Nosenko's case over to the Office of Security for final resolution, and at the same time the FBI began a review of the information it had obtained from Nosenko. The results of these two very thorough investigations were set forth in a memorandum from the Office of Security dated 1 October 1964 and one from the FBI dated 20 September 1964, both of which concluded that Nosenko was what he claimed to be and was a bona fide defector. Since that time this has been and is the position of the CIA.

Nosenko was probably the most valuable source of counterintelligence information that the US government has ever had, and the enormous scope and value of his information attest conclusively to his bona fides as a defector. He identified some 2,000 KGB officers and 300 Soviets who were acting as KGB agents. He provided information on some 238 Americans in whom the KGB had displayed some interest, including many who had been recruited. For example, one of his identifications led to the trial and a sentence of 25 years for US Army Sgt. Robert Lee Johnson. Nosenko also provided information on some 200 foreign nationals in 36 countries in whom the KGB had taken an active interest, and the friendly foreign governments with which he shared this information were able to neutralize a number of important KGB agents as a result. For example, the British were able on the basis of Nosenko's information to identify William John Vassall, a high Admiralty official, as a KGB agent and sentence him to 18 years.[41]

Early on, CIA officials decided to recruit Nosenko and determined

41 RIF No. 104-10534-10165: The Bona Fides of Yuri Nosenko, 1/1/1964.

to let him alone for further intelligence purposes. Nosenko said that he did not wish to defect at that moment because of family considerations. The Agency used Nosenko in that capacity until January 1964 when the situation changed dramatically. Nosenko passed along a message via his secure telephone number to his contacts in Washington saying that he had received a note from his Soviet controller saying that he was being ordered back to Moscow for "consultations." Nosenko, now fearful for his life, demanded to be granted political asylum in the United States. After much debate, the CIA made arrangements for him to be sent to the US. For better or worse, Yuri Nosenko and his "secrets" had arrived.

As Nosenko began to be quizzed by the CIA, his story was met with deep suspicion by the one man in the Agency whose opinion mattered the most, James Angleton. From the beginning of the Nosenko saga, Angleton was deeply suspicious of the newest Russian defector. He was certain beyond a reasonable doubt that Nosenko was on a disinformation mission, as spelled out by Golitsyn. As time went on, the powerful counterintelligence chief became more and more paranoid, seeing conspiracies beyond every corner, and distrusting people he had worked with for years.

Angleton's paranoia concerning Nosenko was rooted in cold hard fact, dating back to the early days after the end of World War II. At that time, Angleton was friendly with Kim Philby, the head of British Intelligence in the United States. The men became champions of each other's causes, sharing all the latest information on the new Soviet threat. Philby worked in Washington, and was the new rising star in British intelligence. What Angleton and the rest of the intelligence establishment did not know was that Philby was a member of the Cambridge Five, a deep cover Soviet mole who had been working for the Russians since World War II. When Philby was finally unmasked in 1963 and defected to the Soviet Union, Angleton was devastated. The man to whom he gave his ultimate trust turned out to be a Russian spy. To Angleton, that was the maximum betrayal. Was Nosenko another Philby?

In time, Pete Bagley, who had interviewed Nosenko in Switzerland and believed that Nosenko was a bona fide defector, reversed his judgement due to the evidence before him. But Angleton's reach did not go far in the agency. Many agents in the Soviet Russia Division did not share Angleton's thesis that Nosenko was a fake defector and huge turf battles concerning Nosenko's bona fides took shape.

As the Nosenko interrogations began in earnest, he dropped a bombshell that only made Angleton even more distrustful of him. He said that while he was in Moscow monitoring American tourists who came to the Soviet Union, he had seen the KGB file on Lee Harvey Oswald, the alleged assassin of JFK. Under further questioning Nosenko said that there was no connection between the Russians and the assassination of President Kennedy. Nosenko said that the Russians had no interest whatsoever in a loner like Oswald, and the only reason they allowed him to stay in the country was his attempt at suicide.

But that was not good enough for Angleton. Despite the fact that the Warren Commission decided that there was no conspiracy, foreign or domestic, in the Kennedy assassination, Angleton was convinced that Oswald was a "dispatched agent," sent to the United States to absolve the Soviet Union of any plot to kill Kennedy. Furthermore, Angleton believed that Oswald was groomed as an assassin by the KGB during his three year stint in the Soviet Union, that he was sent to the United States to kill Kennedy, and that the Nosenko mission was to excise any possible connection to the Soviets in the president's death. The culprit in the whole sordid mess was none other than Yuri Nosenko.

Nosenko's revelations regarding Oswald and other matters fit

KGB agent Yuri Nosenko.

right in with the mindset of FBI Director J. Edgar Hoover who said from the beginning that Oswald was the lone assassin of the president. But if Hoover's FBI was taken in by Nosenko's shocking surprise, others in the CIA were not. From April 1964 to September 1967, Nosenko was put in solitary quarters in a CIA safe house and underwent "hostile interrogation" in order to find out the truth behind his defection.

Many critics of the way the Agency handled the Nosenko interrogations fault the CIA for locking up their prisoner in a small cell, only providing him with the minimal daily necessities, and treating him as less than a person. But what were they to do? Nosenko's arrival in the US was known to only a certain number of people in the intelligence community. Could they just let him walk out in public, attend ball games and concerts, become part of the body politick?

During the years that he was under intensive interrogation, the Soviet Russia Division was tasked with the job of studying all aspects of the Nosenko case. In the end, they wrote a 900-page report that was pared down to 447 pages. Some of their conclusions were the following: Nosenko did not serve in the Naval Reserve at the time he said he did; he did not join the KGB at the time he said he was recruited; he did not serve in the American embassy section as claimed; and he lied about his military rank. Many of his interrogators believed that Nosenko was making up a "legend" for himself, in effect, making up a false identity package for some unknown reason. While they did not come right out and say that Nosenko was a liar, his overall story was taken with a large grain of salt. But the report failed to quell the dilemma that surrounded the Nosenko affair, and Richard Helms ordered another critique of how the agency handled Nosenko's defection which came to yet another conclusion.

Writing this new report was CIA officer Bruce Solie who worked in the CIA's Office of Security. Solie's account was a 360-degree turnaround from the original text. The Solie report was critical of the way the Agency interrogated Nosenko, and said they should have paid more attention to Nosenko's revelations about KGB operations against the United States. In the final analysis, said the Solie report, Nosenko had not been fully debriefed, and until all possible leads were followed up on, the case was not closed. In the end though, the

Solie narrative said, "Nosenko is identical to the person he claims to be." He also stated emphatically that Nosenko was not a "dispatched agent" who had been sent to give counterfeit information concerning Lee Oswald.

In November 1967, the CIA moved Nosenko from his one-man cell and sent him blindfolded and handcuffed to a new safe house in the Washington, DC area. Conditions soon became better for him and the CIA hoped to put the year's long affair behind them.

Late in 1968, the CIA termed Nosenko the genuine article and gave him a "consulting" job with the Agency, with a starting salary of $16,500 per year. The Agency relocated Nosenko to a new home, made him a person in good standing in the community, and said a fond goodbye to their most controversial "defector." But the Nosenko story did not fade away. In the late 1970s, the House Committee on Assassinations was formed by the US Congress to look into the assassinations of President Kennedy and Martin Luther King. One aspect of the HSCA's probe concerned the defection of Yuri Nosenko. When Nosenko came to the US in 1964, his presence, and the information he imparted to the CIA concerning Oswald, was withheld from the Warren Commission.

The HSCA concluded that Nosenko had lied to the CIA about his relationship with Oswald, and that the KGB did indeed take a considerable interest in the activities of Oswald during his stay in the Soviet Union.

But there are still many lingering questions concerning Yuri Nosenko, more than fifty years after the fact. Is there a possibility that he was an agent-in-place long before his defection in 1964? And if that is the case, did he know of Oswald's own "defection" to the Soviet Union in 1959? Did he hoodwink James Angleton and the rest of the Agency into believing his wild accusations concerning Soviet moles inside the CIA?

The documents released about Nosenko are very revealing and fill in a lot of the blanks and the behind-the-scenes goings on regarding his arrival in the United States.

The documents tell the story of just how paranoid and interested the Soviet Union was when they discovered that Nosenko had defected:

On 11 February, the Soviet government delivered a note to the American Embassy in Moscow asking how subject (Nosenko) left Switzerland and requesting an immediate interview with him and his release. On 12 February, Soviet Ambassador to the Disarmament Conference Tsarapkin held a press conference in Geneva in which he accused the Swiss Government of failure to cooperate in locating subject. Although the Swiss categorically rejected these charges, the American Ambassador to Switzerland recommended that Swiss authorities be allowed to interview him to convince themselves that Subject had left Switzerland of his own free will.

On 12 February, on the instructions of the Director, Subject was brought to the United States. He travelled by commercial air, again using alias US Army identification (in true name) on parole under the provisions of Section 212 of the Immigration and Nationality Act.

On 14 February, in Moscow, Soviet Foreign Minister Gromyko called in Ambassador Kohler and protested "impermissible activities" on the part of the US in Subject's case. Soviet press spokesmen took an even harder line to Western correspondents, and accused the US of kidnapping Subject.

When Nosenko arrived in the US he was always accompanied by personnel from the CIA and was even taken to Hawaii on a brief vacation. The documents go on to say:

Evidence continued to mount that Subject was a KGB plant, and at the same time it became obvious that it would be impossible to proceed further to resolve the many suspicious points and contradictions that have arisen without changing the conditions in which Subject was being held. Subject was growing increasingly uncooperative, especially when sensitive areas were touched upon, and constantly pressed for the legalization of his status in the US and the issuance of an alien registration card. At the same time, Subject's heavy drinking and other unruly personal habits were causing increasing difficulties to the security personnel, charged with keeping him under control and out of trouble at all times, and it was clear that it was only a matter of time before he created a public scandal. More important, he was in a position to communicate with the KGB since physical control could not be absolute.

On 4 April 1964, Subject voluntarily underwent a polygraph examination. The results of this examination indicated deception on a number of critical points indicating that he was sent out by the KGB to perform one or more missions which also involved penetration of the Agency and its operations. It was decided, therefore, that the physical circumstances of Subject's stay in this country would have to be drastically changed if the Agency were to carry out its counterintelligence responsibilities and adhere to the terms of the parole agreement. As a result, Subject was moved to quarters where his movements could be more easily controlled, and his outing privileges were suspended, pending resolution of bona fides. He has remained in this status to the present time.

It is worth noting that had we not taken the above action but accepted Subject at face value, it is quite possible that we would have proceeded with a series of operational actions on the basis of Subject's information. The results of some of these actions could have been very embarrassing to the US Government politically and damaging to US national security. For example, Subject's chief operational proposal at that time, one that he was most insistent we should proceed with immediately, involved the sexual compromise of Vladimir Suslov, the most senior Soviet official in the United Nations Secretariat, holding the position of Undersecretary in Charge of Political and Security Council Affairs.

Since April 1964, hundreds of hours have been devoted to interrogations of Subject and a great deal of time has been spent on exhaustive collateral investigations. We conclude that it has been established beyond reasonable doubt that Subject is a KGB agent who established contact with CIA and subsequently defected on KGB instructions, and that he came to the United States on a deception mission. The implications of this mission have a grave and direct bearing on US national security. Although our findings are supported by the results of two polygraph examinations, we must note that the nature of the evidence is inadmissible in a court of law. In any case, it is clear that Subject has not been in a position to perform any overt act of transgression of US espionage laws since 4 April when he was placed in restricted area and deprived of any conceivable means of communication with the KGB.

Subject does not admit that he defected on KGB orders or that he came to the US on a KGB mission. He had admitted, however, that he made numerous lies about his personal history and about the details of his KGB service to US officials, both before and after arriving in the United States.

Among the most important national security officials who were made aware of Nosenko's defection were the following: the Secretary of State, the Attorney General, the Special Assistant to the President on National Security Affairs, McGeoge Bundy, General Carroll, the Director of the Defense Intelligence Agency, and the FBI.

The president was told of the full extent of our suspicions about Subject's bona fides by the then Director, Mr. McCone, on 11 February 1964. The Secretary of State, Ambassador Thompson, and other senior officials in the Department of State were informed of our reservations about Subject's bona fides and our fear that he might be a dispatched KGB agent. In discussions about the possibility of Subject's eventual deportation, the Secretary of State expressed serious concern about the adverse reaction that such a move might have on other potential defectors.

Despite the Agency's total control of Nosenko, press reports soon made the rounds that a high-level Russian had defected. In order to quell more press inquiries, the Agency put out the following statement:

Yuri Nosenko requested asylum in the United States in February 1964. His request was granted. The information Mr. Nosenko is providing is regularly made available to appropriate agencies of the government. However, publicizing this information and its source could only increase the possibility of Soviet reprisal against Mr. Nosenko and others who may seek asylum in the Free World.

Nowhere in the statement was any allusion to the fact that he was being held solitary confinement, was living under harsh conditions and that no one believed his story.

One of the concerns relating to Nosenko was the possibility that he might want to return to the Soviet Union. If that happened, it would be a political disaster for the United States and there were serious discussions about that very possibility. The document relating to this possibility says:

With the passage of time, however, and in view of our much firmer conclusions about Subject's real role and mission and our clearer understanding of what this implies, it is apparent that great practical problems stand in the way of his deportation to either the USSR or a third country.

Subject had categorically stated on numerous occasions that he will never contemplate return to the USSR, and although we suspect that he might secretly welcome such a move, we would expect him to act out his part to the end with loud protests that he was being shipped to his death, etc. When the possibility of expulsion was discussed with Department of State officials in 1964, both the Secretary of State and Ambassador Thompson expressed their concern for the adverse effect this might have on other potential defectors. Forcible repatriation of political refugees is against long established US policy, and would be certain to arouse violent reaction from ethnic groups in the United States and the congressmen representing them. Under these circumstances, any alleged confession by Subject would come under very close scrutiny, and might backfire very badly. Finally, if Subject were accepted by the Soviet's on the basis of forced repatriation, the Soviets might carry through the charade, try Subject as a traitor, and give wide publicity to statements by him about his "maltreatment" by CIA, etc.

The Agency then discussed whether it was feasible to transfer Nosenko to a third country. This was debated but finally put to rest as being impracticable in the long run. "By the same token, it appears very unlikely that any country would agree to accept this dangerous and troublesome Soviet agent if they knew what they were getting into. Finally, even if we were somehow able to induce another country to take Subject off our hands, it is obvious that at best we would have succeeded in exchanging a short term, latent problem for actual and persistent ones."

As the Agency debriefed Nosekno, they came to the conclusion that over time, they would be able to make him confers to his misdeeds:

> Once the Subject confessed, we estimate that we would require approximately a year in which to debrief him, because it would be primarily from minute examination of the details of how and when he was trained and briefed by the KGB that we would expect to obtain a better reading of the true nature of and extent of KGB penetration of US intelligence agencies and activities.
>
> Upon conclusion of this debriefing period-and depending on our estimate of the sincerity and completeness of Subject's confession—we would then be prepared to provide Subject with a new identity and an opportunity to settle in the US or elsewhere. Specifically, we would not contemplate proceeding with any specific plan to dispose of Subject without coordinating this with the Department of State, the Department of Justice, and the FBI.[42]

There was a mountain of paperwork on the Nosenko case generated by the CIA, but one piece that was especially interesting. It was started in October 1978 by Leonard McCoy, Deputy Chief, CI Staff, Subject: Chronology of Effort to Inspire Objective Review of

42 RIF. No. 104-10312-10192: Memo from David Murphy to General Counsel, Subject, Yuri Nosenko.

the Nosenko Case. It traces the development of Nosenko's defection and his later interrogation by the CIA.

The McCoy paper says:

As the Nosenko defection became public and known in the intelligence community, there was pressure for information from Nosenko and access to him, particularly from DIA [Defense Intelligence Agency]. DDP Helms visited DIA Director Carroll to inform him that Nosenko's bona fides were in question and that therefore no further information from him would be published and he would not be made available to DIA for debriefing. In accordance with regulations concerning CIA priority in intelligence officer defector cases, the Inter-Agency Defector Committee was excluded from the Nosenko case.

The McCoy documents tells how he was updated on the Nosenko affair and what steps he took to find out the truth of what had transpired with the defection. He wrote:

Up to this point I was generally aware that Nosenko was judged by the Division to be a deception agent and that he was under interrogation to resolve his bona fides. Upon reading the first few memorandum and noting various contradictions, inconsistencies, and inaccuracies I resolved to note these down and comment on them. As the volume of these problems grew it became apparent that it would not be possible to simply state these orally to C/SR/CI but that they raised a fundamental question that affected the entire issue of Nosenko's bona fides. With this realization I decided to put as much information as possible together in the very short time available so that an alternative on Nosenko's bona fides could be considered.

It seems that there was a lot of arguing among the C/SR staff concerning the report McCoy was writing and he said that at one point C/SR became "highly emotional, shouting and pounding on his desk. He said that he knew I felt very strongly about the

Nosenko matter and that he would call DCCI Helms immediately and we would go together to settle the issue in his presence." The disagreements between McCoy and the top people at C/SR grew and the knives were out on all fronts with regard to Nosenko and the information he imparted.

By the spring of 1966, writes McCoy, a psychiatrist named Dr. Bohrer and a psychologist named Gittinger told him that upon examining Nosenko they had independently arrived at the professional judgement that Nosenko was sociopathic, and therefore could not be reliably evaluated on the basis of substantive information analysis. He wrote, "It seemed to me that these conclusions would now bring the case to a close, placing the bona fides evaluation in permanent suspended animation, leaving us with the job of sorting Nosenko's information for CI and PI use according to the degree to which it was substantiated by collateral reporting."

In April 1966, McCoy met with DDCI Helms regarding his analysis of the Nosenko case. Helms responded that he read the paper and that he was "concerned about the Nosenko case." Helms then gave the report to John Gittinger and asked him to read it. A while later, Helms called Jim Angleton and told him that he was sending Gittinger down to Angleton to be briefed on all sensitive matters which were essential to understanding the Nosenko case. Gittinger went to Angleton's office for the briefing, but Angleton told him nothing, saying that Gittinger knew everything that was pertinent to the case.

Things moved around slowly in the Nosenko case and in December 1966, McCoy prepared another memo regarding the Nosenko probe and had it delivered to Helms. Helms told McCoy to continue his work and stay on the job.

In the March/April 1967 timeframe, McCoy sent a copy of his work to DDCI Taylor who was then told by Helms to hand over the case to the Security Director Osborn for an independent review. McCoy writes that Taylor "only asked how C/SR could have fooled so many people about Nosenko. I replied that C/SR was the supreme confidence man."

In June 1967, things began to come to a head for McCoy regarding his participation in the Nosenko case. He writes that he found out that he was being promoted, then not, and asked to meet with ADDP

Karamessines. "Karamessines said that he and the DDP were fully aware of C/SR's position on the Nosenko case and fully agreed with it. He then directed me to leave CI to those who were responsible for it and to concentrate on doing my own job. In addition, he said that my promotion would go through, and that I should inform C/SR of this decision."

McCoy says in his memo by saying:

> Because of my concern that there might be unfortunate consequences as a result of management learning that I had circumvented the chain-of-command, I prepared and personally typed a chronology of events and took it to Taylor so that he would be informed enough to assure that his Nosenko review did not become complicated by an element of personal or organizational revenge.

McCoy ends his memo by saying that in late 1967, "It became apparent that the Nosenko review was under way and the Division case was coming apart.[43]

The records turn to the claim made by Nosenko to the House Select Committee on Assassinations that he was drugged by the CIA during his hostile interrogation. On July 12 and 13, 1978, members of the Office of Security who served on the teams that were involved in the detention and safeguarding of Yuri Nosenko were interviewed regarding their knowledge of any possible use of drugs by Agency personnel during the entire period of incarceration of Nosenko. We now have a list of the people who were with Nosenko at two locations, one in Clinton, Maryland, and the facility that was known as ISOLATION:

> All of the individuals indicated that they had no knowledge or reason to believe that any drugs other than routine medication were ever administered to Nosenko during the period of his incarceration from April 1964 to October 1967. Several of the individuals recalled that Nosenko complained from time to time that his food was being drugged; however, since they prepared the food they were certain that this was

---

43 Subject: Chronology of an Effort to Inspire Objective Review of the Nosenko Case: October 16, 1978.

not true. The names of the people involved in this operation with Nosenko were the following: Joseph King, John T. Harrington, Billy Hix, and Joseph Mirabile.[44]

On July 20, 1978, another member of this group, Atherton (Pete) Noyes, was interviewed regarding the administration of drugs to Nosenko. Noyes said that he was then a junior case officer on the Nosenko case and was present at the Clinton, Maryland facility, during the hostile interrogation conducted in April 1965. He was also present during the interrogation conducted by Mr. Nicholas Stoiaken at the ISOLATION location during October 1966. Noyes said that he was convinced that no drugs had ever been given to Nosenko during these sessions. Noyes recalled that from time to time Nosenko had complained about being drugged but he did not believe there was any basis for these complaints. A review of these allegations was conducted by security personnel who were in charge of Nosenko while he was in custody, and it was disclosed that no evidence of the use of drugs could be found.

This writer found an interesting page among the Nosenko records that relate to James Angleton and his obsession with Nosenko as it related to the JFK and RFK assassinations and their aftermath. This is what the document says:

> In a more serious vein, files were found on the assassination of President John F. Kennedy and his brother Robert F. Kennedy. These included autopsy pictures of the remains of Robert Kennedy. Although Nosenko's account of the KGB's involvement with Lee Harvey Oswald and his denial that the KGB had anything to do with the murder of John Kennedy might reasonably explain Angleton interest in the John Kennedy assassination, neither Karlis nor Blee, with whom Karlis consulted on this bizarre finding, had any idea why Angleton had the pictures. Neither could they think of any reason why it was appropriate for CI Staff files to contain them. They were accordingly destroyed.

Why did Angleton have the autopsy pictures of Robert Kennedy and where did he get them? The document goes on to say that:

44 Investigation Regarding Any Use of Drugs in the Case of Yuri Nosenko.

Angleton's dogged pursuit, inspired by Golitsyn and his theories, of Soviet intelligence penetration of CIA had led to secret investigations, stretching over a period of many years, of over forty serving CIA officers. Known as the HONETOL cases, and later sometimes referred to in the popular press as the Great Molehunt, this activity had produced extensive files on the CI Staff. In addition, several hundred files were found on American citizens who were not CIA personnel but on whom Golitsyn analysis had similarly cast some sort of KGB shadow. Among the most noteworthy of these were files on W. Averell Harriman and Henry Kissinger. Most of these files were composed entirely of newspaper reports and a few FBI reports.[45]

All these years later the jury is still out on the bona fides of Yuri Nosenko, but many analysts believe Nosenko was not who he made himself out to be. The HSCA concluded that, "In the end, the committee too, was unable to resolve the Nosenko matter. The fashion in which Nosenko was treated by the Agency—his interrogation and confinement—virtually ruined him as a valid source of information on the assassination."

The committee also wrote about Nosenko and his bona fides saying:

Is there evidence of a political or any other type objective which could justify a dispatch of Nosenko by the KGB with permission to speak freely to CIA concerning his knowledge of the KGB and without Nosenko being given a specific mission or missions? The above possibility has been given consideration even though the ultimate ramifications are practically incalculable. The conclusion is that as regards Nosenko with the single exception detailed below, there is no evidence of a political or other type objective which could be considered of sufficient importance by the KGB to warrant the dispatch of a KGB officer with the knowledge of Nosenko to speak freely with CIA without his being given a specific mission or missions by the KGB.

45 Secret Sensitive Noform, date Sep. 28, 1998.

The only area touched upon in any way by Nosenko which might meet the above requirements is the assassination of President Kennedy: the involvement of Lee Harvey Oswald in the assassination and his association with the Soviet Union. Given (a) speculation obtaining at the time that there was Soviet involvement in the assassination, (b) the premise that in fact there was no Soviet involvement, and (c) a hypothesis that the Soviet leadership was deeply concerned lest erroneous conclusions be drawn which could lead to irreversible actions, it is conceivable that the Soviet leadership might have been prepared to take extreme steps to convince the United States authorities of their non-involvement in the assassination. (The passage to the United States government of the allegedly complete Soviet consular file on Oswald was, in itself, an unprecedented act).[46]

The ramifications of the Nosenko case and all it brings to the table regarding the possible Soviet role in the Kennedy assassination the Great Molehunt started by James Angleton still reverberates to this day. Historians will be debating this matter for years to come.

---

46 www.Muckrock.com: "CIA abandoned logic to clear Soviet defector Yuri Nosenko," by Emma Best.

Chapter 50
Roy Cohn

While surfing the Internet, the author found a number of government files on the life of the noted attorney and political fixer by the name of Roy Cohn. While these files do not come from the JFK records, they do add to the knowledge of the time of the Cold War era, the trial of Julius and Ethel Rosenberg, the time of Joseph McCarthy, and the ties that Roy Cohn had to all these important events.

Roy Cohn's name has been in the news since the election of President Donald Trump in 2016. Roy Cohn had been a political fixer and family friend of the Trumps for years (only to be replaced by another lawyer named Michael Cohen—no relation). Michael Cohen and Roy Cohn played similar roles for the Trump family, with Roy getting better treatment than Michael for doing the business bidding of the Trump family. Cohn started working with the president's father, Fred, who began the Trump family real estate business.

Roy Cohn was born in New York City on February 20, 1927, son of Albert Cohn who was a New York judge. At age ten, his father introduced him to President Franklin Roosevelt, and at that meeting, the very young Roy Cohn talked with the president about the goings on with the Supreme Court to which FDR was trying to make major changes. Albert Cohn was deeply involved in Bronx politics and his son would soon follow in his footsteps. Albert Cohn was close to a number of Bronx politicians including Edward Flynn who was the Bronx Democratic Chairman and also a friend of FDR's. In time, Albert rose to the position of assistant district attorney, a chief assistant who prosecuted many high-level cases. As Albert Cohn's career grew, he was appointed for four terms in the New York State Appellate Division of the Supreme Court. Albert was a strong supporter of Senator Joseph McCarthy, as would be his son many years later.

As a young man, Roy attended many primary schools including the Community School for gifted students located on the Upper West side of Manhattan, which never suited his purposes. He later enrolled in the Fieldstone Lower School in Riverdale, New York where he did better. The family then took him out of Fieldstone and enrolled him at the Horace Mann School. In 1944, he enrolled in Columbia College where he studied law. He graduated in June 1947. After graduating, Roy served as a law clerk in the Federal Attorney's office in lower Manhattan. After getting his law license, he was an assistant federal prosecutor on the staff of US Attorney John F.X. McGohey.

It was during his time as an attorney for the federal government that Cohn found his true passion; fighting communism through any judicial means possible. His fight would, in time, bring him face to face with a Wisconsin Senator named Joseph McCarthy who would make it his lifelong political ambition to seek out subversives in the United States government. McCarthy would soon become Cohn's political mentor and together they would wrecak—havoc on anyone they saw as being anti-American when it came to Cold War politics. As he would write in his book called *McCarthy* (1968) about that time in his life:

> My education came slowly. During the years I helped prosecute conspirators while in the US Attorney's Office, I learned that Communists in government presented a far greater threat to the national security than I realized, or than any of my professors at Columbia had told me. I interrogated hundreds of witnesses and as part of my duties was required to read Communist literature from Karl Marx to William Foster. No American can devote himself full time to this subject without becoming fearful of his country's future.

As his anti-Communist law career grew, he took part in the conviction of eleven members of the American Communist Party's politburo. He used this case to propel himself right into the middle of the trial of the alleged Russian spies, Julius and Ethel Rosenberg ,that began in 1951. Cohn examined the Rosenberg's co-conspirator in the case, David Greenglass (who was Ethel's brother), which led to Ethel's and her husband's conviction. It would be many years later, with the release of the so-called Venona transcripts. There would be proof-positive that Julius Rosenberg was an active agent for the

Soviet Union. He was involved in efforts to steal atomic secrets from the United States. The Verona papers showed that Ethel Rosenberg knew of her husband's spying activities but that she did not play a large role in the theft of the atomic secrets.

That is the official version, and as far as it goes, it is not untrue. However, Cohn's conduct during the trial also involved suborning of perjury, using information secretly fed to him by Hoover, among other illegal acts. No matter — the conviction was secured. No one ever heard Roy Cohn regret it.

With Cohn's name now in the national headlines, his next move was certain. In 1952, Senator Joseph McCarthy made Roy Cohn the chief counsel to the Government Committee on Operations of the Senate (the McCarthy Committee). J. Edgar Hoover was the man most responsible for recommending Cohn to McCarthy.

It was at the time of Roy Cohn's appointment as Chief Counsel to the McCarthy Committee that he into contact with another rising star in the Democratic Party's legal/political gang, Robert F. Kennedy. It seems that Joseph P. Kennedy, the former Ambassador to England under FDR in World War II (and an appeaser of Hitler), wanted Bobby in that same job. McCarthy was a friend of Joe Kennedy's but in the end, did not hire Bobby for the job. Bobby Kennedy would now add another name to his enemies list, that of Roy Cohn. McCarthy told Joe Kennedy that the reason he did not hire Bobby was because of his limited legal experience. That did not stop his brother John from appointing him US Attorney General in 1961 after he was elected president. In his book on McCarthy, Cohn wrote that according to a newspaper columnist named George Sokolsky, "Joe [McCarthy] is going to try to talk Joe Kennedy into having Bobby take a lesser spot at the beginning. Then, after a while, he will be moved forward. That should satisfy him." In the end, McCarthy appointed Robert Kennedy as an assistant counsel.

In order to understand the role that Roy Cohn played in the so-called "McCarthy era" of the post-World War II years, we have to go back to the end of the war and the new fight against international communism. When Harry Truman took over after the death of

Senator Joseph McCarthy with Roy Cohn.

President Roosevelt in 1945, the Soviet Union was still an ally of the Western alliance. However all that changed with the end of the war and the realization that the Russians were not our allies anymore. Joseph McCarthy took up the cause of demonizing the Democrats for all sorts of ills, including the supposed infiltration of Communists in the federal government. It is important to realize that the idea of "Communists in government" was not new in the 1950s. "...what came to be known as McCarthyism was grounded in a set of attitudes, assumptions and judgments with deep roots in American history."

The United States did not officially recognize the Soviet Union as a nation until 1933, and throughout the New Deal of FDR, "Americans favored denying freedom of speech, press, and assembly to native communists. In fact, FDR and the rest of his administration had to convince Americans that they were not creating another Soviet Union in this country."

The events that preceded the McCarthy era in the late 1940s had thus set the stage for his brief but powerful career. McCarthy's ceaseless accusations against State Department officials had made him the figurehead of the Republican stand against communism.

McCarthy received support from moderate Republicans, "conservative politicians and publicists, businessmen, and retired military leaders discontented with the New Deal, with bureaucracy, and with military policy." He also received large amounts of money and enthusiasm from conservative Republican policy makers.

McCarthy was not well liked by a number of politicians in his own party, as well as a majority of Democrats in the both houses of Congress, although he did campaign for a number of them in the elections of the early 1950s. He also attacked President Truman for his handling of the Korean War and especially Truman's recalling of General Douglas McArthur who wanted to expand the war into China.

When Dwight Eisenhower was elected president in 1952, he made a decision not to openly attack McCarthy and kept him at arms length. He didn't want to make McCarthy an enemy, as he could probably use him in fights against the Democrats as time went on. With Eisenhower now in office, McCarthy would lessen his attacks on the man in the White House and set out to eliminate the "Communist threat" in the State Department. Still fearing that an attack on McCarthy would harm the Republican Party and thus aid the Democrats, President Eisenhower gave orders not to silence him.

However, as McCarthy's attacks on domestic communists in government grew more strident, the counter attacks by members of his own party grew in scope. As more and more Republicans began to reject these beliefs, McCarthy lost his large power base, and he quickly began to drop from his lofty position within the Eisenhower administration.

McCarthy, now seeing the writing on the wall, turned his attention away from communists in government toward a new foe, the United States Army. One of his first targets was General George Marshall for suggesting that the United States fight a limited war in Korea. He also brought forty-six charges against the Pentagon, claiming that it was responsible for the communist infiltration of the US government.

He now made an about-face and began attacking President Eisenhower. He said he had been wrong in supporting Ike in 1952, because Eisenhower was not taking the communist threat seriously. The same people in the Republican Party who had once supported McCarthy were now trying to undermine him at every turn. As he looked around, he found he had little support among his GOP colleagues and he began railing at one and all.

After the conclusion of the Army-McCarthy hearings in December 1954, Senator McCarthy was censured by the Senate.

One of the members of the Senate, who was absent for the vote due to a recent back operation, was John F. Kennedy.[47]

One of McCarthy's targets during this hectic time was the infant CIA that had been organized in 1947 after the end of World War II. McCarthy alleged that it was riddled with communists.

The choice of the CIA as a target for McCarthy's probes was not all that misplaced. Unknown to the majority of people at that time, during the war years the predecessor of the CIA, the Office of Strategic Services, had been riddled with Soviet agents. Others on the Russian payroll in the Roosevelt administration included Harry Dexter White, and Alger Hiss. So it was that in 1953, McCarthy, seeing a new avenue of opportunity, set his sights on the CIA.

McCarthy announced that there were 200 communists inside the CIA and that it was his duty to root them out. When the senator announced his intention to look into CIA abuses, many people in Washington, and in the Agency itself, became alarmed. According to the senator, the unnamed communists in the CIA were "so adroit and adept" that it was hard to find them. His power was so pervasive on Capitol Hill that many ex-CIA employees with axes to grind told McCarthy anything he wanted to know, including charges of sexual perversions and the use of alcohol, real or imagined.

The senator's charges were backed up by CIA Director Walter Bedell Smith when he testified before the House Un-American Activities Committee (HUAC) on October 13, 1952. According to Smith, "I believe there are Communists in my own organization. I believe that they are so adroit that they have infiltrated practically every security organization of Government." Smith's powerful testimony gave McCarthy enough official sanction to begin his inquiry.

The man Senator McCarthy set his sights on was CIA officer William Bundy. Bundy served as the liaison between the CIA and the National Security Council. Bundy also served as the assistant to the deputy director of intelligence and was well liked in the Agency. On July 9, 1953, Roy Cohn, McCarthy's chief aide, called the CIA's legislative counsel, Walter Pforzheimer to arrange for Bundy to appear before the senators that morning. One of the reasons that McCarthy targeted Bundy was the fact that Bundy had given money

47 Gesualdo, John, "Joseph McCarthy: The Renegade Senator," Back Channels, Volume 2. No.2, Winter 1993, Page 12-13.

to Alger Hiss when he was being investigated on spy charges. According to McCarthy's thinking, anyone who was a friend of Hiss had to be a communist.

Before Bundy could make an appearance, the top brass at the CIA went into action to thwart McCarthy. Pforzheimer contacted Robert Amory, the deputy director of intelligence. Amory devised a plan whereby he contacted Bundy and his wife, told them about Bundy's call to Capitol Hill, and told them to pack their car and leave town as fast as possible. When Cohn called to seek the whereabouts of Bundy, Amory told him that, "Unfortunately, Bundy left on leave on a motor trip."

Director Allen Dulles, who had left a meeting when all this subterfuge was going on, was notified about the Bundy affair and signed off on what actions had been taken.

Roy Cohn.

Dulles further contacted Vice President Richard Nixon, who passed on a message to his close friend, Joe McCarthy, to lay off the CIA. The CIA, unlike other departments of the federal government that McCarthy had set his sights on, refused to buckle. Dulles made it clear to McCarthy that if anyone was going to look into the Agency's dirty laundry, it would be the CIA itself. The Wisconsin senator reluctantly ended his investigation of the CIA, and moved on to other, less threatening targets.

When McCarthy first started working on the committee, he hired a young man named David Schine as a chief consultant without pay. Schine shared most of McCarthy's anti-Communist views and he was perfect for the job that McCarthy asked him to do. Rumors began flying that Roy Cohn and David Schine were lovers but that was never proven.

An FBI memorandum from L. B. Nichols dated May 25, 1953 concerns Roy Cohn and David Schine:

> Roy Cohn called me early Monday evening to furnish me with advice on two points. One, the committee has been seeking to locate [blank] who cannot be found. His attorney [blank] has contacted numerous friends of his and has reported back to the committee he cannot locate [blank] and it appears [blank] has taken a powder.
>
> Secondly, Cohn stated he was having dinner with Bob Morris and Joe McCarthy; that Joe had called the Director today and talked to the Director on two occasions. On one occasion he called the Director in the presence of Senator Jackson; that obviously he could not talk too well, but he wanted the Director to know Senator Jackson was no good. Cohn called Jackson today and told Jackson he heard he was making statements about David Schine and told Jackson he ought to put up or shut up and if he has anything to say he should go to the chairman, whereupon Jackson did go to the chairman, stated he has a report from a newspaper source that Schine was let out of the Army because of a psychopathic personality, when, as a matter of fact, according to Cohn, Dave received an honorable discharge form the Transport Corps as he had a bad back.

The FBI was not the only agency that was interested in Cohn's pal, David Schine. The CIA had also taken notice of the young man and a file was opened on him. The file was not opened on any counterintelligence matter, but Shine had become such an integral part of what McCarthy and Cohn were doing that they wanted to keep tabs on him.

An August 14, 1953 memo regarding Schine was written to Clyde Tolson, who was Hoover's close aide (and some people believed to be his secret lover) from L. B. Nichols. It reads as follows:

> With reference to Bedell Smith's comment that Roy Cohn had requested Smith to intercede with the Army to get a commission for David Schine and also inquired about the possibility of getting Schine a job at CIA, I wish to advise that Cohn has told me an entirely contrary story.
>
> Cohn's story was that in talking to Smith, there was a discussion of some of the difficulties the committee was having, and he mentioned the manner in which Schine was being discriminated against and the unfavorable publicity given him by Pearson. Bedell Smith then raised the possibility of Schine's getting a job at CIA. Cohn promptly vetoed this on the ground that this would present an untenable position for Senator McCarthy in any investigation of CIA, and Schine simply would not be a party to such a move.

During the decade of the 1950s, the FBI had a large file on Schine, much of which has now become public. Some of the Bureau's turned to Schine's army service. A March 30, 1953 memo to Mr. Ladd from a Mr. Rosen spells it out:

> Information has been received from [blank] newspaper columnist, Canaan, New York, that she has heard rumors that subject was able to evade the draft by virtue of his family paying large sum of money. She had no specific information, but stated she heard the statement made by several individuals. She is much concerned because Schine is presently employed by Senator McCarthy's Committee.

David Schine was then President of the Schine Hotels. While the Director was in Florida in December 1950, [blank] of the Schine Hotels in Florida, requested him to see whether a deferment of thirty days or longer could be obtained for subject who had been ordered for induction by his Los Angeles draft board. Mr. Schine's father also spoke to the Director about it. (The Director told him that the most he could do would be to make an inquiry). Subsequent inquiries were made on the national, state, and local levels and it was indicated a rather hostile attitude toward the steps Schine had taken in connection with his Selective Service status existed. The local board indicated some pressure had been brought to bear on them and that rumors had come to their attention that subject would never have to enter the armed services. The local board refused to give subject a hearing and later sent his papers to the New York Board to have subject inducted. Subject personally called the Director on January 31, 1951, and stated he was to report for induction the following morning in New York and had been trying to learn whether he could be deferred a few weeks to adjust his business interests. On February 1, 1951, the subject called the Director by phone and wanted to know how to go about enlisting in the Navy. The Director called SAC Scheidt to make an appointment for subject to see the proper Navy man in New York City as to the proper procedure to enter the Navy. The Director told SAC Scheidt no such discussion had been had and the Director's sole interest was to arrange for subject to see the proper authority in the Navy and from that point on the matter rested with the Navy and Mr. Schine.

The Bureau made a file check on Schine on behalf of Senator McCarthy on January 9, 1953, and the Senator was advised we had no derogatory information. Schine has never been investigated.

The fact that the Director of the FBI, J. Edgar Hoover, was approached to see if he could aid David Shine is a testament to Senator McCarthy's influence with Hoover and his powerful position in Washington on all matters that were of interest to him.

Hoover was not the only one who was trying to pull strings for Schine. Another person was CIA Director of the time, General Walter Bedell Smith.

On August 5, 1953, General Walter Smith advised that Roy Cohn had asked General Smith if he could intercede with his contacts in the Army in order that a commission could be obtained by Schine without Schine's becoming involved in any basic training. According to General Smith, Cohn was advised that this would be almost impossible to do and that Cohn then inquired about the possibilities of arranging a position for Schine in CIA. Your [Nichols'] memorandum to Mr. Tolson dated August 14, 1953, reported that Cohn told you a story entirely contrary to the statements made by General Smith.

The records on this matter continue as follows:

An article in the Washington Post on December 23, 1953, reported that Roy Cohn, Chief for Senator McCarthy's Senate Investigations Subcommittee was bringing pressure to bear on Fort Dix, New Jersey, i\on behalf of Schine, a recent inductee and former Committee colleague. This article reported that Cohn had called Fort Dix as much as four times in one day in this matter.

An article in the Washington Post on December 24, 1953, reported that Senator McCarthy had on that date stated that he had never tried to influence Army officers at Fort Dix, New Jersey, to make basic training easier for Schine.

The records on the Cohn-Schine case say that the Department of the Army Counsellor reportedly had mentioned that Cohn had once called him with respect to special treatment for Schine and that "they could see to it that Secretary of the Army Stevens be removed."

There is more to the CIA-Schine-Cohn story. General Walter Bedell Smith was in a no-win situation:

In this connection he [Smith] claimed that he pointed

out that Cohn's request was very unusual and could place somebody in an embarrassing position. In this connection he claimed that he pointed out to Cohn that Senator McCarthy could be placed in such an embarrassing spot if news ever leaked out that the Senator and Cohn were endeavoring to obtain special privileges for Schine. According to General Smith, Cohn was not at all impressed by the General's comments and Cohn then inquired what the possibilities would be of arranging a position for Schine at the CIA. He informed the General that he was not enthusiastic about such a proposition because Senator McCarthy had found the CIA to be a very "juicy" target and the Senator very likely would not want to be left in the position where he would be obligated to Allen Dulles. General Smith claimed that he then advised Cohn that if he so desired, he would approach Allen Dulles but he explained to Cohn that Dulles very likely would not be particularly cooperative in view of the recent conflicts which McCarthy had had with the Director of the CIA. Smith stated that he also pointed out to Cohn that Allen Dulles has a son who was seriously wounded in Korea last year and it was very doubtful that Dulles would try to arrange a position for Schine in order that he could avoid military service.

There is one other story regarding Cohn and the CIA that is of interest. A memo dated August 5, 1953, mentions a statement from Cohn regarding to a conversation he had with General Smith at which time the General commented that a polygraph examination had revealed that an individual who had been in the FBI for 16 years had been a lifelong homosexual.

The information furnished by Cohn indicated that the foregoing polygraph examination may have developed when an ex-Bureau Agent applied for employment at the CIA. The Director instructed Liaison to inform Smith that there was a story making the rounds to the effect that Smith allegedly had stated that a polygraph test had disclosed that a former Bureau Agent had been a homosexual all his life. Liaison was further instructed to obtain the facts from General Smith.

460

There is no mention of the person's name who was the subject of the Cohn allegation. However, the matter was turned over to Colonel Sheffield Edwards of the CIA in order to ascertain "if he possesses any information which might be related to the story which emanated from Roy Cohn. He stated that he would nevertheless contact his subordinates in order to definitely verify if the CIA has ever uncovered any evidence reflecting that an ex-Bureau agent had been identified as a homosexual as a result of a CIA polygraph examination."[48]

As part of their job working on McCarthy's Senate subcommittee to investigate communist influence in the government, Roy Cohn and David Schine made a trip to Europe in April 1953. They were to look into the goings on of the United States Information Service (USIS). Their trip resulted in thousands of books being removed from USIS libraries in several Western European countries.

Their primary job on their seven-nation European trip was to investigate the workings of the USIS posts, which were foreign offices of the United States Information Agency that had recently been established to serve as propaganda centers of the US government. The USIS posts had regularly hosted speakers and shown movies of the day which put the best face of the United States front and center.

> Cohn and Shine were appalled by the authors they found on the USIS bookshelves. The two men reported that over 30,000 books in the libraries were by "pro-communist" writers and demanded their removal. The authors they targeted were crime novelist Dashiell Hammett, African-American intellectual W.E.B. Du Bois, John Steinbeck, Henry Thoreau, and Herman Melville [what the story by Melville of hunting the great whales has to do with communist literature, is a stretch]. The State Department, which oversaw the operations of USIS, immediately ordered thousands of books removed from the libraries.[49]

The trip by Schine and Cohn to Europe was not unnoticed by the British press who made it their business to follow them around

---

48 Subject: General Walter Bedell Smith, August 5, 1953, to D.M. Ladd, from A.E. Belmont.
49 www.history.com/this-day-Roy Cohn and David Schine.

London and other places. The reporters played a parody of an old vaudeville routine when they saw the men, saying, "Positively Mr. Cohn! Absolutely, Mr. Schine!"

As mentioned in this chapter, David Schine was drafted in the fall of 1953. At this time, McCarthy's committee was in the middle of a highly toxic debate of alleged communist infiltration of the Army Communications Center at Fort Monmouth, New Jersey. The Army Secretary said that Cohn and others were putting undue pressure on the army to give Schine preferential treatment while he was in basic training.

The Schine disclosures then grew in scope and on March 16, 1954, the committee voted to create a special subcommittee—with another Senator named Karl Mundt, Republican of North Dakota, to serve as its chairman—to investigate the accusations. The hearings were well covered at that time including coverage by the ABC and DuMont television networks, as well as the daily papers. As the proceedings went on, the Associated Press said it carried more than a million words about the hearings, and the *New York Times* printed a complete transcript.

The testimony revealed that Private Schine had gone AWOL from Fort Dix, New Jersey. He had received passes every weekend and was allowed to take hundreds of telephone calls while on duty. As the hearings began, Schine was transferred to Fort Meyer, Va., near Washington.

All in all, Schine was in the Army for two years and was sent to a duty posting in Anchorage, Alaska (good move on the Army's part) and was given the rank of corporal. After leaving the Army, he went back into the family hotel business, saying goodbye to his years-long fight against communism. He was the president of the Ambassador Hotel in Los Angeles (the place where Robert Kennedy would be killed in 1968), which was part of a $150 million coast-to-coast theater-hotel and real estate empire which he built. In later years, Schine went into the movie business and was the executive producer for the Oscar-winning movie, *The French Connection* starring Gene Hackman.

In 1977, Schine and Cohn said they had been defamed by a television movie about Senator McCarthy called *Tail Gunner Joe*. They sued Universal Studios and NBC for $40 million. A New York

462

appellate court ruled that they had no case. The title of the movie was based on McCarthy's false claim that he had been a tail gunner during WWII.

On June 21, 1996, David Schine, was killed when a single-engine plane piloted by his son Berndt crashed shortly after taking off from Burbank, California. Mr. Schine was 69 and then lived in Los Angeles. Also killed in the crash was his wife Hillevi, 64.

As one studies that period of time, one can still hear the retort against Senator McCarthy made by Joseph Welch, the Boston lawyer who represented the Army in the hearings. He queried, in an open setting, "Have you no sense of decency sir, at long last."

Roy Cohn and David Schine were part of that setting and were, with Joe McCarthy, at the center of the political storm that was rocking the country at that time. As the years passed, the hunt for homegrown communists faded, only to be replaced by other targets such as hatred against Muslim Americans after 9-11, and the ongoing immigration crisis declared by those who would like to keep our borders secure.

In the end, the McCarthy witchhunts faded just as fast as they began. The American people soon regarded McCarthy as a non-entity, a person whose time had come and was now no longer relevant to the American discourse.

If McCarthy's demise was forgotten by many Americans, there was one man whose rising star would benefit from the McCarthy-Cohn-Schine trio—Richard Nixon. Nixon found his foil in his attacks on Alger Hiss and Whitaker Chambers and rose to the Vice Presidency and finally the White House on that anti-Communist rhetoric.

In his book on McCarthy, Roy Cohn defended his mentor and friend to the end. He wrote that McCarthy had millions of followers in the United States at that time who hung on everything he did and said. But Cohn ultimately wrote, "Those who were adversely affected were the fence-sitters. The actual swing as a result of the hearings was not great. The pro stayed pro, but anti, anti. And they do to this day."

The verdict from the committee regarding the McCarthy-Schine-Cohn affair went along party lines. The Republican majority cleared McCarthy of charges that he "brought improper influence" to bear on Schine's behalf, while the Democratic minority attributed "inexcusable actions" to both the Senator (McCarthy) and Cohn. The findings of the committee majority held:

> ...the charge of improper influence had not been established as a deliberate and personal act of Senator McCarthy's, they stated that he should have displayed "more vigorous discipline in stopping any member of his staff from attempting to make such a move. They found that I was "unduly persistent and aggressive" on Schine's behalf and that Stevens and Adams did try to "terminate or influence" the Fort Monmouth hearings.

Senator Joseph McCarthy died on May 2, 1957 at the Walter Reed National Military Medical Center in Bethesda, Maryland. Roy Cohn died on August 2, 1986 of complications from HIVAIDS.

What President Gerald Ford said on his assumption of the presidency after Richard Nixon's resignation can be related to the entire McCarthy era: "Our national nightmare is over."

Appendix:
The LBJ Connection

As described in Chapter 4 of this volume about the Soviet reaction to the president's assassination, the Kremlin had a lot to say regarding the events in Dealey Plaza. As laid out in that chapter, the Kremlin leaders were very interested in learning as much as they could about the new president, Lyndon Baines Johnson. During Kennedy's term, Lyndon Johnson played a backseat role as far as what the administration was doing and never had the ear of the president. He was given minor jobs, one of which involved the space race but nothing of great interest. The material in Chapter 4 describes the Soviet reaction to the assassination as well as their belief that Johnson played a role in the affair.

According to the documents:

> Officials of the Communist Party of the Soviet Union believed there was some well-organized conspiracy of the part of the "ultra-right" in the United States to effect a coup. They seemed convinced that the assassination was not the deed of one man, but that it arose out of a carefully planned campaign in which several people played a part. They felt that those elements interested in utilizing the assassination and playing on anticommunist sentiments in the United States would then utilize this act to stop negotiations with the Soviet Union, attack Cuba, and thereafter spread the war. As a result of these feelings, the Soviet Union immediately went into a state of national alert.
>
> Our source added that Ivanov also emphasized that it was of extreme importance to the Soviet Government to determine precisely what kind of a man the new President Lyndon Johnson would be. Ivanov said that President Johnson was practically an unknown to the Soviet Government and, accordingly, the KGB had issued instructions to all of its

agents to immediately obtain all data available concerning the incumbent President.

The most important part of this document reveals a deep worry on the Soviets' part regarding the possibility that LBJ was somehow involved in the president's murder:

> Our source added that in the instructions from Moscow, it was indicated that "now" the KGB was in possession of data purporting to indicate President Johnson was responsible for the assassination of the late President John F. Kennedy. KGB headquarters indicated that in view of this information, it was necessary for the Soviet Government to know the existing personal relationship between President Johnson and the Kennedy family, particularly that between President Johnson and Robert and "Ted" Kennedy.

The Soviets were not the only ones who believed that the new American president had some links to his predecessor's death. As interest in the Kennedy assassination mounted over the decades, some people began to take an active interest in what role LBJ had in the assassination. That part of the story gained new momentum with the release of Oliver Stone's blockbuster movie called *JFK* that hit the theaters like a thunderclap. In Stone's movie, New Orleans District Attorney Jim Garrison, when summing up his case against New Orleans businessman Clay Shaw who was on trial for conspiracy in the president's murder, told the jury who would benefit the most from the killing of the president. He mentioned the current president Richard Nixon and the former president, Lyndon Johnson. Both men were corrupt politicians and while there is no evidence that Nixon had any foreknowledge of the Kennedy assassination, the same cannot be said of Lyndon Johnson. Over the years, many assassination researchers have made the case that LBJ was warned beforehand (along with J. Edgar Hoover) that JFK was going to be killed and did nothing to stop it. It is not too much of a stretch to say that JFK liked his archrival in the political wars, Richard Nixon, more than he liked Lyndon Johnson. Kennedy and Nixon came to Congress at the same time fresh from serving in World War

II, and even though their political views were not in synch, they had a grudging respect for each other.

When Kennedy picked Lyndon Johnson as his vice-presidential running mate in the 1960 presidential election, he had no idea how deeply that decision would impact the historical record. Kennedy picked Johnson not because he liked him, but because of the electoral map. He needed Texas in order to win the election and since Johnson was the Senator from Texas, he believed that putting him on the ticket would help his election chances. Kennedy's gamble proved right and he beat Nixon by the slimmest of margins. Once he was in the White House, Kennedy left Johnson in the wind, basically keeping him out of the most important decisions of the day. No more would LBJ, once the powerful Senator Majority Leader, be the power player he once was; he was now relegated to the backbench, an afterthought in the corridors of power in Washington. Kennedy sent him overseas to see foreign leaders and he did an admirable job in that respect. Among Kennedy's top aides, Johnson was referred to in the most derogatory way; the president did not know about much of this talk. Robert Kennedy was one of the most vocal opponents of LBJ, and the feeling was mutual. Bobby never liked the idea that his brother had chosen Johnson for Vice President in the first place, and he let Johnson know about as often as he could.

Throughout his presidency, JFK knew all about Johnson's sordid past but he never used it against him until the last months of his time in office, when one of Johnson's top aids, Bobby Baker, was being investigated for political corruption charges (more on Baker later in this chapter). JFK's secretary, Evelyn Lincoln, said in later years that the president was going to replace Johnson as his vice-presidential candidate in the 1964 election with North Carolina Governor Terry Sanford. The Bobby Baker scandal, which was by then threatening to get out of control and bring Johnson down as well, ended abruptly with the president's assassination in Dallas on November 22, 1963.

Throughout his political career, Lyndon Johnson had been linked to a number of suspicious deaths. Attention focused on him because of his years-long membership in the Senate as well as his powerful position of Majority Leader. He also had a close association with a number of men of questionable reputation such as Bobby Baker and

Billie Sol Estes. It was through these two men that Johnson's secret ties would be investigated, but these probes were to be swept aside when he became the 37th president of the United States.

In order to learn all about the alleged crimes of LBJ, the reader has to understand the man behind all the stories that link him to these sordid tales. The man in question was Billie Sol Estes, a corrupt wheeler-dealer in the decades of the 1940s to the 1960s who was very close to Johnson and who was alleged to have information that LBJ was behind the Kennedy assassination.

Billie Sol Estes was born on a rural farm near Clyde, Texas on January 10, 1925. He was one of six children of John and Lillian Estes. When he was a young man, the Estes family fell on hard times in the Depression years. He had a talent for making deals and money and as a teenager, was able to make a $3,000 profit in the buying and selling of sheep. By age 18, he had made a profit of $38,000, a foretaste of what he would accomplish in later years. He then moved to Pecos, Texas where he began to sell irrigation pumps to local farmers who were having a hard time keeping up their farms. Estes sold ammonia as a fertilizer to local farmers who then began to have better luck selling their crops. Through the selling of irrigation pumps, he soon made a large profit and was on his way to becoming a man to be reckoned with in the Texas business community. However, his luck turned when the Department of Agriculture began to take control of the cotton crop. Agriculture allotments were given out by the federal government, telling local farmers how much cotton they could grow in a season. It was during this time that Estes made contact with Senator Lyndon Johnson, then a mover and shaker in both Washington and Texas politics. Through Johnson's work on his behalf, by 1958, Estes ran a scam allowing him to get federal agricultural subsidies which he was not entitled to. By his own account, he got $21 million a year for growing and storing cotton crops that did not exist.

The Agriculture Department soon found out what Estes was up to and they mounted an investigation of him. The man who was sent to probe Estes' dealings was Henry Marshall. Over a two year period, Marshall found out that Estes had bought 3,200 acres of cotton allotments from over one hundred different farmers. Marshall told his supervisors in Washington on August 31, 1960

Billie Sol Estes.

(during the height of the presidential campaign), "The regulation should be strengthened to support our disapproval of every case." It was alleged that a large amount of money that came from the Estes scam would wind up in the coffers of LBJ's political campaigns. Soon, Marshall's investigation of Estes wound up on Johnson's desk and he took active measures to stop the probe. However, Marshall would not bow to LBJ's harsh tactics and he refused any promotion and instead, redoubled his investigation into Estes' illegal activities. By taking that course of action, Henry Marshall was signing his own death warrant.

Fearing that time was not on his side, Billie Sol Estes and his lawyer, John Dennison, met with Marshall in Robertson County Texas to hash things out. The meeting took place on January 17, 1961, and Marshall told Dennison that his client was involved in a "scheme or device to buy allotments, and will not be approved, and prosecution will follow if this operation is ever used." One week after the meeting between Marshall and Dennison, A.B. Foster, who ran Billie Sol Enterprises wrote a letter to Clifton Carter, who was a friend of LBJ's, describing in detail all that Marshall had alleged that Estes was doing, and asking his help in rectifying the ongoing situation. Estes later said that on that same day (January 17, 1961), he had a meeting with Johnson, Cliff Carter, and Ed Clark regarding Marshall's allegations. At that meeting, Johnson was said to have made this remark regarding Marshall, "It looks like we'll just have to get rid of him." At the same meeting, it was alleged that the person who was to "get rid" of Henry Marshall was a notorious hit man named Malcolm "Mac" Wallace, who was said to be in cahoots

Billie Sol Estes on the cover of *Time* magazine May 25, 1962.

with Johnson.

On June 8, 1961, Henry Marshall was found dead on his farm next to his Chevy Fleetside pickup truck. Police found his rifle next to his body, with five gunshot wounds into his torso. Just how a person was able to fire five gunshots into his body is beyond explanation, evertheless the local County Sheriff Howard Stegall ruled that Marshall had committed suicide and in their investigation, no forensic examination of the crime scene was conducted. Later, the undertaker, Marley Jones, who examined Marshall's wounds said of the circumstances surrounding his death, "To me it looked like murder. I just do not believe a man could shoot himself like that." In 1986, Raymond Jones, Marley's son, told writer Bill Adler, "Judge Farmer told him he was going to put suicide on the death certificate because the sheriff told him to." In the end, Judge Lee Farmer ruled that Henry Marshall's death was "death by gunshot, self-inflicted."[1]

1 Famous Crimes: Billie Sol Estes, Spartacus-educational.com/JFK estes.htm.

Agriculture Secretary Orville Freeman believed that Henry Marshall had died under mysterious circumstances and said he was a man "who left this world under questioned circumstances."

Another man who had serious doubts about the circumstances surrounding the death of Henry Marshall was Texas Ranger Clint Peoples. Peoples had had an exceptional career in Texas law enforcement and was no one to be trifled with. It was during the later stages of his career that he was appointed to be a US Marshall. He initiated a thirty-year investigation that started in 1962 in the case against Malcolm Wallace and his association with LBJ and Cliff Carter.

Another of the cases that Ranger Peoples was associated with was the unexplained murder of George Krutilek in August 1962. George Krutilek was the accountant for Billie Sol Estes and the fraudulent scam he was running. Estes later testified that LBJ ordered that Krutilek be killed at the hands of Mac Wallace. One day after he was questioned by the FBI regarding the Estes matters, Krutilek was found dead from carbon monoxide poisoning. Besides ingesting carbon monoxide, there was a large bruise found on his head indicating that some sort of violent struggle had taken place.

In the early part of 1962, Billie Sol Estes and two other men, Harold Orr and Coleman Wade, were arrested by the FBI and were charged with fifty-seven counts of fraud and conspiracy. Both Orr and Wade died in suspicious circumstances, but it was believed that the men had died by suicide (there's that suicide ruling again). However, in later years, Estes claimed that both men were killed by Mac Wallace at the direction of LBJ.

In Congress, the Senate Permanent Subcommittee on Investigations began a probe into Billie Sol Estes and his corrupt practices. In time, it was revealed that three officials of the Agricultural Adjustment Administration, Red Jacobs, Jim Ralph, and Bill Morris took bribes from Estes and they were fired. In September 1961, Estes was fined $42,000 for his illegal cotton allotments. However, in an unusual move that shook Washington, Estes was appointed by Secretary of Agriculture Orville Freeman to the National Cotton Advisory Board.

It was also revealed that Billie Sol Estes told Wilson Tucker, who was the deputy director of the Agriculture Department's cotton

471

division, on August 1, 1961, that he would "embarrass the Kennedy administration if the investigation were not halted." Tucker later testified, "Estes stated that this pooled cotton allotment had caused the death of one person and then asked me if I knew Henry Marshall." This meeting took place at least six months before questions about the circumstances of Marshall's death began to spread.

At the time that Peoples began investigating the death of Henry Marshall, he reported to Colonel Homer Garrison, who was the Director of the Texas Department of Public Safety. Peoples interviewed Nolan Griffin, who worked in a gas station in Robertson County. Griffin told Peoples that on the day that Marshall died, he came across a man who asked him for directions to Henry Marshall's farm. Mr. Griffin was asked by the Rangers to provide a description of the man whom he saw, and after the sketch artist made a representation, the picture he drew resembled Mac Wallace. Mac Wallace was a suspect in the death of Doug Kinser in 1951. He was tried for the murder but the outcome of the trial was less than satisfactory. Wallace was sentenced to five years in jail but then, suddenly and unexpectedly, he was given a suspended sentence and put on probation. The court stipulated that his probation centered on him staying out of trouble for the next five years. A number of people at that time said a corrupt bargain went down in the sentence of Mac Wallace between the prosecutor and the judge, and that the hidden hand of LBJ was in the background.

With the heat coming from Washington in the form of Secretary Freeman, the body of Henry Marshall was removed from its grave and an autopsy was performed by Dr. Joseph Jachimczyk. The doctor's findings revealed that Marshall did not commit suicide, and Jachimczyk further said that only as much as 30 percent of carbon monoxide was found in his body. Dr. Jachimczyk also said that after viewing the body, that he believed the bruise on Marshall's head had been caused by "a severe blow to the head." He also cast doubt on the suicide verdict by saying that if he had used the rifle to kill himself there would have been traces of soot on his clothes, but none were found.

Billie Sol Estes was sentenced to prison for his participation in the cotton allotment scheme and, if he wanted to incriminate Vice President Johnson, he didn't say a word. However, all that

Billie Sol Estes in his later years.

changed when he was released from prison in 1984. Estes met with Clint Peoples and the Ranger was able to persuade Estes to talk; he appeared before the Robertson County officials that had previously looked into the death of Henry Marshall. In a session that probably made the grand jury blush, Estes told them of his participation in the cotton allotment scheme and much more. He told them that Johnson, Cliff Carter, and Malcolm Wallace had met to discuss what to do with Henry Marshall and his allegations of wrongdoing against Estes. Estes said that Mac Wallace followed Marshall to a secluded place near his farm and almost beat him to death and then shot Marshall five times.

By 1984, the US Justice Department wanted to know more about what Estes knew, and he was contacted via his lawyer,

Douglass Caddy. Attorney Caddy wrote a letter to the Justice Department requesting that his client be granted immunity from further prosecution and, if hewere, he was willing to provide further incriminating information that he had in his possession. However, after much back and forth, Caddy said that Estes would not testify and reveal his bombshell information.

The Estes story might have died on the vine if not for new information that came from a writer named Glen Sample, who wrote a book on the Kennedy assassination called *The Men on the Sixth Floor*. Mr. Sample gained possession of a letter written to Douglas Caddy from Stephen Trott, the Assistant Attorney General of the Criminal Division which was dated May 29, 1984. Trott told Caddy that he'd be interested in hearing what Estes had to say only if he cooperated fully and gave the Justice Department all relevant information, including the extent of his participation in the crimes, as well as the names of his sources. On August 9, 1984, Douglas Caddy wrote to Trott and gave him some startling information. Parts of his letter are as follows:

> My client, Mr. Estes, has authorized me to make this reply to your letter of May 29, 1984. Mr. Estes was a member of a four-member group, headed by Lyndon Johnson, which committed criminal acts in Texas in the late 1960s. The other two, besides Mr. Estes and LBJ, were Cliff Carter and Mac Wallace. Mr. Estes in willing to disclose his knowledge concerning the following offenses:
>
> Murders: The killing of Henry Marshall. The killing of George Krutilek. The killing of Ike Rodgers and his secretary, the killing of Harold Orr, the killing of Coleman Wade, the killing of Josefa Johnson, the killing of John Kinser and the killing of President John F. Kennedy.
>
> In addition, Mr. Estes is willing to testify that LBJ ordered these killings, and that his orders went through Cliff Carter to Mac Wallace, who executed the murders. In the cases of the murders one-to-seven, Estes' knowledge of the precise details concerning the way the murders were executed stems from conversations he had shortly after each event with Cliff Carter and Mac Wallace. Mr. Estes

474

declared that Cliff Carter told him the day that Kennedy was killed, Fidel Castro was supposed to be killed and that Robert Kennedy, awaiting word of Castro's death, instead received news of his brother's killing. Mr. Estes states, that Mac Wallace, whom he describes as a "stone killer," with a communist background, recruited Jack Ruby, who in turn, recruited Lee Harvey Oswald. Mr. Estes said that Cliff Carter told him that Mac Wallace fired a shot from the grassy knoll in Dallas, which hit JFK from the front during the assassination.

Illegal Cotton Allotments: Mr. Estes desires to discuss the infamous illegal cotton allotment schemes in great detail. He has recordings made at the time of LBJ, Cliff Carter and himself discussing the scheme. These recordings were made with Cliff Carter's knowledge as a means of Carter and Estes protecting themselves should LBJ order their deaths.

Illegal Payoffs: Mr. Estes is willing to disclose illegal payoff schemes, in which he collected and passed on to Cliff Carter and LBJ millions of dollars. Mr. Estes collected payoff money on more than one occasion from George and Herman Brown of Brown and Root, which was delivered to LBJ.[2]

These were mind-boggling accusations and if proven to be true, would have led to a major scandal in American history. However, by the time the Estes allegations were made to the Justice Department, a number of the major players in the drama were dead, including LBJ, Cliff Carter, Henry Marshall, etc. As for Billie Sol Estes, he died May 14, 2013, taking his secrets to the grave.

Another wheeler-dealer Johnson relied heavily upon, and who almost brought down his political career, was Bobby Baker who was Secretary of the Senate during the time of Johnson's heyday in that body. He was called "the 101th Senator" by the senators he did favors for, including lobbying for their bills, and procuring some of them "dates" when their wives weren't around. During his time as Secretary of the Senate, Baker was associated with a number of mob figures such as Meyer Lansky, Sam Giancana, and Ed Levinson, and gained a fortune on his meager congressional salary.

2 The Estes Documents: home.earthlink.net.sixthfloor/estes.htm.

Bobby Baker was born in Pickens, South Carolina in 1929 and at the tender age of fourteen, was a page at the Senate. During this time, Lyndon Johnson took a liking to the young man and, as time went on, Johnson turned Baker into a protégé, teaching him the ins and outs of the Senate. He told him whose palms to grease and, over time, made him one of the most influential, unelected members who worked on the Hill. In the 1950s Baker used his influence to help the Intercontinental Hotel chain establish casinos in the Dominican Republic. Using his influence, Baker got mobsters like Ed Levinson, an associate of Meyer Lansky and Sam Giancana, to become partners in the deal, and the first casino was opened in 1955. One of the guests who showed up was LBJ. When Johnson was elected vice president in 1960, Baker became LBJ's secretary and his most trusted political advisor. Baker's deal with the mobsters went south when Rafael Trujillo, the dictator of the Dominican Republic, was killed in a CIA-sanctioned attack by dissidents in that country.

Seeking new avenues of opportunity, Baker, in 1962, started a company called Serve-U-Corporation with his colleague Fred Black and two mobsters, Ed Levinson and Benny Sigelbaum. The firm provided vending machines for companies that operated on federally granted programs. The vending machines were produced by a business that was owned by Sam Giancana, the mob boss of Chicago. As time went on, Baker somehow managed to rake in $3.5 million in profits from Serve-U-Corporation on a salary of $20,000 a year. As time went on, the Baker problem caught the attention of Attorney General Robert Kennedy who heard rumors about Baker's mob ties and his sudden fortune. RFK had the Justice Department start an investigation of Baker, and soon the probe had its sights on the vice president himself. It seems that not only Baker was involved with certain mobsters Robert Kennedy was targeting, but that possibly Johnson was involved on the outskirts of the scandal. This involved the awarding of a $7 million contract for a new jet fighter plane, the F-111, which was based in Texas. There were rumors on Capitol Hill that Johnson was possibly involved in the awarding of the contract to General Dynamics, although it couldn't be proven. Soon, the heat was getting too much for Baker to bear and on October 7, 1963, Baker was forced to resign his powerful Senate post. Another casualty of the F-111 scandal was Fred Korth, the Navy Secretary.

Another scandal involving Baker was the operation of the so-called Quorum Club, a private club on Capitol Hill that Baker created. The club operated out of the Carroll Arms Hotel near the Senate offices, and it provided girls (prostitutes, in some cases) to influential Senators and some people in the Kennedy administration.

One of the girls who was part of Baker's Quorum Club was a German refugee named Ellen Rometsch, who had come with her husband, a West German army sergeant who worked at the West German mission in Washington, to the United States in 1961. Through Baker's intercession, Ellen Rometsch was invited to the White House to see President Kennedy and an affair soon took place. The FBI found out about the Rometsh-Kennedy affair, and it turned out that the beautiful Ellen Rometsch had come from East Germany and had once been a member of a Communist youth organization. The rumor going around Hoover's Bureau was that she was possibly an East German spy who had now bedded the president of the United States. Very quietly, Miss Rometsch was sent back to West Germany.

During the FBI's investigation of Bobby Baker, the Rometsch affair took center stage and an FBI memo dated October 26, stated, "That pertains to questionable activities on the part of high government officials. It was also alleged that the President and the Attorney General had availed themselves of services of play-girls." The news of the Rometsch affair got into the hands of Senator John Williams (R-Delaware) and he threatened to hold hearings in the Senate Rules Committee, the same one that was investigating the Bobby Baker affair. Robert Kennedy now got into the act and he called J. Edgar Hoover to discuss the problem. Hoover briefed Senators Mike Mansfield and Everett Dirksen in a private session, and told them about the Baker-Kennedy-Rometsch affair. To the relief of the administration, the whole sordid affair was hushed up and never saw the light of day. It is not a stretch of the imagination to believe that Bobby Baker told LBJ all about the president's affair with Ellen Rometsch. This would have been fodder for Johnson (and of course, J. Edgar Hoover) if they, at some time, wanted to reveal to the public what they knew about the scandal.

By November 1963, the Baker scandal was about to get ripped

wide open. It seems that *Life Magazine,* as revealed in an issue dated November 8, 1963, was doing an in-depth report on Baker's illegal activities, including information on the Quorum Club and the activities of Ellen Rometsch, and more importantly, Bakers's secret relationship with Vice President Johnson. The headline in the magazine's story read as follows: "Capital Buzzes over Stories of Misconduct in High Places. The Bobby Baker Bombshell." The publication featured a picture of LBJ and the caption underneath said, "Baker was an indispensable confidant of LBJ." The magazine was about to reveal how Baker had gotten rich on his government salary and his ties to Johnson.

Life's editors were now setting their sights on LBJ himself, digging into his past, wondering how he had accumulated so much money from his humble beginnings in Texas to his million dollar fortune in 1963. The reporter who took on the job of looking into Johnson's past was William Lambert whose previous reporting broke the story of the Teamsters Union's association with the mob in the US

A second *Life* article that was dated November 22, 1963 (the day Kennedy was shot in Dallas) went even further in tackling the Johnson-Baker relationship. The main writer for this story was Keith Wheeler who had nine other members of *Life's* staff on hand to assist him in his research. The article went even further in exploring Baker's control of the Quorum Club, the use of girls as prostitutes for certain members of congress, and the relationship of LBJ to the Baker scandal. The reporters wrote, "In a very real sense, the present establishment is the personal creation of Lyndon Johnson who, from the day he took over as majority leader until he went to the Vice Presidency, ruled it like an absolute monarch."

The managing editor of *Life,* George Hunt, took an active interest in his reporters' work and he scheduled a meeting with both William Lambert and Keith Wheeler for the morning of November 22, 1963. As the meeting progressed, word came of the assassination of the president in Dallas and the session was adjourned. At the time of the conference, *Life's* editors were planning to release a third bombshell report on the Baker affair, but with the death of Kennedy and the rise to the presidency of Johnson, the man they were looking into, the Baker-Johnson story was now ended. Thus, in one fell swoop,

LBJ's presidency was free of any further scandal as the country tried to figure out what happened to Kennedy and move on from the nightmare that we'd all been through.

Many Kennedy researchers believe that Lyndon Johnson was the man responsible for the president's death. Of all the people who would benefit the most with JFK gone, the first was LBJ. He would now be president of the United States, instead of being investigated by a possible congressional committee on the Bobby Baker scandal and his relationship to him. Even if he survived the scandal, he would possibly bei dumped by JFK in the upcoming 1964 election. By the fall of 1963, Johnson saw the inevitable end of his powerful political career and he was helpless to do anything about it. Now, all that had changed. The political gods had made their move and Johnson could now go on to implement his own national agenda.

But did Johnson really order the assassination of JFK, or did he have prior knowledge of the event? One week after the Kennedy assassination, the new president created the Warren Commission to investigate his predecessor's assassination. Johnson cajoled Chief Justice Earl Warren to chair the commission, despite his reluctance to take on the position. The Warren Commission did not do a thorough job of investigating all the leads into the assassination, in the end leaving more question than answers surrounding Kennedy's death. Johnson told Earl Warren in no uncertain terms that there were rumors of possible Russian involvement in the assassination, and if they weren't quashed soon, it was possible that nuclear war would break out costing millions of innocent lives. In the end, the Commission said that there was no foreign assistance in the Kennedy assassination.

It wasn't until 1969, six years after the assassination, that Johnson made a rather unusual statement concerning the president's alleged assassin, Lee Oswald. In an interview with CBS News, Johnson remarked, "I don't think that they [the Warren Commission] or me or anyone else is always absolutely sure of everything that might have motivated Oswald or others that could have been involved. But he was quite a mysterious fellow, and he did have connections that bore examination." It was later learned that Johnson asked CBS to withhold that later section of the interview on the grounds of "national security." CBS obliged, and it wasn't until 1975 that the entire remarks of Johnson were publically aired.

As the Warren Commission was being set up, Johnson was influential in appointing as one of its members, his old friend Allen Dulles, who had been CIA Director under JFK and who was at the helm at Langley headquarters during the Bay of Pigs invasion. Dulles agreed with J. Edgar Hoover's findings that Oswald was the lone assassin and that any high-level inquiry into the assassination would be a waste of time. Dulles also knew of the CIA-Mafia plots to kill Castro but, as we have seen, he never informed his fellow commissioners of that most important fact.

Johnson was under tremendous pressure to order a federal inquiry into the president's assassination, as Texas authorities were poised to start their own investigation. After all, the murder had taken place in their jurisdiction. If that happened, Johnson would have very little leverage to control the probe. Johnson ended that possible line of inquiry when he appointed Warren to investigate the crime. Who knows what the outcome of the investigation would have been if the Texas authorities had been able to conduct their own investigation?

Here are some of the people whose stories puts LBJ right in the thick of the Kennedy assassination. One of these people was Madeleine Brown who said that she had a decade's-long relationship with Johnson which resulted in a child being born. Ms. Brown described a meeting that was held by Johnson on November 21, 1963 in Texas with a number of high-profile people that included Texas oil tycoon Clint Murchison, FBI Director J. Edgar Hoover, Dallas Mayor R.L. Thornton, Richard Nixon, John J. McCloy, and H.L. Hunt whose name has been linked to the Kennedy assassination for years. Ms. Brown said that at the end of the meeting, the men all got together and planned the murder of the president that took place the next day. After the meeting, LBJ was said to have told Madeleine Brown, "After tomorrow, those goddam Kennedy's will never embarrass me again-that's no—threat-that's a promise."

Ms. Brown goes further in describing her conversations with Johnson regarding the Kennedy assassination, according to a book on the subject. This event took place on New Year's Eve 1963. The conversation went as follows:

"Lyndon, you know that a lot of people believe you had something to do with President Kennedy's assassination." He shot up from the bed and began pacing and waving his arms, screaming like a madman. I was scared. "That's bullshit, Madeleine Brown," he yelled. "Don't tell me you believe that crap!" "Of course not," I answered meekly, trying to cool his temper. :It was Texas oil and fucking renegade intelligence bastards in Washington."[3]

Another person who had knowledge of LBJ's possible participation in the Kennedy assassination was E. Howard Hunt, the noted spy, writer of spy novels, and one of the men who was arrested in the Watergate break-in.

Shortly before his death in 2007, E. Howard Hunt wrote his memoir called *An American Spy: My Secret History in the CIA*. If anyone really believed that Hunt would reveal something earth-shattering about the Kennedy assassination, they were wrong. That task would fall to his son St. John Hunt who had a rather adversarial, so to speak, relationship with his father.

St. John Hunt took an active interest in the Kennedy assassination years after the event and was shocked to see a photo of the so-called Three Tramps who were arrested in Dallas shortly after the president's death. St. John said that one of the Tramps looked strikingly like his father. E. Howard Hunt always maintained that he was in Washington, DC on November 22, 1963. St. John says that, based on his recollections, his father was *not* at home when he returned from school that day. He also said that he (Hunt) never was really there for him when he most needed a father figure and that Howard Hunt was only interested was in himself. St. John did reveal that he aided his father in destroying a suitcase that contained the electronic equipment that was used in the Watergate burglary. Both son and father went to the banks of the C&O Canal in Hunt's Pontiac Firebird and dropped the suitcase into the muddy water, never to be seen again.

In the months before Hunt's death, he called St. John to his bedside to tell what he knew of his life in the CIA, and more importantly, his knowledge of the Kennedy assassination. St. John

3 Venturea, Jesse, *They Killed Our President,* Skyhorse Publishing, New York, 2013, Pages 271-72.

Hunt took notes, as well as recordings, of the conversations. The elder Hunt mailed the tape to his son in January 2004 and asked that it be kept safe until after he died. In the tape, which was aired in 2007 via a radio interview (none of the mainstream press even mentioned such an important historical event in their pages), and which was given widespread publicity on the web, Hunt revealed the names of the men he alleged took part in the planning of JFK's murder. The names Hunt revealed were: Frank Sturgis, David Morales, David Atlee Phillips, Antonio Veciana, William Harvey, Cord Meyer, a French gunman who was on the Grassy Knoll, and Lyndon Johnson.

Hunt said that he played no active role in the assassination but was just a "benchwarmer" in the discussions. During his confession, Hunt wrote down the names of the people who were involved in the plot in a flow chart, connecting each dot as it went along its natural path. He wrote down LBJ first, followed by lines for each of the other players: Cord Meyer, who became the second highest ranking member of the CIA's Clandestine Service (also, JFK was having an affair with Cord Meyer's wife, Mary); Bill Harvey, who ran the Cuban plots and held a bitter hatred towards the Kennedy brothers; David Morales, a tough, CIA agent who worked in Havana and later in the CIA's JM/WAVE station in Miami, and had numerous connections with the top bosses in organized crime in the US; Frank Sturgis of Watergate fame, and a member of Gerry Hemming's IPF; David Phillips, a CIA propaganda officer, who was stationed in Mexico City at the same time that Oswald was supposed to have been in that city; Antonio Veciana, the leader of the militant anti-Castro organization, Alpha 66; and finally, the so-called French gunman on the Grassy Knoll, possibly Lucien Sarti.

The scenario that Hunt laid out was that LBJ ordered the assassination of the president and passed on his instructions to the rest of the group. By implying that Lucien Sarti, a member of the Corsican underworld, was on the Grassy Knoll firing at the president. Hunt tansformed the Oswald-as-the-lone-gunman theory into a conspiracy. St. John Hunt further stated that his father gave him a document that spelled out how the conspiracy unfolded. Cord Meyer discussed the plot with David Atlee Phillips, who then met with William Harvey and Antonio Veciana. Oswald had a meeting with the above-mentioned men in Mexico City. Veciana then met with Frank Sturgis in Miami who brought David Morales into the plot. There was a change in the location of the assassination plot and it is finally agreed that Dallas was the place where the event would take place.

Hunt went on to describe his involvement in the assassination planning. In 1963, he met with Morales and Sturgis in a Miami hotel room. Morales took his leave and in came Frank Sturgis who talked about a "Big Event" and wanted to know if Hunt was willing to go along with the plans. Hunt asked Sturgis what the plan was and Sturgis replied, "Killing JFK." Hunt then asked Sturgis why he needed him. Hunt told them that he wanted no part in the deal.

St. John writes that he was shocked to hear of his father's confession, believing that he had been lied to over the decades by Hunt's constant denials that he had anything to do with the assassination.

So, Hunt puts Johnson squarely in the middle of the plot to kill his predecessor, if one is to believe him. Can Howard Hunt's deathbed confession be true? If it is, then Hunt was a participant after the fact, knowing just what was going to happen, and doing nothing to stop it. Or was it just a made up story that could be used to sell more books? (It should be noted that these allegations were not part of Hunt's memoirs.) St. John said that prior to his father's death, the elder Hunt was "deeply conflicted and deeply remorseful" that he didn't tell authorities about his foreknowledge of the assassination plot. But can we believe him? The elder Hunt continued by saying that JFK had enemies galore who had the means, motive, and opportunity to kill him. The Hunt allegation just adds fuel to the fire revolving around his probable links to the president's death.

There were further allegations leveled against Johnson, one coming from one of the doctors who were treating Oswald after he was shot by Jack Ruby, Dr. Charles Crenshaw. Dr. Crenshaw was a surgical resident at Parkland Hospital in 1963 and was on hand to treat the alleged presidential assassin. Crenshaw claimed that while he was working on Oswald in the emergency room, he got a call from LBJ wanting Oswald to give a "deathbed" confession to him. That, of course never happened, as Oswald died while being operated on. When asked for comment on the allegation, the Johnson White House never responded.

483

One last point hads to be made regarding the LBJ connection, not necessarily linked to the Kennedy assassination, but his relationship with J. Edgar Hoover and his possible ties to the American Mafia.

During those years, Hoover and Johnson were neighbors, walking their dogs together and talking about the latest hot gossip that was going around Washington, mostly about two of the people they had a large grudge against, the Kennedy brothers. Hoover knew all of the secrets the Kennedys had, and he kept them in his "secret and confidential" files in his office. It is not a stretch of the imagination to believe that the men shared with each other the dirty little secrets of the Kennedy family, beginning with dirt on Papa Joe Kennedy, who started his fortune in the bootlegging operations of the Depression years.

As Johnson rose to power in both Texas and Washington, he made many connections with underworld figures and other sordid people, beginning with Billie Sol Estes and Bobby Baker, who was mobbed up to the gills. Johnson's financial health grew by leaps and bounds in the 1950s using his powerful friends and conduits, no matter what side of the law they were on. Through his connection with Baker, Johnson engaged with a large number of Mafia figures in the United States including Benjamin Sigelbaum, who himself was tied to Mafia figure Ed Levinson. Levinson was associated with off-track betting on (race horses) in Newport, Kentucky, and casino gambling in Las Vegas. In 1959, LBJ and his wife attended the grand opening of the Stardust Hotel and Casino in Las Vegas which was controlled by tons of Mafia money. There were also rumors that Johnson had some sort of relationship with Carlos Marcello, the mob boss who had his powerbase in New Orleans, and who was a prime suspect in the Kennedy assassination.

In his book called *Act of Treason,* author Mark North writes,

> Johnson has always used intermediaries to effectuate questionable goals. While not publically supporting any candidate for the presidency in 1960, Hoover had privately assisted LBJ's efforts to obtain the nomination. Both Hoover and Tolson actually met with him at his Texas ranch on 11/9/59. The Director knows that Johnson, a compromise vice-presidential candidate, does not care for John and Robert

Kennedy and knows they, in turn, hold LBJ in low regard.

In the summer and fall of 1960, Hoover and LBJ wrote effusive letters to each other, giving praise at every opportunity.

Since Hoover had his hand in every conceivable illegal deal that was going on around the country, it is not out of the ordinary to speculate that he knew of Johnson's relationship with Billie Sol Estes and the criminal activity that was going on. As they were close personal friends, it behooved Hoover to cover up his knowledge of the Estes-Baker-Johnson relationship and keep that information on hand for a later time. It is also possible that Hoover told Johnson that he knew of the latter's association with Estes and would do his friend a favor by not revealing it at that time.

The fact that Hoover and LBJ hated the Kennedys was an open secret. Both Hoover and LBJ had heard the rumors that the president was thinking of replacing Johnson in 1964, and if that happened, and Kennedy won as second term, Johnson's and possibly Hoover's influence would be negated. If JFK were gone and Lyndon Johnson was president, Hoover's job would be saved (Johnson would probably have re-appointed Hoover as FBI Director). So, could there have been some sort of plot between Hoover and Johnson (among others) to have JFK removed from office and ensure a Johnson presidency? That question is still open for debate among JFK scholars and conspiracy theorists.

The Kennedy assassination had profound ramifications for the country and the world. Johnson changed JFK's Vietnam policy, creating a war which tore the nation apart and resulted in his decision in 1968 not to seek re-election. All of LBJ's work on civil rights, which profoundly changed the way the United States operated, took second stage to his Vietnam policy.

Robert Kennedy, who himself hated Johnson (the feeling was mutual), summed up his thoughts on the vice president, by telling his friend Arthur Schlesinger, "And my experience with him since then [1960] is that he lies all the time. I'm telling you, he just lies constantly, about everything. In every conversation I have had with him, he lies. As I've said, he lies even when he doesn't have to."

Bibliography: Books

Belin, David, *Final Disclosure,* Charles Scribner's Son, New York, 1988.

Benson, Michael, *Who's Who in the Kennedy Assassination: An A-Z Encyclopedia,* Carol Publishing Co., New York, 1993.

Cohn, Roy, *McCarthy,* The New American Library, New York, 1968.

Dean, John, *The Nixon Defense,* Viking Press, New York, 2014.

Davis, John, *Mafia Kingfish: Carlos Marcello and the Assassination of John F. Kennedy,* McGraw Hill Co., New York, 1989.

Duffy, James, *Who Killed JFK?* Shapolsky Publishers, New York, 1988.

Escalante, Fabian, *Executive Action: 634 Ways to Kill Fidel Castro,* Ocean Press, New York, 2006.

Escalante, Fabian, *JFK: The Cuba Files: The Untold Story of the Plot to kill Kennedy,* Ocean Press, New York, 2006.

Fonzi, Gaeton, *The Last Investigation,* Thunder's Mouth Press, New York, 1993.

Hurt, Henry, *Reasonable Doubt: An Investigation into the Assassination of John F. Kennedy,* Holt, Rinehart and Winston, New York, 1985.

Hinckle, Warren, and Turner, William, *Deadly Secrets: The CIA-Mafia War Against Castro and the Assassination of JFK,* Thunder's Mouth Press, New York, 1992.

Kross, Peter, *Tales from Langley: the CIA from Truman to Obama,* Adventures Unlimited Press, Kempton, Ill., 2014.

Kross, Peter, *The Secret History of the United States: Conspiracies, Cobwebs and Lies,* Adventures Unlimited Press, Kempton, Ill., 2013.

Kross, Peter. *American Conspiracy Files,* Adventures Unlimited Press, Kempton, Ill., 2015.

Kross, Peter, *Target Fidel: A Narrative Encyclopedia on the US Government's Plots to kill Fidel Castro, 1959-1965,* Privately Printed, 1999.

Kross, Peter, *JFK: The French Connection,* Adventures Unlimited Press, Kempton, Ill., 2012.

Kross, Peter, *Oswald, the CIA & and the Warren Commission: The Unanswered Questions,* Bridger House Press, Hayden, Id, 2011.

Minutaglio, Bill and Davis, Steven, *Dallas 1963,* 12 Books, New York, 2013.

Miller, Nathan, *Spying for America: The Hidden History of the U.S.,* Paragon House, New York, 1989.

Mellen, Joan, *Faustian Bargains: LBJ and Mac Wallace in the Robber Baron Culture of Texas,* Bloomsbury USA, New York, 2016.

Newman, John, *Oswald and the CIA,* Carroll and Graf, New York, 1995.

Polmar, Norman & Allen, Thomas, *Spy Book: The Encyclopedia of Espionage,* Random House, New York, 1997.

Pincher, Chapman, *Treachery,* Random House, New York, 2009.

Ranelagh, John, *The Agency: The Rise and Decline of the CIA from Wild Bill Donovan to William Casey,* Simon and Schuster, New York, 1994.

Reibling, Mark, *Wedge: The Secret War Between the FBI and the CIA,* Alfred Knopf, New York, 1994.

Rappleye, Charles & Becker, Ed, *All American Mafioso: The Johnny Rosselli Story,* Doubleday, New York, 1991.

Russo, Gus, *Live By the Sword,* Bancroft Books, Baltimore, Md., 1998.

Strauss, Steven, *The Complete Idiot's Guide to the Kennedy's,* Alpha Books, Indianapolis, In. 2000.

Summer, Anthony, *The Arrogance of Power: The Secret World of Richard Nixon,* Viking Press, New York, 2000.

Summer, Anthony, *Conspiracy,* McGraw Hill Company, New York, 1980.

Ventura, Jesse, *They Have Killed Our President,* Skyhorse Publishing Co, New York, 2013.

Veciana, Antonio with Carlos Harrison, *Trained to Kill: The Inside Story of CIA Plots Agaisnt Castro, Kenendy and Che,* Skyhorse Publishing, New York, 2017.

Magazines and Other References:

Allen, Robert & Scott, Paul, *CIA Withheld Vital Intelligence from Warren Report,* 10-21-1984.

Arana, Marie, *Story of a Death Foretold: The Coup Against Salvador Allende by Oscar Guardiola-Rivera.*

Babcock, Charles, Maheu Admits 54 Anti-Onasis Drive, Washington Post.com, August 2, 1978.

Best, Emma, *No, CIA's Counterintelligence Chief didn't mastermind a JFK assassination cover-up weeks in advance*, www.muckrock.com.

Gage, Nicholas, *Mafia Said to Have Slain Rosselli Because of his Senate Testimony*, New York Times, 2-25-1977.

Gesualdo, John, *Joseph McCarthy—The Renegade Senator*, Back Channels, Vol 2. No.2, Winter 1993.

Horrock, Nicholas, *Rosselli Describes His Role in the CIA Plot on Castro*, New York Times, 6-25-1977.

Kross, Peter, *JFK & The French Connection*, Back Channels, Vol. 1, No. 1, October 1991, Page 3-4.

No author, *American History-The Assassination of JFK-Marina Oswald Biography.* www.spartacus=educational.com/JFK.

No author, *Brilab Jury Convicts Marcello and former Louisiana Officials*, New York Times, 1981.

No author, *Dallas Mayor During JFK Assassination Was CIA Asset*, Who, What, Why, 8/2/2017.

No author, *Cambridge News received anonymous JFK assassination tip-off*, www.bbc.com/news/UK, October 27, 2017.

No author, JFK Files: "British paper got anonymous call just before assassination," The Guardian.com/US-news.

No author, *Ruby Met with Castro Sturgis Says*, Washington Star, no date.

No author, *Maheu Denies Anti-Onasis CIA connection*.

Rivele, Stephen, *Death of a Double Man*.

Roberts, Martin, *Cuban ex-intelligence chief recalls JFK assassination*, Reuters, July 12, 2910.

Scott, Peter Dale, *The CIA's Richard Helms lied about Oswald*, Who, What, Why, December 23, 2015.

Thomas, Robert, *Stravos Niarcho's Greek Shipping Magnate and the Archrival of Onassis Is Dead at 86*, New York Times, April 18, 1996.

Van Gelder, Lawrence, *Crash kills G. David Schine 69, McCarthy-Era Figure*, New York Times, June 21, 1996.

Yates, Ronald, *Mystery Still lingers on Marilyn Monroe*, Washington Star, no date

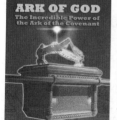

Get these fascinating books from your nearest bookstore or directly from:
Adventures Unlimited Press
www.adventuresunlimitedpress.com

COVERT WARS AND BREAKAWAY CIVILIZATIONS
By Joseph P. Farrell

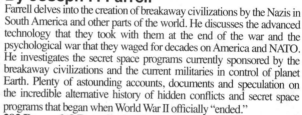

Farrell delves into the creation of breakaway civilizations by the Nazis in South America and other parts of the world. He discusses the advanced technology that they took with them at the end of the war and the psychological war that they waged for decades on America and NATO. He investigates the secret space programs currently sponsored by the breakaway civilizations and the current militaries in control of planet Earth. Plenty of astounding accounts, documents and speculation on the incredible alternative history of hidden conflicts and secret space programs that began when World War II officially "ended."
292 Pages. 6x9 Paperback. Illustrated. $19.95. Code: BCCW

THE ENIGMA OF CRANIAL DEFORMATION
Elongated Skulls of the Ancients
By David Hatcher Childress and Brien Foerster

In a book filled with over a hundred astonishing photos and a color photo section, Childress and Foerster take us to Peru, Bolivia, Egypt, Malta, China, Mexico and other places in search of strange elongated skulls and other cranial deformation. The puzzle of why diverse ancient people—even on remote Pacific Islands—would use head-binding to create elongated heads is mystifying. Where did they even get this idea? Did some people naturally look this way—with long narrow heads? Were they some alien race? Were they an elite race that roamed the entire planet? Why do anthropologists rarely talk about cranial deformation and know so little about it? Color Section.
250 Pages. 6x9 Paperback. Illustrated. $19.95. Code: ECD

ARK OF GOD
The Incredible Power of the Ark of the Covenant
By David Hatcher Childress

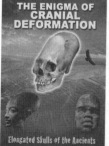

Childress takes us on an incredible journey in search of the truth about (and science behind) the fantastic biblical artifact known as the Ark of the Covenant. This object made by Moses at Mount Sinai—part wooden-metal box and part golden statue—had the power to create "lightning" to kill people, and also to fly and lead people through the wilderness. The Ark of the Covenant suddenly disappears from the Bible record and what happened to it is not mentioned. Was it hidden in the underground passages of King Solomon's temple and later discovered by the Knights Templar? Was it taken through Egypt to Ethiopia as many Coptic Christians believe? Childress looks into hidden history, astonishing ancient technology, and a 3,000-year-old mystery that continues to fascinate millions of people today. Color section.
420 Pages. 6x9 Paperback. Illustrated. $22.00 Code: AOG

HESS AND THE PENGUINS
The Holocaust, Antarctica and the Strange Case of Rudolf Hess
By Joseph P. Farrell

Farrell looks at Hess' mission to make peace with Britain and get rid of Hitler—even a plot to fly Hitler to Britain for capture! How much did Göring and Hitler know of Rudolf Hess' subversive plot, and what happened to Hess? Why was a doppleganger put in Spandau Prison and then "suicided"? Did the British use an early form of mind control on Hess' double? John Foster Dulles of the OSS and CIA suspected as much. Farrell also uncovers the strange death of Admiral Richard Byrd's son in 1988, about the same time of the death of Hess.

288 Pages. 6x9 Paperback. Illustrated. $19.95. Code: HAPG

HIDDEN FINANCE, ROGUE NETWORKS & SECRET SORCERY
The Fascist International, 9/11, & Penetrated Operations
By Joseph P. Farrell

Farrell investigates the theory that there were not *two* levels to the 9/11 event, but *three*. He says that the twin towers were downed by the force of an exotic energy weapon, one similar to the Tesla energy weapon suggested by Dr. Judy Wood, and ties together the tangled web of missing money, secret technology and involvement of portions of the Saudi royal family. Farrell unravels the many layers behind the 9-11 attack, layers that include the Deutschebank, the Bush family, the German industrialist Carl Duisberg, Saudi Arabian princes and the energy weapons developed by Tesla before WWII.

296 Pages. 6x9 Paperback. Illustrated. $19.95. Code: HFRN

THRICE GREAT HERMETICA & THE JANUS AGE
By Joseph P. Farrell

What do the Fourth Crusade, the exploration of the New World, secret excavations of the Holy Land, and the pontificate of Innocent the Third all have in common? Answer: Venice and the Templars. What do they have in common with Jesus, Gottfried Leibniz, Sir Isaac Newton, Rene Descartes, and the Earl of Oxford? Answer: Egypt and a body of doctrine known as Hermeticism. The hidden role of Venice and Hermeticism reached far and wide, into the plays of Shakespeare (a.k.a. Edward DeVere, Earl of Oxford), into the quest of the three great mathematicians of the Early Enlightenment for a lost form of analysis, and back into the end of the classical era, to little known Egyptian influences at work during the time of Jesus.

354 Pages. 6x9 Paperback. Illustrated. $19.95. Code: TGHJ

ROBOT ZOMBIES
Transhumanism and the Robot Revolution
By Xaviant Haze and Estrella Eguino,

Technology is growing exponentially and the moment when it merges with the human mind, called "The Singularity," is visible in our imminent future. Science and technology are pushing forward, transforming life as we know it—perhaps even giving humans a shot at immortality. Who will benefit from this? This book examines the history and future of robotics, artificial intelligence, zombies and a Transhumanist utopia/dystopia integrating man with machine. Chapters include: Love, Sex and Compassion—Android Style; Humans Aren't Working Like They Used To; Skynet Rises; Blueprints for Transhumans; Kurzweil's Quest; Nanotech Dreams; Zombies Among Us; Cyborgs (Cylons) in Space; Awakening the Human; more. Color Section.

180 Pages. 6x9 Paperback. Illustrated. $16.95. Code: RBTZ

TRUMPOCALYPSE NOW!
The Triumph of the Conspiracy Spectacle
By Kenn Thomas

Trumpocalypse Now! takes a look at Trump's career as a conspiracy theory celebrity, his trafficking in such notions as birtherism, Islamofascism and 9/11, the conspiracies of the Clinton era, and the JFK assassination. It also examines the controversies of the 2016 election, including the cyber-hacking of the DNC, the Russian involvement and voter fraud. Learn the parapolitcal realities behind the partisan divide and the real ideological underpinnings behind the country's most controversial president. Chapters include: Introduction: Alternative Facts; Conspiracy Celebrity–Trump's TV Career; Birtherism; 9/11 and Islamofascism; Clinton Conspiracies; JFK–Pro-Castro Fakery; Cyber Hacking the DNC; The Russian Connection; Votescam; Conclusion: Alternative Theories; more.

6x9 Paperback. 380 Pages. Illustrated. $16.95. Code: TRPN

MIND CONTROL, OSWALD & JFK
Introduction by Kenn Thomas

In 1969 the strange book *Were We Controlled?* was published which maintained that Lee Harvey Oswald was a special agent who was also a Mind Control subject who had received an implant in 1960. Thomas examines the evidence that Oswald had been an early recipient of the Mind Control implant technology and this startling role in the JFK Assassination. Also: the RHIC-EDOM Mind Control aspects concerning the RFK assassination and the history of implant technology.

256 Pages. 6x9 Paperback. Illustrated. $16.00. Code: MCOJ

INSIDE THE GEMSTONE FILE
Howard Hughes, Onassis & JFK
By Kenn Thomas & David Childress

Here is the low-down on the most famous underground document ever circulated. Photocopied and distributed for over 20 years, the Gemstone File is the story of Bruce Roberts, the inventor of the synthetic ruby widely used in laser technology today, and his relationship with the Howard Hughes Company and ultimately with Aristotle Onassis, the Mafia, and the CIA. Hughes kidnapped and held a drugged-up prisoner for 10 years; Onassis and his role in the Kennedy Assassination; how the Mafia ran corporate America in the 1960s; more.

320 Pages. 6x9 Paperback. Illustrated. $16.00. Code: IGF

ADVENTURES OF A HASHISH SMUGGLER
By Henri de Monfreid

Nobleman, writer, adventurer and inspiration for the swashbuckling gun runner in the *Adventures of Tintin*, Henri de Monfreid lived by his own account "a rich, restless, magnificent life" as one of the great travelers of his or any age. The son of a French artist who knew Paul Gaugin as a child, de Monfreid sought his fortune by becoming a collector and merchant of the fabled Persian Gulf pearls. He was then drawn into the shadowy world of arms trading, slavery, smuggling and drugs. Infamous as well as famous, his name is inextricably linked to the Red Sea and the raffish ports between Suez and Aden in the early years of the twentieth century. De Monfreid (1879 to 1974) had a long life of many adventures around the Horn of Africa where he dodged pirates as well as the authorities.

284 Pages. 6x9 Paperback. $16.95. Illustrated. Code AHS

HITLER'S SUPPRESSED AND STILL-SECRET WEAPONS, SCIENCE AND TECHNOLOGY
By Henry Stevens
In the closing months of WWII the Allies assembled mind-blowing intelligence reports of supermetals, electric guns, and ray weapons able to stop the engines of Allied aircraft—in addition to feared x-ray and laser weaponry. Chapters include: The Kammler Group; German Flying Disc Update; The Electromagnetic Vampire; Liquid Air; Synthetic Blood; German Free Energy Research; German Atomic Tests; The Fuel-Air Bomb; Supermetals; Red Mercury; Means to Stop Engines; more.
335 Pages. 6x9 Paperback. Illustrated. $19.95. Code: HSSW

PRODIGAL GENIUS
The Life of Nikola Tesla
By John J. O'Neill
This special edition of O'Neill's book has many rare photographs of Tesla and his most advanced inventions. Tesla's eccentric personality gives his life story a strange romantic quality. He made his first million before he was forty, yet gave up his royalties in a gesture of friendship, and died almost in poverty. Tesla could see an invention in 3-D, from every angle, within his mind, before it was built; how he refused to accept the Nobel Prize; his friendships with Mark Twain, George Westinghouse and competition with Thomas Edison. Tesla is revealed as a figure of genius whose influence on the world reaches into the far future. Deluxe, illustrated edition.
408 pages. 6x9 Paperback. Illustrated. Bibliography. $18.95. Code: PRG

HAARP
The Ultimate Weapon of the Conspiracy
By Jerry Smith
The HAARP project in Alaska is one of the most controversial projects ever undertaken by the U.S. Government. At at worst, HAARP could be the most dangerous device ever created, a futuristic technology that is everything from super-beam weapon to world-wide mind control device. Topics include Over-the-Horizon Radar and HAARP, Mind Control, ELF and HAARP, The Telsa Connection, The Russian Woodpecker, GWEN & HAARP, Earth Penetrating Tomography, Weather Modification, Secret Science of the Conspiracy, more. Includes the complete 1987 Eastlund patent for his pulsed super-weapon that he claims was stolen by the HAARP Project.
256 pages. 6x9 Paperback. Illustrated. Bib. $14.95. Code: HARP

WEATHER WARFARE
The Military's Plan to Draft Mother Nature
By Jerry E. Smith
Weather modification in the form of cloud seeding to increase snow packs in the Sierras or suppress hail over Kansas is now an everyday affair. Underground nuclear tests in Nevada have set off earthquakes. A Russian company has been offering to sell typhoons (hurricanes) on demand since the 1990s. Scientists have been searching for ways to move hurricanes for over fifty years. In the same amount of time we went from the Wright Brothers to Neil Armstrong. Hundreds of environmental and weather modifying technologies have been patented in the United States alone – and hundreds more are being developed in civilian, academic, military and quasi-military laboratories around the world *at this moment!* Numerous ongoing military programs do inject aerosols at high altitude for communications and surveillance operations.
304 Pages. 6x9 Paperback. Illustrated. Bib. $18.95. Code: WWAR

SAUCERS, SWASTIKAS AND PSYOPS
A History of a Breakaway Civilization
By Joseph P. Farrell

Farrell discusses SS Commando Otto Skorzeny; George Adamski; the alleged Hannebu and Vril craft of the Third Reich; The Strange Case of Dr. Hermann Oberth; Nazis in the US and their connections to "UFO contactees"; The Memes—an idea or behavior spread from person to person within a culture—are Implants. Chapters include: The Nov. 20, 1952 Contact: The Memes are Implants; The Interplanetary Federation of Brotherhood; Adamski's Technological Descriptions and Another ET Message: The Danger of Weaponized Gravity; Adamski's Retro-Looking Saucers, and the Nazi Saucer Myth; Dr. Oberth's 1968 Statements on UFOs and Extraterrestrials; more.
272 Pages. 6x9 Paperback. Illustrated. $19.95. Code: SSPY

LBJ AND THE CONSPIRACY TO KILL KENNEDY
By Joseph P. Farrell

Farrell says that a coalescence of interests in the military industrial complex, the CIA, and Lyndon Baines Johnson's powerful and corrupt political machine in Texas led to the events culminating in the assassination of JFK. Chapters include: Oswald, the FBI, and the CIA: Hoover's Concern of a Second Oswald; Oswald and the Anti-Castro Cubans; The Mafia; Hoover, Johnson, and the Mob; The FBI, the Secret Service, Hoover, and Johnson; The CIA and "Murder Incorporated"; Ruby's Bizarre Behavior; The French Connection and Permindex; Big Oil; The Dead Witnesses: Guy Bannister, Jr., Mary Pinchot Meyer, Rose Cheramie, Dorothy Killgallen, Congressman Hale Boggs; LBJ and the Planning of the Texas Trip; LBJ: A Study in Character, Connections, and Cabals; LBJ and the Aftermath: Accessory After the Fact; The Requirements of Coups D'État; more.
342 Pages. 6x9 Paperback. $19.95 Code: LCKK

THE TESLA PAPERS
Nikola Tesla on Free Energy &
Wireless Transmission of Power
by Nikola Tesla, edited by David Hatcher Childress

David Hatcher Childress takes us into the incredible world of Nikola Tesla and his amazing inventions. Tesla's fantastic vision of the future, including wireless power, anti-gravity, free energy and highly advanced solar power. Also included are some of the papers, patents and material collected on Tesla at the Colorado Springs Tesla Symposiums, including papers on: •The Secret History of Wireless Transmission •Tesla and the Magnifying Transmitter •Design and Construction of a Half-Wave Tesla Coil •Electrostatics: A Key to Free Energy •Progress in Zero-Point Energy Research •Electromagnetic Energy from Antennas to Atoms
325 PAGES. 8x10 PAPERBACK. ILLUSTRATED. $16.95. CODE: TTP

COVERT WARS & THE CLASH OF CIVILIZATIONS
UFOs, Oligarchs and Space Secrecy
By Joseph P. Farrell

Farrell's customary meticulous research and sharp analysis blow the lid off of a worldwide web of nefarious financial and technological control that very few people even suspect exists. He elaborates on the advanced technology that they took with them at the "end" of World War II and shows how the breakaway civilizations have created a huge system of hidden finance with the involvement of various banks and financial institutions around the world. He investigates the current space secrecy that involves UFOs, suppressed technologies and the hidden oligarchs who control planet earth for their own gain and profit.
358 Pages. 6x9 Paperback. Illustrated. $19.95. Code: CWCC

LIQUID CONSPIRACY 2:
The CIA, MI6 & Big Pharma's War on Psychedelics
By Xaviant Haze

Underground author Xaviant Haze looks into the CIA and its use of LSD as a mind control drug; at one point every CIA officer had to take the drug and endure mind control tests and interrogations to see if the drug worked as a "truth serum." Chapters include: The Pioneers of Psychedelia; The United Kingdom Mellows Out: The MI5, MDMA and LSD; Taking it to the Streets: LSD becomes Acid; Great Works of Art Inspired and Influenced by Acid; Scapolamine: The CIA's Ultimate Truth Serum; Mind Control, the Death of Music and the Meltdown of the Masses; Big Pharma's War on Psychedelics; The Healing Powers of Psychedelic Medicine; tons more.

240 pages. 6x9 Paperback. Illustrated. $19.95. Code: LQC2

TAPPING THE ZERO POINT ENERGY
Free Energy & Anti-Gravity in Today's Physics
By Moray B. King

King explains how free energy and anti-gravity are possible. The theories of the zero point energy maintain there are tremendous fluctuations of electrical field energy imbedded within the fabric of space. This book tells how, in the 1930s, inventor T. Henry Moray could produce a fifty kilowatt "free energy" machine; how an electrified plasma vortex creates anti-gravity; how the Pons/Fleischmann "cold fusion" experiment could produce tremendous heat without fusion; and how certain experiments might produce a gravitational anomaly.

180 PAGES. 5x8 PAPERBACK. ILLUSTRATED. $12.95. CODE: TAP

QUEST FOR ZERO-POINT ENERGY
Engineering Principles for "Free Energy"
By Moray B. King

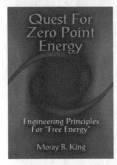

King expands, with diagrams, on how free energy and anti-gravity are possible. The theories of zero point energy maintain there are tremendous fluctuations of electrical field energy embedded within the fabric of space. King explains the following topics: TFundamentals of a Zero-Point Energy Technology; Vacuum Energy Vortices; The Super Tube; Charge Clusters: The Basis of Zero-Point Energy Inventions; Vortex Filaments, Torsion Fields and the Zero-Point Energy; Transforming the Planet with a Zero-Point Energy Experiment; Dual Vortex Forms: The Key to a Large Zero-Point Energy Coherence. Packed with diagrams, patents and photos.

224 PAGES. 6x9 PAPERBACK. ILLUSTRATED. $14.95. CODE: QZPE

AMERICAN CONSPIRACY FILES
The Stories We Were Never Told
By Peter Kross

Kross reports on conspiracies in the Revolutionary War, including those surrounding Benedict Arnold and Ben Franklin's son, William. He delves into the large conspiracy to kill President Lincoln and moves into our modern day with chapters on the deaths of JFK, RFK and MLK., the reasons behind the Oklahoma City bombing, the sordid plots of President Lyndon Johnson and more. Chapters on Edward Snowden; The Weather Underground; Patty Hearst; The Death of Mary Meyer; Marilyn Monroe; The Zimmerman Telegram; BCCI; Operation Northwinds; The Judge John Wood Murder Case; The Search for Nazi Gold; The Death of Frank Olsen; tons more. Over 50 chapters in all.

460 Pages. 6x9 Paperback. Illustrated. $19.95 Code: ACF

PROJECT MK-ULTRA AND MIND CONTROL TECHNOLOGY
A Compilation of Patents and Reports
By Axel Balthazar

This book is a compilation of the government's documentation on MK-Ultra, the CIA's mind control experimentation on unwitting human subjects, as well as over 150 patents pertaining to artificial telepathy (voice-to-skull technology), behavior modification through radio frequencies, directed energy weapons, electronic monitoring, implantable nanotechnology, brain wave manipulation, nervous system manipulation, neuroweapons, psychological warfare, satellite terrorism, subliminal messaging, and more. A must-have reference guide for targeted individuals and anyone interested in the subject of mind control technology.

384 pages. 7x10 Paperback. Illustrated. $19.95. Code: PMK

ANCIENT ALIENS & SECRET SOCIETIES
By Mike Bara

Did ancient "visitors"—of extraterrestrial origin—come to Earth long, long ago and fashion man in their own image? Were the science and secrets that they taught the ancients intended to be a guide for all humanity to the present era? Bara establishes the reality of the catastrophe that jolted the human race, and traces the history of secret societies from the priesthood of Amun in Egypt to the Templars in Jerusalem and the Scottish Rite Freemasons. Bara also reveals the true origins of NASA and exposes the bizarre triad of secret societies in control of that agency since its inception. Chapters include: Out of the Ashes; From the Sky Down; Ancient Aliens?; The Dawn of the Secret Societies; The Fractures of Time; Into the 20th Century; The Wink of an Eye; more.

288 Pages. 6x9 Paperback. Illustrated. $19.95. Code: AASS

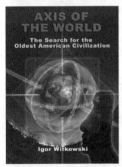

AXIS OF THE WORLD
The Search for the Oldest American Civilization
By Igor Witkowski

Polish author Witkowski's research reveals remnants of a high civilization that was able to exert its influence on almost the entire planet, and did so with full consciousness. Sites around South America show that this was not just one of the places influenced by this culture, but a place where they built their crowning achievements. Easter Island, in the southeastern Pacific, constitutes one of them. The Rongo-Rongo language that developed there points westward to the Indus Valley. Taken together, the facts presented by Witkowski provide a fresh, new proof that an antediluvian, great civilization flourished several millennia ago.

220 pages. 6x9 Paperback. Illustrated. References. $18.95. Code: AXOW

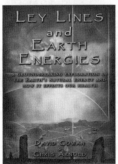

LEY LINE & EARTH ENERGIES
An Extraordinary Journey into the Earth's Natural Energy System
By David Cowan & Chris Arnold

The mysterious standing stones, burial grounds and stone circles that lace Europe, the British Isles and other areas have intrigued scientists, writers, artists and travellers through the centuries. How do ley lines work? How did our ancestors use Earth energy to map their sacred sites and burial grounds? How do ghosts and poltergeists interact with Earth energy? How can Earth spirals and black spots affect our health? This exploration shows how natural forces affect our behavior, how they can be used to enhance our health and well being.

368 PAGES. 6x9 PAPERBACK. ILLUSTRATED. $18.95. CODE: LLEE

ORDER FORM

10% Discount When You Order 3 or More Items!

One Adventure Place
P.O. Box 74
Kempton, Illinois 60946
United States of America
Tel.: 815-253-6390 • Fax: 815-253-6300
Email: auphq@frontiernet.net
http://www.adventuresunlimitedpress.com

ORDERING INSTRUCTIONS

✓ Remit by USD$ Check, Money Order or Credit Card

✓ Visa, Master Card, Discover & AmEx Accepted

✓ Paypal Payments Can Be Made To:

    info@wexclub.com

✓ Prices May Change Without Notice

✓ 10% Discount for 3 or More Items

SHIPPING CHARGES

United States

✓ Postal Book Rate { $4.50 First Item
50¢ Each Additional Item

✓ POSTAL BOOK RATE Cannot Be Tracked!
Not responsible for non-delivery.

✓ Priority Mail { $6.00 First Item
$2.00 Each Additional Item

✓ UPS { $7.00 First Item
$1.50 Each Additional Item

NOTE: UPS Delivery Available to Mainland USA Only

Canada

✓ Postal Air Mail { $15.00 First Item
$2.50 Each Additional Item

✓ Personal Checks or Bank Drafts MUST BE

US$ and Drawn on a US Bank

✓ Canadian Postal Money Orders OK

✓ Payment MUST BE US$

All Other Countries

✓ Sorry, No Surface Delivery!

✓ Postal Air Mail { $19.00 First Item
$6.00 Each Additional Item

✓ Checks and Money Orders MUST BE US$
and Drawn on a US Bank or branch.

✓ Paypal Payments Can Be Made in US$ To:
info@wexclub.com

SPECIAL NOTES

✓ RETAILERS: Standard Discounts Available

✓ BACKORDERS: We Backorder all Out-of-Stock Items Unless Otherwise Requested

✓ PRO FORMA INVOICES: Available on Request

✓ DVD Return Policy: Replace defective DVDs only

ORDER ONLINE AT: www.adventuresunlimitedpress.com

10% Discount When You Order 3 or More Items!

Please check: ✓

☐ This is my first order   ☐ I have ordered before

Name

Address

City

State/Province   Postal Code

Country

Phone: Day   Evening

Fax   Email

Item Code	Item Description	Qty	Total

Please check: ✓

Subtotal ▶

Less Discount-10% for 3 or more items ▶

☐ Postal-Surface   Balance ▶

☐ Postal-Air Mail   Illinois Residents 6.25% Sales Tax ▶
(Priority in USA)   Previous Credit ▶

☐ UPS   Shipping ▶
(Mainland USA only) Total (check/MO in USD$ only) ▶

☐ Visa/MasterCard/Discover/American Express

Card Number:

Expiration Date: Security Code:

✓ SEND A CATALOG TO A FRIEND: